D1806045

Oxford in Asia Historical Reprints from Pakistan
Adviser: Percival Spear

A PARTICULAR ACCOUNT OF THE EUROPEAN MILITARY ADVENTURERS OF HINDUSTAN, 1784-1803

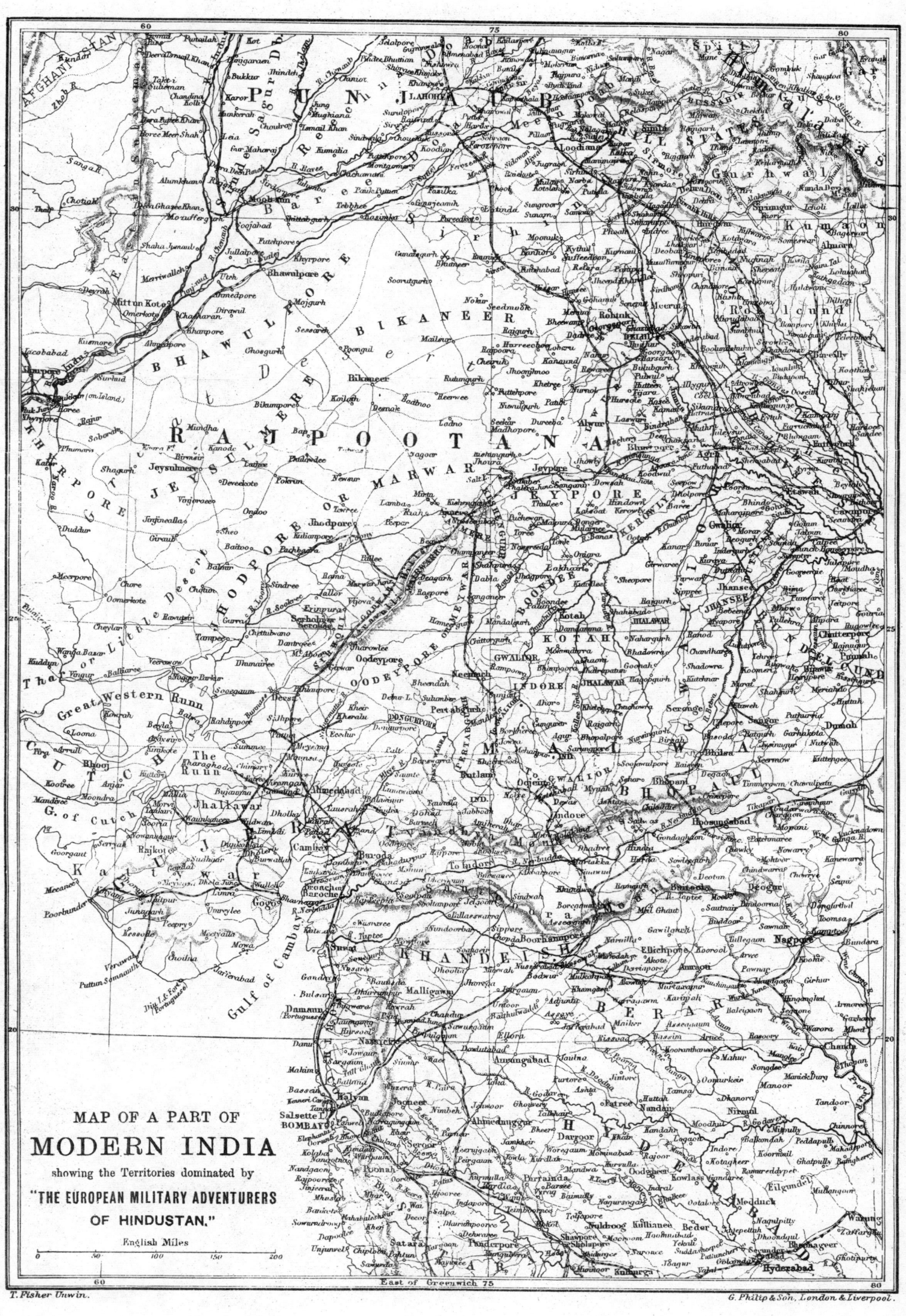

MAP OF A PART OF
MODERN INDIA
showing the Territories dominated by
"THE EUROPEAN MILITARY ADVENTURERS
OF HINDUSTAN."

English Miles

T. Fisher Unwin.

East of Greenwich 75

G. Philip & Son, London & Liverpool.

A PARTICULAR ACCOUNT
OF THE
EUROPEAN MILITARY
ADVENTURERS OF HINDUSTAN

FROM 1784 TO 1803

by

HERBERT COMPTON

With an introduction
by

JOHN PEMBLE

OXFORD
IN ASIA
Historical
Reprints

KARACHI
OXFORD UNIVERSITY PRESS
LONDON   NEW YORK   DELHI
1976

Oxford University Press

OXFORD LONDON GLASGOW NEW YORK
TORONTO MELBOURNE WELLINGTON CAPE TOWN
IBADAN NAIROBI DAR ES SALAAM LUSAKA ADDIS ABABA
KUALA LUMPUR SINGAPORE JAKARTA HONG KONG TOKYO
DELHI BOMBAY CALCUTTA MADRAS KARACHI

First published by T. Fisher Unwin, London 1892
Reprinted in Pakistan, 1976

Introduction © John Pemble, 1976

ISBN   0 19 577227 X

Reprinted by permission of the Government of Sind
under the terms of the
Publication of Books (Regulation and Control) Ordinance 1969

New matter set by
Unique Printers, I. I. Chundrigar Road, Karachi
and the whole work printed by
Civil & Military Press Ltd. Hassanali Effendi Road, Karachi

Published by
Oxford University Press, P.O. Box 5093 Haroon House,
Dr Ziauddin Ahmed Road, Karachi.

INTRODUCTION

In his essay on Clive, Macaulay blamed historians for the apathy and ignorance of the British public about European enterprise in India. Historical writing on India, he decided, was dead and buried beneath the twin tombstones of the works of Mill and Orme. Mill's *History of British India* was 'not sufficiently animated and picturesque to attract those who read for amusement'; while Orme's *Military Transactions of the British Nation in Indostan* was 'minute even to tediousness'. It is a fact that few writers on Indian subjects of this time made any concession to popular taste. Meadows Taylor's authentically based novel *Confessions of a Thug*, which appeared in 1840, seems to have been the only book designed for and accepted by a general audience. Not until John Kaye took up his pen in the 1850's was an attempt made to popularize Indian history. Kaye's work was continued in the 1880's and 90's by William Wilson Hunter, who produced the first concise history of the subcontinent and under whose editorship the Clarendon Press issued the *Rulers of India* series of cheap biographical studies. Public interest was reflected in the large sales of these works, as well as in the commercial success of the Indian memoirs of Lord Roberts (which ran to thirteen editions in one year), the Asiatic epic poetry of Edwin Arnold, and the Indian tales of Meadows Taylor, Flora Annie Steel and Rudyard Kipling. Either because better writing had stimulated the appetite of the reading public or because the shock of the Indian Mutiny and the fever of jingoism had dissipated inveterate torpor, there was a ready market for books on India by the last decades of the nineteeth century, and professional authors qualified to treat

Indian themes set to work to satisfy the demand.

One such author was Herbert Eastwick Compton (1853-1906), who specialized in popular history, biography and stories of naval and military adventure. His interest in India derived from family ties with the country (his father had been in the Bengal army) and the experiences of a twenty-two years' residence there. The European mercenaries who flourished in northern India during the anarchy that followed the collapse of the Mughal and preceeded the rise of the British empire provided him with matter for two books : *A Particular Account of the European Military Adventurers of Hindustan,* an historical monograph which appeared in 1892; and *A Free Lance in a Far Land,* a novel whose title he took from his own earlier work (p. 108) and which was published in 1894.

Despite its obvious meretricious aspects, the subject is one of considerable historical importance. It deserves, and in the present work has received, serious treatment.

These adventurers were agents of Western influence in India, and their activities should be viewed in the wider context of the impact of European ideas on Asiatic society. Their most obvious contribution was of course in the military field, where their work of modernisation changed the style of Maratha warfare and formed a prelude to the second Anglo-Maratha war, the historic conflict which inaugurated 140 years of European hegemony in the subcontinent. Western military technology had appeared in India comparatively early. Guns and long arms were used by the Mughals and the Marathas in the seventeenth century; but they could not be used to advantage in armies composed mainly of cavalry, and it was not until the second half of the eighteenth century, when the European powers operating in India had shown the way, that the native rulers began to employ the disciplined infantry essential for effective musket and artillery fire. Among the Maratha princes, it was the Peshwa of Poona, Balaji Baji Rao, who began the experiment, in the 1750's, inspired by the example of Bussy's battalions in the service of the Nizam of Hyderabad; but it was a nominal vassal of Poona, Mahdaji Sindia of Ujjain (1769-94), who made fullest and most efficient use of infantry of the Western type. He commissioned the Savoyard adventurer Benoit De Boigne to raise three corps ('campos'), which were generally referred to as brigades, but which were in fact more akin to small divisions. Each consisted of infantry, artillery and cavalry and was commanded by European officers. It was these troops that made Mahdaji Sindia guardian of Delhi and its incumbent, Emperor and master of much of the territory that is now the Indian state of Uttar Pradesh; and it was with them that his great-nephew, Daulat Rao Sindia, secured his succession to the family domains in 1794 and went to war against the British in 1803. De Boigne resigned two years after the death of Mahdaji, and the Frenchman Perron took his place as commander of Sindia's regular army and chief lieutenant in the northern territories. He raised a fourth brigade, while the English officer Brownrigg trained a supplementary corps for Daulat Rao's personal use in the Deccan. The Maratha princes of Indore, Tukoji Holkar and his successor Jaswant Rao Holkar, likewise engaged Europeans to raise and train regular infantry, of which there were three brigades in Jaswant Rao's service on the eve of the second Maratha war. Raghuji Bhonsle, the Maratha Raja of Nagpur, raised two regular brigades, which were on the same pattern but which included no European officers.

But the influence of these soldiers of fortune extended beyond the military sphere, and several writers have drawn attention to the broader significance of their work. In three studies produced between 1876 and 1907 (*The Fall of the Mughal Empire, Madhava Rao Sindhia* and *Hindustan Under Free Lances*) H. G. Keene developed the idea that their success represented the triumph of moral superiority over turpitude, and that it prepared the way for the *Pax Britannica* by 'setting up a standard of order (and) preparing men's minds for some vague ideas of discipline and duty'. Less beholden to current racist thought was Malleson's suggestion, in *The Final French Struggles in India* (1884), that De

Boigne's work as a civil ruler laid the basis on which the British later built their own administration in the North-western Provinces. Percy Brown, in his *Indian Architecture (the Islamic Period)*, pointed out that it was Claud Martin, a French adventurer in the service of the Nawab of Oudh, who introduced Western architectural forms into upper India. His priviate palace at Lucknow, 'designed by Martin himself in what may be termed a debased Palladian style...., was one of the first large buildings of a European order to be erected in upper India. Such an important structural undertaking could not fail to impress and, in course of time, to introduce into the building art of those parts an entirely new orientation.' James Skinner, an ex-Maratha officer, built a church of the Palladian style in Delhi, and others must have offered numerous, if less ostentatious examples of Western taste and style of life for native emulation.

Compton's theme, as his title suggests, is the military achievement of these adventurers. His book is mainly concerned with the formation, services and ultimate destruction of the regular army of the Sindia princes under the aegis of De Boigne and Perron. It is in four parts, of which the last is a general appendix of biographical summaries. Part Two, which deals with the career of the Irish freebooter, George Thomas, is in the nature of an interpolation and is a concession to the author's predilection for the picaresque. Thomas's achievement was remarkable enough, and well illustrates the political instability of northern India in this time of interregnum ; but it was a sterile one, of little significance for the future and only tangentially related to the principal substance of the work. This section is also academically the least distinguished, being little more than a résumé of Francklin's *Memoir*. The other parts are based on wide research, and it is this that has ensured for the book a lasting place in the historical literature on its period. Compton was not the first, and he has not been the last, to narrate the story of De Boigne and Perron; but his was the first monograph, and although a few subsequent works have supplemented. they have not superseded his account, which remains the starting point for all who would explore the subject.

This is not to claim that the work is without blemishes. It contains errors that need correction and obscurities that need clarification. Compton is misleading, for example, when he defines the story of military adventure in Hindustan as the story of the Maratha generals of whom he writes. 'These twenty years', he claims of the period 1784-1803, 'saw the rise, the reign and the ruin of independent military adventure in India ... The story of (Sindia's) Brigades is the story of the European Military Adventurers of Hindustan.' (Pp. 8-9). The definition is too narrow, even when enlarged by his brief mention of the European officers in the service of Hyderabad and Mysore. The day of the military adventurer did not end with the destruction of Sindia's brigades. The old areas of opportunity were, it is true, closed after 1805, when the victorious British, following the pattern of their treaties with Oudh (1775), Hyderabad (1798), Mysore (1799) and Poona (1803), required the Maratha and Rajpur princes to forgo the employment of Europeans without special permission; but the Punjab still lay open to free-lance enterprise and a whole new generation of adventurers flourished in the service of Ranjit Singh of Lahore. Men like Allard, Court, Avitabile, Ventura, Holmes and Van Cortlandt modernised the Sikh army in much the same way as De Boigne and Perron had modernised that of Sindia, with the consequence that during the Sikh wars of 1845-6 and 1848-9 the British once again found themselves hard pressed by Indian forces operating with European techniques and resources.

Compton estimates the size of Sindia's combined forces on the outbreak of the war with the British at 90,000 men (p. 297). This is probably near the truth; but his claim that the proportion of regular troops (calculated as 39,000 in the brigades, 5,000 Hindustani horse and 15 battalions under Ambaji Inglia) outweighed that of irregular Maratha cavalry (estimated at 35,000) is almost certainly erroneous. In an autobiographical memoir, quoted by Alfred Martineau in his *Le Général Perron* (Paris, 1931,) Perron himself states that each of his brigades contained only 4,800 sepoys; and since the supplementary brigades under Filoze and Brownrigg were only half as large, even without vacancies, Sindia's regular infantry would have numbered no more than 20,000 men. Allow 360 artillerists per brigade (which had been the figure in De Boigne's day), and the total of men is increased to 22,000. The Hindustani cavalry can have amounted to no more than 4,000 men, made up of 200 per brigade and a separate corps of horse which Perron estimates at 3,000 at the most. The strength of Ambaji's battalions is unknown; but there can be little doubt that the figure of 39,000, which Compton quotes as the strength of the regular army excluding cavalry and Ambaji's troops, was in fact more than enough for all three. The size of Sindia's irregular cavalry, on the other hand, is clearly underestimated at 35,000. Lewis Ferdinand Smith, an ex-Maratha officer to whose book Compton habitually defers but on this issue ignores, reckoned that Sindia had 45,000 Maratha horse; and Sir John Malcolm, who appears to have had access to detailed returns, calculated that the number was 43,000 (excluding freebooters such as Pindaris) at the end of the war, when the corps was much depleted by desertion and casualties. [1]

Irregular horse, therefore, remained the largest component of Sindia's army, and this fact, which holds good for the armies of Holkar and Nagpur, is of more than pedantic significance. It undermines the idea, which has gained wide currency, that interest in infantry and artillery had caused the Maratha leaders to neglect their cavalry. It is true that this ancestral arm failed to produce its usual effect in the war with the British; but the inference to be drawn from this is not so much that the Maratha cavalry had deteriorated as that the British cavalry had got better. Improved size and quality enabled it to neutralize the traditional Maratha threat. The second Maratha war was the first occasion on which the British used cavalry in India on a large scale; and the swiftness of their regular units in pursuits, the success of their irregular, Maratha-style units in protecting convoys, and the demoralizing effect of their horse artillery on the Maratha cohorts all amply vindicated their concern to improve this branch of their service.[2]

The theory was commonly accepted, both at the time when Compton was writing and subsequently, that the Marathas made a fatal mistake in trying to beat the British at their own game, with infantry and guns. Historians like Surendranath Sen (*The Military System of the Marathas*, 1928) and S. P. Sen (*The French in India*, 1958), following the earlier opinions of men like Sir Thomas Munro and the Duke of Wellington, attributed the Marathas' collapse in 1803-5 to their modernization policy, which had caused them to switch from a mobile, predatory strategy to a static, defensive one, and to substitute mercenary forces for a national army. By converting to artillery and infantry they had, runs the argument, discarded their best advantage, which was their elusiveness, and committed themselves to tactics by which they were impeded and at which they were inept. The lightning raid and devastating incursion were replaced by the pitched battle, and the patriotic idealism of their forces was vitiated by extensive recruitment of non-Maratha levies. Compton pays lip service to this theory (pp. 88-9), but has obvious difficulty in reconciling it with the flying speed, stubborn loyalty and excellent fighting qualities shown by Sindia's brigades under De Boigne and at the battles of Laswari and Assaye (pp. 62, 106, 320, 333). Their loyalty was in fact even more remarkable than he realized, since economic difficulties had forced Sindia to reduce their pay shortly before the outbreak of the war with the British. Compton's failure to follow the promptings of his doubts and analyse the theory scientifically detracts from the merit of his book. Had he examined the campaign of Holkar against the British in 1804, for example, he must have realized that artillery had not in practice slowed down the Marathas to any appreciable extent. Holkar's offensive against Colonel Monson showed how a Maratha leader, despite the encumbrance of 200 guns, was able to pursue and harass, at the height of the monsoon, through the black cotton soil of Malwa and across two major rivers, a lightly equipped British force over a distance of 250 miles — an astonishing achievement which, as Lord Lake admitted, 'afforded proofs of a greater degree of efficiency and enterprise than could have been expected'. The strategic error theory is fallacious. It was derived from British helplessness in the face of native cavalry in previous wars and British difficulties in moving artillery and infantry. It took account of neither the recent improvements in the British cavalry, nor the British experience of the loyalty of native mercenaries, nor the remarkable resourcefulness of the Marathas in the matter of transport and supplies.

This resourcefulness, coupled with the contribution of De Boigne and Perron, had furnished them with a formidable fighting machine and ensured that they were defeated by the British only after a desperate contest. Had they done what their critics suggest, and discarded their brigades to fight with cavalry, the margin of defeat would probably have been much wider. The reasons for their collapse are to be sought not in their military strategy, but rather in errors of detail and political failings. De Boigne had trained the Maratha infantry to fight as an adjunct of artillery, which, in the words of his biographer, Saint-Genis, 'became the pivot of the manoeuvre and the centre of attack or defence, with the battalion acting as its framework'. The field gun occupied a much less prominent place in the British dispositions. It was replaced as chief weapon by the bayonet, whose tactical superiority was demonstrated time and time again on the battlefields of the second Maratha war. The loyalty of European mercenary officers, too, proved unequal to the strain of fighting the British, and most (though not all) deserted to the enemy in the initial stages of the contest. But these were weaknesses which only experience could reveal and which might not have proved decisive had the Marathas been less culpable in other respects. They lacked the united leadership which made a high degree of

strategic coordination possible on the British side. Ultimately it was political division and personal quarrels that destroyed De Boigne's creation. Had Holkar played his part
in the first phase of the contest, instead of holding aloof
while Sindia and Nagpur were defeated in detail, the out-
come might have been very different. He was the most able
general among the Maratha leaders, and it was a tragedy
for their cause that he reserved his effort until the British
were free to concentrate all their might against him.

Compton's remarks concerning the number, nationality
and motivation of the European officers who entered Maratha service require amplification and clarification rather
than correction. In two places (pp. 9, 68) he claims that
there were 300 Europeans in Sindia's service — an estimate which is based on a misunderstanding of his source.
The figure is taken from Willam Tone's *Some Particular
Institutions of the Maratha People* (p. 40 in the 1799 edi-
tion), where it refers to the total of Europeans in all the
country services, Hyderabad and Mysore included. Compton assesses the number of commissioned officers at ten
percent of this figure in 1792 (p. 68), and the number of
British officers at 'not less than forty' in 1802 (p. 277). By
using evidence that was not available to him, it is now
possible to give a fairly precise estimate of the number and
nationality of European officers in Maratha employ on the
eve of the war. Among the India Office Records in London
there is a schedule of Europeans from the Maratha services
who received pensions from the British in accordance with
the Governor-General's Proclamation of August 29th 1803.[3]
This contains seventy-nine names. It was drawn up some
time after 1811, when some of the original recipients were
dead; but eight of these can be discovered from the in-
complete but earlier list printed on p. 61 of L. F. Smith's
Sketch. Officers in Maratha service but excluded for one
reason or another from the pension lists include Lieutenant
Lucan, a deserter killed in British service in 1804; nine of
the officers who fought against the British at Assaye (p. 324);
the three officers executed by Holkar and four officers serv-

ing Sindia not mentioned elsewhere (all gleaned from Compton's appendix); the five officers who surrendered after the battle of Delhi (p. 314); and Perron himself. These bring the total of known officers in the services of Holkar and Sindia on the eve of the war to 110, of whom ninety-one appear to have held commissions. This figure cannot be far short of the full number. Even if they had been complete Perron's four brigades would have mustered only 104 officers (twenty-six per brigade), and we know from Perron's memoir that they were not complete. The other brigades had much smaller officer contingents. An examination of the names disposes of the idea that the officers were predominantly French. Of the holders of commissions, twenty-three appear to have been French, eight non-French Continentals, and sixty British or Eurasians of British paternity. This predominance of British and British Eurasians was acknowledged by Perron himself.

Compton is vague about the reasons which drove these men to gamble with their careers and even their lives in such a risky lottery. It is not difficult to understand the motives of those earlier 'men of inferior moral calibre' (p. 26). They had little to lose, as deserters, fugitives from justice, cashiered officers without the means to return home and restless and rootless freebooters of one kind or another from the French, British or Portuguese garrisons in the subcontinent. Less obvious are the motives of those 'Europeans of recognized ability and character' (p. 66) who, as Compton observes, made the Maratha officer corps respectable and professionally competent in the days of De Boigne. There were probably two main impulses. One was growing dissatisfaction with the East India Company's service, which was offering fewer and fewer avenues to fame and fortune. De Boigne himself quitted the Madras Native Infantry for this reason. The appointment of Lord Cornwallis as Governor-General in 1786 inaugurated the rationalization and the purification of the Company's civil and military services; and with the disappearance of extra allowances and irregular perquisites army officers became

unwilling to tolerate a system that offered low pay, slow promotion, no paid leave, no pensions, no high rank and little prestige, and whose independence was made unsure by the constant threat of a take-over by the Crown. Their dissatisfaction culminated in the 'white mutiny' of 1796, which is mentioned by Compton in connection with De Boigne's offer of assistance to the Governor-General (p. 86). This resulted in a victory for the rebels, for the pending scheme of army reorganization was modified in accordance with their demands. Thereafter, service with the Company was still far from ideal; but compared with that with the native states it was advantageous in many respects. In the tract on the Marathas which he published in 1799 William Tone, brother of the Irish rebel Wolfe Tone and one-time officer of the Peshwa of Poona, assessed the respective merits of 'John Company' and the Indian princes as employers and found in favour of the former:
(Native) service is ... very precarious and the expenses are great, as it is almost a constant campaign, which obliges an officer always to keep up a field establishment of servants and animals, both of which occasion very serious deductions from his pay. Very few, indeed, except such as command corps, have any opportunity of accumulating even a moderate fortune; and if you are wounded or disabled in the service, there is no provision allowed from the sircar (government). I would therefore never advise any person to enter a native service, if he can get any situation in the settlements.

It is reasonable to suppose that British officers became less willing to enlist as mercenaries from this time; but Eurasians who aspired to a military career (and they were numerous, since many of this class were sons of British army officers) continued to seek employment with the country powers for the simple reason that they had no choice. In 1791 they were excluded from covenanted office in the civil, military and marine services of the East India Company by a standing order of the Directors, who both feared them as a political danger and resented them as trespassers in the valuable preserve of patronage; and in 1795 an order of the Governor-General in Council extended the ban to all combatant ranks in the Company's armies. These disabilities were not removed until the Charter Act of 1833, and in the meantime many Eurasians sought commissions from the native princes as a welcome alternative to service as farriers or bandsmen with the Company. Compton is undoubtedly right when he claims that they formed 'a very large factor' in Sindia's officer contingent (p. 277).

A Particular Account of the European Military Adventurers of Hindustan dates from a time before professional academics had taken history in hand and applied to it all the apparatus of scientific method, esoteric jargon and sophisticated concepts. Inevitably, a book that is narrative rather than analytical, which is concerned with actions rather than forces and personalities rather than statistics, and whose language owes more to the purple prose of Prescott than the antiseptic ideal of Acton, will seem dated to a modern audience. Nowadays, too, there are bound to be objections to Compton's glib moral inferences and lyrical enthusiasm for men whose motives were, to say the least, selfish and whose stock-in-trade was carnage. But all history is something of a personal vision; and how things seem depends as much on the historian's standpoint as on what he has been able to find out. To Compton, looking back from a 'prosaic age', from 'the civilized Indian Empire of the Victorian zenith', which was steeped in Puritan idealism, whose chronicles were written in bureaucratic black-and-white and whose stability seemed monumental, the success of these self-made men was bound to appear the reward of heroism, just as the violence and volatility of their lives was bound to appear glamorous. His response stamps his book as a product of its age. Likewise, we now look back at the era in which he wrote, and marvel that there ever was such a time, when European bureaucracies ruled Asiatic empires, and men saw glory in mercenary war and wrote of it with such exuberance.

JOHN PEMBLE

NOTES

1. Rughubir Singh (ed.), *Poona Residency Correspondence*, x. 214-5
2. A fuller exposition of the arguments advanced in this and the sub sequent paragraph will be found in John Pemble, 'Resources and Techniques in the Second Maratha War': *Historical Journal*, June, 1976
3. Personal Records, vol. 6 (0/6/6), ff. 95-7. The Proclamation was as follows: 'His Excellency in Council hereby requires all British subjects holding employment in the military service of Daulat Rao Sindia or the Raja of Berar (Nagpur) or of any Maratha chief or other power or state confederated...forthwith to relinquish the service of such chief, power or state...All British subjects who have retired or who may retire from the service of the said chiefs... shall receive from the Honorable Company a provision equal to the amount of (their) fixed pay and allowances..., the said provision to continue during the continuance of hostilities...and so long as such British subjects shall be employed by the Honorable Company; and all such British subjects after having quitted the service of the Honorable Company shall receive a reasonable remuneration and every indulgence which their respective situations may appear to require...' By a subsequent clause the same terms were offered to 'non-British Europeans and Americans' who came over to the British. See House of Commons Sessional Papers, 1803/4, xii. 213, 216, 532-4. Desertion was fairly general among Sindia's officers but was not in all cases attributable to the Proclamation - see Pemble, op. cit.

A PARTICULAR ACCOUNT

OF THE

EUROPEAN MILITARY
ADVENTURERS OF HINDUSTAN

From 1784 to 1803

COMPILED BY

HERBERT COMPTON

EDITOR OF "A MASTER MARINER," &c.

London

T. FISHER UNWIN

PATERNOSTER SQUARE

MDCCCXCII

To

LESTOCK REID, ESQUIRE
(*Of the Bombay Civil Service*)

THIS ATTEMPT TO PERPETUATE

THE MEMORY OF

MANY BRAVE MEN

IS INSCRIBED

WITH

REGARD AND GRATITUDE

INTRODUCTION.

HE European Military Adventurers of Hindustan belong to an heroic age which seems further removed from our's than the mere lapse of a century suggests. It is probable that, saving to the student of Indian history, their names are but as indistinct items on a forgotten scroll, whose record is nearly obliterated by the dust of oblivion. They and their deeds are blended into a barbaric past, when history was written in blood not in books, and of which scarce a vestige remains in the civilised Indian Empire of the Victorian Zenith. And yet only a hundred years ago these dead and gone Adventurers created armies, conquered kingdoms, overturned princes and ruled provinces, winning such distinctions and wielding such personal power as are not within the reach of modern endeavour. Forming a link between the eras of Oriental despotism and European government, they bedizened the introduction of Western enlightenment with the gaudy paraphernalia of the East. But Fate planted them in one of those periods of transition which by their very nature are temporary, and they share with it a short-lived fame. Their individual places in History are limited to a paragraph or, at most, a page. They are but units in the sum of India's story—stray drafts on its capital of achievement which have been retired, filed away and forgotten. None heed these faded personalities now. The whisper of De Boigne's name is as powerless to compel attention as the thunder of his cannon to create terror ; the mention of George Thomas awakens no responsive recognition even in hearts alert to the influence of Romance and Adventure ; the political opinions of Perron have long ceased to affect the price of India stock, or set heads wagging in Leadenhall Street. As for the lesser Soldiers of Fortune—the centurions and the lieutenants of the Mercenary Armies of Native India —they are dust of the common dust, whose memory the greedy march of English enterprise in the East has shuffled out of sight, reducing their achievements to the common level which displays not a headstone to view. Yet each in his different way, designedly or unconsciously, directly or indirectly, worked towards one common end by

assisting in bringing about the conditions that paved the way for the establishment of English supremacy in India; and each, when his personal share in the drama was finished, and the last great act opened, passed off the stage unnoticed and unknown, and left the completion of the task, and the applause it evoked, to other actors.

A word of explanation is necessary concerning the title chosen for this book. The "Hindustan" therein referred to is the circumscribed territory defined by that fine old geographer, Major James Rennell, in his "Memoir of a Map of Hindostan," published in 1785. It was a territory bounded by the Indus on the west, by the "Burrampootra or thereabouts" on the east, by the Himalayan mountains on the north, and "by the countries of the Deccan on the south, so that the whole peninsula to the south of a line drawn nearly from Balasore to Broach is not reckoned Hindostan." It is necessary to thus localise the Adventurers whose lives are sketched in the following pages in order that they may not be confounded with the innumerable European Free Lances, who served the courts of Haidarabad and Mysore and other Native Princes in Southern India.

The period in which the European Military Adventurers of Hindustan flourished began in 1784, during the Government of Warren Hastings, and ended in 1803 during that of the Marquis Wellesley. Those twenty years saw the rise, the reign, and the ruin of Independent Military Adventure in India. To De Boigne belongs the honour of having initiated the wonderful system that took root and grew with the fatal rapidity of an exotic. He created for Madhoji Sindhia—"A Ruler of India"—the first complete army of regular troops employed by the Native Princes of the country. The example was soon followed by the Nizam of Haidarabad, and, in a different degree, by Tipú Sultan. In 1798 there were three great disciplined military establishments in the service of the leading Indian Courts, commanded by Frenchmen in the French interest, and employing European arts and tactics of war. Their destruction and extermination was forced upon the Marquis Wellesley by the political exigences of the times, and was the most important work of his administration. De Boigne's army, which had passed under the command of Perron, was the first of these three organisations to be called into existence and the last of them to be broken up.

The political and, indeed, international importance of the European Military Adventurers of India can be guaged from the following extract from a despatch written by the Marquis Wellesley in 1798 :—

" In the present weak state of the Nizam of Haidarabad's Government, the French corps in his service would (in the event of a war between the English and Mysore, which was anticipated) openly join Tipú Sultan, and by a sudden blow endeavour to seize the Nizam's territories, and to secure them to the Dominion of France under an alliance offensive and defensive with Tipú Sultan. . . . The interest and the inclination of Sindhia, who entertains a large army in his service under the command of a French officer (Perron), would lead him to engage with Tipú Sultan and the French. . . . The junction which might thus be effected between the French officers, with their several corps in the respective services of the Nizam, of Sindhia, and of Tipú, might establish the power of France upon the ruins of the states of Poonah and of the Deccan."

Although this book does not deal with the French Factions or Haidarabad and Mysore, their existence and importance must be noted, because they are intimately connected with the subject treated. In Haidarabad, in addition to the Nizam's irregular soldiery, there was a trained army of 14,000 men and 30 guns under the command of Piron, who had succeeded the famous Raymond. The native army of Mysore numbered 75,000 troops of all arms, and included Tipú's "European or French Force" of 550 officers, non-commissioned officers and men. Finally Sindhia could muster 40,000 disciplined infantry with 380 guns, the whole commanded by Perron, who was assisted by an efficient staff of 300 Europeans. Sindhia's Brigades were one factor, and, as events proved, the most formidable factor in that possible combination which a hundred years ago threatened the existence of the English power in India. The story of those Brigades is the story of the European Military Adventurers of Hindustan.

I am desirous of taking this opportunity of recording my obligations to two gentlemen for help received. Mr. Edmund Neel, C.I.E., the assistant secretary in the political department of the India office, facilitated a search through many volumes of Government records, and kindly assisted in regard to those of a secret nature which were not open to my inspection; and Count de Boigne placed at my disposal a memoir of his illustrious grandsire's life, and cleared up one doubtful point of great interest.

In compiling the following pages a great many authorities have been consulted, but it would be tedious to give in detail the names of all the works from which fragments of information have been gleaned. The principal ones are indicated in the list printed below, to the first four books in which I am particularly indebted. The sketch of De Boigne's life was written before the two French biographies indicated came under my observation, and they have only been used to correct a few minor statements of fact, chiefly of a personal nature. In the life of George Thomas, his memoirs have been very closely followed, but a great quantity of extraneous and uninteresting matter has been eliminated, and a good deal of additional information incorporated. With regard to Perron, so far as I am aware, there is no detailed biography of this adventurer in existence, and the one here presented is compiled from original sources. The lives of the lesser adventurers have been culled from a great variety of works, by far the most important of which is the one written by Lewis Ferdinand Smith.

An earnest endeavour has been made to secure correctness of narrative, but in some cases it has been rendered very difficult, and success rendered doubtful, by divergent statements and contradictory dates bearing on the same incident.

H. C.

LIST OF AUTHORITIES CONSULTED.

A Sketch of the Rise, Progress, and Termination of the Regular Corps formed and commanded by Europeans in the service of the Native Princes of India. By LEWIS FERDINAND SMITH. Calcutta, 1805.

Military Memoirs of Lieutenant-Colonel James Skinner, C.B. By J. BAILLIE FRASER. London, 1851.

The Military Memoirs of George Thomas. By COLONEL WILLIAM FRANCKLIN. Calcutta, 1803.

A History of the Mahrattas. By JAMES GRANT DUFF. London, 1826.

The Despatches, Minutes, and Correspondence of the Marquess Wellesley, K.G., during his administration in India. London, 1837.

Memoire sur la carrière de M. Le Général Comte de Boigne. Chambéry, 1830.

Une page inédité de l'histoire des Indes. Le General de Boigne (1751-1830). Par VICTOR DE SAINT-GENIS. Poitiers, 1873.

Memoirs of the Puthan Soldier of Fortune. . . . Ameer Khan. Compiled in Persian by BUSAWAN LAL. Translated by H. T. PRINSEP. Calcutta, 1832.

Illustrations of some Institutions of the Mahratta People. By W. H. TONE. Calcutta, 1818.

The History of the Reign of Shah Aulum. By COLONEL WILLIAM FRANCKLIN. London, 1798.

The Calcutta Monthly Register, 1790; The Calcutta Monthly Journal, 1798-1800; The Hindostanee Intelligencer and Oriental Anthology, 1801-1802; The Asiatic Annual Register, 1801-1811; The Asiatic Journal, 1831, etc. Selections from the Calcutta Gazette. By W. S. SETON KARR. Calcutta, 1864.

Government Records at the India Office.

Etc., Etc., Etc.

CONTENTS.

CONTENTS.

LIST OF ILLUSTRATIONS.

DE BOIGNE.

CHAPTER I.

HIS EARLY LIFE AND SERVICES. ARRIVAL IN INDIA.

1751-1784.

F the daring and errant military adventurers who, during the last two decades of the eighteenth century, helped to wreck dynasties and establish kingdoms in Hindustan, there is one who towers high and great above the rest. The pride and pomp of Perron, and the delirious ambition of George Thomas, must yield place to the genius and achievement of General Count de Boigne, who, if he never quite touched the political importance attained by the former, or aspired to the actual independence usurped by the latter, must yet take precedence of both as the creator of the military system they inherited or adopted. For De Boigne was the first to raise up disciplined armies from the fierce races of Upper India, and teach them how to fight and how to conquer; he was the first to carry the science of European warfare into the heart of Hindustan; and his famous battalions formed the connecting link between the eras of Mughal Empire and British Dominion in the East. If the extraordinary power De Boigne's brigades exercised, and the brilliant record they left behind them, during a momentous quarter of a century, fill but a single chapter in the turbulent history of India, it is at least one glowing with enterprise and achievement, and worthy of the place it fills between the pages that record the conquests of Clive and Coote and the victories of Lake and Wellesley.

Benoît La Borgne—better known to history as Benoît de Boigne—was born at Chambéry, in Savoy, on the 8th of March, 1751. He was the second son of a large family, and his father followed the calling of a hide merchant. Despite his narrow means, Père La Borgne contrived to afford Benoît a sufficient education at the college of his native town, where, under the tutelage of pious and learned monks, the youth acquired a general knowledge of books and a tolerable proficiency in Latin ; whilst, from the circumstances of his birthplace being situated near the French frontier, he spoke French and Italian with equal fluency.

As a lad, Benoît found his chief pleasure in music and fencing, and his brain was filled with the fanciful ideas of glory in which boys indulge. It was his father's intention to make him a lawyer, but he himself determined at an early age to follow the profession of arms, for which his fine physique and bold spirit eminently fitted him. His desire was to enter the army of his native country, then under the rule of King Charles Emanuel, but in this he was disappointed owing to all its commissioned appointments being monopolised by the nobility of Savoy and Sardinia, and admitting no cadets of less distinguished birth. Perhaps De Boigne lost nothing by this, for the life of an officer in the Sardinian service was often one of inflated poverty wherein a glittering coat covered a hungry stomach during a long and depressing period of uniformed impecuniosity.

But he had not far to look for a more hopeful sphere of action. France was contiguous, and its capital the head-quarters of a body of adventurers famous in history—the Irish Brigade. This corps enjoyed the highest reputation throughout Europe for gallantry in the field and discipline in the camp. Its ranks were open to the merit and talent of all nations, and to belong to it was at once an establishment and a distinction in life. It was, in short, just such a service as appealed to the inherent instincts of young De Boigne, and he determined to enter its ranks if possible.

Tradition says that he left his native country under circumstances which did more credit to his spirit than to his respect for those laws which his father had intended he should expound. A duel with a Sardinian officer, which threatened retribution at the hands of a local magistrate, led De Boigne to accelerate his departure from the paternal roof. Nurturing high aspirations, and without any definite ambition in view, he crossed the frontier and entered France in 1768, and presented himself for employment in the Irish Brigade.

There was a recommendation in his tall martial figure and frank soldierly bearing. His large-boned limbs and massive frame gave evidence of unusual physical powers, and he confronted the world with an air of conscious superiority. His features were stern and

DE BOIGNE.

resolute, lit up with piercing eyes, and surmounted by a lofty brow, not common in the Latin race, and indicating the possession of those qualities from which soldiers are shaped and heroes .hewn. His application was successful, and he obtained an ensign's commission in the Clare Regiment, temporarily commanded by Major Leigh, an officer noted for his discipline. Joining his corps at Landrecies, De Boigne passed the next three years chiefly in Flanders, until his regiment embarked for the Isle of France, where it remained for eighteen months before being ordered back to Europe.

During his stay in the Irish Brigade De Boigne was noted for his professional zeal and general good conduct, and in this famous corps acquired the intimate knowledge of military affairs which proved of such essential use to him in later life. But after some years' service his active and ambitious temperament grew disheartened from want of encouragement ; promotion stagnated, and he found advancement to the higher grades too slow for his restless spirit. He never spared himself, but he expected a suitable reward for his exertions. Despite his zeal and love for his profession, De Boigne was so far a mercenary at heart that he recognised his sword was his sole capital, and desired to invest it to the best advantage. Love of money was strongly engrained in his character, and a subaltern's pay in a foreign legion satisfied him as little as a subaltern's position. When, therefore, he chanced to hear of an opening for volunteer officers in the service of Russia (then at war with the Turks), De Boigne determined to quit the Irish Brigade, and endeavour to advance his fortunes under a new flag where the chances of active service were assured, and the flow of promotion promised to be more rapid.

Resigning his commission in the French service in 1774, De Boigne proceeded to Turin, and obtained from the Marquis D'Aigueblanche, the Sardinian minister, a letter of recommendation to Admiral Orloff, who commanded the Russian forces in the Grecian Archipelago. Equipped with this, he started for the seat of war, and made his way to Paros, where he presented himself before the Admiral, who, with the quick perception of a commander accustomed to read character, was favourably impressed with De Boigne's appearance, and appointed him to a captaincy in a Greek regiment in the service of the Empress Catherine.

But Fate ordained that De Boigne's career of active service should be of short duration. After a few weeks his regiment was employed in an attack on the island of Tenedos, at the mouth of the Dardanelles. The expedition was ill-conceived and ill-executed, and met with a disastrous defeat at the hands of the Turkish garrison, by whom De Boigne, one of the few survivors of the fight, was made prisoner.

As an infidel and a captive of war in the hands of the Moslem he received but scant consideration. One account says he was sent to Scio, where he languished six months in prison till the war terminated. But another authority gives the following somewhat apocryphal but picturesque version of his adventures during the next three years. After being taken prisoner he was sent to Constantinople, and there sold as a slave for fifty dollars, and for a time employed in a menial capacity, being actually set to hew wood and draw water for his master's household. During this period he managed to communicate with his parents, who arranged for his ransom. On regaining his freedom he made his way to St. Petersburg to press his claims for consideration after the hardships he had suffered in the Russian service. After some little waiting he succeeded in obtaining a presentation to the Empress Catherine, who listened graciously and with interest to the story of his slavery at Constantinople, and is said to have predicted a career for him. To compensate for his misfortune she bestowed on him a commission as major in her army, and the war with the Turks being at an end, he was posted to a regiment doing duty on the south-western frontier of Russia, where he was not long afterwards selected for the command of an escort detached to attend Lord Percy, a son of the Duke of Northumberland, on a tour through the islands of the Grecian Archipelago. De Boigne quickly ingratiated himself with this nobleman. In the course of their travels they touched at Smyrna, where De Boigne chanced to meet some European merchants lately returned from the East, whose dazzling descriptions of India, and the prospects it held out to military adventurers so fascinated him that he determined to visit the country. This intention he communicated to Lord Percy, who furnished him with a letter of introduction to Warren Hastings, the Governor of Bengal.

While considering the best way to carry his design into execution, the idea occurred to De Boigne of making the journey to India overland, by way of the Caspian Sea, Tartary, and Kashmir. It was a boldly conceived enterprise, and worthy of his adventurous spirit. Returning to St. Petersburg he solicited an audience with the Empress, and laid his proposition before her. The project was one that appealed to a sovereign who was always ready to encourage travel and exploration, more especially in those countries which Peter the Great had indicated in his will as indispensable objects of future acquisition by Russia. The Empress accorded her countenance to the scheme, and it is interesting to note that, twelve years later, when the relations between Russia and England threatened a rupture, she ordered her ministers to obtain all available information concerning the actual route suggested by De Boigne, with a view to invading India by an advance in that direction.

Such is one version of De Boigne's adventures during this period, but another account merely states that after his capture by the Turks he was confined for seven months at Scio, until the end of the war, which event liberated him, but stopped his promotion; that he then resigned the service of Russia and embarked for Smyrna, where he met certain English traders lately returned from the East, who described India as a veritable political chaos, but withal so marvellous a country that, listening to them, De Boigne felt all the fantastic dreams of his youth revive, and was inspired to go there and search for fortune.

There is nothing incompatible in the two versions, and they both bring the narrative to the same point at Aleppo, where De Boigne found himself about the year 1777, and joined a caravan starting for Baghdad. Unfortunately Turkey was at war with Persia, and the arms of the former having recently suffered some serious reverses, the districts through which the caravan would have to travel were rendered unsafe by the presence of marauding bodies of Persian cavalry, and the leader of the expedition, fearing capture, decided shortly after starting, to abandon the proposed journey and return to Aleppo.

Undeterred by this inauspicious beginning, De Boigne determined to reach India by some other route, and set sail for Alexandria. But misfortune still dogged his path, for the vessel that carried him was wrecked at the mouth of the Nile, and he found himself a castaway on the inhospitable shores of Egypt. He was rescued by a band of Arabs, from whom he expected the inhumanity of treatment they were generally credited with exercising; but it appeared that, however pitiless they might be in plundering the rich, they were precluded by their notions of honour from oppressing the needy, and, so far from ill-treating De Boigne, they succoured him most charitably, and assisted him to reach Grand Cairo.

Here he met his old acquaintance Lord Percy, who introduced him to Mr. George Baldwin, the British Consul, through whose kindness De Boigne obtained a passage in a country ship to Madras, by way of the Red Sea. He was also furnished with letters of introduction to Major Sydenham, the Town-major of Fort St. George, where he landed in January, 1778, just after Sir Thomas Rumbold had assumed the government of the Presidency.

De Boigne was at this time a young man of twenty-seven years of age, ten of which had been spent in military service and foreign travel. And yet he was not so worldly wise but that he expected to find the famous pagoda tree flourishing, whose branches required only to be shaken to ensure the dropping of their golden fruit. He had come to acquire wealth, but he soon learnt that poverty and want existed in the East as well as riches and luxury. War had recently been declared between England and France, and Sir Hector Munro was engaged in laying siege to Pondicherry. It was an inauspicious moment for an ex-officer of the French service to seek his fortune in an English dependency. Month after month passed by, and De Boigne waited for the preferment that did not come. His slender stock of money gradually melted away, and at last, in order to procure the necessaries of life, he was compelled to give lessons in fencing—an art in which he was highly proficient.

That he was very poor, that he was very distressed, and that he was greatly disheartened, is confirmed by his acceptance shortly afterwards of an ensign's commission in the 6th Regiment of Madras Native Infantry. This he obtained through the good offices of Major Sydenham, who found means to overcome the scruples of the Governor. It has been suggested that by entering the British service De Boigne desired to disarm suspicion as to his political relations with the Russian Government, and that this step offered the most efficacious method of doing so. But this theory may be dismissed, for there is little doubt but that it was poverty alone which compelled this ex-captain of the Irish Brigade and ex-major of the Russian army to don the uniform of a subaltern in a regiment of Madras Native Infantry, and swear allegiance to a Company of merchant adventurers.

For nearly two years De Boigne continued in this station, and, but for a fortunate accident, might have ended as well as begun his Indian career as a Company's ensign. His regiment was attached to Colonel Baillie's force at Gantur in September, 1780, when De Boigne happened to be detached on escort duty to convoy up a supply of grain from Madras. During his absence Colonel Baillie was surrounded by the Mysore army, under Tipú Sahib, the son of Haidar Ali, and after a brave, but hopeless, resistance, during which the greater portion of his force was cut to pieces, obliged to surrender.

Just about this time Lord Macartney succeeded Sir Thomas Rumbold as Governor of Madras, and, after the disaster of Gantur, offered De Boigne an appointment in his body-guard It is not improbable that during the next three years De Boigne learnt many particulars concerning the French military adventurers in the service of Mysore, for the deeds of these Free Lances of Carnatic must have been topics of common conversation. Amongst them were many able officers not unworthy successors to Dupleix, Bussy, La Bourdonnais, Lally, and Law. Lally, it may be noted, had served in Dillon's Regiment in the Irish Brigade. Aided by the condition of the times, and the circumstances of the country, these military adventurers attained substantial, and, in many cases, lucrative, commands in the service of Haidar Ali, and were struggling to keep in existence the French influence in Southern India.

Before many months had passed De Boigne came to the conclusion that the Madras Native Army dangled no charms for a soldier of fortune. On the contrary, it confirmed his repugnance for a progressive service. Those were the days of grey-headed ensigns and veteran lieutenants, to whom promotion could never come. Money, not merit, commanded steps, and De Boigne's prospects were the more hopeless because he laboured under the disadvantage of alien birth, which was a bar to his advancement. Yet all this time he was constantly reminded of the possibilities the country offered to men of ability and enterprise, for but a few leagues distant there were Frenchmen—who, in Europe, must have saluted him respectfully—enjoying immense powers, dignity and wealth in a service that was greedy to receive all European applicants who would fight against the English.

The resignation De Boigne decided on was accelerated by two incidents, the one arising out of the other. A charge was preferred against him of taking undue liberties with the wife of a brother officer, and although the accusation was unfounded, and he was honourably acquitted by a court-martial, the circumstance led Lord Macartney to refuse De Boigne's application for an adjutancy, and confer the appointment on an officer of junior standing. Whereupon De Boigne threw up his commission. This induced the Governor to inquire more clearly into the matter, and he was soon convinced that De Boigne had been harshly treated. Anxious now to repair the unwitting injustice, he professed himself ready to sanction the appointment, but De Boigne had made up his mind to leave the Company's service, and declined to withdraw his papers. Lord Macartney was therefore obliged to accept his resignation, but to testify his kindly feeling, he provided him with a letter of recommendation to Warren Hastings at Calcutta.

Captain Edward Moor, in his " Narrative of Little's Expedition," gives another version of the reason that led to De Boigne's departure from Madras. According to this writer he was dismissed from the service for a trivial offence " by the overgrown authority of the Civil power ; " but it matters little whether he resigned voluntarily or of necessity. In 1782 he arrived at Calcutta, where a kind-hearted resident of Fort William—an intimate friend of Captain Moor—took him by the hand, and furnished him with credit to a very considerable amount, which enabled him early in the following year to set out on his journey to Upper India.

Meanwhile De Boigne presented his letters of introduction from Lord Percy and Lord Macartney to Warren Hastings. These secured him a courteous reception, and he confided to the Governor-General his intention of endeavouring to make his way to Europe overland. The boldness of the design interested Hastings, who could appreciate enterprise in all its forms, and he provided De Boigne with letters to the British agents in India, and also to the Nawáb Wazier of Oudh, which assured the recipient great pecuniary advantages, since it was the custom of the Native Courts of India to bestow valuable *Khiluts*, or presents of honour, on all persons recommended by friendly powers. This to a traveller of De Boigne's narrow circumstances was a matter of immense importance.

Early in 1783, after a short stay in Calcutta, De Boigne proceeded to Lucknow, and waited upon Mr. Middleton, the English Resident at the Court of Oudh, and in the course of time was received in audience by the Nawáb Wazír, and honoured with a valuable *Khilut* and letters of credit on Kabul and Kandahar for Rs.12,000. The *Khilut* De Boigne immediately sold for Rs.4,000, and being thus provided with the necessary means, settled down at Lucknow to study the languages for five months, and to prepare a suitable equipment for his journey through Central Asia. During this time he made the acquaintance of General Claude Martine, a remarkable adventurer, who held a post of the highest confidence in the Nawáb's Court, and with whom he formed a friendship that lasted until Martine's death, sixteen years later.

In August Major James Brown, an officer deputed by Warren Hastings on a mission to the Emperor Shah 'Alam, was starting for Delhi, his object being to discover the designs that the Mahratta Prince Madhoji Sindhia had formed in regard to the Mughal Empire. De Boigne decided to accompany Major Brown, but a few days after leaving Lucknow, the march of the mission was arrested by the intrigues of the turbulent nobles of the Court of Delhi, who, having long since reduced their sovereign to a state of impotence, were very averse to oreign interference, and especially dreaded the arrival of the British

Ambassador. In consequence of which they took measures to impede Major Brown's progress; but De Boigne pressed on, and made his way to Delhi, where he arrived towards the end of the month.

The Emperor's Wazír, or prime minister, Mírzá Shafi, being absent from the capital on an expedition against the Játs at Agra, De Boigne found it impossible to obtain an audience with Shah 'Alam, and decided to proceed towards Agra, where Mírzá Shafi was encamped. But when the latter heard that the traveller had been in Major Brown's mission, his fears were aroused and he suspected De Boigne of sinister designs. He therefore accorded him the coldest reception (for Mírzá was at this time intriguing with Madhoji Sindhia), and refused to comply with his application for assistance on his journey towards the west.

Not far from the Wazír's camp lay the army of Madhoji Sindhia, who was engaged in an invasion of the territory of the Ránà of Gohad, and the siege of the fortress of Gwalior. Madhoji was one of the most powerful chiefs of the great Marátha Confederation, and attached to his Court, in the quality of British Resident, was Mr. James Anderson. As soon as this gentleman heard of De Boigne's arrival in the neighbourhood he asked him to visit his camp, and, hopeless of obtaining any assistance from Mírzá Shafi, De Boigne gladly accepted the invitation. But now, in turn, Madhoji's suspicions were aroused by the advent of this stranger, who had been first in the *entourage* of Major Brown, next at Delhi, then in the camp of the Wazír, and was finally coming to Mr. Anderson. It seemed impossible that such a sequence of visits could be altogether innocent in their nature. The re-occupation of Delhi, which the Maráthás had been forced to evacuate after the battle of Pánípat, was the object of Sindhia's present ambition, whilst the encroachment of the British power excited his keenest jealousy. Under these circumstances Madhoji was particularly anxious to discover the real character of the suspicious wanderer, who was moving from camp to camp in a way that suggested intrigue. To obtain this information he had recourse to the usual Marátha expedient of craft, and employed one of the gangs of robbers, with which the country was infested, and whose dexterity in theft was beyond description, to steal De Boigne's baggage during his march to Mr. Anderson's camp, hoping to discover in it letters or credentials that would explain the recent movements or ultimate designs of their owner. His plot was successful, and when De Boigne reached his destination he reported that all his property had been plundered on the march.

Mr. Anderson's resentment was aroused at this indignity offered to his guest, and he demanded the restoration of the stolen baggage. A few days afterwards it was all brought in, with the exception of the letters of recommendation and credit. These were never given up, although every pressure was brought to bear to secure their recovery.

The loss of his money and papers was a fatal blow to De Boigne's schemes of travel and exploration. Without means or credentials he could not hope to pierce the unsettled and disturbed districts that lay between Hindustan and Russia, and he had no other resources on which to fall back. Without friends, without employment, a stranger in a strange land, and penniless to boot, all that was left to him was his sword, his talent, and his determination.

It was of course open to him to return to Calcutta, and Mr. Anderson would have considered it a duty to arrange for his journey thither. But this was a poor and ignominious retreat out of his difficulties, and one that could not commend itself to a man of De Boigne's character and ambition. The spirit of adventure was quick within him, and he scorned surrender. He felt he was on the threshold of an arena where great achievements were possible. Vivid in his memory was the recollection of the French soldiers of fortune in Southern India, whose successes afforded an example of the attainment possible to men fitted for military command, if they once obtained the confidence of the native princes. Instances of similar success were around him: Sombre * and Médoc, Martine and Sangster, Pauly and Baours were adventurers who had commanded, or were at the present moment commanding, small disciplined corps in the service of neighbouring rulers. Here he was, in the centre of Hindustan, amidst contending interests and warlike peoples, each eager to overcome the other. To the north lay Delhi, with its Mughal population nurtured in conquest for centuries past; to the west dwelt the Rájputs, a warrior nation, the bravest and most chivalrous in all India; close at hand were the Játs, staunch and sturdy soldiers, who had recently won their independence; whilst to the southward stretched the great Maráthá Dominion, with its Confederated princes, whose spears had glistened at the gates of Lahore, until the Abdali, carrying the crescent from the north, hurled them back to within their own boundaries from the field of Pánípat.

War was in the hearts of all these antagonistic races, whom rapine ruled, and whose profession was plunder and pillage. Yet they were utterly wanting in the science of war. They relied on the strength of countless numbers, or, at best, on the advantage of surprise by swift advance or safety by rapid retreat. They fought with the ponderous club, whose very unwieldiness carried its blows astray, not with the

* For this, and all subsequent lesser adventurers mentioned, see Appendix.

trained rapier, which pierced the heart almost before its thrust was seen. Their armies were vast multitudes, impossible to manœuvre, subject to panic, ill-armed, and absolutely without discipline. The brute power was there, but it was wasted by reason of the ignorance that could not direct or control it. Its proper organisation opened out to De Boigne a splendid field for his talents. In the strife and scramble for the wreck of Taimur's Empire, a soldier's sword, supported by European intelligence, was a sufficient capital.

De Boigne had already served three masters, and was no novice in the art of swearing allegiance. His fortunes had never been at so low an ebb as they were at this moment, when he found himself derelict in the centre of Hindustan. He was, in truth, a castaway, whose condition might have awakened commiseration in the coldest breast. But herein lay his opportunity. From the lowliness of his beginning must be measured the height of his attainment. He was to prove the resultant of his own works, and before accompanying him on his career to his ultimate success, it is well to note this point from which he started. It was one hedged about with novel and singular difficulties and dangers; but they could not veil from his eyes the possibilities beyond. To a man of his splendid spirit and tireless perseverance obstacles were but the stepping stones to an end. That voyager succeeds in life whose eyes are fixed, not on the troubled waters that intervene, but on the harbour he desires to reach. It was so with De Boigne. He felt that, at last, his career was in his own hands, and with squared shoulders and resolute mien he faced the future that lay before him. Long ago, as a boy, he had dreamed of glory and greatness; but now the reality of his life was dawning, and it was destined to carry him far beyond " the utmost further rim " of youth's imagination.

CHAPTER II.

DE BOIGNE ENTERS SINDHIA'S SERVICE. THE BATTLES OF LÁLSÓT
AND CHAKSÁNA.

1784-1788.

THE value of European direction and discipline in native warfare
began to be acknowledged by the Princes of Upper India about
the middle of the eighteenth century. The Nawábs of Bengal and
Oudh, the Rájahs of Rájputana, the Ját chiefs of Agra and Bhartpur,
and the Imperial Court of Delhi itself, all employed from time to time
the services of several French, and a few English, military adventurers, who found their way westward or northward from Calcutta or
the Carnatic, and sold their swords to the highest bidder. General
Claude Martine, of Lucknow, could have told De Boigne many stirring
and romantic histories, that can never be known now, of European
soldiers of fortune who drilled the troops and led to battle the armies
of alien races, inspiring them with confidence and courage, and teaching
them how to fight fields and win victories. Amongst these daring
men were persons of birth, education, and approved character, who,
from various causes, expatriated themselves, and entered the services
of the Native Courts. Some from dissatisfaction with their prospects,
others—men of less respectability—from caprice or more unworthy
motives; a few were driven to this form of banishment by reason
of their necessities or pecuniary embarrassments, whilst many were
actuated by a spirit of pure adventure, without any aim except a
desire to win distinction in fresh fields, and rise to a pre-eminence
denied them in their own country.

Of this cosmopolitan company two or three achieved high rank and
position at the Courts they served, either through their own abilities
or under favour of fortune. But the majority were men of inferior
moral calibre, who proved unable to resist the temptations around
them, and succumbed to the notorious vices of the East. Having once

given way to debauchery and immorality, they soon fell into the lowest state of degradation, despised by the very people they had purposed to teach.

History has recorded the good and bad deeds of only a few of these early European pioneers in Hindustan.   From time to time their names flit across its pages in desultory transit, to be too often dismissed with perfunctory comment or contemptuous unconcern.   Even the current literature of their day ignores them, and one may search page after page of contemporaneous history without gleaning more than the baldest facts concerning men whose enterprises deserved a fuller recognition, and who in this more civilized and calmer age would have been acclaimed heroes of no common clay.

None of these early soldiers of fortune, who served in the armies of Delhi, Lucknow, Agra, and Bengal, left any permanent mark upon the history of their times.   Some of them were locally successful, and won battles for their several masters, but their victories were isolated incidents leading to no substantial assertion of power.   The doctrine of the highest bidder governed their actions whenever they attained to any temporary importance, and counteracted sustained effort in one direction.   It was left to De Boigne, not only to inaugurate more perfect systems of discipline and superior methods of warfare, but to show how loyalty to a single cause could raise it up to supremacy. His genius and his constancy created a dominion such as those who preceded him never dreamt of, and his career presents a contrast to, rather than a comparison with, the careers of the Military Adventurers who established themselves in Upper India previous to the period in which he flourished.

When De Boigne joined Mr. Anderson's camp, Madhoji Sindhia was engaged in the reduction of Gwalior.   This stronghold had been in the possession of the Maráthás, but was captured from them by the English during the late war, and made over to Chattra Sing, the Rána of Gohad, a Ját chieftain who had created an independent principality for himself on the ruins of Mughal decadence.   The Rána had been assisted by a Frenchman named Médoc, from whom, by a species of transaction peculiar to those days, he purchased a battalion of disciplined infantry.   In 1784 the command of this battalion was in the hands of a Scotchman named Sangster.   It consisted of one thousand disciplined men, and a respectable train of artillery, and was partially officered by Europeans, one of them being an Irishman named Thomas Legge, the hero of a marvellously adventurous life.   But this single battalion was not strong enough to cope with Madhoji Sindhia's immense Marátá hordes investing Gwalior, the siege of which place it had been unable to raise.

De Boigne, smarting under a sense of resentment at the robbery he had sustained, determined to offer his sword to Sindhia's enemy, the Rána of Gohad. But instead of endeavouring to enter the service as an officer under Sangster, he spurned such humble means to an end, and boldly proposed to raise an independent and much larger force of his own. A single battalion would not suit the ambition of this vagrant adventurer, whose pride was not broken by his poverty. He aspired to the immediate command of a brigade of five regiments. It is impossible not to admire the cool audacity which from the depths of recent disaster could deliberately ask for an advance of a lakh of rupees (£12,500) to create an army. This was the actual proposition De Boigne made to Chattra Sing, undertaking in return to recruit five thousand men at Delhi, Jaipur, Gohad, and elsewhere, and withal so secretly and expeditiously as not to arouse suspicion until he was in a position to act in conjunction with Sangster, and relieve the beleaguered fort of Gwalior.

The proposal was an imperial one. But De Boigne had unbounded belief in himself, and did not hesitate to formulate it, even though it should bring him into direct conflict with the might of the Marátá Empire, which at this time was the dominant power in India. A lakh of rupees was all he required. But, alas! for the littleness of human nature and the economy of regal minds, it was over this miserable bauble the scheme was wrecked. Chattra Sing was a prudent and thrifty potentate. He mistrusted the enthusiastic but unknown stranger, and declined to confide so large a sum to his care. But this did not prevent the practical prince from turning the incident to his advantage, by causing circumstantial details of it to be circulated, so that they might reach Sindhia's ears, and intimidate him. The information was soon current in the Marátá camp, and not unnaturally excited Madhoji's enmity against De Boigne. But at the same time it discovered the daring and enterprise of a man who could conceive such an audacious scheme, and marked him as one of more than average ability.

This repulse instead of discouraging De Boigne stirred him to fresh endeavour, for his perseverance was as dogged as his ambition was aspiring. There were other enemies of Sindhia to be appealed to, and first and foremost Partáb Sing, the Rájah of Jaipur, who was jealously watching the movements of the Marátá armies, ready, in his desire to restrain them within their own boundaries, to take the field at any moment. To this prince De Boigne now addressed himself, and his proposals were favourably received. Negotiations followed, and he was engaged at a salary Rs.2,000 a month to raise and discipline a couple of battalions of regular infantry.

De Boigne at once wrote to Warren Hastings, acquainting him of his good fortune. Whether he did so from mere exuberance of satisfaction, or from a sense of duty, it is difficult to say. Possibly he was influenced by the circumstance of his having held a commission in the Company's army, or he may have considered that as he had started from Bengal in pursuit of a fixed purpose, for the furtherance of which he had received credentials from the Governor-General, it was right, now that his original plan was abandoned, to communicate the fact. Unfortunately his letter was official in form, and was read at the meeting of the Bengal Council, whose factious members never neglected an opportunity of opposing the Governor-General; and they immediately expressed disapproval of a European, a *protégé* of Warren Hastings, entering the service of native princes. This opinion was quite in keeping with the petty prejudices of the period, when "interlopers" were regarded with only one degree less suspicion than loafers create at the present day. It resulted in an order for De Boigne to return to Calcutta immediately.

De Boigne received this just as he was entering on his new task, and it is to his credit that he at once obeyed, and started for Bengal. His prompt compliance so pleased Warren Hastings, that after explanations had been tendered, he permitted De Boigne to accompany him to Lucknow, whither he was going, and from thence to return to Jaipur to resume his engagement. But meanwhile the treaty of Salbye had been ratified, and this changed Partáb Sing's policy, and he dispensed with De Boigne's services, salving the disappointment with a solatium of Rs.10,000, with which the latter returned to Delhi, where he found his friend, Major Brown.

Little did the Jaipur ruler suspect what a disastrous effect upon his future fortunes was to follow this decision, or he would never have permitted the departure from his service of a man who was to become his scourge and dictator in the future. It is idle to speculate upon the what-might-have-beens of history, yet it is indisputable that, but for the failure of De Boigne's negotiations with Chattra Sing and Partáb Sing, he would have been arrayed in the field of battle against Madhoji Sindhia, instead of on his side, and this circumstance must, in all human probability, have changed the course of Central and Upper Indian history for the next twenty years.

During these transactions Madhoji Sindhia had been observant of the man whose papers he had stolen, and of whose enterprise he received such constant proofs, and so high was the opinion he conceived of his capacity that he came to the conclusion it would be better to secure his services for himself. In the recent war with the English Sindhia had learnt the value of disciplined infantry. Twice within a fortnight his army of 20,000 cavalry had been attacked and dispersed by Colonel Goddard at the head of a force of 4,000 British troops, whilst Captain Popham, by his brilliant capture of Gwalior, had proved how much could be achieved by Sepoys well trained and heroically led. The Marátha armies of this period mustered no infantry at all, and Sindhia determined to raise a force of this arm. He therefore made advances to De Boigne through Mr. Anderson, and invited the man, who had so deliberately sought to beard him, to enter his service.

With such splendid prospects as were now opened out to him, De Boigne could afford to forget all injuries and bury all animosities, and he accepted the offer without any hesitation. And here a short digression is necessary to explain the political situation in Upper India at the time when De Boigne entered the service of Madhoji Sindhia.

In this year, 1784, the Empire of the Mughal was tottering to its fall. It had, indeed, virtually ceased to exist twenty-two years previously, when 'Alamgír II. was murdered, for Shah 'Alam, who succeeded him, was never anything but a mere symbol of sovereignty, now paraded by one minister in power, now by another, as his patent of authority. Meanwhile the Marátha power was fast recovering from the shock its prestige had sustained at Pánípat, and under the genius of Madhoji Sindhia reasserting its influence at Delhi. Madhoji had good cause to remember Pánípat, for a wound received in that battle left him a cripple for life. Since that memorable day he had been associated with Takúji Holkar in consolidating the Marátha power in the great province of Málwa, whose government they shared equally, and preparing to recover the supremacy of Hindustan. Ten years after Pánípat the two chiefs placed Shah 'Alam on the throne of Delhi, from which he had been driven by the Abdali. Eight years later war broke out with the English, and they were obliged to withdraw their forces southward to protect their own territories. During this campaign, which lasted from 1779 to 1782, Madhoji's fortunes rose and fell, and rose again, until they were finally established by the treaty of Salbye, which recognised his independence, raised him to the head of the confederated Marátha princes, who acknowledged the Peshwá of Poonah as their suzerain, and left him a free hand to deal with the wreck of the Mughal Empire as he willed.

The road was now clear for the fulfilment of those ambitious designs against Delhi, which had been interrupted by late events. Since the withdrawal of the Maráthá protection from Shah 'Alam, the capital had become a prey to internal quarrels and jealousies, which reduced it to a state of absolute anarchy. It was a period when great political and territorial changes were on the *tapis*, and the Emperor's dominions, torn by dissensions, seemed to court invasion. Madhoji only waited a favourable opportunity to advance, whilst behind him crouched the enormous power of the Marátha nation. To be associated with such a prince at such a time was to woo fortune by her most certain path.

De Boigne was so associated, and how well he used his opportunities these pages will attempt to show. The commission he received from Madhoji was to raise two battalions of disciplined infantry, with a suitable complement óf artillery. He was to receive eight rupees a month for each soldier in the force, and his own pay was fixed at Rs.1,000 per mensem. The battalions were to consist of 850 men each, and to be formed as nearly as possible upon the lines of those in the Company's service, with similar accoutrements, arms, and discipline. In short, the corps was one calculated to give fair scope to De Boigne's powers of organisation and his military ability.

In 1784 De Boigne began this task with characteristic energy. Recruits soon flocked to his enlisting centres, for in such warlike times, and amongst such warlike races, soldiers were an abundant ready-money commodity. He fixed the pay of a Sepoy at five and a half rupees per mensem, thus leaving a sufficient surplusage from which to offer attractive inducements to European officers to join his standard. Sangster was one of the first to do so, having recently left the Rána of Gohad's service on that chief submission to Sindhia. The Scotchman was a man of considerable ingenuity, and skilful in the art of casting cannon, and De Boigne appointed him superintendent of his arsenal, where he was soon busy turning out excellent artillery and small arms. Another officer was John Hessing, a Dutchman by nationality, and a gallant man by nature. He commanded one of the battalions, and a Frenchman named Frèmont the other.

During the time he was engaged in raising his corps De Boigne's energy was inexhaustible, and in vivid contrast to the sensual indolence which too frequently characterised the military adventurers of the period. From morning to midnight he was continuously at work, superintending every detail of the new force. He examined and

passed recruits, drilled the raw levies, organised the companies and
divisions, and selected and appointed the native officers. Amongst
others who offered their services about this time was a certain
Rohillá, named Amír Khán, whom De Boigne rejected because of
his youth. It was not often that he was at fault in selecting his
native subordinates, but in this instance he failed to detect the merits
of the applicant; for Amír Khán rose to an eminence which, in
comparison, was as great as that attained by the European who
declined his services. As soon as his muster roll was full De Boigne
turned his attention to succeeding details, choosing the uniforms,
deciding on the accoutrements and armament, and providing a
suitable equipment for field service. He never spared himself, but
grappled with the work he had undertaken strenuously and enthu-
siastically. The result was that in less than five months he had
brought into readiness for active service two excellent battalions of
regular infantry. Those only who have had experience of the interior
economy of a native state, which nowadays is but a reflection of the
chaos existing in India a hundred years ago, can form an idea of the
magnitude of the work accomplished by De Boigne within this short
space of time.

As soon as his new-fledged battalions were ready to take the field,
Madhoji Sindhia ordered them to join the army of Appa Khándi Ráo,
one of his leading generals, who was engaged in the subjugation of
Bundelkhand. Appa's force consisted solely of cavalry, that being
the only arm of service engaged in the predatory system of warfare
which the Maráthás affected. There was at first a prejudice, amounting to a contempt, displayed towards De Boigne's new battalions, but
this did not prevent him from making their value felt; and when the
siege of Kalinjar, a strong fortress a few miles south of Allahabad,
was undertaken, the whole brunt of the attack devolved upon his
infantry and artillery, who distinguished themselves so signally that
they evoked the highest tribute of praise from Appa Khándi Ráo.

But the Bundelkhand campaign was brought to a premature close
by events at Delhi. Madhoji Sindhia had long been watching the
dissensions in progress at the Court of Shah 'Alam, which culminated
in the assassination of two successive Wazírs. Paralysed by the
difficulties around him, and after vainly seeking help from the
English, the luckless Emperor appealed in his extremity to the
Marátha prince to subdue his mutinous nobles and seat him in
security on the throne of his forefathers.

This was the opportunity Madhoji had so long desired. He at once
crossed the Chambal River, which formed the northern boundary of

the Marátha dominions, and joined the Emperor at Agra in October, 1784, and early in the following year escorted him back to Delhi, from which he had been forced to fly. Some of the rebellious nobles evacuated the city on his approach, and others submitted, and in January, 1785, the unhappy monarch was once more elevated to the regal state, if not the sovereign power, of Emperor of Hindustan.

The power remained in Sindhia's hands, for he was the master of the situation. In his gratitude Shah 'Alam desired to invest his deliverer with the title and dignity of Amir-ul-Umrah, or Chief of the Nobles, but this honour was declined. The titular distinction was not accompanied by corresponding practical advantages, and the empty leadership of such a factious aristocracy was to be avoided rather than accepted. The crafty Hindu prince—a great soldier, but a greater statesman—had other objects in view than the impossible post of keeper of a Muhammadan emperor's unruly kin. With a sycophantic assumption of humility, which he always carried to excess throughout life, Madhoji declined all honours for himself, but for his suzerain, the Peshwá, who was nominally the vassal of Delhi, he requested the dignity of Vakil-i-Mutluq, or supreme deputy of the Emperor, a post which carried with it paramount authority. This was accorded by Shah 'Alam, who thus signed away his regal power. As a natural consequence Madhoji, the Peshwá's local representative, assumed the office, and with it the control, of the Imperial army, the sole machine of government in Oriental politics. Soon afterwards the chief command of it was conferred on him as a personal distinction.

Hindustan was now in Sindhia's hands. His arms and his diplomacy had made him its master. The rich Mughal districts in the Doáb, a fertile tract of country between the Ganges and Jumna, soon surrendered with the fortresses of Aligarh and Agra. On the fall of the latter, regarded as the key of Hindustan, the Deccan Hindu was paramount lord of the Mughal Empire.

But Fortune had been too lavish with her favours. In his career of conquest Madhoji Sindhia was aided by circumstances too fortuitous to be permanently relied upon. The ancient aristocracy of Delhi, awed into submission at first by his masterly advance, and the weakness of their own internal chaos, began to foregather and recover spirit. Sindhia's necessity, possibly his cupidity, could not resist the temptation of sequestrating the estates of the leading nobles, and thus, to the intolerable insult of a despised infidel being placed in command over them, was added the positive injury of the loss of their property. Misfortune made them kin, and they determined to sink for a time all their private enmities, and concert measures to expel the invader. To which end they entered into communications with the Rájahs of Jaipur and Jodhpur, in Rájputana, to whom they proposed an alliance, and these princes, mindful of the heavy exactions they continually suffered as tributaries of the Maráthás, turned a favourable ear to their overtures.

Directly Madhoji Sindhia heard of this combination he determined to anticipate its action. The Rajputs had long been nominal vassals of the Empire, and seizing on this as a pretext, he called upon them, in his capacity of Vakil-i-Mutluq, for payment of tribute. The demand was only partially obeyéd, and in order to enforce it, Madhoji prepared to lead the Imperial army against the rebels.

But Sindhia's power now showed the unstable basis on which it was builded. His weakness lay, not in his will, but in his weapon. The Imperial army was necessarily the instrument of his purpose, but it was officered by those very nobles who had entered into intrigues with the enemy, and its ranks filled with their own personal following. It was obviously unsafe for Madhoji to place himself in the power of such a force. In order, therefore, to strengthen his hands, he recalled the army of Bundelkhand, and, on being joined by Appa Khandi Ráo and De Boigne, set out for Rájputana early in the year 1787.

Near the village of Lálsót, some miles to the south-east of Jaipur, the allied forces of the Rajput princes were found drawn up for battle. The untrustworthiness of the Imperial army soon discovered itself, for two of the leading generals at once went over to Partáb Sing, taking with them all their troops. Their names were Muhammad Beg Hamadáni, and his nephew, Ismáil Beg, who was destined to become one of Madhoji's most redoubtable foes for the next seven years.

This early example of treachery created a spirit of mutiny amongst the Mughal soldiery, whose sympathies were naturally with the deserters, and the aspect of affairs soon became threatening. In this dilemma Madhoji was compelled to avail himself of that desperate panacea for internal trouble—action. He determined to give battle before there was time for any further desertions to take place, trusting to fortune for victory, and knowing that halting indecision always sides with the stronger party.

Accordingly he disposed his army for attack, and gave the order to advance. On the left De Boigne's battalions were stationed, and the right was entrusted to the Marátha Cavalry, both supporting, or more probably coercing, the Imperial army in the centre. The Rajput princes at once accepted battle, and the action began. At the very outset Muhammed Beg Hamadani was killed by a cannon-shot, which so disheartened his troops that they began to retreat, and it seemed as though the day was lost. But at this juncture Ismáil Beg came to the rescue. Rallying his uncle's wavering soldiery he placed himself at their head and charged the Mahratta Cavalry with such impetuous gallantry that he drove them back in disorder.

Observing this, the Chief of Riah, one of the Rája of Jodhpur's generals, was encouraged to advance, and collecting his 10,000 Ráthor Cavalry, led them against Sindhia's left wing, where only De Boigne, with his little body of infantry, stood to oppose him.

The Ráthors of Jodhpur were the very flower of Rajput bravery, and celebrated throughout Hindustan for their splendid courage and their handsome mien. They were a warrior clan whose past achievement had marked them out as the first and finest of all the fighting races of the East, and won for them the proud distinction of being without fear.

As they came within sight of De Boigne's two battalions, drawn up ready to receive them, they converged upon the little band, rending the air with fierce and exulting shouts of anticipated victory. Their flags flaunted in the breeze, the sunshine glistened on their plumed helmets and chain armour, and their swords and spears flashed aloft as they thundered over the sun-baked plain. Never yet in the history of battle had footmen dared to oppose the might of Márwár mounted for the fray, and when the Chief of Riah saw the compact formation, steady as the stones around, awaiting his onslaught, he determined to punish this insolence of courage.

It was a terrible baptism of battle for De Boigne's young battalions. Armies had melted and dispersed before these on charging warriors, who seemed as if they had but to ride over to annihilate the little square that held its place and awaited the shock with splendid courage. In the midst of his men rode De Boigne, calm and fearless. He had formed them into a hollow square (a formation Wellington and Quatre Bas were to make famous in after years), with his guns hidden from view in the centre. Not for a moment was his presence of mind disturbed, and as he issued his orders and completed his dispositions, his confident bearing gave his men that sense of security which Asiatics' have ever derived from the presence and co-operation of European leaders.

Nearer and nearer came the advancing squadrons, until the supreme moment arrived and only a few paces intervened. Then the word of command rang out, and with the precision of the parade ground, De Boigne's front line fell back behind the guns, which, before the amazed Ráthors could realize what the movement signified, belched out a murderous discharge of grape into their ranks.

The huge moving mass staggered at the shock, but, carried forward by its own impetus, completed its charge. Reckless of everything except the honour of the day, the sons of Márwár rode to the cannons' muzzles, cutting down the gunners as they served their pieces, and attempting to break into the centre of the stubborn square. For a few seconds all was inextricable confusion; then, as the smoke cleared away, high above the roar of battle, the word of command rang out again, and from nearly two thousand muskets, at closest quarters, a death-dealing volley was directed against the Ráthor ranks.

Their horses refused to face the awful sheet of flame that flashed out and strewed the field with corpses of men and beasts; and riderless steeds, stampeding back in terror through the main body, added to its confusion. De Boigne's military instinct seized the decisive moment, and the advance was sounded. It was the turning-point of the fight. The enemy were rallying for a second charge, infuriated at the insult of a repulse from infantry. But before they could reform De Boigne and his battalions were on them. Again the flames flashed forth in the very faces of the horses, and like lightning from the heavens above dealt death and dismay. The despised infantry could not only resist, it could attack! A revelation burst upon these warriors of the West, and before that small disciplined force the chivalry of Rájputana wavered and broke, till finally, like driven cattle, they streamed out in flight, conquered by the genius, the resolution, and intrepidity of a single man.

It needed but a general advance of the Imperial army to complete the victory assured by the valour of De Boigne's corps. The Mughal centre was ordered to follow in pursuit, but intrigue and treachery had been at work, and they refused to stir. And so the enemy made good their retreat, and De Boigne found that the heroism of his men had been expended in vain, and that the blood so freely shed on Lálsót's plain had been sacrificed to the accomplishment of an empty victory.

Two days later Sindhia prepared to renew the battle, but even as he was forming his line, the whole of the Imperial army, by a *volte face* indigenous to Asiatic soil, passed over to the enemy, taking with them eighty pieces of cannon. De Boigne's indignation was aroused beyond endurance as he saw the Mughal deserters marching away with drums beating and flags flying. Galloping up to Sindhia he asked permission to charge them with the Maráthá Cavalry, but Madhoji with a more prudent appreciation of the danger their defection involved, preferred the doctrine of discretion and decided to leave them alone.

There was nothing left but to retire, for the Maráthá troops could not hope to resist the overswollen ranks of the enemy. The danger was critical, but it served to bring into operation all Madhoji's finest qualities of fortitude and resource. A line of retreat to Ulwar was quickly decided upon and the march commenced, the defence of the rear being entrusted to De Boigne. Ismáil Beg at once prepared to follow, but his Rajput allies, having satisfactorily asserted their exemption from tribute, and recovered their lost province of Ajmir (which the Maráthás were obliged to abandon), declined to take up another's quarrel and withdrew into their own territories. The Mughal noble, collecting all the cavalry he could muster, followed in pursuit of the retreating enemy with the intention of destroying them, but in this he was foiled by De Boigne, who proved himself as skilful a general in retreat as he had been in action, and with his two battalions successfully defended the rear of Sindhia's army for eight days, meeting and repulsing every attack made by Ismáil Beg, until Ulwar was reached and refuge found within its walls.

The Mughal noble now relinquished the pursuit, and made his way to Agra, and shortly afterwards Madhoji Sindhia, convinced that he could no longer hold Hindustan, collected his vanquished forces, and crossing the Chambal, fell back upon the fortress of Gwalior, whence he wrote urgent letters to the Peshwá at Poonah to send reinforcements to aid in retrieving this tremendous disaster to Maráthá prestige.

Meanwhile Ismáil Beg, in his design to recover Delhi, found himself forestalled by a Rohillá chief named Ghulám Kádir, who had seized the opportunity afforded by the distracted state of affairs in Upper India, and the defenceless condition of the capital, to drive out the Maráthá garrison and take possession of it. The only individual who attempted to oppose him was the Begum Somru, who had succeeded to the command of the regular troops her late husband raised ; but although she displayed great courage and spirit she was obliged to retire. Ghulám Kádir next captured Aligarh, whereupon Ismáil Beg, finding the Afghan master of the situation, and not feeling strong enough to oppose him, made overtures for an alliance, offering to share with him all the conquests their joint forces might effect ; and these terms being accepted, a plan was formed for the immediate recovery of the Mughal-Doáb provinces from the Maráthás.

The capture of Aligarh was soon followed by that of the surrounding districts. This accomplished, the two chiefs were able to concentrate their forces on the siege of Agra, Sindhia's sole remaining stronghold in Hindustan, but here a stubborn resistance was opposed to them by a Brahmin named Lakwá Dáda, one of the bravest and best of the Maráthá generals, and a prominent figure in the history of the country for the next fifteen years.

With the Imperial city wrested from him, the Doáb Provinces lost, Aligarh captured, and Agra closely invested, the fortunes of Madhoji Sindhia were indeed dark. After his brief blaze of triumph, he had in one short campaign lost nearly everything his arms had previously won, and now found himself apparently further off than ever from the attainment of his ambition. His army was beaten and dispirited, and he had proved as weak in holding Hindustan as he had been bold in seizing it. For some months he remained at Gwalior, anxiously awaiting help from the Deccan; but it was a far cry from the Chambal to Poonah. Not only many leagues, but many jealousies intervened. Poonah politics were directed by a crafty Brahmin named Nána Farnavis, who has been denominated the Machiavelli of the Maráthá Empire. He had long been hostile to Sindhia, whose enormous and growing power aroused mistrust, and had no difficulty in persuading the Peshwá that his vassal of Ujjain was aiming at the establishment of an independent kingdom for himself. Beneath the cloak of servility, under which Sindhia always disguised his intentions, there existed designs of the most imperial nature. In his excess of humility he called himself a Patél, or village mayor, and vowed that to carry his master, the Peshwá's, slippers was his hereditary duty; but under this artificial assumption of modesty there lurked far-reaching aims and ambitions. Nána Farnavis was aware of this, and in the hour of Sindhia's need, deemed it the wisest policy to withhold assistance. To the urgent appeals for reinforcements replies of a temporising nature were sent, and it soon became apparent to Sindhia that no help could be expected from Poonah at present, and that he must depend upon his own exertions to re-establish his shaken fortunes.

The relief of Agra was of the first importance, in order to secure a base of operations for the reconquest of the lost territory. In proximity to this fortress lay the country of the Játs, a low caste Hindu tribe, originally from the banks of the Indus, who possessed a tolerable army, which included a battalion of regular infantry, commanded by a Frenchman named Lestineau. After his defeat at Lálsót, Madhoji, with diplomatic generosity, had made a virtue of necessity, and restored to the Játs a considerable tract of territory and the fortress of Díg, which had originally been conquered from them. This paved the way for an alliance which he now entered into with their ruler, Ranjít Sing. Calling in all his scattered detachments, Sindhia concentrated his army at Bhartpur, where a junction was formed with his new allies, and in the spring of 1788 he prepared to take the field again.

Whereupon Ismáil Beg and Ghulám Kádir raised the siege of Agra, and marched to oppose him, and on the 24th of April the two armies met at Chaksána, or Cháksu, about eight miles from Bhartpur. Sindhia's troops were commanded by Appa Khandi Ráo and Rána Khán. The latter was a favourite officer, who had saved Madhoji's life at Pánipat more than a quarter of a century before, in gratitude for which he had been raised to high military command. Although of humble birth Rána Kkán proved himself worthy of the confidence reposed in him, and was moreover a very capable general. Appa Khandi Ráo, as a reward for gallantry and enterprise, had recently obtained the estates sequestrated from Ismáil Beg, but only to lose them by his master's present reverse of fortune. He had every reason to desire the re-establishment of the Maráthá rule, and was entrusted with the chief command in this battle. In the disposition of his forces he placed the Maráthá troops in the centre, supported on the right by De Boigne's battalions, and on the left by the Ját army and Lestineau's regular infantry.

The action began with a heavy cannonade opened by Ismáil Beg, and chiefly directed against De Boigne's corps, in the hopes of shaking the solidity of the phalanx which had so successfully resisted all attacks in the battle of Lálsót, and during the retreat to Ulwar. On the other wing Ghulám Kádir, spurning such incidental aid, charged the Játs, and soon put all to flight, except Lestineau's infantry, who maintained their ground. Seeing the enemy's left wing in retreat, and anticipating that their example might be contagious, Ismáil Beg now suspended his artillery fire, and collecting his cavalry bore down upon De Boigne.

But the same discipline and resolution which had saved the two battalions when they stemmed the torrent of the Ráthor charge animated them now. Ismáil Beg's onslaught was met with firmness and fortitude, and all his efforts failed to shake the square of trained men, who, standing shoulder to shoulder, proved themselves impervious to panic, and withheld their fire until their leader gave the word of command. Then was repeated the lesson of Lálsót: a hail of bullets tore into the ranks of the enemy, and strewed the ground with dead and wounded. Calm discipline again proved its superiority over mad valour, and the science of war triumphed over the advantage of numbers. Before De Boigne's musketry fire the Mughal squadrons fell back dazed and decimated, and it needed but the assistance of the Maráthá Cavalry to secure the day. But again Fate snatched the laurels from the adventurer's grasp, for when the critical moment arrived the Deccan warriors were not at hand to charge. De Boigne's and Lestineau's infantry alone kept the field, until unsupported in the unequal fight, they were obliged, after sustaining heavy losses, to fall back and seek shelter within the walls of Bhartpur, whither their cowardly allies had preceded them.

The defeat of Chaksána completes a chapter in De Boigne's career, for with it closes the record of his military misfortunes. The signal personal distinction with which he emerged from the two disastrous battles recorded served to establish his reputation in a more sensible degree than if he had merely shared in a general victory. His gallantry in action, his presence of mind in crisis, and his resource in retreat, marked him as a great and gallant leader, and impressed his high merits on the mind of Madhoji Sindhia, whilst the ordeal through which his young battalions had triumphantly passed, completed the confidence of his men in their commander, and in themselves.

CHAPTER III.

1788-1790.

IMMEDIATELY after their victory at Chaksána, dissensions broke out between Ismáil Beg and Ghulám Kádir. There was little in common between them except their creed. The former represented Mughal respectability, whilst the latter was an Afghan adventurer, emasculated in his youth, and vindictive and truculent by nature, who represented a purely foreign element in Hindustan. News of the quarrel was conveyed to Sindhia, who learnt at the same time that the Sikhs had made an incursion into Ghulám Kádir's own territory of Saharanpur. So he sent a force to assist them, and this obliged the Rohillá to proceed at once to the protection of his property, whilst Ismáil Beg returned to the siege of Agra, which still held out under Lakwá Dáda. Taking advantage of this division of the enemy's forces, Rána Khán and Appa Khándi Ráo were encouraged to resume the offensive, and marched to the relief of Agra, which place they reached on the 18th of June, 1788.

It was the height of the hot season, just before the breaking of the monsoon rains, when the heated air was like a furnace breath, and the sun scorched with the fierceness of a flame. The opposing armies were drawn up on a large plain outside the city. Behind Ismáil Beg's camp flowed the river Jumna, its waters swollen by the melting of the Himalayan snows. To the far right the dazzling dome and slender minarets of the Táj rose in exquisite symmetry over the grave of Mumtáz-i-Mahal, a monument to the past glory of that empire which could raise such a monument to one of its queens. Behind the red stone battlements of the beleaguered fortress the gallant Lakwá Dáda still held his own, and watched with anxious eyes the result of the coming contest that was to decide the fate of Hindustan. It was an historical day, on which, for the last time in

41

the annals of the house of Taimur, its army was to stand in battle array, fighting for the faith against the great encroaching power from the south, begotten of its own overgrown empire.

A long and desperate battle ensued. Around De Boigne's battalions the strife raged fiercest. But his men were veterans in warfare now, trained in the hard school of defeat, and met and repulsed each succeeding charge, till the Mughal Cavalry reeled backwards beaten. Then De Boigne advanced, with serried ranks and compact formation, and before the sun had set Ismáil Beg's army was dispersed in full flight, its guns abandoned, and its camp given over to flame and pillage. When he saw the day was lost, the Mughal noble, who had been twice wounded, mounted a swift horse, and spurred to the Jumna. Plunging into its swollen waters, he swam to the other side, and so made good his escape, whilst the remnants of his routed army flocked in straggling bodies to Delhi.

The battle of Agra was the most important and decisive that had taken place between the two parties engaged for many years. It extinguished for ever the last flickering hope of independence that remained to the Mughal, and completely established the ascendency of the Maráthás. It assured the easy reconquest of the Doáb Provinces, and made Madhoji Sindhia the undisputed master of Hindustan. That the success of the day was due in the first degree to De Boigne, every historian has admitted, and from this time forward the force which his genius had created, became a recognised power in the political history of the country, and the chief factor in framing its course during the next fifteen years.

Ismáil Beg fled at once to Ghulám Kádir's camp, where an apparent reconciliation was effected between them. As soon as Shah 'Alam heard of the Maráthá victory he wrote to Madhoji Sindhia, throwing himself on his protection ; but this letter fell into the hands of Ghulám Kádir, who immediately proceeded to the capital, where he found the gates closed against him. Corruption and treachery soon opened them, and seizing the person of the Emperor, the Rohillá chief deposed him from power, and placed a youth named Bédar Shah on the throne. He then sacked the palace, not even sparing the *Zenána*, or women's apartments ; but being disappointed by finding less than was expected, he sent for Shah 'Alam and commanded him to disclose the place where the concealed treasure was deposited. The monarch pleaded in vain that he knew of none. Inflamed by a continued debauch, which had thrown him into a paroxysm of rage, the brutal Rohillá seized Shah 'Alam, who was an old man of nearly seventy years of age, and throwing him to the ground, gouged out his eyes with a dagger, heedless of the holy but impotent protest that appealed against the sacrilege of destroying " eyes which for a period of sixty years have been assiduously employed in perusing the sacred Korán." For two months this bloodthirsty ruffian continued to hold sway in the capital, during which it became the scene of the most barbarous atrocities and foulest excesses consequent on his inhuman efforts to extort money from the inmates of the palace.

During this time Madhoji Sindhia, with a supineness that has been reprobated, halted at Gwalior awaiting the reinforcements from the Deccan, which were at length being sent to him. It was not until three months had elapsed that he ordered Rána Khán to march to Delhi. On the approach of this chief, Ghulám Kádir at once evacuated the capital, whilst Ismáil Beg, who had quarrelled with him over the spoils of the palace, and was further disgusted by his brutal conduct, tendered his submission, and came over to the Maráthás, who took possession of the fort and city without firing a shot. De Boigne's battalions were entrusted with the charge of the citadel, and the blind emperor was released from confinement, and soon afterwards, on Sindhia's arrival, elevated for the third time to his unstable throne. The office of Vakil-i-Mutluq was now confirmed on the Peshwá, and the deputyship to Madhoji, whilst Ismáil Beg was rewarded with the territory of Hariána and Rewari, which he was sent to administer.

Ghulám Kádir fled to Meerut, whither he was pursued by Rána Khán and Lestineau. The city being surrounded and all supplies cut off, the chief's followers became mutinous, and as a last resource, he placed himself at the head of 500 faithful cavalry, and one night made a sortie from the fort and cut his way through the investing lines. He would doubtless have made good his escape, but for his horse falling into a well, by which the chief was disabled, and his followers, unaware of the accident, left him behind. This led to his capture, and he was shortly afterwards shockingly mutilated, his body being dismembered, and his trunk, whilst he was yet alive, placed in a cage for the purpose of being conveyed to Delhi. But death mercifully released from his sufferings one who had never shown mercy to others. His saddle-bags, stuffed with valuable jewels looted from the emperor's palace and harem, fell into the hands of Lestineau, who conceived the opportunity of retirement from active service too auspicious to be neglected, and on his return to the capital, drew a large sum of money for the pay of his troops, and then decamped to British territory, whilst his bilked battalion relieved its feelings by breaking into mutiny.

The victorious termination of a long campaign that had opened so disastrously, proved beyond doubt the value of De Boigne's disciplined infantry, which had done so much towards retrieving the earlier reverses of the war. Their commander now began to press his claims for suitable recognition. In an army like Sindhia's, a corps of 2,000 men counted as nothing, numerically speaking. They were lost in the enormous multitudes of Maráthá soldiery, and their leader prejudiced by the insignificance of their numbers. Moreover, De Boigne was subject to the control and authority of the native generals, and although he saved them in defeat, and won their victories for them, he still remained subordinate to men for whom he could not but feel a professional contempt and a racial superiority. His *amour propre* rebelled against a continuance of these conditions, and the false position they placed him in. It was customary to measure the merits of a military adventurer by his success, and to reward him in like ratio. It has been observed that De Boigne was impatient of the slow promotion of a progressive service; but his present service was not even progressive, for his command remained precisely the same now as when he was first appointed to it, although in the interval his battalions had been instrumental in saving Sindhia from annihilation, and had mainly helped to restore to him a lost kingdom. One cannot wonder that De Boigne began to expect a reward commensurate with the results he had achieved, and proposed to Madhoji to augment the two battalions into a full brigade of 10,000 men-at-arms. In urging this he could point to the justification of past achievement, for Lálsót, Chaksána, and Agra were credentials upon which almost any claim might have been based by one whose share in them was as glorious as De Boigne's.

It is difficult to understand why Sindhia declined to accede to this proposal. He was fully aware of the value of De Boigne and his two battalions, and that the honours of the victory of Agra belonged to them; for not even the jealousy that surrounded the European commander could hide his merits or depreciate his success. Possibly it was the circumstance of this jealousy that influenced Madhoji, who could not afford to quarrel with his countryman at this crisis. An acquiescence in De Boigne's proposals would certainly have raised up a host of dangerous malcontents. The time was not appropriate for the introduction of such radical measures, for it was imperative for Sindhia to conciliate all hostile influences and consolidate his power. Another substantial argument against the suggested increase of the force was its expense, for the chief was gravely embarrassed by pecuniary difficulties, and the disturbed and devastated condition of the districts he had just reconquered made it impossible to collect any revenue from them. Lastly, it is not unlikely that there lingered in his heart some deeply rooted Maráthá prejudice in favour of cavalry ; for although his experience and observation had taught him the value of infantry, he was at this time a man convinced against his will. All these causes operated against an immediate consent to De Boigne's suggestion, and Madhoji declared himself in favour of the existing establishment and opposed to any augmentation.

Whereupon De Boigne, with the independence of character he had often displayed before, tendered his resignation, and Sindhia, not altogether displeased at the opportunity of gratifying his own country-men, accepted it. But there was no personal ill-feeling displayed or aroused. Madhoji was conscious that he owed much to De Boigne, who on his part had innumerable pecuniary favours to remember. And so the prince and his general parted with friendly compliments and regrets, that augured an early *rapprochement* ; and whilst the former settled himself down to the consolidation of his power in Hin-dustan, the latter determined to forsake the hazardous paths of war, and devote himself to the cultivation of the quiet fields of commerce.

Leaving Delhi in 1789 De Boigne proceeded to Lucknow, where he was welcomed by his old friend Claude Martine, by whose advice he entered into trade as a cloth and indigo merchant, embarking in these ventures the very considerable sum of money he had saved in Sindhia's service. He soon laid the foundation of a successful and lucrative business, which he continued to conduct after he resumed his military career, utilising it as a means of transmitting to Europe the large fortune he made in the East.

But he was not long permitted to pursue a peaceful life at Lucknow. Madhoji Sindhia, having established himself at Delhi, and completed the subjugation of the Doáb, turned his attention to army reform, and early in the year 1790, began to introduce several innovations with the view of making his forces better adapted for the requirements of the service on which they were now employed. Amongst the first of these was the enlistment of Rajput and Muhammadan soldiers for garrison work, his own countrymen being too independent by nature and too lawless by habit to perform the duties of a standing army. Before long Sindhia's judgment convinced him that, however suitable his hordes of cavalry might be for predatory warfare, for the invasion of countries and the sack of cities, those objects once attained an infantry force was indispensable for the maintenance of a permanent occupation, where fortresses had to be garrisoned, and large centres of population controlled. For such duties his wild Deccan horsemen, with their impatience of restraint, and their irresistible craving for plunder, were altogether unsuited, and to detach them for service of this description was almost tantamount to billetting a pack of wolves on a fold of sheep.

Moreover, there was another danger which began to make itself apparent. Madhoji was illegitimate by birth, and this tended to diminish his influence with his countrymen, and afforded a handle for his enemies, of whom he had many, to intrigue against him. Mughals Rohillas, Rajputs, and Játs, all resented his dominion at Delhi, and were prepared to oppose him at every opportunity. But there were more dangerous foes than these, for amongst his own countrymen were many whose hostility was scarcely veiled, and chief amongst them his great rival 'Takúji Holkar, who was consumed with jealousy at Sindhia's success. In order therefore to strengthen himself Madhoji determined to create a special force, bound to him .by the strongest ties possible, and more completely under his control than his unruly Maráthás.

Early in 1790 he sent an agent to Lucknow, to invite De Boigne to return to his service, and promising that the proposals originally made should be accepted in every detail. De Boigne was discovered deeply immersed in his new business; but he was a soldier before everything else, and the call to arms fell upon willing ears. A few days sufficed to regulate his affairs at the Oudh capital, after which he accompanied the Vakil back to Madhoji's camp at Mattra. In a single interview an understanding was arrived at, for the prince was liberal, the soldier not exacting, and both imbued with feelings of mutual confidence and esteem that had not been disturbed by anything in the past.

The commission with which De Boigne was entrusted was the creation of a *Campoo* or Brigade of ten battalions of infantry, with a suitable train of cavalry and artillery, the whole to be disciplined in the English style, and officered by Europeans. In the execution of this task he was left a perfectly free hand.

Thus, after ten years of endeavour and perseverance, De Boigne found himself with the means of accomplishing the object he had long desired, and empowered to create a force worthy of his ambition. The future was now his own to make: the materials required but the moulding. With characteristic energy ·he set to work carrying into execution the scheme whose details he had so long considered and matured in his mind. His two battalions were still in Sindhia's service, and formed the nucleus of the new brigade. Lestineau's regiment had been disbanded as a punishment for its mutiny, but, at De Boigne's request, the men were permitted to re-enlist. Thus there were at his disposal trained soldiers sufficient for three battalions. The remaining seven were raised in Rohilkhand, Oudh, and the Doáb with but little difficulty. It was a time of war and battle, when the arts of peace had fallen into desuetude. Every peasant was perforce a soldier, and every artisan could wield a sword. The inducements of regular pay and the anticipations of plunder were irresistible attractions to men whose lives had been spent in defending their property or fighting for existence against the exactions of tyrants and the incursions of invaders.

The engagement of a staff of European officers presented greater difficulties than the enlistment of the men. Sangster was still in the service, and able to continue his work of casting cannon and manufacturing small arms, in both of which branches he was an expert. During the next few years he supplied most of the best artillery in Sindhia's army, whilst his muskets, turned out at a cost of ten rupees each, were far superior to anything then in the hands of the native powers, and almost equal in finish and durabilty to weapons made in Europe. His arsenal was established at Agra, which fortress Sindhia assigned to De Boigne as a depôt for his arms and munitions of war.

Frèmont the Frenchman and Hessing the Hollander still remained in their original posts, and the former was now promoted to second in command of the Brigade. Of the other European officers engaged at this time the names of at least six survive—Perron, Baours, Pedron, and Rohan, all Frenchmen; and Sutherland and Roberts, who were British subjects. They were posted to the command of the different battalions which were named after forts and cities, such as the Ujjain, Burhanpur, Delhi, and Agra regiments.

With the assistance of these officers, De Boigne rapidly organised his Brigade. It consisted of ten battalions of infantry of 750 men each. Of these, seven, known as Telingas, were uniformed and accoutred in the same way as the Company's Sepoy regiments and armed with muskets and bayonets. The other three, designated Najibs, were recruited from Pathāns, and at first armed with matchlocks, shields, and swords, but later on their efficiency was much increased by the substitution of bayonets for the latter. These Najibs wore Persian uniforms, and their matchlocks were of a new invention. All the infantry were exercised in the drill and manual according to the old English system of 1780, and although one ultra-patriotic historian avers that the word of command was given in Irish, it is agreed by the majority of commentators that English was the language in use.

To increase the mobility of the Brigade 500 Mewátis, or irregular soldiers, were incorporated, who performed the ordinary routine duties of camp, thus leaving the regular troops available for combatant work. The cavalry consisted of 500 regular horsemen, called *Trokesuwars*, and the artillery of sixty pieces of cannon, three, six, and twelve-pounders, with a proportion of howitzers, all excellently appointed and drawn by capital cattle. When brought to its full strength the entire brigade numbered very nearly 10,000 men-at-arms, and formed a compact, well-organised fighting machine, immeasurably superior to any hitherto existing in the native states of India.

De Boigne was promoted to the rank of General, and his pay, at first fixed at Rs.4,000 per mensem, was subsequently raised to Rs.10,000, and he enjoyed in addition many other services of emolument. In his agreement with Madhoji Sindhia he made but two stipulations ; one that he should never be called on to carry arms against the English, the other that his troops should be regularly paid. Herein he showed his wisdom. The history of all previous military adventurers employed by native princes pointed one moral, and that was the failure that invariably attended unpunctuality in paying the men. Eastern potentates were as poor in their pecuniary performances, as they were prodigal in their preliminary promises, and Madhoji Sindhia was no exception to the rule. He had a reluctance to, amounting to a positive horror of, parting with hard cash from his treasury. De Boigne was a prudent man, especially in money matters, and recognised that silver was the sole power that could control a mercenary army, and that without a fixed and certain revenue it was idle to attempt the establishment of a serviceable force. He therefore insisted upon a sound financial arrangement for the upkeep of his Brigade, and Sindhia whose prejudices did not include indirect disbursements, made over to De Boigne a *Jaidad* or military assignment of territory, the revenues of which were to be devoted to the expenses of the corps. This system of assigning land for the payment of troops was almost universal in India, where districts were always apportioned to the native chiefs and generals for the upkeep of their troops.

The *Jaidad* which De Boigne received comprised a large and rich tract of country in the Doáb, and within its boundaries, he was paramount, exercising and enjoying sovereign rights and privileges. When he first assumed the administration of this province its revenues amounted to sixteen lakhs of rupees a year (£200,000) ; but by subsequent additions and good management the area was increased to fifty-two *pergannahs* or districts, and the income to thirty lakhs. De Boigne's civil administration was as successful, and, in its way, as remarkable as his military one. He introduced a system of order and regularity, adopted a fixed and equitable scale of taxation, and created special departments for collecting and checking the same, by the simple but efficacious expedient of two revenue offices, the accounts in one being kept in French, and in the other in Persian. By a firm, but just government he created confidence amongst the peasantry, and without harassing or squeezing them, drew from the land larger and more punctually paid revenues than had ever been obtained before. He was allowed a commission of 2 per cent. on all collections, and so xcellent was his administration that not only were his troops regularly and liberally paid, but his own private fortune was materially increased.

Early in the summer of 1790 the Brigade was brought to its full strength and reported ready for service. This prompt accomplishment of a really great undertaking was due to De Boigne's i..defatigable exertions. His enthusiasm and energy were marvellous, and he neither stopped nor rested until he had completed his work. When at length everything was ready, and he paraded his new-formed army in review for the first time, prompted by a sentiment, that must touch all patriotic hearts, he unfurled above it, in that wild and heathen spot, so far removed from his native land, the flag of his own country —the White Cross of Savoy.

When Madhoji Sindhia inspected his new Brigade for the first time, he must have been struck with the contrast between it and his own undisciplined Marátha army. The Deccan soldiery of the last century were perhaps the most irregular ruffians in all India. Every individual trooper asserted his independence and freedom from control; he was the proprietor of his horse and arms, and whilst agreeing to give his services in return for a certain payment, he did not consider it any part of the contract to imperil his property. Warfare, he regarded, as a legitimate means of plundering, but as his steed and spear represented his entire capital, and constituted his sole claim to employment, he sedulously avoided all conflict (which somewhat detracted from his merits as a combatant), and preferred flight to fight on every occasion of danger.

The camps of these immense armies of discreet, and yet, at times, dashing warriors, were vast halting places, formed without any idea of order or regularity, and covering extended tracts of ground. Every trooper slept with his horse picketed beside him, and there were generally three camp followers to each fighting man. A teeming bazaar accompanied the armies in their line of march, wherein all trades and professions of city life were represented, and which included every accessory of Asiatic civilisation from bevies of dancing girls to bands of professional thieves, who plied their licensed callings

4

under privilege of a trade tax. The multitudes which a Marátha prince led to war consisted of a vast medley of conglomerate elements, as far removed in appearance from a military expedition as it is possible to conceive, and powerful only in their overwhelming numbers, their wonderful endurance, and the almost incredible rapidity, with which they could move from place to place, either for attack or in retreat.

De Boigne's Brigade was the very antithesis of a Marátha army. It was a small, solid, compact, slow-moving body, in which obedience and discipline were the guiding principles. Every military operation was carried out with precision and routine ; the men marched and manœuvred in the methods that obtained in European armies, and in camp afforded a spectacle of order and system that would have done credit to a Company's Sepoy regiment.

This result had not been accomplished without labour. De Boigne's life was far from one of Oriental ease and luxury. He rose each morning with the sun, and until midnight devoted himself to the multifarious duties of his position. Every day he inspected his *Kharkhána,* or arsenal, drilled his troops on parade, and issued the orders of the day. To the enlistment of recruits he paid especial attention. The equipment and armament of his force were designed and provided by him, and he was his own quartermaster and adjutant general. The medical department and ambulance service had his care, and both were arranged for. He never delegated administrative duties to subordinates, for he was a somewhat morbidly, independently man, who insisted on doing everything himself, and distrusted the deputation of authority. Active and laborious to an astonishing degree, he seemed capable of performing the work of half a dozen men, and his example infected those under him, with much of his own energy and diligence. Before his zeal and determination to succeed, difficulties faded away, and apparent impossibilities became accomplished facts. The highly organised and disciplined army, of which this first Brigade was the earnest, was a monument no less to his military genius as a great soldier, than to his personal industry as an able administrator.

CHAPTER IV.

THE BATTLES OF PÁTAN AND MERTA.

1790.

THERE was soon work for the new Brigade. Madhoji's old and redoubtable enemy, Ismáil Beg, renounced his allegiance, and having induced the Rájahs of Jaipur and Jodhpur to assist him, appeared in arms in the Ajmir district. Sindhia, with his accustomed preference for intrigue, tried at first to corrupt the following of the Mughal noble, but failing in the attempt, detached an army from his camp at Mattra, under the command of Lakwá Dadá and De Boigne, to punish the rebel and crush the Rajput princes.

They came upon the enemy near Pátan Tanwar, in the Shaikháwáti country, on the 20th of June, 1790. It has been stated that a secret understanding existed between Lakwá and Partáb Sing, by which the latter agreed to stand aloof during the fight on the condition that his territory of Jaipur, adjoining the Marátha boundaries, should not be devastated. To this cause is attributed the defeat of the famous Ráthor Cavalry in a bloody and obstinate conflict, in which Ismáil Beg and his Páthan horse behaved with signal gallantry, thrice charging through De Boigne's line and cutting down his artillery men at their guns. It was only the personal courage of the general, and the staunchness of his troops, that secured victory. There exists an authentic description of the battle, written by De Boigne himself four days after it was fought, and which appeared in the *Calcutta Gazette* of the 22nd of July, 1790. It reads as follows:—

"*Extract of a Letter from Major De Boigne.*

"CAMP PÁTAN, *June* 24, 1790.

"Our various little skirmishes since the severe cannonade of 8th and 9th *Ramzan,** are not, I hope, unknown to you. I have often

* Ramzan : the ninth Mohammedan lunar month. The month of the Fast.

tried to harass and surprise the enemy, but their naturally strong and almost impregnable situation, added to their very great superiority in numbers, both in troops and artillery, rendered all my exertions fruitless. At last, tired out with vexation, I determined to march from our ground in three columns, so as to form the line from the centre of each with ease and celerity. In that way I advanced to a little more than cannon-shot distance from the enemy, where I formed my little army, consisting of two lines and a reserve, the Maráthá horse in the rear and on our flanks. After waiting the best part of the day with impatient hopes to see them marching against us, as they had threatened; at last, about three o'clock, a few Maráthá horses began to skirmish with the enemy's right wing, consisting of horse, which shortly increased from five to six thousand, but they were soon beaten off. I was now encouraged to try if something better could not be done by our side, and in order to induce them to come out from their stronghold, I ordered the line to advance after a warm cannonade of about an hour from both sides. The enemy not appearing to come out, I still advanced till we came within reach of grape-shot; then, halting, we gave and received from each gun nearly forty rounds of grape, which made it a warm business, we being in the plain and they in the trenches. The evening was now far advanced, and seeing at the same time such numerous bodies of the enemy's cavalry in motion, and ready to fall on us if they could find an opening, I thought it prudent to move on rather quicker, which we did till the firing of platoons began. But we had already lost such numbers of people, principally clashies,* that those remaining were unable to drag the guns any further. I, therefore, gave immediate orders to storm the lines, sword in hand, which was as soon executed. Upon which the enemy, not relishing at all the close fighting, gave way on all sides, infantry as well as cavalry, leaving us in possession of all their guns, baggage, bazaar, elephants, and everything else. The day being now closed put an end to the slaughter of the enemy, which must have been very considerable if we had had an hour's more daylight. However, it was a complete victory. Their cavalry, after losing about 2,000 men and horses, saved themselves by flight; the infantry, who could not run so fast, took refuge in the town of Pátun, strongly fortified. But in the morning they thought proper to give themselves up, and surrendered to me all their arms, colours, etc. Nine battalions and irregular troops, making above 12,000 men, are now prisoners of war; I have promised

---

* Clashies : native artillerymen.

to allow them a safeguard to conduct them to the other side of the Jumna.

" The enemy's force consisted of 12,000 Rhattore Cavalry, 6,000 from Jeypore, 5,000 Moguls under Ismail Beg, and 2,000 under Allyhar Beg Khan ; of foot they had 12,000 men, and 100 pieces of artillery, and with Ismail Beg 5,000 *Tellengas,** and matchlock men, with twenty-one pieces of artillery, 4,000 *Rohillas*, 5,000 *Fakirs*,† called *Attyles* and *Brakys*, and Rajpoot *Sybundees*, ‡ with eight pieces of cannon, and 4,000 *Minahs*, § who were of great service to the enemy, as the battle was given at the foot of the hills.

" My Brigade was 10,000 strong. The Mahratta Cavalry stood on our flanks as spectators ; they began the skirmish, in which they had only six men killed and forty wounded. Had it not been for two battalions of mine, who changed frcnt when the enemy's cavalry were charging ours, the Mahrattas would have seen fine play.

"Our victory is astonishing ! A complete victory gained by a handful of men, over such a number in such a position ! It may surprise you when I say that in less than three hours' time 12,000 round and 1,500 grape shot were fired by us, and by the enemy much more, as they had two guns to our one.

" During all the engagement I was on horseback encouraging my men. Thank God I have realised all the sanguine expectations of Sindhia. My officers, in general, have behaved well ; to them I am a great deal indebted for the fortunes of the day.

" We have had 129 men killed and 472 wounded. The enemy not more, perhaps not so much, as they were entrenched ; but they have lost a vast number of cavalry.

" I have taken 107 pieces of artillery, 6,000 stand of arms, 252 colours, fifteen elephants (amongst them are Ismael Beg's five elephants) 200 camels, 513 horses, and above 3,000 oxen. I intend to send the whole to Sindhia as soon as it may be practicable. All their camp was burnt or destroyed ; they have absolutely saved nothing but their lives.

" The terror of our arms alone put us in possession of the town of Patun, in which the troops found a great deal of plunder, and near 2,000 horses. It would have required at any other time a month to take it, its fortifications being very strong, and defended by three hills close to each other. The place was never taken before."

* Tellengas : regular soldiery.
† Fakirs : religious fighting mendicants.
‡ Sybundees : irregular infantry,
§ Minahs : hill men from the districts near Ajmir.

It is difficult which to admire most in this letter,* the lucidity of the narrative, or the modesty of the gallant soldier in his description of an achievement in which he played the principal part. Another account of the battle, also published in the *Calcutta Gazette*, enables one or two interesting details to be added. It appears that the attack on Ismáil Beg and the Rajputs was commenced on the 23rd of May ; but owing to their strong position and numerous artillery, no impression could be made on their lines, " it being full nine *kos* round the mountains to come even at their foraging parties." At last De Boigne received information that the enemy's council of war had fixed on the 20th of June as an auspicious day, and, taking them in the humour, he sent word to Ismáil Beg that he would meet him half way. For this purpose the general marched out of camp an hour before day-break, but the battle was delayed until three o'clock in the afternoon, owing to the reluctance of the enemy to join issue. The fight then followed, as described by De Boigne, until " about six o'clock in the evening, our intrepid General, placing himself at the head of one of the battalions, and giving orders to the rest to follow, rushed forward, sword in hand, to the mouth of the enemy's cannon. This vigorous proceeding animating all our troops, had the desired effect, as we almost instantaneously got possession of their first line. Their second was forced about eight o'clock, and by nine the enemy were entirely routed. The General's courage and judgment on this occasion were equally conspicuous. . . . In the course of three days we took the strong town of Patun by storm, which was afterwards razed to the ground, and so intimidated the Rájah, who commanded Patun Fort (a place resembling Gibraltar from its almost impregnable position), that he submitted to become a vassal of Sindhia, and is now (1st July) with us on the march to Jaipur. Our signal victory was gained with only the loss of 700 men killed and wounded ; but the number of the enemy who have fallen must be immense, for it is said that, beside those left on the field, the road from here to Jaipur, about thirty-two *kos*, is covered with the dead carcases of men, horses, camels, and bullocks. Their camp, which was three miles in length and one in breadth, we burned and left not a stick standing. Our success affords a strong proof of the amazing power of discipline under a brave and skilful commander."

Directly the result of the battle was placed beyond doubt, Ismáil Beg accepted the inevitable, and attended by a small retinue, galloped from the field. When news of this great success reached Sindhia at

* It is probable the original was written in French and translated into English for the *Calcutta Gazette*.

Mattra, he determined to press home the advantage, and complete the subjugation of the Rajput states, which had asserted, and maintained, their independence since the battle of Lálsót, and he now ordered De Boigne to invade Jodhpur, and reduce the Rájah to submission. On receiving these commands, De Boigne decided to first attempt the capture of Ajmir, which, lying as it did, half way between Jaipur and Jodhpur, was the key of the country. On the 15th of August he reached it, and at once completed the investment, but, owing to the impregnable nature of the fort, was unable to take it by a *coup de main.* So he left 2,000 cavalry, and a sufficient force of infantry to cover it, and marched with the rest of his army towards Jodhpur.

The following extract of a letter from an officer in De Boigne's Brigade, published in 1790, refers to this incident :—

> "AGIMERE CAMP,
> "*September* 1, 1790.
>
> "Although we have invested this fort for fifteen days very closely, yet we can make no impression upon it ; our guns, from the very great elevation they are placed at, and the distance, make no visible impression, and the narrow paths which lead to the fort are so defended by nature, that a few large stones thrown down must carry everything before them. The noise they make in rolling I can compare to nothing but thunder. Indeed, I am afraid we must turn the blockade into a siege, as they have six months' water and a year's provisions in the fort. I fancy we shall divide our forces, leaving some here, and the rest proceeding to Mairtha, where the enemy have taken the field. Bijai Sing offered the fort of Agimere and country for fifty *Kos* * round to General de Boigne, if he would desert Sindhia ; but De Boigne's reply was that Sindhia had already given him Jodhpur and Jaipur, and that the Rájah would not be so unreasonable as to expect he would exchange them for Agimere."

The latter paragraph is interesting as confirming the assertion often made that De Boigne was on several occasions solicited to enter the service of Sindhia's enemies.

To turn for a moment to the course of events in the Rajput states, it must be noted that Bijai Sing, the Rájah of Jodhpur, had sustained a terrible disgrace by the defeat of his Ráthor Cavalry at Pátan. The flight of those redoubtable warriors, even though it was due to the treachery of their Jaipur allies, had given rise to a ribald rhyme, which accused them of abandoning on the field of battle the five

* *Kos*: an elastic measure ; probably a mile and a half in this instance.

attributes of manhood, namely, horse, shoes, turban, moustachios, and the "Sword of Márwár." This was tantamount to taunting them with having degenerated into women. None but those who can enter into the exaggerated sense of pride which is the ruling passion of a high caste Rajput, and understand his precise views concerning womankind, can appreciate the keenness of this taunt. To wipe out the shame of Pátan, Bijai Sing summoned to his standard every Ráthor between fourteen and sixty years of age capable of wielding a sword. From hamlets and villages they came, from towns and cities, eager to blot out with their blood this evil stain on their national honour. In response to this call to arms, 30,000 warriors, burning to repel the invader and efface the memory of the past, collected at Merta, a large walled city, standing on high ground in the centre of a vast grassy plain, thirty miles to the east of Ajmir. It was an historical place, and had been the scene of many desperate battles, in the annals of Márwár, in which the crown of Jodhpur had oftentimes been lost and won. The plain around was fat with blood, poured out, sometimes in internecine strife, but more often in opposing foreign invasion, and was covered with altars and memorials, erected to the manes of the doughty dead who lay there. Here, in September, 1790, the Ráthor army assembled to meet their Marátha enemies, who, forty years before, had defeated them on the very spot, with a loss of 40,000 men.

Owing to the failure of the annual rains, all the ordinary sources of water supply, never plentiful in the best of seasons, were exhausted, and De Boigne was obliged to make a considerable detour to approach Merta. On September 8th he reached a village called Riah, on the banks of the Lúni, and began the passage of the river. But soon his cannon became embarrassed in its muddy bed, and this occasioned considerable delay. Whereupon he sent the Marátha Cavalry forward to reconnoitre, who, after proceeding a few miles, suddenly came upon Bijai Sing's army.

The Ráthors were drawn up on the plain of Merta, their right flank resting upon the village of Dangiwas. Bijai Sing was not present, for he had remained at his capital, and entrusted the direction of the war to his commander-in-chief, Gángaram Bhandari. But, unfortunately, he had associated with this general one of his ministers, and the introduction of a civil element into an essentially military matter proved fatal. Directly Gangaram Bhandari saw the Marátha Cavalry, unsupported by those terrible battalions that had done all the fighting at Pátan, he desired to engage them. But the Rájah's minister insisted upon waiting until they were reinforced by Ismáil Beg, who was hurrying to form a junction with them. Owing to this unhappy divergence of opinion, the golden opportunity was lost. For it cannot be doubted but that the Ráthors dying to redeem their honour, would have made short work of the Maráthá Cavalry, whose cowardice was notorious, and after defeating them, might have fallen upon De Boigne's Brigade during its passage of the Lúni river, with every prospect of destroying the force, or, at least, obliging it to retreat.

As it was, the Marátha Cavalry were permitted to retire unmolested, and so to remain for the next thirty-six hours. It was not until midnight of the 10th that De Boigne completed the crossing of his guns. The next morning he advanced slowly in the direction of Merta, his march across the sandy plain being much impeded by the heaviness of the ground. Towards midday he came in sight of the enemy, drawn up in line of battle, and a heavy cannonade was at once opened upon him. Lakwá Dadá, the Marátha General, was anxious to engage forthwith, but De Boigne, profiting by the experience of Pátan, where nightfall robbed him of the full meed of victory, determined to defer the battle till the next morning, in order that he might have a long day for the work in hand. He accordingly decided to fall back, and the Ráthors, who still awaited Ismáil Beg's arrival, made no effort to force on an action.

During the afternoon, De Boigne carefully reconnoitred the ground, and after deciding on his plan of battle, gave orders for the Brigade to be under arms before dawn, hoping to take the enemy by surprise. Whilst it was yet dark the troops began to assemble, and in the silence of the sweltering autumn night fell into their places and prepared for action. As day broke, the sleeping hosts encamped in front of them were awakened from their slumbers by showers of grape, followed by the advance of the regular infantry, who rapidly stormed and occupied their outer lines. All in confusion and haste, the Ráthors formed and opened a cannonade. But the advantage was already with the attacking army, and the Jodhpur infantry was beginning to waver and break, when a misadventure overtook De Boigne, which nearly proved fatal in its results.

Captain Rohan, a French officer in command of the left wing of the Brigade, took upon himself, without orders from the General, to advance, and the battalions on either side of him following his example, the line was broken, and a weak point afforded for attack.

In order to show how the Ráthors took advantage of this error, it is necessary to revert for a moment to the events occurring in their camp. When its occupants had been surprised in the early morning by De Boigne's attack, their principal chiefs were wrapped in the

lethargic slumber of opium—a narcotic universally consumed by the
governing classes of Rajputana. Slowly they were awakened from
their drowsy sleep, one of them—the Chief of Ahwa—being aroused
with the utmost difficulty. When they regained possession of their
senses, they found, to their shame and humiliation, the camp in confusion, and the infantry a disorganized rabble on the point of being
routed.

Then did these chiefs, twenty-two in number, decide on a great
atonement. Girding on their swords, they called four thousand *
chosen followers to arms, and, as the clan was collecting, prepared
and drank opium together for the last time. It was not the final
carouse of weak debauchees, but a stern and solemn sacrament. For
they drank it as the draught of death. They wrapped themselves
around with shawls of yellow silk, the certain token that they rode to
victory or death, and so gave the order to mount.

It was at this moment that Captain Rohan advanced out of De
Boigne's line. The Chief of Ahwa saw the opportunity presented for
attack, and in the act of imprudence recognised a propitious omen.
Standing up in his stirrups, he encouraged his clansmen with a few
spirited words, calling on them to follow him, and concluding with the
pregnant exhortation : " *Remember Pátan !* "

Then he led the way, the squadrons following after, at full gallop.
The scene of conflict was soon reached, and charging straight against
De Boigne's three detached battalions, he took them at disadvantage,
and drove them back in disorder. The moral effect of this temporary
triumph inspired the Ráthors with hope and excitement. Their Chief
now turned his attack upon the main body of the Brigade, and when
he neared it his body of horse divided and trailed out, and, as if acting
on a preconcerted plan, wheeled round until De Boigne was completely
surrounded ; awhile they rent the air with the war cry they had accepted, and which was at once a confession and an inspiration.

Peradventure the God of Battle, as he looked down upon that heathen
host, smiled grimly in anticipation of the rich sacrifice about to be
offered up before his altars. The parched plain gaped for the coming
red flood that would drench it so darkly, and force forth richer pasture
growths than any springing from the rain which fell from above. The
steel-blue sky interposed no clouds between that awful arena and the
high heavens. The rugged Aravallis, towering on the horizon, caught
the first rays of the morning sun, and hung out crimson banners on
their mountain-tops. Oft had they looked down on Merta's fields, and
seen human strife and human carnage ; oft from their grey steeps and

* Some authorities quote this number as only four *hundred.*

stony fastnesses the roar of battle had re-echoed back in angry thunder tones ; oft had their shadows fallen, as a pall, on ghastly heaps of mangled men. And now the cycle of war had come round again, and the wind that blew from Merta's plain was soon to be hot with the breath of battle.

" *Remember Pátan !* "—Onward swept the squadrons of Márwár ; out rang the battle cry, as with uplifted swords and lances poised to thrust, they hurled themselves upon De Boigne's battalions.

But the genius of the great general had anticipated the danger, and prepared to meet it. With "incomparable presence of mind " De Boigne rapidly formed his men into a hollow square, and as the Ráthors dashed on to them they found a magic change had ranged serried rows of bristling bayonets and long lines of gaping guns ready to receive them at every point. Up to the very muzzles of the cannon, they charged and recharged, those valiant sons of *Marowar,* "The Land of Death." Dwellers in the Land of Death were they, and death they despised. Theirs to retrieve a lost honour ! Theirs to give the lie to that stinging jest of false Jaipur ! Theirs to " *Remember Pátan !* "

Again and again they charged, each time with ebbing effort and weaker effect. Again and again they flung themselves against that hedge of bayonets with merciless madness. There is a limit to human endurance, but to-day that limit was *Death.* To the bravest man there comes a time when conscience confesses, " Enough," and justifies it ; but to-day the command of conscience was *Death.* Great gaps yawned in the ranks, where grape and shot ploughed their furrows, only to be at once closed up by the valour of a frantic fanaticism, as the Ráthors reformed under the destroying fire, and rode back to the charge with the abandon of despair. But the disciplined Brigade confronted them, unmoved as the rocks against which the succeeding storm waves are shattered, and they reeled back broken, but unbeaten. And so the ghastly sacrifice was consummated until only fifteen remained alive, and these, steadfast to the end, returned for the last time to the shambles of self-immolation, and found the death they sought.

The God of Battle smiled grimly down, and the incense of war rose to his nostrils. A holocaust of self-doomed devotees lay prone before his feet. The plain reeked with blood, but it flowed not from alien veins, but from hearts that claimed Merta as their mother earth. The echoes of the cannon, booming sullenly back from the grey Aravallis, thundered out no salute of national victory, but sounded the minute guns that proclaimed the end of Márwár's chivalry. Thus was the atonement of the Chief of Ahwa accomplished.

Before midday the Jodhpur army was in full flight, and an hour later De Boigne's battalions in possession of their camp. After allowing his troops a short rest upon their arms, he ordered the storm of the town of Merta, and before sunset the colours of the Brigade were flying over that formidable place.

There is an account of the battle of Merta, written by an officer in De Boigne's army, and printed in a Calcutta paper, which must be quoted here, for the description already given is mainly based on Colonel James Tod's record in his "Annals of Rajas'than." This letter is dated from Camp Merta on the 13th of September, 1790, and reads as follows :—

" We had laid close siege to Agimere for seventeen days, when the General, finding that the spirits of the army were upheld by the enemy taking the field at Mirtah, left 2,000 horse to blockade Agimere, and marched against the enemy. Owing to a scarcity of water, following on a famine and dry season, we had to make a circuitous route, and did not reach Rie till the 8th. About midnight we recommenced our march, and having marched very near to the enemy, a heavy cannonade commenced about nine o'clock in the morning. The Mahratta chief was eager to advance upon the enemy, but De Boigne objected, not only on account of the fatigue of the troops, after a march of ten *kos*, but because of the intense heat and lateness of the hour, which would have prevented him reaping the fruits of success. The enemy's force consisted of 30,000 cavalry, 100,000 infantry, and 25 pieces of cannon. On our side the same number of horse, 6,000 to 7,000 rank and file, and 80 pieces of artillery. On the 10th at break of dawn we were ordered to advance on the enemy, the disposition of our troops being the same as at the memorable battle of Pátan. A heavy cannonade soon commenced, supported on both sides with great vigour. Our first line of 50 pieces of cannon shortly after began to fire with grape, and, by means of our superiority of guns, drove the enemy from their lines. But a French officer of Sindhia's, elated with success, advanced without orders of the line of battle at the head of three battalions. The enemy soon took advantage of his imprudence, and charged him so vigorously that it was not without great difficulty he effected his retreat. They then charged our main body in front, flanks, and rear, but General De Boigne's foresight and incomparable presence of mind were the means of saving us, for upon perceiving the error which his officer had committed, and no doubt aware of the consequences, he formed us into a hollow square, so that upon being surrounded shortly after-wards, we on all sides presented a front to the enemy.

"About nine o'clock they were obliged to quit the field; about ten we got possession of their camp; and about three p.m. took the great and formidable town of Mirtah by storm. The pillage lasted three days, and to mention all the particulars attending it would make your teeth water. The ladies at first seemed displeased with our coming abruptly into the town, but at length grew more kind, acknowledging with good grace that none but the brave deserve the fair.

"The town of Mirtah is much larger than Benares, surrounded by a thick mud rampart and parapet thirty feet high. It has two minarets, and the houses are all *pucca.** In this engagement the attacking army lost six to seven hundred men, killed and wounded, mostly by the sabre. Gangaram Bhandaree, the Commander-in-Chief of the Rhattores, was taken on the 11th at night, endeavouring to make his escape in the disguise of a servant. It is impossible for me to describe the feats of bravery performed by the *Jerd Kopperah Wallahs,*† or Forlorn Hope, of the enemy. I have seen, after the line was broken, fifteen or twenty men return to charge a thousand infantry, and advance to within ten or fifteen paces before all were shot. Captain Bahore (? Baours), who commanded the right wing, was wounded in the thigh, and died; Lieutenant Roberts was also severely wounded by a missile, or weapon called an *Organ,*‡ which is composed of about thirty-six gun barrels so joined as to fire at once. The Rhattores lost five chiefs, including a nephew of the Rájah, and the *Buxee* § of the army. These five, finding they could not escape, quitted their horses, and fought with eleven other followers on foot till they were all cut to pieces. This great victory is solely to be attributed to the coolness and intrepidity of our general in making so complete a disposition of his forces in time to repel the rapid charge of the most courageous cavalry in the world. Ismáil Beg arrived the day after the engagement at Nagora, about two *kos* distant."

Merta was a decisive victory, and was won by the bravery of De Boigne. "But for his skill and presence of mind," writes Colonel James Tod, who describes the battle from the Jodhpur point of view, "his Brigade would infallibly have been annihilated." His trained intelligence recognised the impending danger before it was apparent

---

* *Pucca* : substantial, built of stone or burnt brick, in contrast to the usual buildings, which are *kutcha, e.g.,* built of mud.

† *Jerd Kopperah Wallahs :* men in yellow raiment, the garb of doom.

‡ *Organ* = query, a *mitrailleuse ?*

§ *Buxee* = the paymaster of the army, a most important personage in Oriental armies.

to any one else, and his military genius made the dispositions that
met and overcame it. The battle was recognised at the time as a
remarkable one. "De Boigne's battalions," writes the *Calcutta
Chronicle* of the 14th of October, 1790, "have certainly all the merit of
the victory of Mairtha. De Boigne has shown such ability and courage,
that the corps seem to act as if they thought themselves invulnerable."
Another writer, with a juster appreciation of the man he was describing, thus refers to him in another journal, " M. de Boigne's history
will make an important figure in future times in the annals of India
that will immortalise his name, and add celebrity to the European
character." Six months later, in March, 1791, the deeds of this
adventurer were recognised in a debate in the British House of
Commons.

Merta won for De Boigne's Brigade the name of the *Cherri Fouj*,
or Flying Army, for it showed that infantry could not only protect
fortified places and act in pitched battle, but were able to undertake
extended campaigns, and invade distant territories. It converted
Madhoji Sindhia to a complete belief in his regular troops, and led
to the creation of the huge standing army which, before a decade had
passed, became a menace to the British power in India.

The day after the battle Ismáil Beg joined Bijai Sing, bringing
with him a hurriedly-collected force. He endeavoured to persuade
the Jodhpur prince to renew the contest, and an attempt was made
to reassemble the scattered soldiery, and form a new army. But in
December discreeter counsels prevailed, and Bijai Sing sent a Vakil
to Koápur, where De Boigne was encamped, to sue for peace. The
terms imposed were severe, and included, in addition to an indemnity
of three quarters of a million sterling, the cession of the province of
Ajmir, which was granted as *Jaidad* to Lakwá Dáda, the Maráthá
Commander-in-Chief.

As soon as the treaty was concluded, De Boigne marched his brigade
back to Mattra, which he reached on the 1st of January 1791. Here
he was welcomed with an unique salute of the entire park of artillery,
and a *feu de joie* of all the small arms in the Maráthá camp, whilst
in the jubilation of his heart Madhoji loaded his victorious general
with honours and rewards commensurate with his great services.

CHAPTER V.

1791–1793.

THE immediate result of the victories of Pátan and Merta was the formation of a second brigade in 1791 and a third in 1793, the enlistment and organisation of which occupied much of De Boigne's time and attention till the summer of the latter year. Establishing his headquarters at Koil, he threw himself with heart-whole energy into the new work Madhoji Sindhia had entrusted to him, determined to fulfil the expectations of his master and deserve the unlimited confidence reposed in him. Koil was situated close to Aligarh, the fortifications of which were considerably strengthened, and beneath its ramparts arose an extensive cantonment capable of holding a large body of troops, whilst under De Boigne's fostering administration the town itself became an emporium of commerce. The spot was well chosen for the headquarters of an army, for its position in the centre of De Boigne's districts secured to him supplies of all descriptions necessary for his troops, whilst the equi-distance from Delhi and Agra enabled him to dominate both cities by the rapidity with which he could concentrate a force at either point.

When increasing his army, circumstances induced De Boigne to somewhat remodel the constitution of the brigades, each now consisting of 6,000 Telingas, or regular infantry, 1,000 Najibs, or irregulars, and 1,000 Rohillas, called "Allygools," who were men of proved bravery, and recruited for the special work of leading storming parties. Attached to each brigade were 800 regular cavalry, 3 battering guns, 10 howitzers, 2 mortars, and 36 field-pieces. There was also a small body of Persian Horse, mounted and armed at De Boigne's expense, and regarded as his personal bodyguard. The regular cavalry were well mounted; some were armed with matchlocks and swords, others with carbines, pistols, and swords, and all were well disciplined to perform the European evolutions.

To military readers the composition of a complete battalion in De Boigne's army may be interesting. It was as follows :—

Infantry.

1 Captain (European)
1 Lieutenant (European)

		Rs.	
1 Adjutant, or Subahdar	paid	35.	per mensem.
8 Jemadars	,,	20.	,,
1 Havildar Major	,,	12.8	,,
32 Havildars (sergeants)	,,	10.8	,,
32 Naïks (corporals)	,,	8.8	,,
2 Colour Bearers	,,	12.	,,
2 Cymballs	,,	12.	,,
10 Drummers	,,	12.	,,
10 Fifers	,,	12.	,,
416 Sepoys, Grenadier Companies, 6. ; others	,,	5.8.	,,

Artillery.

		Rs.	
1 Sergeant Major (European)	paid	60.	per mensem.
5 Gunners (European)	,,	40.	,,
1 Jemadar	,,	30.	,,
1 Havildar	,,	15.	,,
5 Naïks	,,	9.	,,
5 Sarangs (bullock sergeants)	,,	9.	,,
5 Tindals (park sergeants)	,,	6.8	,,
4 Blacksmiths	,,	6.	,,
4 Carpenters	,,	6.	,,
85 Golundars (native gunners)	paid 6., 7., and 8.		,,
85 Clashies (native artillerymen)	paid 4.8 and 5.		,,
20 Béldars (sappers)	paid	4.	,,
24 Garewáns (bullock drivers)	,,	4.	,,

Native Staff.

		Rs.	
1 Pandit (accountant)	paid	60.	per mensem.
2 Matsaddis (writers)	,,	20.	,,
11 Beesties (water carriers)	,,	4.	,,
7 Armourers	,,	7.	,,
2 Hirkarrus (messengers)	,,	5.	,,
4 Gurreealas (time-keepers)	,,	5.	,,
1 Surgeon (native)	,,	10.	,,
1 Masalchi (torch-bearer)	,,	5.	,,

Each battalion was provided with—

    408 stand of arms.
    4 field-pieces (four- and six-pounders).
    1 howitz.
    5 tumbrils.
    120 bullocks.
    18 camels.
    2 bullock carts.
    300 round of shot for each gun.
    100 round of grape for each gun.
    50 stone shells for each howitz.
    50 rounds of grape for each howitz.

Each tumbril was drawn by twelve bullocks, under charge of three drivers; and each gun by eight bullocks, with two drivers.

The irregular infantry were similarly equipped, but while the Telingas were clothed in scarlet uniforms, obtained from Calcutta, with black leather accoutrements and cockscombs in their blue turbans, the Najibs wore garments of blue quilted country-cloth.

The companies fired by platoons independently, but as the fire of the matchlock battalions was much heavier than that of the musket battalions, De Boigne gave an extra " caronade " or " howitz " to each of the latter. The Rohillas, recruited for fighting in hill country and attacks on fortified villages, were paid Rs.5.8 *per mensem.* There were also 400 *Méwattis* attached to each brigade, whose duties were to forage, furnish guards, escorts, wood-cutters, &c, and two hundred and forty recruits, who drew two annas a day each until incorporated in the rank and file.

The details concerning the Cavalry are not quite so explicit. The number attached to a brigade appears to have been 800, and their uniform was a green one, with red turbans and *kammarbands* or belts. De Boigne's bodyguard, the pick of the mounted troops, was made up of four Risálas or troops, each consisting of—

		Rs.		
1 Risáldar	... ... paid	40.	per mensem.	
1 Naib Risáldar...	... ,,	30.	,,	
4 Jemadars	... ... ,,	18.	,,	each.
4 Daffadars	... ... ,,	12.	,,	,,
64 Troopers	... ... ,,	8.	,,	,,
1 Kettledrum	... ... ,,	7.	,,	
35 Gunners	... ... ,,	8.	,,	,,
4 Galloper guns				

It included also a special body of 75 skirmishing horse, mounted on the fleetest and hardiest animals, and recruited from the bravest and most active men, who were not disciplined like the troopers of the other squadrons, but employed as irregulars.

Two Risálas of similar cavalry, composed of the bravest and best mounted men, were attached to each brigade for skirmishing purposes. The ordinary cavalry, who had to provide and feed their own horses, were paid as follows—

			Rs.	
Risáldars	...	...	paid 80.	per mensem, each.
Jemadars	...	...	,, 40.	,,
Daffadars	...	...	,, 30.	,,
Kettledrums	...	...	,, 24.	,,
Troopers	...	...	,, 24.	,,

The number of men in each brigade was about 9,000, so that when his army was brought to its full strength De Boigne had under his command, including garrison troops, about 30,000 men. The monthly cost of a brigade was Rs.56,000 in Hindustan, increased by a special *batta* or allowance of 50 *per centum* to Rs.84,000, when serving south of the Chambal river.

The difficulty of obtaining competent officers was in a measure overcome by the pay and allowances offered. But it is probable that these were not so liberal at first as the scale ultimately sanctioned, which bore favourable comparison with that obtaining in the Company's army at the same period, and was certainly good enough to tempt Europeans of recognised ability and character to enter the service. This could hardly have been the case in 1792, as the following pay-list of De Boigne's officers, supplied to the Government of India, will show—

OFFICERS IN COLONEL DE BOIGNE'S BRIGADE IN 1792.

Commander of First Brigade.

PAY PER MENSEM.
Rs.

Major Frèmont (Frenchman) 1,400

Commander of Second Brigade.

Major Perron (Frenchman) 1,200

Brigade Major of First Brigade.

Captain James Gardner (Scotchman)... ... 450

Brigade Major of Second Brigade.

Captain Drugeon (Savoyard) 400

Officers in the First Brigade.

Captain Lyenite (France)	700
,, Felose (Italy)	300
,, Allamunde (England)	200
,, Baleman (Pohlman ?), (Hanover) ...	200
,, Butterfield (England)	200
,, Le Marchant (France)	300
Captain Lieutenant Robert Bell (England) ...	250
Lieutenant Sutherland (Scotland)	200
,, Jumeon (Holland)	150
,, Rennick (Ireland)	200
,, Abbott (England)	200
,, Lewis (Bourguien ?), (France) ...	200
Ensign Harvey (Ireland), (deserter from Company's Artillery at Cawnpore)... ...	•120

A footnote mentions that promotion and pay entirely depended on Colonel De Boigne's favour.

In this list the loaves and fishes are few and far between, but a considerable improvement was made in the pay and allowances of the officers when the third brigade was raised, as the following amended scale of salaries then introduced indicates—

RANK OF OFFICER.	PAY PER MENSEM IN HINDUSTAN. Rs.	PAY PER MENSEM IN THE DECCAN. Rs.
Colonel	3,000 ...	... 4,500
Lieutenant-Colonel ...	2,000 ...	... 3,000
Major	1,200 ...	... 1,800
Captain	400 ...	... 600
Captain-Lieutenant ...	300 ...	... 450
Lieutenant	200 ...	... 300
Ensign	150 ...	... 225

Besides their pay, all colonels, lieutenant-colonels, and majors commanding brigades drew Rs.100 a month from the Bazaar as table allowance. It is also easy to understand that there were many other sources of emolument open to the officers besides their pay, especially when they rose to positions of command and responsibility, and as time passed certain privileges accrued which increased their position and respectability. For instance, no ordinary person presumed to set up a palanquin in the Maráthá dominions, and in the Mughal provinces the right of riding in a yellow elephant howdah was confined exclusively to the aristocracy; yet De Boigne's Europeans were permitted to use both unquestioned. In travelling through the country their baggage was carried from place to place free of charge, and all goods imported for their personal use were exempted from the payment of customs dues. As for the duties of these officers, except in the case of a commander of a battalion, they were far from onerous. But, on the other hand, the service was admittedly a precarious one, depending solely upon success in the field. So long as fortune smiled upon their arms, pay and position were assured; but in the event of a defeat, it was tacitly understood that there was no compensation for, or appeal against, loss of employment. The expense of living was considerable, requiring the upkeep of a large establishment of servants, camp equipage, and transport animals.

That fortunes could be, and were, made by the officers in De Boigne's Brigades is a matter of fact, for they had opportunities of acquiring large sums of money apart from that which the ordinary exercise of their profession brought them. The Pagoda tree still flourished in the native states of India. De Boigne himself, in his old age, was wont to remark of many of his old subalterns, " Such a one, if he had not drunk, or such a one, if he had not gambled, could have done as I have done. It was his own fault that he did not save £100,000. It depended on himself to make a fortune equal to mine."

When the Second Brigade was completed Major Perron was appointed to its command, whilst Major Frèmont received that of the first. On the formation of the third Major Sutherland obtained the command. As showing the value attaching to commissions in the service, it is interesting to note that an officer named Pedron, who joined as a captain-lieutenant, soon after *purchased* his majority. By the time the three brigades were brought to their full strength there were about three hundred Europeans of different nationalities—English, French, German, Swiss, Italian, Hanoverian, Portuguese, and half-castes—in the force, of whom 10 per cent. held commissions. The rest were drill-sergeants and artillery-men, chiefly recruited from runaway soldiers and sailors of the Company's service, or half-castes. Their pay was very small, ranging from 30 to 60 rupees a month. They were generally dissolute and degraded in their mode of life, forming connections with native women, and in times of peace reflecting but little credit on their European birth. But during active service they constantly exhibited extraordinary courage, and sustained their reputation for brave fighting.

De Boigne's pay was raised, first from Rs.4,000 to Rs.6,000 a month, and subsequently to Rs.10,000. Moreover, this was nearly doubled by various perquisites, including a commission of 2 per cent. on the revenue collections of his *Jaidad*, which could not have brought him in less than Rs.60,000 a year. He enjoyed the income of a modern British Viceroy.

Soon after its establishment De Boigne's force received the title of *The Imperial Army*, for although it was absolutely of Madhoji Sindhia's own creation, and subservient to his orders alone, he preferred, perhaps from a sense of exaggerated humility, or more probably from motives of policy, to invest it with a titular designation which accorded the shadow of authority to the blind emperor, and left the substance in his own hands.

Of course these radical changes and innovations, creating as they did for Sindhia a formidable standing army of 30,000 men, were not introduced without causing enmity and dissatisfaction in many quarters. In the first instance, the assignment to De Boigne of a vast and fertile district in the heart of the Doáb as *Jaidad*, made him an object of universal jealousy. Soon, in addition to this, a large *Jaghir*, or personal estate, was conferred on him by his grateful master, to the intense chagrin of the Maráthá chiefs, who realised, with impotent anger, that the European interloper had obtained their prince's ear and favour, and, having discredited their own military pretensions, was completely superseding them. The power and authority De Boigne enjoyed were equal to those of a sovereign ruler, and his orders carried the same force as if they had been issued by an independent Mughal Emperor.

Thus in nine short years, by perseverance and determination, by ability and industry, by the valour of his sword and the wisdom of his conduct, De Boigne raised himself from the inconsequence of an ensign in a regiment of Madras native infantry to the position of Commander-in-chief of the army of Hindustan. Assisted by none, dependent solely on his own exertions and talents, he attained this pre-eminence through sheer force of character and merit. In the great city, which had for centuries been the capital of the most potent and gorgeous empire in India, this wandering Savoyard was paramount. It was an elevation that exceeded his wildest aspirations— one which in his old age he could never look back upon without exclaiming, " It all appears as if it were a dream ! "

After the formation of the Second Brigade De Boigne was for some time employed in consolidating Sindhia's power in the Shaikbáwáti district, but the service was of a comparatively unimportant character, and chiefly confined to extirpating robber bands and reducing petty chiefs to submission. No detailed chronicle of this period appears to exist, but the following extract from a letter printed in *The World* newspaper, published at Calcutta, in September, 1792, is so far interesting that it localises his actions about this time, and conveys information regarding the state of his health. The letter was written by an officer in the First Brigade, under Major Frèmont, who was engaged in punishing the Rájah Devi Sing, a tributary chief of Jaipur, and compelling him to pay the amount of tribute due from him. The first portion will be found in the appendix in the sketch of Frèmont's life : the concluding part reads as follows :—

" This country is called the Sheikawutty District, and if properly, or even moderately, cultivated, would yield seven lakhs' revenue, whereas it is not estimated at more than three. It is still populous, and the ruins of vast cities and towns dispersed through all our route, convey a strong impression of former and vast opulence. But want stares through every village, and while the little that the wretched inhabitant of a hut possesses is subject to be wrested from him by numerous bands of banditti on the one side, or by the oppressions of his chief or his servants, or both, on the other, heaven has afflicted this unfortunate land with a drought of two years' continuance. The country is very mountainous, but the valleys, notwithstanding the niggardness of the elements, give still a display of verdure not to be expected, and almost incredible.

" We left the First Brigade with De Boigne at Rohtak on the 22nd of June (1792). De Boigne was then just recovering from a dreadful dysentery, which has deprived us of some of our officers. Colonel Martine's brother died at Jedger (Jhojjar ?), and Lieutenant Stewart at Rohtak, the day prior to our march, and we came at the rate of eight and nine cos each day. Grain was nine seers a rupee, and coarse flour six pice the seer yesterday. It is now more moderate.

" Liqua Adda (Lakwa Dáda) commands the division of Mahratta Cavalry attached to this Brigade. He is a man of great respectability, and a favourite of Scindia's. The second in command is Jaggo Cappoo (? Bappoo) Dada, a man of ability and trust.

" De Boigne with his First Brigade is now at Ulwar, in the Mewatte country, about fifty cos from Delhi. The position of our camp is in a more westerly direction, but only fifty cos from Delhi. The country is in such a state that subjection seems almost chronic; for plunder is the universal system, and become so habitual as to be spoken of with as much indifference as we talk of a purchase in a mercantile way. As soon as a party has plundered a district, the plundered directly make an incursion on their neighbours, and so it continues with as great regularity as trade, only that it operates in the contrary course, ruining instead of supporting nature.

" The superior politics, as you call it, has been some time out of my way, or rather I have been out of its way, on this active tour. Scindia continues at Poonah, and a letter of yesterday from De Boigne (August 9th) mentions that he is not to be expected speedily. At Oojeen Major Palmer (the English Resident) has taken up a partial abode. He will make it such so long as the subtle Mahratta continues with the Peishwa. The situation is particularly favourable for keeping the communication of correspondence complete between your presidency and our friends in this quarter. It keeps the circle perfect. It is certain that there had been some secret stroke in meditation between the British and the lately hostile Sultan.* Almost Dutchlike slowness and Oriental indecision delayed the stroke till, to use an old adage, *the iron cooled.* The opportunity is passed, and to prevent its return will be the true British policy. Various ideas are entertained by the delay of Scindia. It has been asserted in our camp that he aimed at measures tending to fix a claim to the Mogul tribute of two and a half lakhs of rupees, agreed to be paid by the Company to the Dewanni. But I can scarcely credit it, although I know that Scindia's power at Delhi is all, and that of the Mogul is nothing. Beside, by the king's determination in 1771 to reside at Delhi instead of Allahabad, that claim was forfeited.

" The Sikhs hold the northern balance of India. Intrigue cannot act on them from the unsettled nature of their living. But if Scindia had youth to reduce them, as he has spirit and resolution, their weight would soon again restore the throne to the worshippers of the Hindoo Theogony."

During the period that De Boigne was raising the Second and Third Brigades, and establishing his master's authority, the enormous growth of Sindhia's power was being watched with rancorous jealousy by Takúji Holkar, his partner in the province of Malwa, and his great compeer in the Marátha Confederation. Holkar had been associated with Madhoji in the extension of the Marátha power over Hindustan. Politically the two were equal, and the former clung to his prescriptive share in the conquest with great tenacity. But Pátan and Merta, and the completion of De Boigne's army, disturbed the balance of power, and the shrewd and enterprising policy of Sindhia outran the slower and more conservative course that Holkar steered, and carried him to the front. Takúji realised this, and, in order to combat it, raised a disciplined corps of his own. Its organisation was begun in 1791, and the Chevalier Dudrenec, a gallant French gentleman, but a singularly unfortunate soldier, was chosen for its command.

* Tipú Sultan of Mysore.

Had Holkar merely confined himself to the establishment of an infantry brigade, modelled on the lines of De Boigne's, Sindhia might have regarded his endeavours with tolerable indifference. But simultaneously cabals and intrigues were set on foot at the Peshwá's Court at Poonah, and every craft brought to bear to undermine Madhoji's influence. So successful were the conspirators that Sindhia soon found it necessary to proceed to the capital to protect his own interests, and counteract the schemes of his enemies. The step was a serious one, but the necessity was great ; for Sindhia's ambition comprehended an assertion of power, not merely in Hindustan, but over the whole of the Maráthá dominions, and Holkar's hostility neutralised in the south all that De Boigne's successes had wrought in the north.

Hindustan was secure while De Boigne's brigades held it in an iron grasp, and of this Madhoji felt satisfied. So he appointed Gopál Ráo Bháo his Viceroy, and prepared to start for Poonah. But in order to allay suspicion he announced that the object of his journey was to invest the Peshwá with the insignia of the office of *Vakil-i-Mutluq,* or supreme deputy of the empire, which had been confirmed on him three years previously by the Emperor. Moreover, with diplomatic moderation, he confined his escort to a single battalion (the one chosen to accompany him being that commanded by Michael Filoze), and a bodyguard raised for the occasion by Colonel John Hessing, who had quarrelled with De Boigne after the battle of Pátan, and resigned his command. In the spring of 1793 Madhoji Sindhia commenced his journey, and marching by slow stages arrived at Poonah on the 11th of June following.

CHAPTER VI.

THE BATTLE OF LAKHAIRI. DEATH OF MADHOJI SINDHIA.

1793–1794.

THE departure of Madhoji Sindhia from Hindustan was the signal for Takúji Holkar to commence operations in that quarter. He had long considered himself unjustly used by the small share awarded him of the territory conquered from the Mughal, and his indignation was greatly increased when he learnt that one of the principal objects of Sindhia's visit to Poonah was to procure the recall of his rival from the conquered provinces. This was not an unnatural step for Madhoji to take. In the battles that had led to the annexation of Hindustan, and the subjugation of the Rajput States of Jaipur and Jodhpur, Holkar had studiously, and on one notable occasion, treach rously, kept aloof; but, as not unfrequently occurs, when the fighting was over, he desired to share the plunder. In Hindustan he had been less insistent, or less successful, but he had made up for this in Rájputana, where he had carefully avoided conflict until Pátan and Merta had been fought and won, when he sent his troops across the Chambal, pretended that in the division of the spoils the tribute of Jaipur had passed to him, and Jodhpur to Sindhia, and asserted his equal right to occupy, with Madhoji's forces, the newly-annexed territory of Ajmir. This, of course, led to disagreements and difficulties; but, before drawing his own sword, Holkar sought for some other instrument to use against Sindhia, and in the restless and rebellious spirit of Ismáil Beg found the very weapon he desired.

He at once determined to make a cat's-paw of the Mughal noble, and push him forward to disturb the tranquillity of the new conquests, trusting in any disturbance that ensued to find an opportunity to further his own interests. A plausible chance soon presented itself. Before the Marátha occupation of Delhi, one of the Emperor's most trusted ministers had been a nobleman named Najaf Kuli Khan,

This person had recently died, leaving a widow, who still maintained her independence in the fortress of Kánaund. Being a woman of brave and masculine spirit, she refused to surrender her stronghold to Sindhia, and as such rebellious conduct could not be overlooked, it was deemed necessary to take forcible measures to reduce her to submission, and De Boigne ordered Major Perron to proceed against Kánaund with a small force and capture it. Najaf Kuli Khan during his lifetime had formed so high an estimate of the power of De Boigne's battalions, that previous to his death, although exhorting his Begum to hold out resolutely against the Maráthás, he advised her to surrender at once if De Boigne's troops were sent against her. With this warning fresh in her memory the widow was prepared to sue for peace, but before she actually did so, Ismáil Beg, who had remained inactive after his defeat at Pátan, instigated by Takúji Holkar, collected a force, and, marching to Kánaund, persuaded the Begum to oppose resistance.

A description of the battle which ensued between Ismáil Beg and Perron's forces will be found in the sketch of the latter's life, to which it rightly belongs. Here it is sufficient to record that the fort of Kánaund was captured and the Begum killed, whilst Ismáil Beg, in order to save himself from a shameful treachery premeditated against him by the garrison, surrendered to Perron, under promise of his life being spared. Directly Madhoji Sindhia heard that his old enemy was at last in his power, he sent orders for his immediate execution, but De Boigne chivalrously resisted the mandate, and saved the life of the gallant but unfortunate noble, whose energy in the field and heroic resistance to the invaders of his country was the one bright spot in the miserable history of incapacity and defeat that brought about the downfall of the Mughal Empire. Ismáil Beg was sent as a state prisoner to Agra, where he was treated with the respect due to his rank and courage, and awarded a subsistence of Rs.600 a month. But his spirit was broken by his misfortunes, and he never lifted his head again. He died in 1799, and with him passed away the last worthy warrior that sought to sustain the dynasty of Taimur in independence on the throne.

The failure of Ismáil Beg's final effort left Holkar with only himself to depend upon for the accomplishment of his hostile designs against Madhoji, and it was not until the latter had proceeded to the Deccan, in 1793, that he dared to bring matters to a crisis. In July of that year a rupture took place between his troops and those of Sindhia, when the two factions were engaged in levying tribute in Rájputana. A quarrel over the spoils of a certain district led to an appeal to arms, and this was at once followed by active preparations for war between the two great rival chiefs.

Gopál Ráo Bháo, Madhoji's Viceroy in Hindustan, having summoned Lakwa Dáda and De Boigne to join him, advanced against Holkar's army, which was in the vicinity of Ajmir. The latter endeavoured to avoid a pitched battle, and some time was lost in marches and counter-marches, but he was at length brought to bay in the pass of Lakhairi in September, 1793.

Gopál Ráo's army consisted of 20,000 horse, and De Boigne's First Brigade of 9,000 infantry, with 80 guns, whilst Holkar brought into the field 30,000 cavalry, and his four newly-raised regular battalions under the command of the Chevalier Dudrenec. De Boigne, on whom the command devolved, found the enemy strongly posted in a defile in the hills, where the nature of the ground was such that only a very small force could be utilised in attack. The battle that ensued has been described by the General as the most obstinate and bloody one he was ever engaged in. He began the action by sending forward three battalions of infantry and 500 Rohillas to storm the narrow, wooded pass which led to the enemy's position. But scarcely had these advanced than a terrible disaster overtook his main body. A chance shot struck an open tumbril of ammunition and exploded it, and this was immediately followed by the explosion of twelve others standing near. The catastrophe threw the Brigade into the greatest alarm and confusion, but fortunately, owing to the wooded and hilly nature of the country, Holkar's Cavalry were unable to take full advantage of it. With the wonderful presence of mind and resource in moments of crisis that never failed him, De Boigne retrieved the disaster. Returning to his main body he collected and reformed the broken soldiery in time to meet the onslaught of the enemy's cavalry, who, as soon as they came under his fire began to waver. De Boigne then ordered his regular horse forward, and leading them in person, attacked the hesitating foe, and turned a doubtful day into a complete victory.

The punishment of the battle fell on the Chevalier Dudrenec's corps. These were unable to keep up with the cavalry in their rapid flight, and in self-defence faced round and attempted to stem the pursuit. With the utmost determination and gallantry they contested the ground until they were practically annihilated. Dudrenec alone escaped unhurt, every European officer in his force being killed or wounded,. whilst thirty-eight of his guns were captured. The shattered wreck of Holkar's army made a precipitate flight across the Chambal into Malwa, where their prince, in impotent rage, swooped down upon Sindhia's undefended capital of Ujjain and sacked it.

The battle of Lakhairi decided for seven years the doubtful contest that had hitherto smouldered between the houses of Ujjain and Indore. It made Sindhia the sole master of the Maráthá acquisitions in Hindustan, and humbled the pride if it did not actually break the heart of Takúji Holkar, who never showed fight again, and died four years later. The one redeeming feature of the defeat was the valour displayed by the Chevalier Dudrenec's disciplined brigade. Short-lived and ill-fated though it had been, it had still proved its worth, and shortly afterwards Holkar was induced by this officer to raise another corps on similar lines.

The quarrel between Sindhia and Holkar, and the absence of the former from Hindustan, now prompted Partáb Sing of Jaipur to throw off the yoke of a tributary and declare his independence. He was a ruler not wanting in spirit, nor deficient in judgment, but on this occasion his conduct was both impolitic and pusillanimous, for he lacked the courage and the energy to carry into effect a determination he had arrived at too hastily. No sooner was De Boigne informed of Partáb Sing's refusal to pay his tribute, than, with his usual vigour and promptitude, he marched from Lakhairi to Jaipur. The Rájah fell back before him, and shut himself up in his capital, and at the last moment, rather than sustain a siege, tendered his submission and paid the fine demanded of nearly a million sterling.

Matters being thus settled Partáb Singh invited De Boigne to his capital, and entertained him in a style of unparalleled magnificence. From Jaipur the General marched his Brigade back to the Doáb, stopping on the way to visit the Rájah of Ulwar at Macheri. Here he narrowly escaped assassination whilst attending the chief's durbar. During the ceremony one of the Rájah's attendants, approaching his master, asked, in a whisper, if he would authorise the assassination of De Boigne, which could be accomplished when he was leaving the palace. To his credit, be it recorded, the Prince of Ulwar recoiled in horror from the foul suggestion, and in consequence no attempt was made to carry it out. De Boigne's Vakil overheard the proposal, which was whispered in a vernacular the General did not understand, and communicated it to him, but De Boigne not only made no comment, but never alluded to the incident in any way afterwards.

De Boigne had now reached the zenith of his greatness, and when he returned to Delhi at the head of his victorious army, he was the autocrat of Hindustan. He had vanquished all Sindhia's enemies, and there was not one left that dared to so much as raise a hand. The power of Holkar was broken, and the rebellious spirit of Rájputana reduced, whilst Delhi was humbled to the position of a city occupied by an enemy. Shah 'Alam, the blind Emperor, was suffered to exist—a mere symbol of authority—in order that the fiction of governing in his name might be preserved. All the power lay in De Boigne's hands, for Gopál Ráo had recently been suspected by Sindhia of participation in the hostile intrigues of Nana Farnavis, and deposed from his office of Viceroy of Hindustan, which was conferred upon De Boigne, with whom the Bháo, in his misfortunes, had taken refuge, and by whom he was protected, even as Ismáil Beg had been, from the malice of a wanton and cruel revenge.

With Sindhia De Boigne was paramount, for the Maráthá Chief although treacherous by nature and suspicious by disposition, trusted his European General implicitly, and treated him as honourably as he trusted him. Never did any European gain from a native prince such confidence and esteem as De Boigne won from Madhoji, who frequently remarked that though he owed his being and his heritage to his father, it was De Boigne who taught him how to enjoy the one, and make use of the other. Assuredly this was the case, for it was De Boigne's battalions "before whose bayonets terror recoiled, and whose grape scattered armies in flight" that raised up Sindhia to his supreme position, and kept him there.

That De Boigne was worthy of the great responsibilities to which he was called, history bears witness. Although surrounded by temptations which appealed to his ambition, his vanity, and his cupidity, he never abused his opportunities, but, on the contrary, made the noble use of them, that stamps him as a good as well as a great man. In the exalted rank he had attained, the power for evil was as potent as the power for good, and he chose to exert the latter. Foremost in war, he was also foremost in peace, and the welfare and social improvement of those he ruled, were his sincere aim. In battle his fearless courage and military genius inspired with confidence the ignorant and barbarous peoples he trained to arms, but when the fight was finished he tempered the brutality of the times by an exercise of humanity that made its mark on the decade. The ferocity of war, and the savage reprisals of victory were curbed by the enforcement of a rigid discipline; and slaughter, devastation, and rapine were sternly repressed. He never suffered the disgrace of defeat, and he never permitted the greater moral disgrace that too often attached to the unlicensed excesses of conquest in the East. Loyal as he was to Sindhia, he was equally loyal to his own sense of rectitude, and feared not to champion the claims of humanity when the occasion arose. Often did he stand between Madhoji and the hasty wrath that would have been guilty of a mean or wicked action, shielding those whom the despotism of an Oriental revenge threatened, until the fierce storm of passion had passed and justice was allowed to resume its sway. That De Boigne could so act, and did so act, and yet to the last retained his master's esteem and confidence, proved that his moral victories were even greater than those which he won with his sword.

From June, 1793, to February, 1794, Madhoji remained at Poonah, endeavouring to gain over the young Peshwá, and circumvent the crafty machinations of his many enemies at Court. The signal defeat of Holkar at Lakhairi made the task even more difficult than before, for the universal jealousy it aroused increased Sindhia's unpopularity in the Deccan capital, whilst his schemes were too ambitious to find immediate adherents. The time passed in intrigue and counter intrigue, plot and counter plot, until at last his efforts began to be rewarded, and the young Peshwá, chafing under the austere direction of Nana Farnavis, evinced a decided inclination to throw off the yoke and submit himself to the more attractive guidance of his great vassal. Madhoji was rough, but he was genial, and he cloaked his shrewdness under an apparently open and hearty nature. There was a certain freedom in his manner which was attractive, and he assiduously laboured to please. It almost seemed as if the same good fortune that had crowned his arms in the north was going to crown his diplomacy in the south, when, in this moment of success, there came a sudden summons to him—a summons that kings and subjects alike must obey, and which shatters all hopes and ambitions, even as it terminates all fears and sufferings. Early in February 1794, the old Patél, whilst residing at Wanaoli, near Poonah, was seized with a violent fever, and on the twelfth of the month, in the sixty-fourth year of his age, Madhoji Sindhia, the greatest prince, with the exception of Sivaji, that the Maráthá nation ever produced, breathed his last.

Gifted with great political sagacity, skilled in artifice, and a master of intrigue, Madhoji's schemes were ambitious, but practicable. Had he lived there is little doubt but that he would have fulfilled a portion, at least, of the task he set himself, and founded an independent dynasty which might have claimed a place by the side of the greatest in India. His military talents were of the first rank, and he was not less a great statesman than a great soldier. It was the combination of the highest qualities of each that enabled him to recognise the merits of De Boigne and adapt them to his purpose. Boldly breaking free from the trammels of long-established custom, he superseded an untrained multitude with a comparatively small, but compact and highly disciplined army, which formed a powerful weapon in his

MADHOJI SINDHIA.

[From a plate in Francklin's "History of the Reign of Shah-Aulum."]

hands. His enterprise met with its due reward, for it raised him up to a position which knew no compeer, and feared no rival. The fighting machine he called into existence made him invincible. Before his death, in addition to his vast possessions in Central India and Malwa, across the Chambal Rájputana was his vassal, and Hindustan his own. From the Deccan in the south to the Siwaliks in the north, from the valley of the Ganges in the east to the deserts of Bikanir in the west, the sway of the old Patél was undisputed. The kingdom he left behind him was the most powerful in all India, and it owed its circumstance not less to the statesmanship of Madhoji Sindhia than to the battalions of Benoît De Boigne.

MADHOJI SINDHIA left no children, and was succeeded by his grand nephew, Daulat Rao Sindhia, a youth of fifteen, who was entirely under the influence of a crafty Brahmin named Baloba Tantia, whom he appointed his minister. Tantia, in common with most of the leading Maráthá chieftains, was inimical to De Boigne, and jealous of his enormous power. But it was impossible to attempt any change in the complicated military and political machine that controlled Hindustan, and the General was confirmed in the command of the army, the guardianship of the Emperor's kingdom, and the government of all the Maráthá possessions north of the Chambal.

On his accession Daulat Rao Sindhia decided to remain at Poonah and continue his uncle's policy, which had been directed towards the attainment of a preponderating influence at the Court of the Peshwá. His position was soon considerably strengthened by the arrival of De Boigne's First Brigade, under the command of Major Perron, which had been ordered down to the Deccan by Madhoji shortly before his death. This secured the young chief a force sufficient to awe the Peshwá, and assure the ascenuancy of his own views. Moreover, about the same time Hessings's and Filoze's corps were considerably augmented.

On the death of his old master De Boigne's conduct was governed by those principles of honour and rectitude which distinguished his whole career. So great was his power that it is no exaggeration to say he might have made Hindustan his own ; but the temptation was rejected, and the soldier of fortune who had so loyally served Madhoji Sindhia wavered not for an instant in his allegiance to the boy prince who succeeded him.

Often throughout his career had De Boigne been the recipient of tempting overtures from neighbouring powers, who sought to detach him from the Maráthá interest, and secure his services for themselves, and many of these offers were now repeated. Shah 'Alam, who in his impotent blindness and degrading confinement, still hugged the delusion of majesty, proposed to confer on De Boigne the high office of Wazír, if he would employ his Brigades in restoring an independent Mughal Empire. Zemán Shah, the king of Cabul, sent his ambassadors to the General, with offers so dazzling, that they amounted to an equal share in his throne if De Boigne would set up the dominion of the Abdali in India. But these and many other overtures were all declined, and De Boigne remained true to the young master of the house he had so long served, and whose fortunes he had raised to such a commanding eminence in the community of Indian nations.

It was a noble decision that recognised the path of duty so clearly and followed it so unhaltingly. For it was the decision of a proud, ambitious man in the flood tide of his successful career, on whose actions no restraint was placed save that of conscience. De Boigne was at this time but forty-three years old, and in the very prime of life, and there was afforded to him a possibility of obtaining independent sovereign power. But he rejected the temptation; and in the renunciation there was a finer credit than any which the grandeur of an usurped crown could have conferred.

Upon the accession of Daulat Rao Sindhia De Boigne's overwhelming strength enabled him to keep the peace in Hindustan, and overawe those projected rebellions against existing authority which always follow the succession of Oriental rulers. Three small outbreaks occurred at Datia, Narwár, and Soháwalgarh, but were speedily suppressed by Majors Frèmont, Sutherland, and Gardner, who were severally detached to reduce the refractory chiefs implicated. With these exceptions no record exists of any extensive military operations undertaken north of the Chambal, during the period that intervened between Madhoji Sindhia's death, and the General's departure for Europe.

But although his sword was allowed to rest in its sheath there were many civil and political duties which claimed De Boigne's attention at this time, and two of them are especially interesting. One was the condition of the *Táj* at Agra, the other the circumstances of the Emperor Shah 'Alam. An interest in both matters was evinced by Colonel John Murray, an officer of the Company holding a high post under Government at Calcutta, who, on the 22nd of February, 1794, wrote to De Boigne, inquiring if any steps were being taken to preserve the unique mausoleum raised to Mumtaz-i-Mahal at Agra,

and stating that " he had repeatedly heard that this monument of
Eastern magnificence and refinement was likely to'fall soon into
irrevocable decay, unless means were taken without loss of time to
prevent it."

De Boigne, in reply to this inquiry, wrote :—" I have been honoured
with your kind favour of the 22nd ultimo, which has given me much
pleasure in finding myself noted by you, and thought capable of
effecting the liberal views and honourable wishes you have in the
preservation of the Tage." He then went on to state that he had
already once or twice spoken to Madhoji Sindhia on the subject of
preserving the mausoleum " but he did not appear to value more than
the richness of the material." A small allowance had been sanctioned
for the expenses of keeping it in good repair, " but the avarice and
parsimony of the Hindoo caste in general, and the Mahrattos in
particular, as also their abhorrence of all that is Mahomedan will for
ever impede the application of the allowance to its real purpose . . .
I shall certainly use my best endeavours, and take advantage of the
little influence I have with the Prince, to have the allowance already
made, applied to the repairs of it, and if possible to have something
more added to it, if the former is thought insufficient. . . . Was ever
Scindia endowed with those noble principles you possess, and which
guide your actions in this desire of yours, yet the Pundits, who have
the management of all business at Court, will never put aside the old
way of embezzling the half of what is to pass by their hands, which is
so familiar in every transaction, that it is not thought so much as to
take any notice of it. . . . If I am so happy as to meet with success
in my exertions to execute your commands, that honour shall be
yours, and positively to you alone shall be indebted for the pleasure
they shall enjoy in the admiration of that superb monument. If
otherwise, and that the decay of it cannot be much retarded, you shall
have the self-satisfaction of having wished and done your utmost for
its preservation, and I, at your request, to have followed your steps in
that noble career. Requesting the favour to be at all times honoured
with your commands, and with a place in your acquaintance, permit
me to be, with unfeigned regard, Sir, your most obedient and very
humble servant, BT. DE BOIGNE."

The " Dream in Marble " still stands to witch all pilgrims to Agra
with its exquisite beauty. It's costly splendour may be estimated
from the fact that upon this single edifice over three million pounds
sterling were expended, and this, too, in a country where labour was
the cheapest item in building work. It is formed of the finest white
marble inlaid with precious stones, and although bearing many marks

of Vandal Maráthá hands, still the *Táj* exists in all its original exquisite symmetry of form. For their share in its preservation posterity owes a debt of gratitude to Colonel John Murray and Benoit De Boigne.

Colonel Murray was evidently encouraged by the tone of De Boigne's letter to address him on another subject which he had at heart. This was the ill-treatment the Emperor Shah 'Alam was experiencing at the hands of his Maráthá appointed custodian Nizam-ul-Din. This man was by profession a Dervish, and often alluded to as the " *Cowrie* Father," from the circumstance that alms in the shape of *Cowries*, or shells (the lowest form of currency in India), were often thrown to *fakirs* of his persuasion. Writing on the 10th of October, 1794, Colonel Murray thanks De Boigne for the attention paid to his letter regarding the preservation of the *Taj*, and now begs to enlist his sympathies on behalf of the blind Emperor, asking him " to use his pious endeavours to mitigate the sufferings of this fallen and ill-used family," and enclosing the following extract from a letter, written by a friend of De Boigne at Delhi, to a correspondent in the Company's service :—

" Scindia sets Shah Nizam-ool-Deen over the Badshaw as the greatest scoundrel they could find. He does not give a farthing of money to the Badshaw, or any of his people, affecting to console the poor old king that it is all the better for him, as no temptation can remain for another Gholam Cadir to seize upon him for the sake of plunder. Regularly every day he furnishes the old King with two *seers* (4 lbs.) of pillaw and eight *seers* of meat for himself to get cooked as he likes. This, with two loaves of bread, about the length each of a cubit, to suffice for breakfast, dinner, and supper, and he may get *masála* (spices and condiments) where he can. This, however, though it is to serve for five persons, and the poor servants who can pick at it a bit afterwards, is living in clover in comparison with the rest of the Royal Household. They, poor creatures, without distinction, Princes and Princesses, nay Queens and all eunuchs and female slaves, have exactly delivered out to them to bake into cakes two *seers* a day of barley flour for every three of them, which they are to bake for themselves, and are thus afforded two-thirds of a seer of food a day. For liquors, from the King to the turnspit, they have nothing but water. The King's quincuncial party at dinner every day is made out of himself and his doctor, his son and heir, and a little favourite daughter, and the mighty boon of being one at this fine extra fare is fairly allotted to his 200 Begums, one after another in turn ; so that of the poor Queens each has a prospect, of what to them, after their miserable fare, must be a high treat indeed, a dinner and a half a year ! I asked if the old gentleman would not wish to regale himself with beef now and then ? Yes, he longs for it, but where is he to get it ? The servants often apply in great misery to the unfeeling father (Nizam-ool-Deen) for a little wages, when, after having been three or four months without a farthing, he will perhaps only bestow on them three or four annas, on another perhaps as much as eight annas. The old Nizam (of Hydrabad) sent the King six years ago 6,000 gold mohurs. They every farthing got into the *Cowrie* Father's hands, and remain there ! "

Such was the pitiful condition to which the Emperor of Hindustan was reduced when Colonel John Murray, impelled by a feeling of humanity, wrote to De Boigne. It was not until the month of March in the following year that the latter replied to the letter, for it reached him during a time when he was prostrated with illness, and incapacitated from work. But as soon as he had recovered, and instituted the necessary inquiries, he sent the following answer to Colonel Murray, dated from Koil, the 12th of March, 1795 :—

" DEAR SIR,—I can't but with propriety begin by making you strong and warm apologies for my having been so long in acknowledging your kind favour last received in its due time, and delivered to me by Lieutenant Robert Murray. Be pleased to believe, my dear sir, that the cause don't come from any neglect or forgetfulness. Too proud in the honour of your remembrance and correspondence, I have had so bad a state of health for these six months, that with the greatest difficulties have I been able to attend in part to the duties of my station, which, indeed, are too great to leave me a moment's quietness of mind or body. On that account, and confiding in your kindness and liberality, I have some hope that you'll be pleased to forgive me.

" In regard to your observations of the King Shah Allum and family's situation, they are but too right. However, not quite so bad as by the paper you have been pleased to send me, the author having somewhat exaggerated or been misinformed. Could the old man know the interest you take in his misfortunes, which are great indeed, he could not but admire the goodness and sensibility of your heart, which is above all praise ; and myself, as if informed with your liberal intentions, feel as you do for the unfortunate. I have been for near these two years past endeavouring to alleviate the miseries of that family, and have been perhaps rather troublesome to the late

Madhajee Scindia in that respect. I will not disguise that the principal motives of my exertions were not so pure as yours, they being rather intended to the reputation of the prince, my master, and perhaps my own, knowing that the king's miseries could not but tarnish it in the eyes of the world. He always promised me that at his return in Indostan he would certainly attend to my application in ameliorating his situation, and had he lived no doubt something would have been done. After his death I have continued my importunities to the young prince, which has occasioned, as you may have heard, some advances to the Soubahdar of Delhy, Shawjee, that Fakir having been obliged to pay lately 150,000 rupees, which the Mahratta chiefs have taken from him without the king's benefitting by it, except about 25,000 in nuzzars and goods presented to him. At the same time it has been settled that the former, or present allowance of the king, should be increased by 5,000 rupees a month. A few villages have been ceded in *Jaghir* to some of the Begums and Princesses, and I have put myself Mirza Akber Shah's eldest son in possession of a province called Kotte Kassim, producing about 30,000 rupees per annum, which he held also in *Jaghir* before the late troubles in Indostan. All this, which is not much, has been done now, and not, I assure you, without my encountering the greatest difficulties, the present government and the Mahratta chiefs having not the smallest intention or wish to ameliorate the situation of that poor old man ; and it may be said the little already done to have been done entirely by deference to him than to the King—which brings us to say, *O! Tempora! O! Mores!* The province in Shawjee's possession intended for the support of the royal family may produce about seven lakhs *per annum.* Should that sum be employed to that purpose, it would be quite, if not above, sufficient. But Shawjee, as a *Fakir,* takes the greatest part of it for himself, and a great deal must be given to the Mahratta chiefs, to be supported and continued in his office. Who is not acquainted perfectly with the Mahratta character—particularly the Pundits—can have no idea of their avarice and insensibility and bad faith. It may be said they have all the vices known, without any of the virtues, which gives reason to suppose that the Empire is soon to fall. Being forced, against my wish, to enter into all the details of government since the death of Madhajee Shah, I have the opportunity to know them better than I have been able to learn in ten years before.

" Being so far advanced in your wishes and good intentions in regard of that miserable family, I shall continue to employ my best exertions, and the little influence I have in the Government, to do what may put them out of physical want, and which 50,000 rupees a month will entirely do. Where so fortunate, I shall with a heartfelt satisfaction give you due intimation of it, persuaded that it will be an enjoyment to you.

"Do me the honour of your remembrance and of your commands. My punctuality in the execution of them will prove to you my being with regard and esteem,

"Your most humble and very obedient servant,

"Bt. De Boigne."

In this letter it is important to note De Boigne's opening statement regarding his ill health, for the time was now approaching when its continuance obliged him to resign his post, although other reasons were advanced for his retirement. The letter is pervaded with a spirit of modesty, almost approaching humility, which to English ears sounds strangely, when coming from one who wielded such immense power as the writer. A great deal of this is, no doubt, to be traced to what has been conventionally termed "French politeness," and it certainly would not have been so noticeable if the letter had been expressed in French. Its whole tone conveys indisputable evidence of the cordial feeling existing between De Boigne and the East India Company, and the establishment of a friendly correspondence between him and one of the leading Government officials at Calcutta.

It is not improbable that it was this established and friendly communication which gave rise to an incident that occurred about this time, and requires special mention ; for it illustrates the remarkable consolidation of De Boigne's power, and adds a crowning prestige to his career. In 1795 a mutiny broke out amongst the officers of the Company's army in Bengal, due to circumstances into which it is not necessary to enter here, and in this emergency either the Governor-General Sir John Shore applied to De Boigne for assistance, or it was offered spontaneously. Colonel Meadows Tayler, in his admirable history, states that the Company was the applicant, but from Lord Cornwallis's correspondence it would appear that in the first instance the offer came from De Boigne. It matters little which, for the fact remains that a cavalry regiment, officered by Europeans, was placed at the disposal of the Governor-General. No incident in De Boigne's life is so significant as this, and yet, with customary indifference to all matters relating to independent military adventure in the East, it is left unmentioned by many of the historians of India, and slurred over by nearly all the rest. But it was assuredly no slight circumstance that, in a serious crisis of its affairs, the Great Company *Bahadur* accepted from this Soldier of Fortune assistance with which to quell a mutiny in its own army, and found it accorded with a promptitude which testified both to De Boigne's power and his friendly disposition towards the English.

Although Hindustan was peaceful, trouble soon broke out in the Deccan, where a demand for *Chout*, or tribute, by the Maráthás led to a war between them and Nizam Ali Khan, of Haidarabad. De Boigne's First Brigade, under Major Perron, was ordered by Sindhia to co-operate with the Peshwá's forces, and mainly through its instrumentality a great victory was gained by the Maráthás on the 11th of March, 1795. A detailed account of the contest will be found recorded in the life of Perron. Although the actual loss on the field was slight, Kardla (or Parinda, as it is sometimes called) was one of the most noteworthy battles of the period, not only from its results, but because of the number of disciplined and European-led troops engaged in it. These amounted to nearly 40,000 men, and included on the side of the Maráthás De Boigne's First Brigade, the independent corps of John Hessing and Michael Filoze, the former by this time increased to four and the latter to six battalions, and the Chevalier Dudrenec's brigade, which was contributed by Holkar. On the side of the Nizam there were eleven battalions of Colonel Raymond's army, and the independent corps of Majors Boyd and Finglass. With the exception of Lakhairi, which bore very much the aspect of civil war, Kardla was the only occasion on which the native powers of India employed large bodies of trained infantry and European tactics in their contests with one another, and the victory, gained chiefly by De Boigne's battalions, over an enemy similarly armed, drilled, and commanded, and admirably handled, added very considerably to the reputation of the famous Brigades of Hindustan.

But Kardla did more than this. It confirmed a disposition which many of the Marátha chiefs had long evinced for entertaining disciplined bodies of regular infantry, and hereafter most of them are found employing corps trained and commanded by Europeans. Holkar increased his establishment by the addition of two brigades, under Majors Plumet and William Gardner. Major W. H. Tone was ordered to raise a force for the Peshwá, into whose service Major Boyd also entered. Lakwa Dáda engaged Captain Butterfield and the younger Sangster for a similar purpose, and Ambáji Inglia commissioned James Shepherd and Joseph Bellasis, both excellent officers, and worthy of a better master, to drill battalions for him. Appa Khandi Ráo was singularly fortunate in securing such a commander as

George Thomas, Ali Bahadur, of Bundelkhand, and Raghoji
Bhonsla, of Berar, each had their trained battalions, and Daulat Rao
Sindhia, in addition to the formidable army created by De Boigne,
entertained no less than four other independent corps under the
commands of Colonels John Hessing, and Michael Filoze, Captain
Brownrigg, and Colonel Saleur, who was at the head of the Begum
Somru's contingent. Within five years a complete change took place
in the various armies of the Marátha Confederation, and the Western
system of military organisation superseded the old native method.
No chief of importance considered his army complete unless it contained disciplined infantry and European officers.

In the face of this almost universal adoption of the European
system it is strange to find that the innovation proved of doubtful
advantage. Regular corps were delicate machines, requiring special
knowledge and expert handling to keep them in order. They were
apt to become dangerous to those who employed them when not
punctually paid and properly controlled. The radical changes their
introduction brought about in Marátha warfare were not suited to
the national character of the people. The Maráthás were essentially
cavaliers, fitted only for predatory campaigns. Rapid retreats formed
as important an element in the economy of their operations, as daring
incursions, and a horse was a *sine quâ non* for any display of confidence and courage, of which they possessed but a very moderate
share. The introduction of infantry and artillery involved pitched
battles, and afforded no scope for those marvellously quick, and hence
demoralising advances, and those equally swift strategic movements
to the rear, which distinguished the wild Deccan horseman of the
past. The result was that before long the Maráthás, as a nation,
began to lose that which they could least spare—their courage, and
also much of their former mobility, and confidence in distant enterprises. And there were those who prophecied that the very innovations which had created Madhoji Sindhia's power, would in the end
prove the ruin of his race. Colonel James Skinner describes an
incident which admirably illustrates this distrust of the new military
policy. When Daulat Rao Sindhia gave orders for the erection of a
permanent Cantonment at Ujjain, Gopál Ráo, who had been restored
to favour after Madhoji's death, and was now Commander-in-chief of
the Marátha army (a term used in these pages to distinguish the
national cavalry from the mercenary trained infantry), made a striking remark in open Durbar. " Our fathers," he said, " the first
founders of the Marátha power, made their houses on the backs of
horses ; gradually the house came to be made of cloth, and now you

are making it of mud. Take care that in a short time it does not turn to mud, and is never built again." Daulat Rao Sindhia laughed, and replied, " Who is there dare oppose me so long as I have my infantry and guns ? " " Beware," answered the old Maráthá general, " it is those very infantry and guns which will be your ruin."

A similar prediction came from a source even more illustrious. In a speech in the House of Commons Sir Philip Frances quoted an opinion on this point passed by Warren Hastings. " Sir," said the great Pro-Consul to him, " the danger you allude to in the progress the Maráthás are making in the art of casting cannon, in the use and practice of artillery, and in the discipline of their armies is imaginary. The Maráthás can never be formidable to us in the field on the principles of an European army. They are pursuing a scheme in which they can never succeed, and by doing so they detach themselves from their own plan of warfare, on which alone, if they acted wisely, they would place dependence." A similar opinion was expressed by the Duke of Wellington.

But history proves that the Maráthás, or at least the mercenaries they employed, could be, and were, formed into excellent armies, drilled and disciplined to a high state of efficiency. Nevertheless, Warren Hastings' condemnation of their unwisdom in deserting their own military system found ample illustration in the Pindari Wars, and in Laswari and Assaye. The genius of De Boigne, whilst it transformed savage irregulars into staunch and disciplined soldiery, created an enormous standing army, that raised the fear and jealousy of the English, and proved a vulnerable body, capable of being attacked and brought to bay. It was unable to elude flight as the mounted Marátha hordes of the past had done, and as Jaswant Rao's Pindaris were yet again to do, and when it passed under the command of a leader who lacked the political prudence of De Boigne, it became a menace, and by courting the very danger he warned it against, met the doom the greybeards of the nation predicted.

Kardla was the last battle in which De Boigne's Brigades were engaged during the period of his command. Towards the end of 1795 his health began to fail and his constitution to show signs of yielding to the enormous strain imposed upon it. Rest and change of climate were imperative. For eighteen unbroken years he had laboured under an Indian sun. There existed for him no snow-fanned Simla, no breezy Utakamand, where he might snatch annual reprieves from the furnace blasts of the plains. Imagine a modern Indian Viceroy spending eighteen years in the plains ! Conceive a contemporary commander-in-chief completing eighteen annu   tours

of inspection without a holiday to the Hills. Yet this was what De
Boigne had done. Little wonder that the time had arrived when he
felt he must relinquish the reins of power, or risk their dropping from
stiffened fingers, never to be picked up again. It has been asserted
that he resigned his post because some fancied storm was brewing,
and that his departure was the result of a prudent discretion. But
what storm could have shaken the foundations of the power that
absolutely ruled Hindustan? Perron — base, braggart Perron—
boasted in after years that by his intrigues he had compelled his
general to resign. But to this vainglorious assertion the lie is given
in a letter written to De Boigne by Daulat Rao Sindhia within a few
months of their parting. " You are the pillar of my State, the right
arm of my victory," runs a passage in it ; " your presence is required
in my councils and my Brigades. Come, with all speed. Without
fail. It is my order and my petition to you."

All suggested reasons for De Boigne's resignation may be dismissed
save the one that really occasioned it—his broken health. It was not
without a deep regret that he bowed to the inevitable necessity, and
asked to be relieved of his command. At first Daulat Rao Sindhia
refused his consent, or to allow his general to depart. But De Boigne
persisted, and sanction was unwillingly accorded on the understanding
that if his health was re-established by a change to Europe he would
return and resume his post. His parting admonition to the Prince
was to avoid all contest with the English, and disband his battalions
rather than excite their jealousy, or risk a war with them.

And thus it came to pass that in December, 1795, the curtain drew
up on the last scene of the romantic drama of Indian military
adventure which these pages have attempted to depict, and on the
plain of Agra, where seven years before he had fought that stubborn
battle which won an empire for Madhoji Sindhia, De Boigne paraded
his battalions in review for the last time.

It was no ordinary occasion that witnessed the solemn parting
between the chief and the army of his creation. The scene is one imagination can help to depict. The General, tall, gaunt, and martial, his
rugged features showing signs of failing health, is seated on his charger.
He watches with sadness in his piercing eyes his veterans passing
before him for the last time. The sword, that has so often led the way
to victory, now, and for the first time, trembles in his hand as he brings
it to the salute. Rank after rank, regiment after regiment, file past,
of dusky Asiatics who deem this man their God, and cannot comprehend why he should leave them now. Before him they would
seat themselves down, and pressing their foreheads to his feet, call

him "*Father*," and appeal to him to stay, but for that stern discipline which he has taught them, and which bids them to face
neither to right nor to left, but march obediently on.

And he who watches them? What stirring memories the sight of
those serried ranks must have aroused! What ghosts of dead soldiers,
perchance, stalked after them, summoned by that last *reveillé* from
their forgotten sepulchres in the wind-swept deserts of Rájputana,
the sultry plains of Central India, or the fertile valleys of the Green
Doáb! And, ah! what spectre hosts of slaughtered foemen—gallant
Mughals and chivalrous Rajputs, fierce Rohillas and stubborn Játs—
could have crept into the presence of that great white chief, had he
possessed the power to call the dead from their graves. In the
accomplishment of his high career there was much to rejoice over,
much to be proud of; but the course of conquest is marked by many
monuments, and there are those which are crowded with the records
of the dead, as well as those which commemorate the achievements
of the living.

CHAPTER VIII.

DE BOIGNE RETURNS TO EUROPE.—HIS MARRIAGE, OLD AGE, AND DEATH.

1796–1830.

ON Christmas Day, 1795, De Boigne left Koïl under escort of his bodyguard, and set out for the Company's territory. "He was attended," writes a correspondent of one of the journals of the day, "by 610 cavalry, 4 elephants, 150 camels, and many bullock-waggons laden with his effects. His cavalry cut a good appearance, being dressed in a uniform of green jackets with red turbans, the folds of which were intermixed with silver wire. They seemed to be very well disciplined, and each horseman was armed with a pair of pistols, a gun, and a sword."

Making his way to Lucknow, De Boigne halted some time at that place arranging his affairs, which he left in charge of General Claude Martine. From thence he proceeded to Calcutta, where he was honourably received by the Governor-General. The horses and equipment of his bodyguard were purchased by the British Government, and the troopers enlisted in the Company's service, in which they remained for two years, until Lord Wellesley, in an hour of retrenchment, transferred the corps to the Nawab Wazir of Oudh.

It was not until September, 1796, that De Boigne finally quitted India. He sailed in the ship *Cromberg*, and reached England early in the year 1797, carrying with him a fortune of £400,000, the result of nineteen years of adventure in the East.

On his arrival he took up his residence near London, for the war on the Continent offered little prospect of repose in his native Savoy. His health, much improved by the long voyage, was soon completely re-established, and it seemed probable that he would return to India, for he had actually commenced preparations for so doing, when a pretty face and a musical voice—"A voice which must be mine," as he remarked even before he saw the face—changed his destiny.

It happened one day that he was at a concert where a young girl—Mdlle. Eleonora Adèle D'Osmond, daughter of the Marquis D'Osmond, afterwards French Ambassador to England—was one of the performers. Her beauty and her sweet singing conquered the heart of the war-worn old soldier; and, although she was only seventeen years old, he proposed for her hand and was accepted. They were married on the 11th of June, 1798. There was a fitting touch of romance in the union not out of keeping with De Boigne's past; but unfortunately the marriage did not turn out happily. They lived together in London and Paris for some years, but the disparity in age was too great, and in 1804 they separated, no children having been born. De Boigne provided handsomely for the Countess, and she returned to her father's home, and accompanied him to London when he was appointed French Ambassador to the Court of St. James. In 1819 she settled at Paris, and became the centre of a select *coterie* in high life, her salons being thronged with the most distinguished people of the period. Once every year she visited her husband at Chambéry for a few weeks, assuming her position as mistress of his house and entertaining his numerous friends. She always expressed the highest respect for his character, and it is said that the honours which were subsequently conferred upon him by Louis XVIII. were due to her solicitations as much as to De Boigne's well-known royalistic principles. The Countess De Boigne survived her husband many years, and died as recently as 1866.

De Boigne's history for the six years succeeding his marriage, has been the subject of remarkable and persistent misrepresentation at the hands of English writers. It has been stated, and repeated with circumstantial detail, that in 1802 the General, at the invitation of Napoleon Bonaparte, removed to Paris, and became the First Consul's Privy Counsellor and Adviser in those designs against the English power in India, which led to the second Maráthá war, and the extermination of Sindhia's regular army. After a long and laborious investigation of the matter, it seemed to the compiler that this statement was fairly well attested, even though he failed to find it corroborated by any of the records in the India Office, opened to his inspection, and which he carefully searched for its confirmation. It was not until the view was accepted that De Boigne did actually assist Napoleon Bonaparte with his counsel, and this chapter was in print, that a refutation was received. It came from the best living authority, the present Count de Boigne, whose letter is printed *in extenso* later on.

As the excision of the discredited passages would greatly interfere with the construction of the story, and render unintelligible several references in the sketch of Perron's life, it has been thought best to leave them as they originally stood—for they contain much historical narrative that is correct—and to refute the personal misrepresentation they contain by the publication, side by side with it, of Count de Boigne's denial of his grandfather's alleged transactions with Bonaparte.

In the year 1802, the peace of Amiens—if, indeed, that term can be applied to a cessation of hostilities that was little more than an armistice—had just been concluded, and the opportunity was favourable for the perfection of those designs against India which the First Consul had long premeditated. The conquest of the British possessions in the East was one of his most cherished ambitions, and towards the furtherance of this object he had undertaken the Egyptian campaign, and entered into intrigues with the ruler of Mysore ; but the battle of the Nile and the capture of Seringapatam put a period to both these attempts. By the Treaty of Amiens, through an inconceivable oversight on the part of English diplomacy, Pondicherry and the other possessions in India which had been wrested from her during the late war were restored to France. This gave Bonaparte a foothold in the country sufficient for his purpose. Hitherto the French had been foiled in every endeavour to re-establish their power in India. In direct conflict with the English they had been defeated and driven out of the land. After Raymond's death his army, which practically dominated Haidarabad in the French interest, was disarmed and disbanded by Lord Wellesley in 1798. In Mysore, Tipú Sultan was dead, and the French auxiliaries prisoners of war in the hands of the English. Southern India was swept clean of Frenchmen. But Bonaparte, undiscouraged and indefatigable, projected fresh schemes of conquest in 1802, and began to build sanguine hopes of success in a quarter hitherto untried. Generel Perron, who succeeded De Boigne, was paramount at Delhi, and had recently opened communications with the French Government, and made certain proposals which commended themselves to the First Consul. De Boigne was now in Paris, and in touch with Hindustan, being in correspondence with Perron and other of his old officers, whilst his local knowledge and experience were unique. Of his ability and advice Bonaparte is reported to have availed himself, for it appeared to him that the Marátha nation, from its constitution, its habits, and its territorial importance, held out the most hopeful prospects that had yet offered for the furtherance of French ambition and the destruction of the English power in India,

The great want that existed in Perron's army was that of trained officers. To supply this deficiency Bonaparte, under the colourable pretext of colonial defence, despatched to Pondicherry a fleet of six men-of-war, which sailed from France under Monsieur Lenois, a distinguished naval officer. It transported 1,400 picked troops commanded by General Decaen. Amongst these were 200 young Frenchmen, who, although they shipped in the guise of private soldiers, were gentlemen by birth, thoroughly trained in the duties of officers, and provided with a proper equipment. They were, in addition, one and all fired with a determination to follow in the footsteps of De Boigne, and carve out for themselves kingdoms and principalities. It was intended that after landing at Pondicherry these young adventurers should make their way to Delhi in small bodies, through the territories of the Rajah of Berar, whose seaboard of Cuttack could be reached by country boats in forty-eight hours during the south-west monsoon. At Delhi they were to take service under Perron, so that, when the time was ripe, the army of Hindustan, efficiently officered and led, might co-operate with Bonaparte in his intended invasion of India, and crush by one concerted blow the English power in the East. War was to be declared and carried on in the name of the Emperor Shah 'Alam, whose rescue from British tyranny was assigned as the ostensible object of this disinterested scheme.

Unfortunately for these aspiring young cadets, their hopes were blighted by the sagacity and acumen of the Marquis Wellesley, who mistrusted their coming, and whose suspicions were subsequently confirmed by the copy of a secret document obtained from one of General Decaen's officers. This was entitled "A Memorial on the present importance of India, and the most efficacious means of Re-establishing the French Nation in its ancient splendour in that Country." It detailed the French scheme in full, and after denouncing "the treatment received from a company of merchant adventurers by the Emperor of Hindustan, the sole branch of the illustrious house of Taimur," went on to assert that "the English Company, by its ignominious treatment of the great Mughal, has forfeited its rights and privileges in Bengal," and that "the Emperor of Delhi has a real and indisputable right to transmit to whomsoever he may please to select the sovereignty of his dominions, as well as the arrears (of tribute) due from the English." . . . "These arrears," concluded the ingenuous document, "with the interest of the country added, amount to four hundred and fifty-two *livres Tournois*, a sum which greatly exceeds the value of the Company's moveable capital."

" A pretty comfortable prospect," comments a contemporary historian, "for the new legacy hunter, Bonaparte, of a bequest, at the demise of an old man past eighty years, of All Hindustan and nineteen millions seventeen hundred and seventy-five pounds sterling ! "

Lord Wellesley thus deals with this document in one of his dispatches, or rather with the scheme by which Bonaparte hoped to constitute himself legatee of the Mughal's millions : —

" The system of introducing French adventurers into the armies of the Native States, for the improvement of their discipline and efficiency, has been found 'the readiest and most effectual means of establishing the influence and authority of the French in the government of those States, and of erecting an independent territorial and military power, within the limits of a foreign dominion. . . . Under the continuance of peace between England and France, and between the British Government and the Mahratta States, the progress of French intrigue and aggrandisement of the French power in India would be most rapid and dangerous to our security. In the prosecution of these views the French would manifestly derive essential aid from the possession of the person and family of the Emperor Shah Allum, and under the plea of restoring that monarch to his hereditary dominion, the power of France in India might be directed to the subversion of every state, and the appropriation of every territory unprotected by alliance with the British Nation. . . . By successful intrigue M. Perron has obtained the office of Commandant of the Fortress of Delhi, which is the residence of the royal family, and thus secured the person and nominal authority of the Emperor. The Mogul has never been an important or dangerous instrument in the hands of the Mahrattas, but the augmentation of M. Perron's influence and power, and the growth of the French interest in Hindustan, have given a new aspect to the condition of the Mogul, and that unfortunate prince may become a powerful aid to the cause of France in India, under the direction of French agents."

The practical application of these views was found in the precautions Lord Wellesley took to prevent any member of General Decaen's Expedition from finding his way to Delhi. On their arrival at Pondicherry the two hundred French officers found, to their intense disgust and mortification, that they were virtually " *en cage* " within its narrow boundaries. They never left the desolate strip of territory, and, when a little later hostilities broke out again between England and France, these miserable men were all made prisoners of war.

Meanwhile it has been stated that De Boigne, seduced from his former sympathies with the English, became a highly distinguished personage at the Tuilleries, and was elevated to the dignity f a Privy Counsellor. Doubts have, however, been thrown upon this episode in his history. His biographer, M. St. Genis, omits mention of it, although he makes allusion to " an unfounded remark of Bonaparte " which had obtained currency and conveyed the impression that the First Consul had been angered at a refusal on De Boigne's part to proceed to India at the head of an invading expedition. St. Genis adds that although De Boigne had taken up his abode within the limits of the Empire, he had no sympathy with Napoleon, and probably distrusted the solidity of his power ; and that notwithstanding the advantageous opening his military talents might have found in the Imperial service, he was averse to such employment on several grounds, and the Emperor knew him too well to spare him the necessity of a refusal. On the other hand it is asserted that De Boigne did actually advise and assist Bonaparte in his designs against the English Empire in the East. In a pamphlet printed in 1804 and entitled " Brief Remarks on the Mahratta War, and the Rise and Progress of the French Establishment in Hindustan under Generals De Boigne and Perron," which, though published anonymously, bears evidence of particular knowledge, there is a circumstantial account of the matter as herein narrated, and one of the principal points put forward seems to be corroborated by a passage in a letter from Perron to De Boigne, dated the 28th of February, 1802, and published in M. St. Genis' work. Perron writes as follows (the letter will be found quoted in his life):—" Yes; I will receive with great satisfaction all the persons you recommend for appointments in the Brigades."

Again, in " A Letter on the Present Crisis of Affairs in India," written in 1807 by Major Ambrose, who had been an officer in Holkar's service, and who refers to De Boigne's residence at Paris as a matter of common notoriety, one of the arguments put forward is, that " Napoleon possesses the advantages of De Boigne's abilities to guide him." In a third "India Tract,"—to use the generic name by which these publications were known—written in 1812 by " A Field Officer on the Bengal Establishment of thirty years' service," and entitled " A Dissertation on the Defence of the British Territorial Possessions in Hindustan," the following passage occurs :—

" When a single adventurer like De Boigne, with but slender talents (*sic*), and without the countenance or support of any European prince, was able to raise and discipline, in the North of India, such an army as we had to contend against in 1803–4, we cannot surely be

7

surprised if men of genius and talents, selected by Bonaparte, and supported with all the influence of his great name and extensive resources, should succeed in forming a powerful army in that country. That De Boigne was received with distinguished attention, and consulted on this very point is well known ; and that he recommended the measure as easy and practicable, and the first and most certain step towards the conquest of Hindustan, there can be very little doubt."

But perhaps the most important reference is contained in a chance, but significant, remark in a letter of Lord Wellesley to General Lake, under date of the 8th of July, 1803, which concludes with the sentence :—

" M. Du (*sic*) Boigne (Sindhia's late General) is now the chief confidante of Bonaparte. He is constantly at St. Cloud. I leave you to judge why and wherefore."

Recent information has denounced these assertions and suggestions as incorrect. In June, 1892, the following communication was received from the present Count de Boigne, and is inserted with peculiar satisfaction, for it is pleasant to be assured that his grandfather was innocent of the hostility towards the English with which he has been charged :—

" In 1802 the General was in Savoy, and signed authentic deeds, which I have in my possession, together with letters which General Perron wrote to him from Hindustan.

" He was never a Privy Counsellor to Bonaparte, and in all his family papers I do not find a single word which might lead one to suppose that he ever saw him, or had anything to do with him.

" During the whole of the reign of Bonaparte the General led a perfectly secluded life. It was only at the Restoration that he was appointed Marshal, Knight of St. Louis, and of the Legion of Honour, by King Louis XVIII. He had married Mdlle. D'Osmond, and his father-in-law was the first French Ambassador in London after the return of the Bourbons.

" In 1815, after Savoy was united to the kingdom of Sardinia, he was appointed Lieutenant-General, and received the Grand Cross of St. Maurice et Lazarre.

" All this proves he never had any transactions with Bonaparte.

" As to his connection with the English and the advice he gave to Sindhia, the General felt that, in spite of the splendid army he had created for him, the Prince would be beaten if he waged war against the English. When he left him, he told him that, notwithstanding the pride he felt in the Brigades, he advised the Prince to disband them rather than go to war with the English.

" It seems to me, therefore, that the information you have received is not correct. It is in contradiction to the facts, and I can understand why you failed to find any confirmation of it in the Records of Government.

" CTE. DE BOIGNE."

This disposes of an accusation, which, with the marvellous fertility of falsehood, has blossomed from the dust of nearly ninety years ago.

Early in 1803 De Boigne purchased a fine estate on the outskirts of his native town of Chambéry, in Savoy, where he built himself a magnificent mansion named " Buisson," wherein he spent the last twenty-seven years of his life, enjoying the princely fortune he had acquired. During this period his bounties to the poor, the sick, the aged, and to religious institutions were immense, and conceived in a spirit of the broadest philanthropy. The principles which governed him cannot be better illustrated than by a quotation from an address he delivered in 1822, on the occasion of opening a hospital with which he had endowed his native town. " If Divine Providence," he said, " deigned to crown with a special grace the career of arms I followed, He also loaded me with favours far greater than my poor talents could have expected, and, I may add, greater than I deserve. My wants were never great, and I experienced no particular ambition for riches. From my forefathers I inherited nothing, and all that I have, I received from heaven. For this reason I consider I should use these gifts in a way acceptable to Him who gave them. Gratitude and our Holy Religion enjoin this as a duty, and suggest that the proper use to make of my wealth is to succour the unfortunate. Therefore, on my return to my native land, to which my heart has ever clung with affection, my first work, my first thought, was to invite my fellow citizens to share the benefits so liberally entrusted to my keeping by Providence."

These are noble words, and how nobly De Boigne acted up to them, a list of his charities can testify. During the latter years of his life the sums he expended on philanthropical objects reached the enormous total of 3,678,000 francs. He built and endowed two hospitals, a lunatic asylum, an institute for teaching trades to young girls, an almshouse, a college, and a public library. Nor did his benefactions cease with his life, for in his will he supplemented them with further princely bequests.

Honours were heaped upon De Boigne in his old age. King Victor Emanuel of Sardinia created him a count and a lieutenant-general in his army, and decorated him with the Grand Cross of the Order of St. Maurice and St. Lazarus. Louis XVIII. appointed him a *Marechal de Camp*, and a knight of the Legion of Honour, and conferred on him the Order of St. Louis. His native town of Chambéry delighted to honour him. During his life time his bust in marble was unveiled by the King in the public library, and one of the finest streets in the city perpetuates the name of her greatest son, and contains a beautiful monumental fountain erected to his memory.

It has been mentioned that De Boigne had no children by his marriage with Mdlle D'Osmond. But there were two born to him by a marriage contracted " according to the usages of the country, with the daughter of a Persian colonel in India." These were a son named Ali Bux, born at Delhi in 1792, and a daughter named Bunoo. They accompanied their father to Europe, and were subsequently baptized, receiving the names of Charles Alexander and Anna. The latter died at Paris in 1810, but Charles grew up and married the daughter of a French nobleman, by whom he had a family. He succeeded his father in the title, and lived a life of unostentatious benevolence, dying in 1853, when the estate passed to his son, the present Count de Boigne.

In his old age De Boigne dispensed a lordly hospitality, and especially welcome to his house were any English officers who had been in India. Both Colonel Tod and Grant Duff, in the works with which their names are associated, make special mention of this, and each pays a tribute to the courtesy and hospitality experienced at Buisson. As illustrating the simplicity of De Boigne's *ménage*, it may be mentioned that to the end of his days his sole *Major Domo* was an old native servant whom he had brought from India, and who directed all his household arrangements.

One who knew De Boigne well has thus described his appearance two years before his death ;—" His frame and stature were Herculean, and he was full six feet two inches in height. His aspect was mild and unassuming, and he was unostentatious in his habit and demeanour, preserving at his advanced age all the gallantry and politeness of the *vielle cour*. He disliked, from modesty, to advert to his past deeds, and so seemed to strangers to have lost his memory. But in the society of those who could partake of the emotions it awakened, the name of Merta always stirred in him associations whose call he could not resist. The blood would mount to his temples, and the old fire came into his eyes, as he recalled, with inconceivable rapidity and

eloquence, the story of that glorious day. But he spoke of himself as
if it were of another, and always concluded with the words, ' *My past
appears a dream !* ' "

But it was no dream—that glorious past of his—which he looked
back upon. The vista of many years stretched between him and the
epoch his deeds made memorable, but through its gathering shadows
vivid, distinct and brilliant, glittered the star of victory—the splendour
of actual accomplishment.

Almost on the fortieth anniversary of the battle of Pátan, Death
came and gently summoned away the brave old Adventurer whom he
had so often spared on Indian battlefields. On the 21st June, 1830,
amidst the prayers of the aged and the helpless, and the blessings of
the sick and the needy, full of years, full of honours, peacefully, in
his bed, died Benoît La Borgne, Count De Boigne.

CHAPTER IX,

THE CHARACTER AND ACHIEVEMENT OF DE BOIGNE.

DE BOIGNE'S Indian career has been described as a series o
ambitious plans; yet however exalted their aim they all found a
justification in results. To a high intent he added a sustained diligence and a determination that never faltered until each design he
undertook was completed. He scorned delights and lived laborious
days. Work—sheer hard work—was the secret of his success. Without it even his genius must have failed in achieving the ends he
attained. Moreover, he weighed those ends well. A certain practical
caution governed all his enterprises, and his prudence never permitted
him to be carried away by his enthusiasm. This characteristic he
exhibited in his financial arrangements, in his business aptitude, and
in his attention to detail. No mutiny occurred in the army he
created, yet the histories of prior and contemporaneous corps teem
with instances of insubordination, desertion, and revolt, consequent
upon irregularity of payment. De Boigne's penetrating perception
marked this weak spot, and discounted its danger by obtaining from
Madhoji Sindhia the territorial assignment that supplied him with a
fixed income, secured him from dependence on an untrustworthy
treasury, and placed his Brigades from the very first on the only sound
footing possible to a mercenary army.

The amount, as well as the variety, of work accomplished by De
Boigne was astonishing. Lewis Ferdinand Smith thus describes his
routine of daily duty :—

" De Boigne was active and persevering to a degree which can only
be conceived or believed by those who were spectators of his indefatigable labours. I have seen him daily and monthly rise with the
sun, survey his arsenal, view his troops, enlist recruits, direct the vast
movements of three brigades, raise resources, and encourage manu-
factures for their arms, ammunition, and stores; harangue in his
durbar, give audience to ambassadors, administer justice, regulate the

civil and revenue affairs of a *Jaidad* of twenty lakhs of rupees, listen to a multitude of letters from various parts, on various important matters, dictate replies, carry on an intricate system of intrigue in different courts, superintend a private trade of lakhs of rupees, keep his accounts, his private and public correspondence, and direct and move forward a most complex political machine. Such was his laborious occupation from sunrise till past midnight, and this was not the fortuitous avocations of a day, but the unremitting employment of nine or ten years. To this exhausting and unceasing toil he sacrificed one of the firmest and most robust constitutions ever formed by nature."

Living in sovereign magnificence, and wielding quasi-sovereign power, De Boigne was called upon to exercise the most important duties of State. For this he was fitted, for he was a consummate diplomatist, skilled in directing the most complicated affairs, and he added to a complete mastery of Oriental intrigue the political subtlety of the Italian school. His knowledge of the world was profound, and he understood the art of moulding to his purpose the minds of those he had to deal with. He was an acute observer of the dispositions of men, a rapid judge of character, and gifted in a remarkable degree with the power of gaining the confidence of others. But he never divulged his own affairs, and, as one of his commentators has observed, " there is this remarkable thing about him, that during the whole of his Indian career his only secretary was his writing-desk, which knew neither his business nor his fortune, for both of those he kept completely to himself."

To the end of his stay in India De Boigne carried on the mercantile business he established at Lucknow in 1789, the books and correspondence of which he wrote up with his own hand. All these multifarious occupations, military, political, administrative, and commercial were conducted without assistance from others, for it was a frequent assertion of his that any ambitious person who reposed confidence in another risked the destruction of his own views. He never deputed authority, preferring to labour eighteen hours a day, and day after day, rather than delegate to a subordinate the control of any matter of importance.

It has been stated that this tenacity of power degenerated at times into a positive greed of authority, and led him to view in an unworthy light the successes and efforts of others, and he has been taxed with a jealousy that on occasions administered ungenerous rebuke where commendation was justly due. How far this was true it is impossible to estimate now, but it is certainly not corroborated by the singular

esteem evinced towards him by his subordinates. In considering
these charges it must not be forgotten that the men who filled the
higher appointments in De Boigne's Brigades were in many cases
illiterate persons of humble birth, whose mental calibre unfitted them
for positions of responsibility, although doubtless in the artificial
exaltation of their lives they considered themselves equal to any duty,
and entertained opinions of their own qualifications not shared by
their chief.

De Boigne has also been accused of greed and avarice, and described as mean and grasping in pecuniary matters, and this by one
who knew him well and respected him highly. How far this failing
was a part of his nature, and how far it was due to the spirit of the
times and his surroundings is a moot point. India of the last century
was above everything else the Land of the Pagoda Tree, and the
raison d'être of the Pagoda Tree was to be shaken violently. Men
went to the East to make fortunes as quickly as they could, and then
return to Europe. The intention was never disguised. The question,
therefore, of De Boigne's avarice, may be fairly judged by the degree
of his fortune. Let us compare the harvest of his life with that of
others. In eleven years he saved from his pay, from his administration of a vast territory, and from his commercial speculations, a sum
of £400,000. But Perron, who succeeded him, accumulated in nine
years a capital which has been variously assessed at from three-quarters of a million to two millions sterling, and this without any assistance from the profits of business. Bourguien, who merely commanded
a brigade under Perron, was credited with taking " an equal sum "
out of the country, but this refers to the actual amount Perron succeeded in conveying to Europe, which was not more than £500,000.
But these examples of money-minting pale before the financial
achievements of a certain Colonel Hannay, who entered the service
of the Nawáb Wazir of Oudh in 1778. Hannay was a Company's
officer, and for very cogent reasons obtained permission to serve on
the further side of a boundary which creditors could not cross and
where writs did not run. He received the command of a considerable
force, and was assigned the districts of Baraitch and Gorakhpur for
its support. These he depopulated in three years by his exactions.
" He entered the Nawáb's service," remarks a contemporary writer,
" a man in debt, and left it three years afterwards with a fortune of
£300,000." With such instances before us the savings that De Boigne
amassed appear reasonable when his length of service, his enormous
income, the gifts he received from Sindhia, his mercantile business at
Lucknow, and all his incidental sources of emolument are considered.

Finally, the accusation of "avarice that verged on the contemptible" may fairly be met by a reference to the princely philanthropy of his declining years, and in this connection it is proper to quote the remarks of the Marquis de Faverges, who, in discussing his character, says: "He gave coldly, but always decidedly. He counted the money which came and went, more from business habit than from actual avarice, but he never withheld a halfpenny. He gave much and unostentatiously, but without any desire to hide it, although his secret charities were considerable."

It is difficult to reconcile this conflicting testimony, but whilst the accusation rests on individual statements, the refutation exists in the charitable gifts and bequests enjoyed to this day by the inhabitants of Chambéry. And it must be noted that in the speech De Boigne made on the occasion of opening a hospital in that town, he categorically disclaimed "any particular ambition for riches."

On the other hand, against these possible detractions must be set many good and noble qualities. Above all stands De Boigne's staunch and unswerving loyalty, which, in the face of the many enticing offers that appealed especially to the avarice he has been charged with, never faltered for a moment. His sense of justice was singularly well balanced between severity and mildness, and his orders commanded respect, no less from the firmness with which he enforced them, than for the impartiality he displayed in arriving at a decision. His manners were polite and elegant, his disposition affable and vivacious, and he was not wanting in a sense of humour. He was modest, and good-natured in his behaviour towards his subordinates, although he could show himself stern and implacable if opposed or thwarted, but he possessed an entire command over his passions, and was an adept in the art of dissimulation—gifts of inestimable advantage in dealing with the natives.

De Boigne's achievements are the best testimony to the high order of his military talent. As a general he may take his stand amongst the greatest India has ever produced. In times of crisis and sudden danger his presence of mind was incomparable, and his judgment in guaging difficulties and deciding on the course to follow was as quick as it was correct. His retreats were the result of cowardice, treachery, or incompetence on the part of those with whom he was associated, for he never lost a battle, nor was himself worsted in fight, while his victories were all of his own winning. Pátan, Merta, and Lakhairi, although hidden from view in the turbid flood of Indian strife, were achievements that can be compared with the most brilliant the Company's Sepoy regiments ever performed, and if their particular

record is lost in the tumult of Eastern warfare, they deprive its annals
of a glorious chapter, that might fitly preface the victories of Laswari
and Assaye.

As a general De Boigne was not only successful in carrying out
extended campaigns of conquest, and directing battles splendid with
vigour, but could inspire mercenary armies with courage and confidence, and, above all, with patience. No troops in Asia suffered
greater proportionate losses in war, or underwent more trying fatigues
than his famous brigades, which, during twelve years of incessant
activity, were constantly marching and fighting. And yet they were
sustained by no patriotic spirit, inspired by no national sentiment,
bound together by no common cause. They were merely a hireling
soldiery, risking their lives for stipulated payment, and as often
opposed to men of their own creed or caste as allied with them. Notwithstanding which they conducted themselves with a loyalty and
heroism that could not be excelled by any national army. The conquests between the Chambal and the Siwaliks were of countries
inhabited by savage and warlike peoples, from whose very midst De
Boigne raised the battalions that held the territory in an iron grip,
and drew from it revenues richer and more regular than had been
extorted by any previous conqueror.

A noble trait in De Boigne's character was his earnest endeavour
to mitigate the horrors of war and minimise its evils. His humanity
evoked blessings from the battlefield, where only despair had moaned
before. Officers and soldiers who were wounded in his service
received pecuniary compensations commensurate with the severity of
their sufferings, and men permanently disabled were awarded grants
of land, which passed to their heirs, whilst special provision was made
for the relatives of those who were killed in action. The tortures of
the battlefield were ameliorated by the establishment of a medical
department, to which an ambulance corps was attached. These re-
forms were half a century in advance of the times, and were benign
innovations such as no native powers had ever dreamt of before.

What wonder that his soldiers loved this chief, whose heart was
so full of solicitude for their welfare! What wonder that one of his
old officers, in writing to him, expressed himself in the following
terms: "You must return to us. We await your coming as that of
the Messiah. You will be like a saint, so highly are you venerated
and adored. Above all by the troops, who, in their songs, invoke
your name only." Do not the echoes of these songs, chanted by a
rude soldiery around their Indian camp fires, come floating over many
years to tell us what manner of man their leader was? Does not

that message, with its unlaboured eloquence, touch our hearts to-day, even as it must have touched the heart of him to whom it was addressed nearly a century ago? It is very plain to see that, above and beyond the respect his military talents commanded, there existed an affection for De Boigne that made every individual soldier in his army an adherent, and inspired his battalions with the magic strength of a personal devotion. When he left India he carried with him, not only the esteem of his master and the admiration of his officers, but the love of the humblest soldier who served under him.

By his enemies De Boigne was respected, for in the hour of their defeat he treated them with mercy and consideration. " It is not the least merit of General De Boigne as a military man," writes the *Bengal Journal* in 1790, " to have tempered, by an admirable perseverance, the ferocious and almost savage character of the Mahrattas. He subjects to the discipline and civilisation of European armies troops hitherto deemed barbarians; and licentiousness and rapine, heretofore so common among them, have now become infamous even in the estimation of the meanest soldier." Despite this humane departure from the repressive customs of the times, when slaughter followed victory, and pitiless oppression stalked in the path of conquest, De Boigne's personal prestige suffered no diminution, and " latterly the very name of De Boigne conveyed more terror than the thunder of his cannons."

De Boigne's genius in war and his abilities in diplomacy more than quadrupled the extent of Madhoji Sindhia's dominions and influence. The unbroken successes of his " Invincible Army "—as it came to be called—inspired that prince with a belief in the European methods of warfare, and weaned him from his racial prejudices in favour of cavalry to an appreciation of infantry for heroic defence and irresistible attack. His conversion was not without fruit, for " the military talent of De Boigne and the valour of his battalions were the grand instruments which made Madhoji Sindhia the most powerful prince in India."

De Boigne was a born leader of men. "There was something in his face and bearing," writes the authority so often quoted, " that depicted the hero, and compelled implicit obedience. In deportment he was commanding, and walked with the majestic tread of conscious greatness. The strong cast of his countenance and the piercing expression of his eyes, indicated the force and power of his mind. On the grand stage, where he acted so brilliant and important a part for ten years, he was at once dreaded and idolised, feared and admired, respected and beloved."

Certes in the history of the decade in which he flourished De Boigne stands out, a splendid solitary figure, distinct and distinguished above all others. We recognise in him an adventurer of a rare and noble type. Nor is that glamour of romance wanting which can invest with a certain heroic charm the personalities brought under its influence. The circumstances of his career always remind us that he was a free lance in a far land. We see him organising armies, winning battles, conquering countries, and ruling territories in a picturesque scene, rich with Oriental colouring, martial with pagan hosts, peopled with dusky races, and instinct with barbaric splendour. He carries us away out of our cold, conventional European climate, into the warm glow of an Asiatic land, where the conditions of life are strange and startling, and its possibilities illimitable. We follow him, step by step, across arid deserts, through tropical jungles, over desolate hills, past districts prodigal in their fertility, to that stately marble palace on Jumna's bank, where a blind Emperor, the colophon of one of the greatest empires Asia has ever seen, finds in this self-made soldier of fortune a protector, a patron, and the regent of his throne. More wondrous than a fairy tale, more dazzling than a dream, stranger than the strangest fiction, it is difficult to realise the magnitude of De Boigne's achievement. In this prosaic age, when the daily occurrences of a generally humdrum East are read at our breakfast tables the next morning, and we are reconciled to a Government that prosecutes sedition in a police court, and exercises self-restraint as an election sop, it is hard to realise that less than a hundred years ago India was a dark continent to our forefathers. Yet such it indubitably was when De Boigne carried the military systems of Europe into the heart of Hindustan, and without favour of political opponents or license of a criminal procedure code, established his sway in the Empire of Akbar and Aurangzebe.

GEORGE THOMAS.

*[From a medallion in Francklin's " Military Memoirs of
Mr. George Thomas."]*

GEORGE THOMAS.

<hr/>

CHAPTER I.

GEORGE THOMAS LANDS IN INDIA.   EARLY VICISSITUDES.   ENTERS THE
BEGUM SOMRU'S SERVICE.

1756-1793.

[Although in the chronological order of events the Life of General Perron
should follow that of De Boigne, there is a career—that of George Thomas—so
overlapped by both, that it is most conveniently inserted between the sketches of
the two greater Adventurers.]

EORGE THOMAS was born in Tipperary in the year
1756.   His parents were people of humble position,
unable to afford him any education, and at an early
age he adopted the seafaring profession, and came out
to India whilst he was quite a boy.   The circumstances
under which he left this calling are variously related.
He has been described as " a quartermaster in the Navy, or, as some
affirm, only a common sailor, who landed at Madras in 1781 or 1782";
whilst another account states that he was a cabin boy on board a
trading ship on the Coromandel coast, from which he ran away.
Whatever his exact condition when he arrived in India, it is certain
he began life in a very humble capacity as a sailor.   On leaving his
ship he made his way " up-country "—an expression synonymous with
" inland " in India—and spent some years in the Karnatic with the
Poligars, a semi-independent and exceedingly lawless class of chiefs
inhabiting mountainous and jungle districts, and of whom there were
a considerable number in the hill tracts of Southern India.

After a residence of about five years amongst these people, Thomas
appears to have found his way to Haidarabad, in the Deccan, where

he took service as a private soldier in the army of Nizam Ali Khán. But he did not stay here long, for in 1787 he left the Deccan and made his way to Delhi. It is a pity there is no record of this journey, for it must have been full of adventure and incident. Even in these modern days the march of a solitary European from one capital to the other would not be altogether free from danger. A hundred years ago the undertaking must have been perilous in the extreme, and nothing but a stout heart and a strong frame could have successfully traversed the thousand miles between the two cities, through countries which were in a constant state of disturbance and commotion, and infested with numerous bands of robbers and predatory chieftains, who levied blackmail on every traveller, and acknowledged allegiance to no authority.

Despite all dangers and difficulties, Thomas completed his journey, and arrived at the Mughal capital in safety. This was before the final occupation of Delhi by the Maráthás, and when the influence of Ghulám Kádir and Ismáil Beg was paramount there. The only body of regular troops in Hindustan was that belonging to the Begum Somru, to whom Thomas offered his services. She held the fief of Sardhána, a district lying about forty-five miles north of Delhi, where her troops were cantoned. Thomas's application was entertained, and he was appointed to a subordinate command in the Begum's army. Before long the handsome Irishman attracted his mistress's attention. He was a tall, soldierly fellow, endowed with a pleasing address for one of his station, and gifted with the honied speech of his countrymen, and, except when his temper was aroused, gentle in his manners, though not without that dash and spirit which always commends itself to womankind.

Before long he obtained the Begum's confidence and favour, and she gave him in marriage a slave girl whom she had adopted, and promoted him to the command of a battalion in her force. He soon found an opportunity of distinguishing himself. In 1789 the Begum, in her capacity of feudal vassal to Shah 'Alam, was engaged in assisting the Emperor to reduce certain revolted districts which had been restored to him when he regained his nominal independence after the defeat of the Maráthás at Lalsót. These were in the possession of a discontented noble named Najaf Kuli Khán, who refused to render allegiance, and took up a position of defiance in a strong fortress named Gokalgarh, a little to the north-west of Agra, which latter place Ismáil Beg was engaged in besieging. Shah 'Alam had invested the rebel's stronghold, and erected trenches around it. But the Imperial army was in a shamefully demoralised condition, and one night the officers and soldiery having recklessly abandoned themselves to a debauch, Najaf Khan, determined to profit by the enemy's folly, and, marching silently out of his entrenchments, attacked the royal troops as they lay buried in a drunken slumber. The investing lines were quickly carried, and a dreadful slaughter commenced. The terror excited by the sudden and vigorous attack was so great that a panic seized the royal army, which was soon in confusion and on the point of flight. The Emperor himself was exposed to the greatest danger, many persons around him being killed, and he was preparing to withdraw from the field, when the Begum Somru, whose camp was pitched a short distance off, perceived his peril, and, unaffected by the panic, determined to support her sovereign. A hundred men and a six-pounder gun, under the command of Thomas, were hastily ordered to advance, whilst the Begum, seated in her palanquin, accompanied them to the scene of conflict, and gave the order to open fire. Thomas's native sense of chivalry was aroused by the spectacle of a woman on the field of battle, and he supported her with such determination that after a short but desperate struggle, Najaf Khan was beaten back and the Emperor rescued from his critical position. In grateful recognition of assistance so timely rendered, Shah 'Alam summoned the Begum to his Durbar, and, after praising her for her gallantry, and thanking her for her service, loaded her with honours, and bestowed on her the title of "His most beloved daughter." Nor was Thomas unrewarded, for not only was his reputation established by the incident, but he received a very valuable *khilut*, or present, from His Majesty.

Not long after this the Begum was entrusted with the defence of the northern Mughal districts against the incursions of the Sikhs, and a valuable *Jaidád* assigned to her as payment for this special service, to the management of which she appointed Thomas, who took up his quarters at a fort called Tappal, the principal place in it. It was a wonderful piece of promotion, for it elevated him to the position of Military Governor and Civil Administrator of an extensive territory. Despite his inability to read and write, he seems to have handled the reins of management with considerable ability, for he doubled the revenues of the *Jaidád* before long, and established the Begum's authority in a district which had never previously acknowledged any master but the drawn sword. In the intervals of collecting rents and dispensing justice Thomas was frequently called away northwards to repel the periodical incursions of the Sikhs, a task in which he distinguished himself no less by his personal prowess than by his uniform success. Unfortunately no chronicles exist of these border frays of a past century. Advanced or retired boundary pillars formed the only records of frontier warfare in India. But in various and successive actions against the Sikhs Thomas, by his courage and energy, made his rule respected, and for long years after tradition handed down the legendary deeds of the mighty *Jehazi-Sahib*, or sailor, who first taught the sons of Nanak to respect the marches of the Great Mughal.

By these successes Thomas gained considerable influence over the mind of the Begum, but there were many Europeans in her force, chiefly Frenchmen, between whom and him a violent hatred soon developed. They monopolised the chief posts, and drew large emoluments, although, as he quickly observed, they were of little use except to keep their mistress in a chronic state of pecuniary difficulty. Their jealousy of and hostility to the English interloper were undisguised ; but in spite of their machinations he retained for a considerable time the place he had gained in the Begum's favour, for he was always ready to fight, which her other officers were not, and when he fought he won. This in itself made him a valuable acquisition to a force whose records in the tented field were none too glorious ; but as, in addition to his military abilities, Thomas possessed the charm of personal attraction, he soon became chief adviser and counsellor to the "Witch of Sardhána," as the Begum was called. But this success, obtained at the expense of others, increased the circle of his enemies and made them desperate. Envy and jealousy entered into a plot, and under the leadership of an officer named Le Vassoult a cabal was formed to bring about Thomas's ruin. The season chosen was during one of his periodical expeditions against the Sikhs. Taking advantage of his absence, the conspirators presented themselves in a body before the Begum, and by artful arguments persuaded her that Thomas harboured treacherous designs against her independence, and that his reason for desiring to procure the dismissal of her French officers was that he might make himself sole and undisputed master of her possessions.

This plot, which was brought to a head in 1792, was entirely successful. It was cunningly contrived, being calculated to raise the Begum's fears by suggesting a danger that bore an air of probability, for the subversion of authority was at the root of every conspiracy in those times. The Begum at once became alarmed, but, on being assured of their protection and fidelity by her French officers, anxiety gave way to anger, and she visited her wrath upon Thomas's wife, who communicated with her husband. Back he came at once from the frontier, rescued his family, and carried them to Tappal, where he erected the standard of rebellion.

No doubt he was driven to this by the force of circumstances, for George Thomas's worst enemy could never have accused him of treachery. But still his conduct seemed to confirm the accusations made against him, and the Begum Somru forthwith marched with an overpowering force to regain her district. Tappal was invested, and Thomas compelled to surrender. And then the Begum, with a magnanimity which could hardly have been expected of her, and had in it a touch of both inconsistency and tenderness, spared his life, and permitted him to depart unmolested.

When Thomas evacuated Tappal his worldly wealth did not exceed fifty pounds. It was not much to show for five years' meritorious service, but it may fairly be adduced as evidence of his integrity; for during his administration of a district producing a revenue of nearly £10,000 a year, many opportunities must have occurred of enriching himself by methods which, however deprecated in the West, were regarded in India as not only fortuitous, but legitimate.

His prospects, as he summed them up, were far from encouraging. After eleven years of active adventure he found himself little richer than when he began. Heroic measures were necessary, and he adopted them forthwith. Having expended his small capital in arming a band of desperate followers, he stormed and captured a large village near Delhi, from which he plundered a considerable sum of money. With the sinews of war thus obtained he increased his force to 250 mounted men, and marched them to Anúpshahr, the frontier British station, there to await events. After putting his followers through a course of training until they presented a semblance of discipline, he offered the services of his party to Ali Bahadur, one of the leading Marátha princes, who had established an independent rule in Bundelkhand. But a difficulty arising about terms, the negotiations were broken off, and shortly after this Thomas received proposals from a chief named Appa Khandi Ráo, with promise of a suitable provision, and these being acceptable, he entered his service early in 1793.

CHAPTER II.

UNDER APPA KHANDI RÁO.

1793-1797.

APPA KHANDI RÁO was one of Madhoji Sindhia's principal chieftains, and had played an important part in the conquest of Hindustan. More recently he had been engaged in the invasion of Bundelkhand, but his arms had not met with success, and owing to this his troops were several months in arrears of pay, and when their leader's continued ill-fortune seemed to destroy all hopes of recovering what was due to them, they broke out into mutiny. This so angered Sindhia that he summarily dismissed the chief from his service, and Appa's proud and haughty spirit was brooding over this disgrace when he sought the assistance of George Thomas.

It will be remembered that it was under Appa Khandi Ráo that De Boigne—now in his zenith—entered Sindhia's service with the two battalions which comprised his first command. His extraordinary success, and the power he had attained, inspired Appa with confidence in the merits of European courage and intelligence. Although Thomas's small band of ragamuffins must have presented a ludicrous contrast to De Boigne's trained and equipped battalions, the chief remembered how modestly the latter began his career, and Thomas's impoverished condition and needy appearance did not necessarily prejudice him. Vicissitudes of fortune were the rule, not the exception, in Hindustan—only a few weeks previously Thomas himself had been thrashing the Sikhs in the northern provinces of Delhi, and enjoying a position of importance and confidence in the service of the Begum Somru. It mattered little his being temporarily under a cloud. What he had done in the past, that he could do in the future, and Appa was in urgent need of some one to collect his revenues, since his own mutinous troops could no longer be depended upon for that very essential service. The man who had enforced taxes from the Tappal

114

districts, could extort them from Appa's, which adjoined them in the Mewatti country.

So Thomas was engaged, and ordered to raise a battalion of 1,000 regular infantry and 100 horse. But this required money, a commodity Appa could not command, and, therefore, in lieu of a monthly payment, he assigned to his new commander the districts of Tijára, Tapúkra, and Firozpur, the revenues of which were to be applied to the expenses of the corps. They formed a portion of Appa's own territory of Rewári, which had formerly belonged to Ismáil Beg, and lay about forty miles south of Delhi. Their assignment answered a double purpose : it secured the payment of a battalion by which Appa hoped to re-establish his fortunes, and it brought the districts themselves under his authority, which was comforting to his feelings and agreeable to his dignity, for, as a matter of practical finance, he had never been able to collect any revenue from them himself, owing to their chronic state of rebellion. They had, indeed, been to him a bane rather than a blessing, for whenever he sent a force against them, the peasantry fled for refuge to the hilly tracts around, and directly his troops retired, sallied forth and committed fresh depredations on the surrounding country. This unsatisfactory state of affairs made it both cheap and profitable to sublet the district to any one who would undertake to pay himself out of the proceeds, and keep the unruly inhabitants in peace and subjection.

Thomas had no misgivings as to his ability to collect revenue, for his methods were as sure as they were summary, and he accepted the proposal, with the single stipulation that accounts should be balanced every six months, and the difference adjusted. This being agreed to, he received two cannons and a supply of ammunition, and began the enlistment of men. Service under European commanders was popular with the natives, and there would have been no difficulty in filling his ranks had he enjoyed the command of a little ready cash. As it was, the problematical revenues of Tijára, Tapúkra, and Firozpur did not pass current, and it was with great difficulty he recruited 400 men. With these he decided to take possession of his *Jaidad*, hoping to extract a reality out of its shadowy resources ; but scarcely had he marched half way toward it than he was recalled in hot haste by Appa, and ordered to accompany that chief to Delhi, to guard against any possible commotion that might arise owing to the death of Modhoji Sindhia, news of which had just reached Hindustan.

There were several chiefs collected at the capital, who joined in maintaining the Marátha authority under General De Boigne. They were honourably received by the Emperor, to whom Thomas, in due turn, presented his *nazzar*, or offering, and from whom he received a valuable *khilut*. He remained at the capital for some time, during which he was successful in recruiting his force up to 700, and then obtained leave to depart in order to take possession of his assigned districts, and raise from them the funds, which were now more urgently needed than ever. But scarcely had he marched his party out of the capital than they mutinied for their pay, and began to disperse and plunder the surrounding country, after the manner fashionable at that period.

It was with the greatest difficulty Thomas whipped in his riotous pack, and returned with them to Delhi, where he represented to Appa the impossibility of doing anything without means. The chief found a truly Oriental escape out of this difficulty by getting very angry; but Thomas, who seldom avoided a fight if he could help it, gave his master back word for word, and a rupture seemed imminent, until Appa compromised the matter by advancing Rs.14,000, and executing a bond for the rest of the claims, which, it is perhaps superfluous to add, was never honoured. The payment on account, however, enabled Thomas to satisfy his mutineers, and in July, 1794, he set out for the third time to take possession of his *Jaidad*.

His route lay through the Jumna Jaghir of the Begum Somru, which Thomas had administered for such a long time. The opportunity was irresistible, and he plundered it, exacting a heavy fine from a village called Garáth. It was a very sorry return for the generous treatment he had received from the Begum; but it is probable his vindictiveness was directed, not against her, but against the French faction, which directed affairs at Sardhána, and had brought about Thomas's downfall.

Continuing his march after this little interlude, Thomas duly reached his domains. It was a dark and rainy monsoon night when he arrived at Tijára, the place of chief importance. He pitched his camp a short distance from its walls, and his men, fatigued after a long and harassing march, lay down to rest. That night his new subjects gave him a taste of their quality by creeping into his encampment and stealing a valuable horse, which had been picketted in its very centre.

The impudence of this proceeding aroused Thomas's wrath, and he instantly determined to inflict condign punishment on the vagabond thieves who were so wanting in veneration for constituted authority. So he detached a party to discover the village to which the horse had been taken; but they had not gone far before they were attacked, and obliged to retire. Seeing this, Thomas ordered his cavalry to advance and cover the retreat of the detachment, whilst he himself led out the main body of his infantry; but by this time the enemy had been considerably reinforced, and showed a formidable front. Thomas, taking the lead of his centre column, boldly advanced and set fire to the village, which was the point of attack, but as he was doing so, his right and left wings were seized with a sudden panic, and fled in precipitation. Their example affected the centre, who immediately followed, abandoning their wounded, and leaving Thomas with only a dozen faithful men and a few cavalry to support him.

It was a moment of extreme peril. But it was in such crises that Thomas displayed those splendid qualities of audacity and defiance which distinguished his whole career. Falling slowly back on one of his guns which had become embarrassed in the bed of a stream, he encouraged his small party to exert themselves in extricating it, and had just succeeded, when the enemy, confident of victory now, renewed the attack with furious energy.

The native commander of Thomas's cavalry, a man of distinguished bravery, stood nobly by his master, and, with a few others, threw themselves between the enemy and the gun which was the object of their charge. Their intrepidity cost them their lives; but their gallant effort allowed time for the piece to be loaded, and the next minute a well-directed fire of grape was poured into the advancing foe. The timely discharge saved Thomas and the few brave fellows that survived, and after half a dozen more rounds the enemy drew off and retired into the surrounding ravines.

Thomas now collected his fugitives, but when he had mustered them, found his force reduced to 300 men. With these he again advanced to give battle; but the enemy, satisfied of his prowess, declined to renew the contest.

Although his first experience had been so disastrous, the gallantry and ability with which he retrieved the reverse created a great effect, and spread a dread amongst the people who had opposed him. Serious as was Thomas's loss in action, the Mewáttis had suffered more, and the immediate consequence was that their headmen made overtures for peace, which led to an amicable adjustment of terms. It was agreed that a year's revenue should be paid, and the stolen property restored, hostages being given for the performance of these conditions.

Tijára was the strongest place in the district, and inhabited by the most refractory people. Only a few weeks before the date of Thomas's victory the Begum Somru's whole force had failed in an attack upon the town, and been compelled to retire. Its occupation by Thomas led to the immediate submission of the rest of the district; but he was so pleased with the spirit and fighting qualities of the people that he offered to enlist any of them who chose to serve him, and this being well responded to, he had no difficulty in bringing up his battalion to the sanctioned strength.

Orders now reached Thomas from Appa to assist the collector of the district of Kishnagar in getting in the revenue due. Having no belief in conciliatory measures, but holding the opinion that the turbulent people of the province could only be coerced into obedience, Thomas at once entered into a vigorous punitive campaign, carrying fire and sword into their midst. His expedition concluded with the subjugation of the town of Jhajjar, a place of considerable importance, after which he returned to Tijára.

Upon the surrender of Jhajjar, Appa gave Thomas an order on the collector of that town for a sum sufficient to pay the arrears due to the battalion ; but just at this time the chief's own troops mutinied for their long-withheld pay, and the money was diverted to satisfy their claims. Whereupon Thomas marched to the Bahadurgarh district, to raise a contribution to meet his needs. In his route he found the smaller villages all deserted, and considerable numbers of armed persons collected in a threatening manner in the larger ones. His force, thinned by frequent desertions, had dwindled down to 300 men, whose discipline was extremely unsatisfactory. Notwithstanding which, having arrived at a place called Mandáka, and found the inhabitants ready to resist him by arms, he attacked them without a moment's hesitation, and after giving them a severe beating, sacked their village of Rs. 4,000.

The extraordinary vigour and success of Thomas's short campaign began to arouse the apprehensions of the Marátha authorities at Delhi, who felt obliged to take note of the influence he was acquiring within such a short distance of the capital. At the instigation of the Begum Somru, whose resentment had been aroused by the recent attack upon her Jumna *Jaghir*, a combined force was sent to watch Thomas, who thereupon deemed it prudent to remove to a distance, and, in consequence, retired to headquarters.

Scarcely had he reached Tijára than he received an urgent message from Appa, calling on him to advance with all speed to Kôt Pútli, a fort about forty miles distant, where the chief was detained by his mutinous troops, who had been tampered with by Gopál Ráo Bháo, Daulat Ráo Sindhia's viceroy in Hindustan. Appa was fearful of being delivered up to his enemies, and implored Thomas to rescue him without fail, for he could no longer rely on his officers, who had all been bought over by Gopál Ráo.

Although it was raining heavily, and the afternoon far advanced when Thomas received the summons, he did not hesitate for a moment in obeying it. The fall of his master meant his own ruin, for if Sindhia resumed Appa's territory, as he seemed inclined to do, Tijára, Tapúkra and Firozpur would naturally go with it. Instantly collecting his men, Thomas marched all night and the greater portion of the following day and night, through constant rain and over heavy roads, and at two o'clock on the second morning arrived before Kôt Pútli. His sudden appearance, and the inclement state of the weather, prevented any opposition from the mutineers, who had surrounded Appa and his few faithful followers, and Thomas was able to march up to the fort, encamp under its walls, and send in a supply of provisions, of which the chief stood in great need.

As nearly all Appa's troops were in mutiny, it was impossible to re-establish his authority with the small force remaining loyal, and under these circumstances Thomas recommended that an effort should be made to come to terms with Sindhia. Of this advice Appa approved ; but he, nevertheless, sought an early opportunity of placing himself and his family in safety, and the next day made his way to Thomas's camp, a-proceeding not unattended with danger. It was now determined to fall back upon Kánaund, Appa's principal stronghold, and the order was given to strike camp and march. But no sooner had a start been made, than the mutineers began to follow in pursuit, and in a short time overtook and surrounded Thomas's force. The position now became very critical, and as a last resource Thomas urged Appa to mount his elephant, and lead an attack, believing such behaviour would have an inspiriting effect upon the men who defended him, and who were disheartened at the position in which they found themselves. Appa, who was a courageous chief, at once adopted the suggestion, which met with complete success. No sooner was a bold front shown than the mutineers first came to a halt, and then retreated, leaving the way clear for Thomas to conduct his master in safety to Kánaund.

The danger had been great, and the deliverance dashing, and in gratitude for his exertions, Appa presented Thomas with a *khilut* of Rs.3,000, with which to purchase an elephant and palanquin suitable to his dignity. Furthermore, to mark his appreciation of the gallant and faithful conduct of the regular troops, he ordered a considerable increase in their numbers, and assigned to Thomas in perpetuity the districts of Jhajjar, Bairi, Mandoti, and Pathoda, which were situated to the westward of Delhi, and yielded an annual revenue of a lakh and a half of rupees.

This marked a distinct step in Thomas's fortunes, for in all the changes and vicissitudes he subsequently experienced, he clung to

Jhajjar to the end, and only surrendered it at the termination of his career.

Appa being safely established at Kánaund, where he was in a position to hold his own, Thomas was permitted to depart in order to take possession of his new territory, but before he had completed doing so, a serious disturbance broke out in one of his master's frontier districts, which was under the charge of a Brahmin official named Ganga Bishen, who possessed great influence, and was able to bring 14,000 fighting men into the field. Discontented with the exacting rule of Appa, and encouraged by recent events, Ganga Bishen entered into negotiations to transfer his allegiance to Gopál Ráo Bháo, and surrender to Sindhia the district he held from Appa. This intelligence being communicated to the latter, he sent orders to Thomas to seize the rebel, who at once retreated to a mountainous part of the Mewátti country, and shut himself up in a strong hill fort.

In order to lull suspicion, Thomas allowed a short time to elapse before making any movement. He then, after a sudden and swift night march, presented himself before the rebel's stronghold, and by a clever stratagem, secured his person, and sent him to Appa. But the fort still hold out, being occupied by a garrison of 1,000 men, under the command of Ganga Bishen's nephew ; and it was necessary to reduce it. As it was known to be well supplied with provisions and ammunition, nothing but a long and tedious blockade seemed possible, and the better to ensure success, Thomas began the construction of a chain of posts or redoubts around the place.

Whilst employed in erecting these, he experienced a desperate adventure, in which he narrowly escaped losing his life. Shortly after the completion of one of his principal redoubts, he had retired to rest one night, when he was awakened by a great shouting and commotion. Hurrying to an eminence near at hand, he saw that the garrison had made a sortie, and possessed themselves of this redoubt, in which was stored all his reserve arms and ammunition. Whilst he was reconnoitring the position, a small band of the enemy caught sight of him, and immediately bore down towards where he was standing. In his haste Thomas had not armed himself, but at this moment a faithful servant rushed up with his sword, which he had just time to grasp when the attackers reached him, and he found himself confronted by half a dozen dangerous men.

These discharged their matchlocks, and threw several spears at him, but fortunately with an unsuccessful aim. Perceiving a stand of colours, which his own men had abandoned, Thomas stooped down to pick them up, and the enemy, concluding from the motion of his body that he was wounded, dashed forward, hoping to overpower him by force of numbers and a simultaneous onslaught. But they had under-estimated the prowess of the *Jehazi Sahib.* Nothing daunted by overwhelming odds, he gallantly met them, and although he was obliged to loose his hold of the colours, he succeeded in beating his assailants off, and on being reinforced by his men, drove them back into the fort. Faint from loss of blood, he could not follow up the advantage, but was compelled to retire to his trenches, where his wounds were dressed, and his pusillanimous followers recalled to a sense of their duty.

The principal points in the lines of investment were now strengthened, and the siege vigorously enforced ; but Ganga Bishen's nephew held out as resolutely, and Thomas's troops soon began to suffer hardships. Supplies ran short, and sickness broke out. The camp equipment was of a miserable description, Thomas's tent being the only one in the field, and this, with characteristic generosity, he gave up for use as a hospital. The weather was inclement, with incessant rain, and was made the harder to bear from the great scarcity of blankets and warm clothing. As usual Thomas's funds were exhausted, and in order to raise sufficient money to purchase the more urgent necessaries his men required, he sold his horses. It was by such generous sacrifices as these that Thomas endeared himself to his soldiers, and won from them that personal devotion which he always enjoyed. In the piping times of peace his liberality was prodigal, and in seasons of adversity, when there was no pay in the treasure chest, and no grain in the camp bazaar, he never failed to identify himself with his followers, sharing with them their trials, their discomforts, and their dangers.

The siege of Ganga Bishen's fort lasted for some time, but after two mines had been sprung with considerable effect, the garrison capitulated, and Appa's authority was asserted. Thomas then returned to Jhajjar, where he collected the revenue due, paid his troops their arrears, and allowed them the rest needful after their late severe exertions.

Towards the end of 1794, Gopál Ráo Bháo, Sindhia's viceroy in Hindustan, was disgraced, and superseded by General De Boigne, who delegated much of his authority to Lakwa Dáda, a distinguished and favourite chief of the late Madhoji Sindhia. Lakwa now appeared in the vicinity of Appa's territory at the head of a large Marátha army, and the latter, considering it politic to pay his respects in person, visited his camp.

But although Appa was well received, the occasion was taken to demand from him arrears of tribute which were stated to be due ; and when he desired to depart permission was withheld, and he was practically detained a prisoner pending the settlement of what was claimed from him. Although the whole amount was only two lakhs of rupees, and many persons in Appa's family could easily have afforded him assistance in his distress, not a man was found who would advance anything. Being unable to raise the required sum, Appa, to secure his freedom, was obliged to make over his districts in mortgage to a Maráthá chief, named Bapu Farnavis, and furthermore to enter into an agreement to pay the troops Bapu proposed to keep up to collect the revenue. "In short," observes Thomas in his memoirs, "it was plain to see that whoever might hereafter, by chance of war, obtain possession of the districts in question, it was evident that by these concessions Appa had for ever done away with his own right." Amongst the *pargannahs* thus surrendered were these of Tijára, Tapúkra and Firozpur, which belonged to Thomas, to whom the loss was a severe one, but with a magnanimity highly to his credit he observed that "since his principle was ruined he had no cause for complaint," and made no claim for compensation from that part of his master's territory still remaining to him.

Appa Khandi Ráo's prestige and authority were much shaken by this sequestration of his property, and his detention in Lakwa Dáda's camp, and the inhabitants of his remaining districts deemed the opportunity a good one for refusing the payment of their taxes, and breaking into rebellion. But they had reckoned without their master's tax-gatherer. Thomas at once marched against them at the head of 800 men, and in a short time captured several of their principal places, some by day and others by night assaults, and soon reduced them to submission. His promptitude in planning, and vigour in executing, punitive expeditions of this description were remarkable. Having exacted heavy fines from a large portion of the malcontents, he came at length to a place called Bairi, where he met with a desperate resistance, the description of which is best told in his own words.

"In the fort of Byree, exclusive of the garrison, were 300 Rajpoots and Jhats, who had been hired for the express purpose of defending the place, and it was here that I was in the most imminent danger of losing the whole of my party. We had stormed the fort and were beat back with loss. One of my *sirdars* (officers) was wounded, and from the confusion that occurred was left behind in the hands of the enemy. The danger was every moment increasing, the town being set on fire in several places, and our retreat nearly cut off by the flames that surrounded us.

" In this situation we had the additional mortification to perceive the merciless enemy seize on the wounded officer, and with savage barbarity precipitate him into the fire. Equally animated and enraged by the spectacle, my troops now rushed forward to the attack, with an ardour that was irresistible. Having gained entire possession of the fort, the soldiers, with clamorous expressions of revenge, insisted on the death of every one of the garrison that remained, and I was not inclined to refuse. But it cost us dear, the enemy to a man making a brave resistance. This contest was continued so long as to afford time to those who had retreated to return ; by these means we were engaged again, and at one time almost overpowered, but receiving a reinforcement of our own party, the enemy by slow degrees began again to retreat. I pursued with the cavalry : the enemy once more made a stand in the jungles adjoining the town, when, after a second desperate conflict, they gave way on all sides, and most of them were cut to pieces."

The expedition which was concluded by this vigorous exploit had been a short but severe one. Now that it was finished, the recognition awaiting Thomas was not such as he expected, for scarcely had he completed the objects of his march than he received a communication from Appa, informing him that, owing to his straitened means, he found it impossible to retain the services of the battalion, and he therefore desired it to be dismissed, and Thomas to repair to his camp in the country of the Ráo Rájah.

It was certainly a brief and summary way of terminating the contract that existed between the soldier and his master, and had the merit of simplicity ; but it quite ignored the fact that Thomas's troops were in considerable arrears of pay, and that without a settlement of their claims it was impossible to disband them. Their commander, therefore, marched to Appa's camp, which was pitched near Ulwár, and in the interview which followed, was informed by the chief, who spoke with visible uneasiness, that the Marátha commanders noticing Thomas's influence and his energetic conduct, considered him a dangerous personage, and one who might, if occasion arose, act against Sindhia himself, and they had therefore requested Appa to discharge him.

Thomas, on hearing this, at once repaired to Lakwa Dáda, whom he taxed with endeavouring to procure his ruin ; but the Marátha general not only denied that he had ever disapproved of Thomas's conduct, but offered him the command of 2,000 men in Sindhia's service, if he felt inclined to leave Appa.

This was putting a new complexion on affairs, for the proposal embraced a promotion which few men would have hesitated to accept. But it failed to tempt Thomas, whose idea of duty stretched before him straight as a die. Mercenary soldier and adventurer though he was, no truer or more faithful servant than this wandering Irishman ever pledged his word. Appa's districts had now broken out again into a state of open rebellion, and Thomas " considered himself under obligations which could not be passed over ; for if he now quitted his master it would in all probability prove his utter ruin, and he there-fore resolved to adhere to Appa Khandi Ráo, and endeavour to retrieve his affairs."

On Thomas's return from Lakwa's camp, he went to interview Appa, who excused himself for his late conduct, the reasons for which are hard to understand. But he managed to satisfy Thomas (who on more than one occasion in his career gave evidence of a confiding and complacent disposition), and induced him to undertake the sub-jugation of the revolted districts. Before he could start, however, there came a request from Lakwa Dáda, for Appa's battalion to assist in the reduction of the fort of Soháwalgarh, which had refused to pay its stipulated tribute to the Maráthás, and, with his master's consent, Thomas marched his men to join the forces already engaged in besieging the place.

On his arrival Thomas's post was assigned to him, but his men, being now several months in arrears of pay,* refused to fight, and in order to satisfy their demands he was again compelled to sell his property, and distribute the proceeds before his soldiers would return to their duty.

Soháwalgarh had been for some time invested by four of General De Boigne's battalions, under command of Major Gardner. The enemy, in the hopes of compelling the Maráthás to raise the siege, had taken possession of the ravines in the neighbourhood, which led to several skirmishes, occasioning losses on both sides. Soon after Thomas's arrival a council of war was summoned to consider the best means of reducing the place, and Major Gardner proposed the advance of a second parallel, but this could not be effected without first capturing a very strongly fortified outpost, which no one appeared inclined to attack.

Thomas, who was present at the council, volunteered no advice, but his mind was already made up to take the redoubt. That same evening he carefully reconnoitred its approaches, and decided how to

---

* The chronic state of arrears in which Thomas's troops seemed to exist is difficult to understand. It is probable that his frequent assertions of having " paid them up " meant only small payments on account.

assault it, and early the next morning, without acquainting any one of his design, mustered his troops, formed them into columns, and, advancing whilst the enemy were off guard, completely surprised them. Having stormed the outworks he effected an entry into the redoubt itself, and maintained his position until he was reinforced from the Marátha camp, whereupon the enemy evacuated the place, and he established himself in the position he had won.

The second parallel was now advanced, and the fort so closely invested, that the commandant, despairing of succour from without, negotiated for terms, and a ransom of two lakhs of rupees was demanded, which he agreed to pay. Thomas received a share sufficient to reimburse him for all the expenses he had incurred, and then returned to his own country. This he found in the usual rebellious state, and the better to keep it in order, he divided his force into two battalions, one of which he employed in the collection of revenue, and kept the other stationed at Jhajjar.

And now another danger threatened him. For some months past the Begum Somru had been trying by every means in her power to effect Thomas's ruin, and had even gone so far as to bribe the Marátha officials to advise his dismissal. To this hostile course of action she was incited by her French officers, and especially by Thomas's old enemy, Le Vassoult, to whom, about this time, the Begum was secretly married. His influence being now paramount, he persuaded her to attack Thomas's districts, and she accordingly ordered her army to Tháru, a place about twenty-five miles south-east of Jhajjar. The force consisted of 4 battalions of infantry, 400 cavalry, and 20 guns, and it was publicly given out that the object of the expedition was a war of revenge against her former officer.

Thomas immediately called in his detachments to headquarters, where he concentrated all his troops, which now amounted to 2,000 regular infantry, 200 cavalry, and 10 pieces of artillery. With these he prepared to meet the threatened invasion; but before the Begum could put her intention into execution, a mutiny broke out in her army, and she was obliged to return to Sardhána, whilst Thomas, freed from the impending danger, once more turned his attention to the ever-constant necessity of keeping his own districts in order.

Since Appa's reverse of fortune his country had been placed under a joint management, as Lakwa Dáda insisted on his officials being associated in the collection of the revenue. This surveillance was strongly resented by Appa, whom it greatly humiliated, and he therefore intrigued to sow dissensions between Lakwa and his local deputy Bapu Farnavis, and having succeeded in setting the two quarrelling, determined, whilst they were occupied with one another, to reassert his own independence.

Withdrawing into his stronghold of Kánaund, which he fortified very strongly, he sent orders to Thomas to summarily dismiss the Marátha collectors and officials employed by Lakwa Dáda. These instructions were promptly carried into effect, although their execution gave rise to much severe fighting and loss of life. Appa next marched out and laid seige to Narnál, a large and populous town sixteen miles south of Kánaund, where Thomas joined him, and the chief was so delighted with the thorough way in which his work had been performed, that he presented him with several valuable presents, including an elephant and a palanquin.

Narnál was under the command of one of Lakwa Dáda's Brahmin officials, who, on hearing of Thomas's arrival, came to him secretly at night, and offered to surrender the town and fort if the safety of his own person and property were guaranteed. To this Thomas agreed, and the gates were opened the next morning to the besiegers. But now a difficulty arose, for Appa, being in desperate want of money, desired to extort a heavy fine from the Brahmin, who was known to be a rich man, and demanded his surrender from Thomas. The request was at once refused, with an explanation of the circumstances under which the man had given himself up. Upon this Appa became very angry, and declared that the slight lowered him in the estimation of his followers, and that it was not within Thomas's power to grant terms and protection to the chief's enemies. But Thomas, whose loyalty to his word of honour was his finest trait, refused to yield, and the result was a serious rupture between him and Appa.

A few days later Thomas was requested to attend his master, and at once complied. Having arrived at the house where Appa had taken up his quarters, he was informed that the chief was ill and confined to his bed in an upper chamber, to which Thomas was desired to ascend. Suspecting no treachery, and anxious to avoid giving any cause for offence, he left his escort below and went upstairs unattended, when, to his surprise, he found Appa apparently perfectly well, and waiting to receive him.

A conversation ensued, and it soon became evident that the surrender of the Brahmin was the main object of the interview. Thomas listened to all his master had to say, and then replied that his pledged word involved his personal honour and could not be broken, and that no consideratian would induce him to yield to Appa's request. On hearing this the chief, making some excuse, rose and left the room, from which he had no sooner departed, than it was filled with armed men.

The trap he had fallen into was now apparent to Thomas, but so far from showing any alarm or timidity, he calmly retained his seat with an air of imperturbability—a course of conduct that was not without its effect upon the intruders. Presently a letter was handed him from Appa, which proved to be a sort of ultimatum, demanding the immediate surrender of the Brahmin.

This brought matters to a crisis. Many a man in such a dilemma would have salved his conscience with the reflection that he had done everything in his power to keep his promise, and that to resist any longer was only to wantonly imperil the one life that stood between the proposed victim and his destruction. But this was not the view Thomas took of the matter, for he spurned such a surrender of principle as it involved, and instantly refused compliance. Then, rising to his feet, he demanded, in an imperious tone, to be conducted to Appa's presence. His audacity saved him, and before any one could interpose he strode out of the room and into the adjoining chamber, where the chief had retired.

At the sudden apparition of the tall resolute Irishman, whom he had imagined a prisoner, Appa was completely taken aback. There was danger in Thomas's flashing eye, and an actual threat in the action of his hand, as it sought the hilt of his sword. Before this exhibition of daring the Marátha chief quailed, and seeing his hesitation, Thomas, with the exquisite guile and gallantry of his countrymen, relieved himself of a conventional compliment, and accomplished his departure unmolested.

On his return to camp he despatched his *diwán*, or head native official, to Appa to inform him that, "compelled by a just indignation against the treachery of his proceeding, he would no longer serve him." In this determination Thomas was supported by his troops, who, fired at the insult offered their leader, declared they would no longer remain in Appa's service.

The incident illustrates very vividly the dangers that surrounded a soldier of fortune in India in those days. Craft and treachery were component parts of the Marátha nature, and the European, with his code of honour, was at a disadvantage in dealing with men who had none. Appa's original request was one that would have been complied with by any native without demur or hesitation, and the means he took to try and enforce it was consistent with established custom, and would probably have been considered rather clever. The fact that Thomas had for a long time devoted himself with uncommon energy and fidelity to the chief's cause, weighed as nothing against the gratification of avarice or malice, and Appa would have sacrificed his officer without a sigh rather than forego the accomplishment of his personal desire.

And now that he had failed to coerce or intimidate him his conduct was equally despicable. He feared losing not only his European, but the regular infantry as well. So he began to invent excuses for his treachery, trying to explain it away, and in order to re-establish confidence came the next day in person to Thomas's camp, and succeeded in persuading him to withdraw his resignation and return to his allegiance. It is difficult to comprehend how Thomas could have consented to overlook what had occurred, but it is possible that he hesitated before relinquishing an established position with a chief of standing, and one that was not without certain substantial advantages. At any rate matters were amicably adjusted, and before Appa left he and Thomas were on their old footing.

The collection of the revenue in the Mewátti district was the next task that engaged Thomas's attention. Here he found the Marátha officials again interfering and quarrelling with Appa's, but by punishing some, and conciliating others, he brought matters into a favourable train for settlement. In the course of these proceedings, however, he was under the necessity of storming a fort, in which he captured a valuable booty of cannon, bullocks, and other transport animals. On hearing of this success Appa claimed as his right the artillery taken, but Thomas as strenuously insisted that the guns belonged to the troops who had fought for them. This divergence of opinion led to another rupture, and Appa, highly incensed at his officer's insubordination and growing ideas of independence, determined, if possible, to finally effect his downfall.

To this end he entered into communication with a body of Ghussains, who were proceeding on their annual pilgrimage to Hardwar, and happened to be encamped in the neighbourhood. These people belonged to a formidable sect of Hindu mendicants, accustomed to engage in military service when any offered, and large bodies of them were frequently to be met with travelling from place to place, and levying contributions wherever they went. They often attached themselves to the service of a particular chief, and for sudden attacks or reprisals no men could be found better fitted, for they were inured to pain and privation by the nature of their calling, and were absolutely indifferent to death.

In consideration of a reward of Rs.10,000 the leader of this band of Ghussains agreed to make an attack on Thomas; but, luckily, particulars of this atrocious arrangement were communicated to him by the agents he employed in Appa Khandi Ráo's camp. Deeply incensed at the premeditated treachery Thomas determined to defeat it, and making a night march against the Ghussains, fell upon them unawares, and completely turned the tables on the would-be assassins, for he routed them with immense slaughter, and sent the few survivors in headlong flight to Delhi, as though the devil himself were after them. Having thus asserted himself, Thomas wrote to Appa, denouncing his base conduct, and declining to remain any longer in the service of one who could be guilty of such a shameful act.

A Marátha is seldom at a loss for an excuse, and Appa absolved himself from all responsibility for the deed, by laying the blame on his servants ; vowing that they alone were guilty, he himself having been ill, and unable to attend to any business. He then went on to expatiate upon the gravity of his disorder, which had taken a dangerous turn and was growing worse every day, and capped all by expressing a wish for a personal interview with Thomas, before it was too late, in order that he might place under his charge the heir and successor he had chosen, and for whose youth and inexperience he desired to enlist his officer's favour.

This invitation was both surprising and awkward, for though it was true that Appa's health was failing, Thomas was not prepared to place any further reliance on his word. On the other hand, it was difficult to refuse such a request from so powerful a chief. Happily the necessity of coming to a decision in this difficult dilemma was obviated by intelligence of a raid made by a numerous body of Sikhs into the Doáb districts north of Delhi, where, after defeating and almost exterminating the Marátha troops stationed for the defence of the frontier, they were committing great depredations in the vicinity of Saharanpur.

Although Appa Khandi Ráo had no particular connection with Saharanpur, he thought that, in common with the other Marátha chiefs, he ought to exert himself to prevent further incursions, the more especially as his own districts would in all probability be the next to suffer from these desperate marauders. He therefore ordered Thomas to march his whole force northward, and attack the Sikhs wherever he encountered them in Marátha territory.

The commission was one to Thomas's taste. He had the Irishman's irresistible love of a row, and never lagged when fighting was in prospect. Moreover, the expedition relieved him from his quandary with regard to Appa's invitation. Crossing the Jumna, a little to the north of Delhi, he advanced rapidly towards the enemy. But the Sikhs knew the *Jihazi Sahib* of old, having often felt the weight of his sword when he was in the service of the Begum Somru, and entrusted with the defence of these very districts. To quote Thomas's own words, "he had on more than one occasion given them samples of his method of fighting," and the information thus conveyed sufficed. They had no stomach now to meet the fiery Irishman, whose prowess was already a password along the frontier, and on hearing of his approach effected a rapid retreat into their own territory.

When Lakwa Dáda heard how promptly and efficiently Thomas had retrieved the disgraceful defeat of the Maráthá troops and cleared the country of the Sikhs, he requested Appa to allow his officer to raise a body of 2,000 men for the protection of the province of Saharanpur and other parts of the Marátha possessions. To this Appa, unable to disoblige so powerful a chief, reluctantly consented, and the districts of Pánipat, Sónpat, and Karnál, were assigned to Thomas in *Jaidad,* for the upkeep of a special frontier force of 2,000 infantry, 200 cavalry, and 16 guns. These districts were contiguous to Thomas's own *jaghir* of Jhajjar, and their acquisition made him paramount lord over an extensive domain. Pánipat itself was an historical city of great antiquity. It stood in the centre of a large plain, which had been the scene of two decisive battles in the history of Hindustan, and although it had ceased to be an emporium of commerce, as it had once been for the caravans of Kabul, Lahore, and Persia, it still remained a place of considerable importance.

No sooner had Thomas established himself in this new territory than a pathetic appeal for help reached him from his old mistress the Begum Somru. Her marriage with Le Vassoult had led to a mutiny in her force, and in a vain endeavour to escape from Sardhána, her husband met his death, and she herself was deposed from authority, and confined a prisoner at her capital, her step-son, Zaffar Yáb Khan, otherwise known as Balthazar Sombre, being elevated to the government. The Begum now wrote to Thomas in most abject and desponding terms, throwing herself on his clemency,.and begging him to come to her aid, as she had no one else to look to. She declared that she was living in imminent dread of being poisoned, and offered to pay any sum of money he might demand if he would only reinstate her in power.

Thomas possessed in a very marked degree the virtues of chivalry and generosity, and could never turn a deaf ear to the pleadings of lovely woman in distress. According to his recorded description the Begum was at this time forty-five years of age, small in stature and inclined to be plump. Her complexion was very fair, and her eyes black, large, and animated. Her dress "perfect Hindostany" and of the most costly material. She spoke the Persian and Hindustani languages with fluency, and in conversation was " engaging, sensible and spirited." He resolved to help her, and on receipt of her letter induced Bápu Sindhia, the Marátlá governor of Saharanpur, by an offer of Rs.120,000 (£15,000), to move some troops towards Sardhána. From his former experience Thomas felt convinced that unless he' could gain over a portion of the Begum's rebellious soldiery, who had now sworn allegiance to Balthazar Sombre, not only would his exertions be fruitless, but the Princess herself would be exposed to the greatest personal danger. So he set on foot an intrigue for this purpose in which he was successful. He then marched with his force, and encamped at the village of Kataoli, twelve miles to the north of Sardhána, where he publicly announced that unless the Begum was reinstated in authority, he would accord no mercy to those who resisted ; and to give additional weight to his proclamation he stated that he was acting under the authority of Sindhia.

This intimation was at first attended with the desired effect, for a portion of the troops belonging to the Sardhána State immediately responded by confining Balthazar Sombre and declaring for the Begum. But Thomas knew well that no reliance could be placed on their capricious temper, for mutiny came to them as a periodical relaxation in the monotony of life : so he lost no time in pinning them to their declaration by advancing towards Sardhána. But before he reached the place a counter revolution had already proclaimed the restoration of Balthazar Sombre.

Thomas now determined on a *coup de main.* Ordering four hundred of his infantry to follow with all expedition, he galloped forward, escorted by only fifty cavalry, on whom he could thoroughly depend. Balthazar Sombre on seeing the weakness of this escort at once jumped at the conclusion that he had got Thomas into his power, and gave orders for an attack, but at this moment the infantry were perceived in the distance, and the mutineers believing the whole Marátlá army was at hand, sought safety in a third revolution, deposed Balthazar *nemine contradicente,* and tendered their humble submission to Thomas. Before sunset the Begum Somru was restored to power, and an oath of fidelity—such as it was worth—extracted from her troops, whilst Balthazar Sombre, who was a poor debauched semi-imbecile half-caste, was plundered of all his property, and conducted a prisoner to Delhi, where he was incarcerated.

After reinstating the Begum Thomas marched his force to a large town named Samli, situated on the Sikh frontier, the commandant of which place had encouraged the Sikhs in their late incursion, by communicating to them the defenceless condition of the Upper Provinces. Samli was situated forty-five miles from Sardhána, and Thomas covered the distance in twenty-four hours. An action took place in the open, in which the commandant, after a stubborn resistance, was defeated and compelled to retreat into the town, and Thomas, anxious to bring the affair to a speedy conclusion, gave orders for an assault the same evening, when the fort was carried by storm, and nearly all the garrison put to the sword.

It was by these long and rapid marches, and by these sudden and vigorous attacks, that Thomas won most of his victories. There never existed a man who more conscientiously observed the maxim " Never put off till to-morrow what you can do to-day." Fearless, impatient, impetuous, the *Jehazi Sahib* could brook no delay when his fighting blood was aroused, and his very audacity imposed on his enemies, so that they came to regard him as irresistible and invincible.

Having arranged affairs at Samli, and appointed a new governor, Thomas next repaired to Bápu Sindhia's camp, to whom, under orders from Appa, he was now attached. Bápu was engaged in the reduction of Laknoti, a place of considerable strength, situated on the east bank of the Jumna a little to the north of Samli, and occupied by the Sikhs. A practicable breach having been effected, preparations were made for an assault, but the commandant, seeing he was likely to be unsuccessful in defending the fort, in order to save effusion of blood, came privately to Thomas's tent, and made terms for the surrender of the place, which were faithfully and punctually carried out on the following morning.

The next matter of importance in Thomas's career was the receipt of a letter from Appa, in which that chief informed him that from continued illness his pains were augmented to a degree which had become intolerable, and no hope remaining of recovery from his cruel distemper, he had determined to put a period to his misery by voluntary death. For this purpose he was on his way to the Ganges, but he requested Thomas to come to see him once more before the scene closed for ever. On receipt of this intelligence Thomas set out immediately to afford, such consolation as he could to his desponding chief ; but he had not marched far when intelligence reached him that Appa had committed suicide by drowning himself in the river Jumna.

Thus perished, in 1797, one of Madhoji Sindhia's most intrepid and enterprising chieftains, and a man who had played no inconsiderable a part in the Marátha conquest of Hindustan. Appa had been engaged in the battles of Lálsót, Chaksána, and Agra, and the occupation of Delhi. He was a typical Marátha, whose mind was never free from intrigue and treachery, and his conduct towards Thomas had at times been as base as it was unintelligible, for he had no abler or more loyal soldier in his service than the European whose life he twice attempted to take. On the other hand Appa was a brave and skilful general, whose later misfortunes were due to political causes, and who, during a troublous time in the history of Hindustan, held his own against many and powerful enemies, and retained his distinguished position until his death.

CHAPTER III.

THE CONQUEST OF HARIÁNA.

1797–1798.

THE death of Appa Khandi Ráo was a severe blow to Thomas. Although the chief had often been capricious and treacherous in his conduct, he had at times shown he could appreciate the high qualities of his European officer, and as he represented an established power in Marátha politics there was a substantial advantage in being connected with him. A great deal could be done in India under the name of authority, even though the power invoked was a shadowy unreality. For twenty years Hindustan had been ruled in the name of Shah 'Alam, and notwithstanding that he was blind, helpless, and a prisoner, edicts continued to be issued in his name, and rewards, titles, and privileges conferred by his favour.

Appa Khandi Ráo was succeeded in his possessions by his nephew Váman Ráo, or Báwan Rao as the name is sometimes written. Váman Ráo was a vain, inexperienced youth, better fitted for the calling of an accountant than the career of a soldier. He was entirely in the hands of intriguing Brahmins and crafty courtiers, who crowded his capital at Rewári, and were jealous of the authority and influence of Thomas, to whom Appa, in his last moments, had entrusted the protection of his heir. They soon persuaded the young chief to renounce his guardian, and demand from him the restitution of the district, which had been granted as a reward for honourable services. Thomas was naturally indignant at this treatment, and peremptorily refused to surrender his *Jaidad*, but conscious that a quarrel between Váman Ráo and himself could only involve both in very serious difficulties, he endeavoured to compromise matters by offering to pay a sum of money to be confirmed in his possessions, this species of succession duty being in accordance with the custom of the country.

But Váman Ráo, instigated by his advisers, would not agree to this, and was foolhardy enough to resort to force. Without notice or warning he occupied with his undisciplined rabble a large village called Kosli, which formed part of Thomas's possessions. The latter, with a forbearance not usual with him, curbed his inclination to fight, and endeavoured to avoid a breach of the peace. This encouraged Váman Ráo, who on being joined by large bodies of local peasantry, became too formidable to be ignored, and Thomas felt obliged to bring the business to an issue. He accordingly attacked the chief's troops, and the affair was quickly decided. Váman Ráo's soldiery broke at the first onslaught and fled in all directions, and the greater part of them having taken refuge in the fort of Kosli were besieged therein. After erecting batteries, Thomas ordered grates for heating shot to be made ready, and this being done, fired so successfully with red hot balls as to quickly set the place on fire, and compel a surrender at discretion.

It was now agreed that an interview should take place between Thomas and Váman Ráo at Kánaund, for at the first sign of defeat the chief had shut himself up in that stronghold. But when Thomas arrived, Váman Ráo pretended to be fearful of treachery, and refused to come out of the fort, whilst Thomas, for similar reasons, was unwilling to enter it. The negotiations were in consequence broken off, and leaving matters *in statuo quo* the latter marched his troops north, where his presence was required to repel an incursion of the Sikhs. He took the precaution, however, of leaving a force to defend Jhajjar against any attack that might be made on it in his absence, and then directed his way to Karnál, where he soon had his hands full of fighting. Four successive actions took place, which resulted in a loss of 500 men on Thomas's side, and 1,000 on that of the enemy. A mutual desire for peace was the result of this blood-letting, and a treaty was concluded by which the Sikhs agreed to evacuate the villages they had taken possession of.

Váman Ráo did not neglect the opportunity of attacking Jhajjar during its master's absence, but the garrison left in it resisted him successfully, and on Thomas's return the chief thought fit to retire.

The differences between Thomas and his old master's heir had been fomented in a great measure by a specious and wily native named Kashmiri Bholi, who was the *zemindar*, or headman, of a large and populous district called Dádri, which lay to the west of Jhajjar. Thomas now determined to punish this individual, and falling upon him suddenly extorted a heavy fine. No sooner had he effected this than he was summoned by Bápu Sindhia, the governor of Saharanpur, to assist in repelling an invasion of Rohillas on the eastern frontier of the province, to which they had been incited by a Sikh chief named Nihál Sing, who had himself assembled a large body of his countrymen to assist by a diversion on the western boundary. On Thomas's approach the latter at once withdrew, and meanwhile Bápu having driven back the Rohillas, Thomas's assistance was not required, so he turned aside to Sónpat, one of the districts recently assigned to him, and encamped there a short time, making himself acquainted with its resource. Soon rumours of the arrival at Lahore of Zemán Shah, the King of Kabul, created general consternation in Hindustan, and caused Bápu Sindhia to summon a council of war, to which Thomas was invited, the districts he was deputed to guard being in the very path of the projected invasion, and the place where the Afghan army should most properly be met.

Unfortunately at this critical juncture Thomas's troops, being in arrears of pay, became clamorous for their dues. This, at a time when their services might at any moment be urgently required, gave the greatest offence and dissatisfaction to Bápu, and caused a serious misunderstanding between him and Thomas. The result was that the latter marched away in disgust, and was at once followed and attacked by a force sent after him by the Marátha chief, but in the action that took place Bápu's general was wounded, and drew off his troops. An amicable arrangement might now have been effected had not the Sikhs, delighted at the breach between the governor of Saharanpur and his Warden of the Marches, intrigued successfully to widen it and bring about a renewal of hostilities.

This was a serious matter, for with Bápu Sindhia against him on one side, and Váman Ráo on the other, each threatening to sequestrate his assigned districts, Thomas was placed in a dangerous predicament. After considering his situation, he determined to fall back on Karnál; but in order to accomplish this he had to cross the Jumna, and Bápu, who was determined to dispute his passage, having strongly reinforced his defeated troops, took the command in person, and getting between Thomas and the river opposed his progress. A desperate engagement ensued, but the latter, although greatly outnumbered, was successful in holding his own and eventually effected his object.

Bápu Sindhia was now joined by many of the country people, and further reinforced by troops sent out by Ragoji, the Marátha general at Delhi, as well as by some of the Begum Somru's battalions —a poor reward to Thomas for the aid he had recently afforded that princess. As Sardbána was a tributary state to the Maráthás, she was probably acting from necessity not choice. With this combined force Bápu crossed the Jumna, and by a rapid march took up a position between Thomas and Jhajjar with the intention of cutting off his retreat to his *Jaidad.*

Thomas's position was now very critical, for he was short of provisions and completely isolated, and there was only one resource left to him, namely, to fight his way through the enemies' forces. This he at once determined to do, and forming his men into line, gave battle. Bápu now looked upon success as assured, and engaging Thomas's front with his infantry, sent his cavalry to charge him in flank. These attacked him again and again, but were on each occasion driven back by steady and well-directed volleys, poured into them by Thomas's right and left wings, who changed front to repulse them. After each charge Thomas moved his force forward, and as the attacks became weaker and weaker gradually made good his advance, until at length he found the road to Jhajjar clear and effected his escape. Bápu, disheartened by his heavy loss, made no attempt to pursue, but contented himself with re-occupying the districts of Pánipat, Sónpat and Karnál, which Thomas, of necessity, had to abandon.

Dispossessed of his principal source of revenue, Thomas was now completely crippled, and left with no adequate means to pay his troops, who numbered 3,000 men. He had hitherto occupied a position analogous to that of other European adventurers in the Marátha service, to whom territory was assigned for the upkeep of their corps. But his summary dismissal from his appointment of Frontier Warden, and the resumption of his districts by Bápu, left him not only without a master, and without a territory, but encumbered with an army heavily in arrears of pay, which had recently mutinied and might at any time mutiny again, and with only the revenues of the comparitively small district of Jhajjar to draw upon. These were altogether insufficient for the support of such a large force as he had enlisted.

This reverse marks a distinct departure in Thomas's career. Hitherto he had been a mercenary, fighting other peoples battles for stipulated payment; and acting under such authority or license as passed current in those wild times and places. But the fountain of remuneration was now dried up, and he was thrown solely on his own resources. Needs must when necessity drives, and from this hour Thomas threw off all disguise, and became a freebooter pure and simple. There was no attempt at concealment. He began forthwith to support himself by fillibustering raids on the towns and villages of his neighbours, without any regard whatever to the elementary laws of *meum* and *tuum.* He sold his troops for specific reward, or let them out "by the job," with license to pillage and plunder like any Pindari. His attacks were indiscriminate, the occasion of his impecuniosity being the certain signal for a foray in the nearest territory where he could hope to levy fines.

This course of life which he now entered upon cannot be defended or excused. The most that can be said for it is that it was in keeping with the ideas of the times, and in harmony with the Maráthá system which dominated Hindustan. Thomas, in his isolated and adventurous career, surrounded by enemies and befriended by no one, was fighting for very existence. Both his livelihood and personal safety depended upon the men who followed his standard ; had they rebelled against him his life would not have been worth an hour's purchase. Money was the sole power able to control them, and when his assignment was forfeited his only means of raising money went with it. There were but two courses open to him : flight into British territory, or a bold bid for independence. His daring and ambitious nature rebelled against the ignominious escape offered by the former : to achieve the latter it was necessary to throw all conventional restraint to the winds, and boldly usurp a position, which, whilst raising every man's hand against his, would make him his own master. This was the course George Thomas chose.

Upon his arrival at Jhajjar the troops at once demanded their pay, and in order to satisfy their claims he marched them against Harichu, a large and populous town belonging to the Rájah of Jaipur, and "levied a contribution" from it. Without reason or right other than his own necessity, he called on the governor of the town to pay him a "ransom" of a lakh of rupees, which being denied, he stormed and took possession of the place. The fort, which defended the town, and stood separate from it, still held out ; but when Thomas prepared for a second assault, the commandant offered Rs.52,000, and this was accepted. But during the negotiations the town had " unfortunately been set on fire, and burnt so fiercely that goods to the amount of several lakhs of rupees were totally consumed."

This episode is related by Thomas with a candour which, in a less reprehensible matter, would be a naïve. There is a directness of description and a precision of narrative in his treatment of the subject which has a copybook simplicity. He volunteers no explanation, advances no theory of justification, attempts no excuses, but merely mentions that he wanted money to pay his men, and so he went to Harichu and took it.

Perhaps this bold and lawless action had an effect on Váman Ráo, whose adjacent territories might be the next to tempt " contribution."

At any rate he chose the moment to re-open negotiations, and conducted them in such a conciliatory spirit, that the differences between the two were adjusted and Thomas was confirmed in his possession of Jhajjar. In return for this he employed himself in reducing several of the chief's refractory *zemindars* to obedience, and in forcing from them the payment of their arrears of revenue. This incidental expedition carried him again towards the borders of the Jaipur territory, the proximity of which suggested another raid. And so he repeated his former experiment, this time under a pretence of punishing, what he was pleased to call, " a nest of banditti," who had at some remote date invaded Váman Ráo's country, the memory of which iniquity aroused a virtuous indignation in Thomas's bosom, and compelled him to attack them in force, and annihilate "the thievish tribe" before returning to his headquarters at Jhajjar.

He now determined to allow his men a short rest and recreation after their sixteen months incessant campaign, the more especially as it was the month of May, and the intense heat of the season militated against operations in the field. It was during this short period of inaction that there came to Thomas's imagination the ambitious design of erecting for himself an independent principality, over which he might rule with sovereign power.

To the north-west of Jhajjar lay a tract of territory known as Hariána, or the Green Land. Perchance the name reminded him of the Green Isle far away, from which he had come, and for which he felt the passionate devotion of an Irishman. Although at the present day a populous and settled district, replete with railways, roads, jails, court-houses, and missionaries, and hallowed with the privileges of local self-government, Hariána at the end of the last century was a veritable No Man's Land, acknowledging no master, and tempting none. In turn the prey of many succeeding invaders, it had for many years been a recognised battle-field for contending powers. It covered an area of nearly three thousand square miles of country so wild and barren that it had been a favourite hunting ground for Firoz Tughlak, a renowned king of Delhi, the ruins of whose buildings were still to be seen, and also the remains of a canal, excavated in the year 1356, to supply the place with water from the Jumna. This was rendered necessary by the natural dryness of the region—the name Hariána being appropriate to only a small portion of it—for there was little or no surface water to be found, the only supply, not brackish, being obtained from wells, most of which had to be sunk to a depth of over a hundred feet.

So far back as 1036, Hánsi, the capital town of Hariána, had been in existence, and was, indeed, a place of considerable importance. When Massoud, the son of the famous Mahmud of Gazni, invaded India, he found it fortified and strongly garrisoned by Hindus, who believed it could never fall into the hands of the Muhammadan. It was, however, taken by storm after a short siege of six days, and plundered of the immense treasures it contained. Lying as it did in the direct road of the Western approach to India, it became thereafter the victim of many invading armies, and owing to this cause was almost a depopulated wilderness when Thomas determined to make himself master of it.

Having matured his plans and waited until the approach of the rainy season, Thomas reinforced his army, provided it with everything necessary to ensure success, and commenced his march. His first attack was directed against the town and fort of Kanhori, the inhabitants of which were notorious for "thievish depredations," which shocked Thomas. Advancing with his usual celerity, he attempted, according to his custom, to take the place by storm, but was prevented by the spirited resistance of the enemy, who compelled him to retreat with a loss of 300 men.

This was an unfortunate prelude to his scheme of conquest, and would have induced most aspirants to forego such ambitious designs. But Thomas was a man whose persistence equalled his courage. Like an illustrious fellow-countryman of his, who, half a century later, distinguished himself not many miles from this very spot, he " never was *bate* and never would be *bate !* " A repulse only raised his fury and stirred him to fresh endeavour, and when his troops fell back, baffled and defeated from the walls of Kanhori, he issued orders for the fortification of the camp, with the stern determination of retrieving the disaster.

A regular siege of the fort was now commenced, but constant and heavy rain prevented the erection of batteries, and so a fortified chain of posts was erected round the town, by which it was cut off from all external aid. Before long the garrison were in straits for provisions, and began to suffer great distress, and they made several fierce sallies, attempting to fight their way through in investing lines.

During one of these encounters Thomas experienced another of those desperate adventures and escapes with which the history of his life abounds. A sortie was directed against the redoubt which he himself occupied, and in the confusion of the attack a sudden panic seized his troops, and the greater portion ran away, leaving him in a most critical position, for only five of his infantry remained with him, these being selected soldiers to whom had been allotted the particular charge of his firearms, consisting of pistols and blunderbusses of a large size. With these, and the assistance of a few cavalry who came to his aid, he maintained the post for a considerable time against every effort of the enemy to dislodge him, and at length by repeated and well-directed discharges compelled them to retire.

A few days after this occurrence, the weather becoming finer, Thomas was able to erect a battery, from which he fired with such good effect as to bring down a portion of the wall of the fort. This emboldened him to attempt another assault, but night coming on, he was obliged to defer it till the following morning, when he found the enemy had evacuated the place.

The best and bravest inhabitants of the Hariána district resided in the fort of Kanhori, men of desperate courage, nurtured in battle, and inured to invasion, and who lived by the sword and recognised no other form of government. The defeat of so formidable a faction had a salutary effect on the rest of the district, which offered but a slight resistance. In a short time Thomas gained complete possession of the whole of the southern portion of the territory; but it cost him much trouble to extend his rule over the north-western parts, which were occupied by the Sikhs and a predatory tribe called Bhattis. These he successfully engaged and defeated, driving the former back across the river Ghaggar, which he made his boundary in that direction.

The conquest of Hariána was now complete, and Thomas proclaimed his rule over an extent of territory which had formerly contained nearly a thousand towns and villages, and produced an annual revenue of Rs.1,430,000 (£178,750). But the number of the former was now reduced to little more than a quarter, and only yielded Rs.286,000 a year. The products of the country consisted chiefly of grain, and were dependent upon the rainfall. In favourable seasons the Ghaggar—of evil reputation to Simla-bound travellers of the present day—overflowed its banks and inundated the northern *pargannahs*. On the subsiding of the waters a rich greasy deposit remained on the land, which produced amazing crops of wheat and grass. So stimulating were the effects of this pasturage that the cattle grazed on it were celebrated for their excellence, and this character they retain to the present day. In the southern and western parts of the country the soil was sandy and the rainfall small, the consequence being that cultivation was very sparse. During the summer months the heat was intense, but upon the whole the climate was sufficiently salubrious, and in the winter very cold and bracing.

For the capital of his new domains Thomas selected the town of

Hánsi. The state of desolation into which this place had fallen may be estimated from a legend which long ran current in the Panjab that, when Thomas occupied the city, its sole inhabitants were a *fakir*, or holy mendicant, and two lions—emblems of its poverty and its deserted state. It had, however, the advantage of being centrally situated on an elevated spot of ground, the highest for many miles round. The ruins of the former city lay at the foot of the fortress, which was built on one of those huge mounds of earth common to this part of the Panjab and the mud walls of the citadel were of such enormous thickness as to prove impervious to shot. A large reservoir in the centre caught and retained the rain-water, and there were several wells in the immediate vicinity, although the surrounding country was an arid waste of desert, through which approach for any large body of men was rendered almost impossible by the absence of water. The district harboured many tigers, and a few lions, it being the only place in India, except Guzerat, where the latter species of *ferae* existed. Even as late as 1830 they were to be found there.

The plain around Hánsi might almost be termed a cemetery, for it was computed that not less than 40,000 of the followers of the Prophet had found a resting-place within a short circuit of its walls during the centuries of warfare it had witnessed between Hindu and Muhammadan. The inhabitants of the district were endowed with great personal bravery, and were expert in the use of arms, particularly in the exercise of the lance, sabre, and matchlock. Many instances of their resolution and courage were recorded, and in recent years they had successfully resisted the attacks of Mughals and Maráthás, and forced their armies to retreat. But, although fearless in fight, they were cruel, treacherous, and vindictive, and singularly callous of shedding blood or taking life in their domestic quarrels. The greater part of the population at the time of Thomas's annexation were Hindus, and their occupation agricultural.

Thomas's first care was to rebuild the walls of the fort, which had long fallen into ruin, and repair the defences of the town that lay under its ramparts. The decay of ages had eaten into the red-brick masonry, so that it crumbled to the touch, the streets were empty and the houses roofless and tenantless. But by degrees and by gentle treatment Thomas attracted nearly 6,000 people to take up their residence in the place, and to these he allowed every lawful indulgence, and guaranteed the protection of their lives, liberty, and property.

What more he did is best told in his own words, by quoting the following famous passage in his memoirs, which has been reproduced by nearly every writer who has had occasion to mention him :—

" At Hánsi I established a mint and coined my own rupees,* which I made current in my army and country. As from the commencement of my career at Jhujhur I had resolved to establish an independency, I employed workmen and artificers of all kinds, and I now judged that nothing but force of arms could maintain me in my authority. I therefore increased their numbers, cast my own artillery, commenced making muskets, matchlocks, and powder—and, in short, made the best preparations for carrying on an offensive and defensive war, till, at length, having gained a capital and a country bordering on the Sikh territories, I wished to put myself in a capacity, when a favourable opportunity should offer, of attempting the conquest of the Punjaub, and aspired to the honour of planting the British standard on the banks of the Attock ! "

One other act of Thomas's must be mentioned. Very early in his rule he instituted a system of pensions and compensations for his soldiers, and those who were wounded in his service received sufficient for their wants, whilst half of the pay of their rank was granted to the

* Through the kindness of General Sir A. Cunningham the following engraving of a George Thomas rupee has been obtained :—

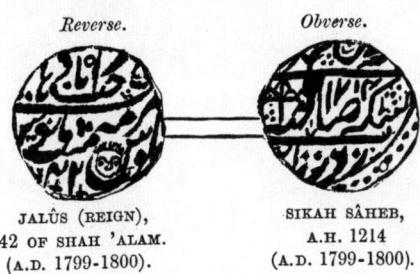

Reverse.   *Obverse.*

JALÛS (REIGN),   SIKAH SÂHEB,
42 OF SHAH 'ALAM.   A.H. 1214
(A.D. 1799-1800).   (A.D. 1799-1800).

General Cunningham writes : —
" I believe this rupee to have been struck by George Thomas.
" The middle line of the obverse reads *Sikah Sâheb*, which is never used for the money of a king. *Saheb Kirân Sani* is used as a title of kings, but always in combination with the name of the king.
" The Hegira date on the obverse is 1214=A.D. 1799-1800.
" The Reign (Jalûs) date on reverse is 42 of Shah 'Alam=A.D. 1799-1800.
" I hope this coin may be proved to belong to George Thomas. The date is correct. The beginning of the name of *Hánsi* is at the left hand of the top line of the Reverse. The mint city of the kings was *Hisâr ;* but *Hánsi* was a very famous fortress which resisted the arms of the early *Ghazni* kings, and was accordingly known as the ' Maiden Fortress.' "
An additional interest is attached to this engraving, from the fact that the coin it is copied from is probably unique.

widows and children of men killed in action.   These liberal provisions
absorbed a sum of Rs.50,000 a year, which was more than a tenth of
Thomas's entire revenue—a proportion far in excess of that allotted to
such philanthropical purposes, even in the most civilised countries.

It is a pleasant page in his chequered career to dwell upon.   And
so let the chapter close on George Thomas, emancipated from his lust
of battle, and settling down for a brief space in his erratic life to
cultivate the paths of peace and improvement, and patronise the rude
arts of those rude days.

CHAPTER IV.

THE JAIPUR CAMPAIGN.

1799.

BY the time Thomas had established himself at Hariána, and outlined a system of administration, his exchequer was exhausted, and he was called upon to solve the problem of finance. When he had money at his command he was a lavish paymaster, and in cantonments spoilt his men with kindness, often in his improvidence expending his last rupee on them with cheerful recklessness. At this particular time he had extremely heavy calls on his resources, for he was preparing for the great project which had become the central idea of his mind and his ambition. This was the conquest of the Panjab, or, as he expressed it, the planting of the British standard on the banks of the Attock river. With this object in view, he commenced casting cannon, manufacturing small arms, and purchasing warlike stores and material, and these expenses soon brought him to the end of his means. Whereupon he took stock of his position to see if he was properly prepared for the great undertaking he aspired to carry through; but on a review of his troops his force appeared insufficient. He therefore decided on what he pleasantly terms an " excursion " into Jaipur territory, which place, he gratefully adds, "had hitherto afforded a never-failing supply to his necessities, and whose ruler was, in consequence, become his bitter enemy."

It happened just about this time that the Rájah of Jaipur was in arrears with the payment of his tribute to the Maráthás, and Váman Ráo was ordered to invade his country and collect what sums he could. Of the amount so realised he was authorised to retain ten-sixteenths to pay himself for his trouble and exertion, and the balance was to be remitted to the Maráthá treasury.

For the delicate detail of accounts, and especially for crediting himself with a bigger ten-sixteenths than so exact a science as mathematics legitimately allows, Váman Ráo was most admirably qualified. But the coarse and brutal preliminary of invading Jaipur territory and by force of arms coercing a nation of warriors into paying tribute was quite out of his line. Partáb Sing's army consisted of 30,000 cavalry and 18,000 infantry, with a numerous and well-appointed artillery. The order to compel the lord of so many legions to pay up tribute quite staggered the little quill-driving, copper-counting chief, and he immediately wrote pressing letters to Thomas urging him to assist in the proposed expedition. Thomas, however, possessed with the delirium of Panjab conquest, was unwilling to enter into a campaign which he knew must prove an extended one, preferring the small but quick profits of rapid raids, and partly from this reason, partly from prudential motives, declined the invitation. He foresaw that to put into the field a body of troops sufficient for an invasion like the one proposed could only be accomplished with a full treasury, whereas his was as dry as the sands of his own deserts. This he explained to Váman Ráo, but the chief had become fascinated with the commission and was not to be denied. It seemed to him that if Thomas could be prevailed upon to do the fighting, he himself could cope with the accounts, and as this promised substantial pecuniary results (Jaipur being rich in resources of every kind) he pressed his proposals home, and finally sent a Vakil to Thomas with the offer of a sum of money down. This argument was irresistible, and Thomas consented to accompany the chief on his expedition.

The Hariána force at this time consisted of three battalions of 400 men each, 300 Rohilla irregulars, 200 Hariána irregulars, 90 cavalry, and 14 pieces of artillery—in all nearly 2,000 men. Váman Ráo's troops numbered one battalion of infantry, 600 irregulars, 900 cavalry, and four guns; so that the combined forces amounted to about 4,000 strong. Having effected a junction, the march for Jaipur territory was commenced early in 1799.

On entering the country a detachment of the Rájah's troops, stationed on the frontier to collect revenue, retreated, and the headman of the district sent a Vakil into Thomas's camp and agreed to pay two lakhs of rupees as tribute. This offer was accepted, and the march being resumed several other chiefs were compelled to submit, and for a month the invaders continued their progress without opposition, their mere presence sufficing to enforce their demands.

But meanwhile Partáb Sing had not been idle. Having collected his troops, he now marched to the relief of his northern districts, wherein Thomas and Váman Ráo were disporting themselves, with a resolution to punish them and give battle whenever he met them. Nearly the whole of the Jaipur mercenary and feudal troops were assembled in this army, which amounted to not less than 40,000 fighting men.

Buoyed up by a false sense of security begotten of their unopposed progress, Thomas and Váman Ráo had pushed on too far, and suddenly discovered they were cut off in the middle of a hostile country without any source of supply or base of operations to fall back upon—a disregard of military caution which involved their small flying column in a very hazardous position. In this dilemma Váman Ráo counselled retreat, deeming it impossible to encounter so large a force as that threatening them, and which was, moreover, composed chiefly of Rajputs, whose bravery was traditional. In combatting these arguments and frustrating so pusillanimous a design, Thomas remonstrated strongly against a retrograde movement, and reminded Váman Ráo that he had in the first instance insisted on undertaking the expedition, and that there existed no cause to prevent at least one trial of strength with the enemy, the troops being faithful and eager to engage. As for a retreat, without an exertion on their part, "This," Thomas declared, "would be a dishonour to myself and my progenitors, who never turned their backs on an enemy." But the argument which finally prevailed with the chief was the warning that he could never again expect to be employed by Sindhia, or any other chief under his authority, if he retreated now without striking a blow. In the end, Váman Ráo agreed to risk an engagement, and with this determination marched to Fatehpur, a prosperous and important town in the Shekhawati district, where there was a prospect of finding a supply of grain sufficient for the troops, and securing a strong defensive position.

Early information of Thomas's approach was conveyed to the inhabitants of this place, who, as a preliminary measure of resistance, filled up all the wells in the surrounding country, and thus rendered it waterless in the direction from which the invaders were advancing. Unaware of this, Thomas pushed on, only to discover, when it was too late to rectify his mistake, the serious danger to which his force was exposed. For on the last day he was obliged to make a forced march of twenty-five miles over deep sand, through which, as the long, hot afternoon wore on, his jaded troops could scarcely plough their way, their feet sinking ankle-deep into the yielding surface. When at length the walls of Fatehpur loomed in sight, the town was found fully prepared to resist, and the last well outside its gates was just being filled up by a body of 400 men, who had been detached for the task.

The capture of this solitary water supply now became an object of supreme importance, as Thomas at once realised. It was no time for hesitation, and without further ado he collected his little band of regular cavalry, who needed no stimulus beyond the cravings of their own unendurable thirst, and charged the force defending the well. The skirmish was at first obstinate, but two of the enemy's officers being killed, their men fell back, and the well was happily preserved. It was a narrow escape from a great disaster, for if the comparatively unfatigued cavalry had failed in their attack, the exhausted infantry, who had toiled on foot during the whole of a day, "the service of which was uncommonly severe," could not have retrieved defeat, and Thomas's army must either have been annihilated in an unequal fight, or in an almost impossible retreat have perished from thirst and fatigue.

The camp was now pitched, and the troops obtained the rest and refreshment needed, and by morning were ready for work again. But the city being full of people, Thomas desired to treat for its surrender, in order to save the effusion of blood which must necessarily ensue from an assault. He therefore suggested the payment of a ransom, but no sooner was the word "negotiation" whispered than Váman Ráo came to the front, and demanded ten lakhs of rupees. The townspeople, being encouraged to hold out by the hope of receiving assistance from the Rájah of Jaipur, who was rapidly advancing to their relief, responded by offering to pay one lakh, and nothing definite was arrived at when night put a stop to the negotiations. Whereupon Thomas, who disbelieved in the policy of procrastination, formed his troops, and stormed and captured the place the next morning.

This was scarcely effected than intelligence of Partáb Singh's approach was announced. Thomas, in consequence, decided to fortify his camp, which he did in the following ingenious way. There grew in the neighbourhood an abundance of a species of wild thorn-tree common to that part of India, and he caused a large number of these to be cut down and piled one upon another in the front and flanks of the camp, with their branches closely interwoven. Being strengthened and secured with ropes, they formed an almost impenetrable *chevaux de frise*, the weight and solidity of which were increased by a large quantity of sand thrown between the branches and piled up over their butts. It was not practicable to dig trenches, as the soil was too loose, but the abattis, or breastwork, described was found ample both to ward off the charge of the enemy's horse, and to protect the camp generally. Some of the wells in the vicinity having by this time been cleared out and opened afresh for use, batteries were erected for their defence. In the immediate rear of the camp stood the town of Fatehpur, which was fortified in the best manner the shortness of the time admitted. Nor did Thomas neglect the precaution of collecting a large supply of provisions and grain, and by the time he had completed these preparations the vanguard of the Jaipur army appeared in sight.

Partáb Singh encamped at a distance of six miles, and then pushed forward a strong detachment of cavalry and infantry to clear the wells in his front. He was allowed to do so for two days without interruption, whilst Thomas further secured his position; but on the second night the latter marched out to attack the enemy's main park of artillery with two battalions of infantry each 400 strong, 8 guns, and his 90 regular cavalry, whilst he detached his third battalion to disperse the advance party engaged in clearing out the wells. He had kept his intentions hidden from Váman Ráo, whose troops were, in point of fact, asleep when Thomas left camp. The reason for this secrecy was the knowledge that if he acquainted the Maráthás with his scheme the enemy would certainly hear of it; for Váman Ráo's countrymen were quite unable to hold their own counsel, and the gossip of their camps always reached the ears of the enemy. So Thomas contented himself with leaving a letter for the chief, explaining his plan of action, and requesting him to follow with his cavalry in the morning, and leave his infantry to guard the camp.

Unfortunately, soon after Thomas started an accident happened to one of his tumbrels, and occasioned such delay, that dawn began to break before the mishap was repaired. This rendered it impossible to carry out his original design of a surprise, for, to Thomas's mortification on arriving within sight of the Jaipur main camp, he perceived the enemy assembled under arms and ready to meet him. He therefore diverted his attack and advanced against the party at the wells, which numbered about 7,000 men. These received him with a show of resistance, but the spirit and vigour with which he made his attack soon obliged them to fall back upon their main body, after sustaining considerable loss. Having obtained possession of the wells, which they had cleared out, Thomas filled them up again, and after capturing several horses and many head of cattle, returned to camp. On his way back he met the Maráthá cavalry, who seemed much out of humour at not having been consulted on so important an occasion, but Váman Ráo rebuked them,

telling them plainly that their delay in preparing for action and following Thomas was the real cause of their having missed sharing in
the victory. Thomas and his officers received *khiluts* from the chief,
and to prevent animosities and jealousies similar marks of honour
were bestowed, though with reluctance, on the commanders of the
Maráthá cavalry.

Thomas now determined to force on a general engagement, but
found his intention anticipated by the enemy, who, at daybreak the
next morning sallied out in order of battle. In returning to his
encampment on the previous day he had prudently reconnoitred the
ground, and determined in his own mind the spot on which he would
engage. Towards this he now made his way; but aware that no
reliance could be placed upon the Maráthás, he left a battalion of his
infantry and four six-pounder guns to defend the camp and protect
his rear, which would otherwise have been open to attack by the
enemy. The force with him consisted of 800 regular infantry, 200
Rohillas, 90 cavalry, and 10 pieces of artillery. Váman Ráo's Maráthá
cavalry accompanied him at the start, but no sooner did they see the
immense host with which they had to contend than they gave themselves up for lost, and left Thomas to fight the battle alone, nor once
during the whole day did they afford him any assistance.

After some manœuvring on either side Thomas was glad to find the
Rajput forces voluntarily distributing themselves in a manner conformable with his plan of battle. Their right wing, consisting of the
feudal cavalry, was directed against his camp, and so certain were
they of victory that on catching sight of the defences which had been
built up, they laughed at the idea of "a few bushes," as they contemptuously termed them, retarding their progress, or resisting the
impetuosity of their attack. The left wing, consisting of 4,000
Rohillas, 3,000 Ghussains, and 6,000 irregular infantry, commanded
by the chiefs of their respective districts, advanced at the same time
with hasty strides and loud shouts to take possession of the city, the
loss of which would have been attended with the most serious consequences. The main body, or centre of the enemy, was composed of
10 battalions of infantry, 22 pieces of artillery, and the body-guard of
the Rájah, the latter numbering 1,600 chosen men, armed with
matchlocks and sabres. This division was commanded in person by
Rájah Roraji Khavis, the generalissimo of the Jaipur forces.

It was fortunate for Thomas that he had chosen such a strong
position, for this alone enabled him to sustain the unequal combat.
No sooner did the Maráthás, who were posted in the rear, observe
the Rajput cavalry advancing against them in close and compact

order, than they sent urgent entreaties to Thomas for reinforcements. Although it was imprudent to spare them, he ordered four companies from the battalion which had been left for the protection of the camp to march out and strengthen the troops in the field, whilst with five companies and three guns he advanced to repel the attack of the Rájah's body-guard, leaving his main body under the command of an Englishman named John Morris, who, though a brave man, was better adapted to conduct a forlorn hope than direct the movement of troops on the field of battle. Thomas, by a skilful manœuvre, obtained possession of a high sand bank, whereby the enemy were placed between two fires, and could neither charge him nor attack the camp without exposing their rear to danger. Whereupon they began to draw off, sullenly and slowly, but presently, perceiving the weakness of his small squadron of regular cavalry, made a sudden and furious charge upon the little body of ninety mounted men, killing the commander and several of the troopers. Thomas instantly advanced two companies of grenadiers to their assistance, and these brave fellows, after giving a single volley, charged the great body of cavalry with their bayonets, and compelled them to retreat, thereby affording the extraordinary illustration of infantry attacking and routing a mounted force.

During this time the enemy's left wing had advanced and made an assault upon the city, from which they were driven back by the troops Thomas had posted for its defence. These consisted of his Hariána infantry and 100 Rohillas, who, having occupied the highest and strongest of the houses, were able to maintain themselves against all attacks except those of artillery. Of this circumstance the enemy now became aware, and summoning reinforcements of six pieces of cannon to their aid, returned to the assault. Whereupon Thomas, having beaten off the cavalry, proceeded to the relief of the garrison defending the town, and attacked the enemy's left flank so vigorously that he compelled them to limber up their artillery and retire again. By this time their main body had become a confused mass, without regularity or method, having been in turn disordered by the retreat of the right and left wings, which Thomas had defeated one after another. But notwithstanding this Roraji determined to risk the final issue of the day in a general charge. The ardour of his troops, however, proved unequal to the call, and Thomas, perceiving them wavering, opened a heavy artillery fire of grape shot upon them, before which they precipitately retreated. He now desired to pursue them with those of his companies which had suffered least during the fight, but unfortunately the bullocks attached to his artillery had been stationed for protection behind a sandbank some distance in the rear, and could not be brought up quickly enough. On perceiving this, the Maráthá cavalry, who all through the action had stood aloof, galloped up and offered their services, and Thomas, having procured a sufficient number of bullocks for one gun, advanced with that and a battalion of infantry, whilst the Marátha horse made a great show of accompanying him.

The enemy were now retiring in all directions, and Thomas first turned his attention to a pair of 24-pounder guns which they had abandoned, and directed them to be taken to the rear. But at this moment a large body of Rajput cavalry, under the chief of Chúmu, rallied, and fired with a determination to redeem their honour and recapture the lost guns, formed a *gól*, or dense band of feudal chivalry, and charged down on Thomas. Whereupon his cowardly Marátha allies, without waiting to sustain a single impact, turned and fled. Thomas immediately drew up his infantry as well as the shortness of the time admitted, but before the line was completely formed the panic-stricken cavalry, reckless of where they were riding, dashed through his left wing, closely followed by the Rajputs, who began to cut down a great number of his men. These gallant fellows made a heroic resistance, many of them, even in the agonies of death, seizing hold of the bridles of the enemies' horses, in their attempts to impede their progress. The moment was critical, and it seemed as if the battalion must be exterminated. But Thomas, ever resourceful and undaunted, loaded his single gun up the very muzzle, and with about 150 of his men, who bravely resolved to conquer or die with him, awaited the event with fortitude. After permitting the enemy to approach to within forty yards, the order was given to fire, and simultaneously with the discharge of the 6-pounder, the men delivered a volley of musketry with such cool precision and effect, that great numbers of the enemy were killed or wounded. Twice, before they could recover themselves, did Thomas's little force reload and fire, and after their third discharge the Rajputs turned and fled, bearing away with them the chief of Chúmu, sorely wounded, from the field.

Meanwhile the Marátha cavalry, who had been the chief cause of this disaster, were flying helter-skelter towards the camp. But here, by Thomas's orders, previously conveyed, they were refused admittance, and in consequence fell into the hands of a small party of the Rajputs, who had followed in their rear, and put many of them to death without mercy.

The enemy's infantry, when they saw the success which had at first attended the charge of the chief of Chúmu, seemed disposed to return to the contest, and Thomas, collecting the remains of his gallant battalion, prepared to receive them. But by this time the day was drawing to a close, and the exhibition o᛫ his dogged resolution convinced Roraji that it was best to retire ; and so he drew off, leaving Thomas to return to his fortified camp with the remnants of his force. The casualties during the day on Thomas's side amounted to 300 men, or 25 per cent. of his troops actually engaged in the open. Amongst the wounded was the gallant John Morris. The enemy lost 2,000 men, and were compelled to abandon a vast number of horses and other valuable effects.

Thus ended the battle of Fatehpur, in which Thomas, with less than 2,000 men, successfully defended a large city, and an extensive fortified camp, and defeated in the open field an army of 40,000 men well supplied with artillery. In reviewing this achievement there are many points to admire : the engineering skill with which he protected his encampment; the ability with which he defended a hostile town with a mere handful of irregular soldiery; his strategy in occupying the advantageous position from which he gave battle ; his generalship in dividing the enemy and defeating them in detail ; the marvellous resolution with which he retrieved disaster; and the courage and vigour he displayed at all times throughout the day. When the overwhelming numerical superiority opposed to him is considered, and the ever-present consciousness of danger which he laboured under from the cowardly and untrustworthy conduct of his allies, we must accord to him the merit of having won a very remarkable victory by the display of the highest qualities of a soldier and a general.

On the following morning Thomas notified to Roraji that he might send proper persons to bury the dead, and carry away the wounded without interruption on his part. This civility was received with attention, and presently a request came to treat for peace. At the prospect of renewed negotiation, Váman Ráo, whose name, it will be noted, does not appear once in the description of the battle, came forward again, and took the conduct of it into his own hands. As a preliminary stipulation he insisted on a heavy payment to indemnify him for the loss he had sustained, but Roraji objected, saying he was not authorised by Partáb Sing to disburse so large a sum without express orders. On receiving this answer Thomas suspected that the enemy only desired time to procure reinforcements, and urged Váman Ráo to renew the attack. Although the Marátha chief was averse to this proposal, fearing the risk of another engagement, and overruled Thomas's advice, in the end the negotiations were broken off, and the enemy, having collected the scattered remains of their forces, took post on their former ground. A resumption of hostilities was now imminent, but at this juncture orders came from Daulat Ráo Sindhia for Váman Ráo to discontinue the war, and others of similar import from General Perron, who had recently been invested with the government of Hindustan.

And now the enemy of their own accord offered to pay the sum of Rs.50,000, but this was most unaccountably rejected by Váman Ráo, who soon had cause to repent his folly, for during the recent negotiations considerable reinforcements had arrived in the Jaipur camp, and, despite Sindhia's instructions, hostilities were recommenced with redoubled vigour on both sides.

Soon Thomas's troops began to suffer great inconvenience from the scarcity of forage, which they were obliged to collect from a distance of twenty miles, and were sorely harassed by detached parties of the enemy when bringing it into camp. To add to their difficulties the Rájah of Bikanir arrived with reinforcements of 5,000 men for the Jaipur army. The Maráthás in Thomas's camp were useless, except to plunder and destroy the unresisting peasantry, and he had only his own decimated troops on which to rely. In this situation, and forage continuing to decrease, a council of war was called, and it was unanimously agreed to attempt a retreat to their own country.

In accordance with which resolution camp was struck, and before daybreak the next morning the troops began to file off. But scarcely were they in motion than the enemy advanced to the attack in great force. While it continued dark confusion prevailed everywhere, none being able to distinguish foes from friends, but on the appearance of daylight Thomas collected his men, and forming them into proper line of battle, compelled the enemy to sheer off. The march was then resumed, but the Rajputs continued to hang on his rear, annoying it with the fire of artillery and an immense quantity of rockets. He pushed on, however, at a rapid rate, and soon left their heavy guns behind, the rocket and matchlock men alone continuing the pursuit.

The day was intensely hot, and the disheartened troops suffered severely from want of water. The fiery desert wind blew over the sandy plain in furnace breaths, whilst on the horizon a delusive mirage dazzled and glittered, presenting alluring pictures of green islands floating amidst lakes of cool water, which faded away or receded, even as they appeared to be within reach. The tramp of shuffling feet over the loose sand churned up clouds of impalpable dust, which aggravated the thirst and discomfort the column suffered. Fortunately these trials operated as much against the pursuers as the pursued. For fifteen weary hours Thomas's little army fought its desperate way, with certain death behind it, and in front an uncertainty of relief almost as terrible. "The service was severe," writes Thomas, in his brief, soldierly language, "and in the highest degree fatiguing. At length, after a toilsome march, we arrived in the evening at a village where we fortunately met with two wells containing plenty of excellent water."

So great was the rush to these that two men were precipitated into them, one of whom was drowned, and the other rescued with the greatest difficulty. After this an armed force was stationed to protect the approaches till, by degrees, most of the troops received a small supply, the confusion ceased, and order was restored.

The enemy had meanwhile encamped three miles in the rear, and Thomas made up his mind to attack them on the following day. But when morning broke he plainly realised that his men had lost their accustomed bearing, and were too dispirited for fighting. All he could do was to continue the retreat. Before long many began to succumb to exhaustion, for the march was accompanied by circumstances fully as distressing as those of the previous day. The enemy, encouraged by their advantage, frequently appeared inclined to charge, and Thomas was forced to keep up a constant fire from his artillery in the rear. So disheartened were his men that, in order to encourage them, he dismounted from his horse and marched on foot at their head during the whole of the day.

This is a characteristic incident, and displays at their best those personal qualities which made Thomas so greatly beloved by those who followed his fortunes. A native general in retreat either spurred away on a fleet horse, or was carried along on the fastest elephant, regardless of everything except his own safety or comfort. Not so with this fighting Irishman, who in his career never proved false to a friend, or deserted a dependent in distress or danger. He shared with his soldiers their perils and their privations, as well as their victories, and never asked them to undertake a task he was not ready to join in, or a risk he was not prepared to undergo.

There is the material for a fine picture in this retreat from Fatehpur. At the head of his dispirited army marches Thomas with lifted head and determined stride. Behind him plods the long straggling column of soldiery, the men turning their eyes first to the illimitable waste of desert around, and then to their indomitable leader, who holds his steadfast compass course, and in whom all their hopes are centred. The jaded cattle drag the guns slowly and toilfully through the deep sand. Anon a halt is called, a gun unlimbered, and a few defiant shots fired at the enemy. Like minute guns the dull reports die away after each discharge, and the heavy smoke hangs sullenly in the still air. Then the order is given to limber up again, and once more assuming his position at the head of the column, the tall, fierce Irishman leads the way into the desolate expanse ahead.

Towards sunset a large town was reached, where the distressed troops were gratified by the sight of five wells of water, and were able to assuage their thirst, while the enemy, who had by this time outmarched their enthusiasm, gave up the pursuit, and returned to Fatehpur.

Thomas was now able to direct his attention to the condition of his men. The locality was a favourable one for a halt, and he determined to camp here till they were recovered from their recent fatigues. The sick and wounded were conducted to a place of safety, and properly cared for. Supplies and water being in abundance, all fared well, and a few days' rest made a wonderful change. Before a week had passed, with bodies fortified and spirits revived, and, above all, with an increased faith in the *ikbál*, or good fortune, of their commander, Thomas's battalions were ready for a renewal of active operations.

He desired nothing better, for fighting was his second nature. Hostilities were recommenced in the enemy's country, and by a succession of exactions and fines, sufficient money obtained to defray the expenses of the expedition, and satisfy the arrears of pay due to the troops. Before long the Rájah of Jaipur, sensible of the injury his territory would sustain by a prolongation of these depredations, sent persons to sue for peace, and the evacuation of his territory, and Váman Ráo, having been reduced to a more moderate frame of mind, accepted the terms now offered, and peace was declared.

Thomas was now free to return to Hariána, but instead of doing this he determined to retaliate on the Rájah of Bikanir, and punish him for the assistance he had recently afforded to the Jaipur prince. Súrut Singh, the ruler of Bikanir, kept up a very respectable army of mercenaries and feudal levies, the whole amounting to 8,000 men, two-fifths of whom were cavalry, and the remainder infantry and artillery. There were several European officers in his service, who resided in the fort of Bikanir, and disciplined his troops. The country was a dry and waterless one, the approach to which must be attended with privations similar to those Thomas had recently experienced. Profiting by the past, he took measures to protect himself against a recurrence of misfortunes by preparing a number of water bags, made of skins, for the use of his army, whereby he overcame the difficulty of traversing waterless deserts.

Súrut Singh, on receiving intimation of the intended invasion, prepared to repel it, but being weak in artillery, and knowing he could not stand against Thomas in the plain, confined his defence to strongly garrisoning his frontier towns, hoping to tire the invaders out with repeated attacks on entrenched positions and fortified strongholds. But assaults of this description never came amiss to Thomas. The first he made was upon the village of Jeitpur, which was about seven marches north-east of the Rájah's capital, and defended by 3,000 men. Resolving on an immediate storm, Thomas carried it with a loss of 200 men, and exacted a heavy ransom before consenting to spare the lives and property of the inhabitants. This example of his methods of warfare was sufficient to intimidate the country round. Hereafter he met with but little serious opposition, for the Rájah's troops deserted in great numbers, and only a few Rajputs remained faithful to his cause.

Under circumstances so unfavourable Súrut Singh despatched a Vakil to Thomas's camp to sue for peace, agreeing to pay an indemnity of two lakhs of rupees, half of which was to be delivered on the spot, and for the remainder bills given upon certain wealthy bankers of Jaipur. These terms Thomas accepted, and commenced his return to Hánsi; but when, a short time afterwards, he presented the drafts for encashment, they were dishonoured. He contented himself with a protest at the time, but in his soul he determined that when occasion offered he would severely punish these reprehensible frauds upon his confiding nature.

CHAPTER V.

1799–1800.

IT was early in the summer of 1799 that Thomas returned to Hánsi from the Jaipur and Bikanir campaigns, and about this time Lakwa Dáda, the Marátha commander-in-chief, being suspected of sympathy with the rebellion of the Bhais, fell into disgrace with Daulat Ráo Sindhia, and was superseded by another chief named Ambaji Inglia. Lakwa's downfall suggested to Thomas the feasibility of regaining possession of the districts which had been sequestrated from Appa Khandi Ráo, and these he now occupied, intending to present them to Váman Ráo. But Ambaji and General Perron, hearing of this action, requested Thomas to withdraw; and he, after consulting with Váman Ráo, who advised compliance, consented to do so. In recompense for this the Marátha government gave Thomas the district of Badhli, which he added to his other possessions.

By this time Thomas had become a confirmed filibuster, whose restless spirit could not endure peace, or brook inaction. Rather than remain idle, he now turned his attention to the Sikh states on his northern frontier, and marched against Jhind, a town belonging to a chief named Bágh Singh, who had evinced hostility to Thomas from the first moment of his establishing himself at Hariána.

Following his usual tactics, Thomas made a sudden march, and attempted to storm Jhind by surprise. But he had underrated its strength, and, after a stubborn conflict, found himself driven back with a loss of 400 men. The defeat was as serious as it was unexpected; but Thomas was undismayed, and instead of retreating, he fortified his camp and settled down to blockade the place, in the hopes of compelling the garrison of 3,000 men to surrender.

Adjacent to Jhind lay the territories of Sahib Singh, the Sikh chief of Patiála. He was himself an indolent, weak-minded man, but possessed a sister named Kunúr, a woman of masculine and intrepid spirit, and she now marched at the head of a large force to the relief of the besieged town. On the way she was joined by an individual, who, according to Thomas's etymology, rejoiced in the name of Bugheel Sing, and several other Sikh chiefs. Directly these arrived within striking distance Thomas attacked them, and compelled them to retire, driving them in panic through their own camp, which being built of straw huts was easily set on fire, and consumed.

After a few days Kunúr rallied the enemy, and returned to the contest with increased numbers, and, by the shameful supineness of two of Thomas's officers, surprised and obtained possession of two of his redoubts, in which many of his best men were cut to pieces. This reverse encouraged the country people, who had hitherto been held in awe, to declare openly against Thomas, and cut off his supplies of provisions, so that he was compelled to raise the seige of Jhind and commence his return to Hánsi. By this time the enemy had increased to 10,000 strong, and directly he began his retreat they followed in his rear, and simultaneously the Chief of Patiála took the field against him, with a large additional force and several pieces of heavy artillery.

A retrograde movement in these countries was always deemed equivalent to a defeat, and the peasantry now rose in a mass to oppose Thomas's progress. In order to allay their increasing hostility he publicly gave out that he was going to Jaipur, hoping thereby to induce them to relinquish the pursuit. But they were not to be imposed upon by this ruse, and hovered on his rear and flanks, repeatedly attacking him, and as often being repulsed. By a forced march the Sikhs managed to get between him and Hánsi, and encamped at a place called Narnaund, with the intention of stopping his way. In this crisis, Thomas, with his usual defiance, resolved on assuming the offensive again, and suddenly ordering a night march, arrived by daybreak before the enemy's camp. Instantly attacking them, he inflicted a severe defeat. Their tents, baggage, the howdahs of their elephants, their bazaar, 1,000 saddles and 200 horses fell into his hands, and had it not been for his troops getting out of control and dispersing for plunder, he would have captured their artillery and elephants as well.

The Sikhs fled to Jhind, but on their arrival there were refused admittance by Sahib Singh's sister, who taunted them for their cowardice, and offered to take the field in person herself, to show them how to fight. Ashamed in being exceeded in spirit by a woman, they returned to attack Thomas, whom they found encamped near a large town, where he had left his heavy baggage. Their resolution now was to conquer or perish ; but whilst deliberating overnight on the tactics they should employ, their camp was unexpectedly attacked by a numerous and daring banditti, who sounded their trumpets with such loud alarms, that the Sikhs thought it was Thomas himself, and abandoned the place with great precipitation.

Their panic was so ludicrous and humiliating that it lost for them the reputation for prowess they had previously enjoyed. They were now as desirous of peace as they had before been impatient for war, and made overtures which resulted in an accommodation being arrived at, by which each side remained in possession of the districts they held before the siege of Jhind. This treaty satisfied everybody except the Rájah of Patiála, who refused to ratify it, although his spirited sister did so, in spite of his remonstrances. Whereupon he displayed his resentment by seizing her person and placing her in confinement ; but Thomas, on hearing of this, deemed it his duty to interfere, and by threats compelled the release of the brave lady.

Thus ended Thomas's first offensive campaign against the Sikhs. Begun impetuously, at one time it nearly found a premature end in defeat ; but his own right hand retrieved reverse, and turned disaster into victory. Although the war led to no substantial results, it illustrated Thomas's qualities in danger, and the amazing vigour with which he could turn upon an exultant and victorious foe, and scatter them in flight at the very moment when they believed they had him in their power.

Shortly after his return to Hánsi Thomas received a proposal of temporary employment from Ambaji Inglia, who offered him a subsidy of Rs.50,000 a month, to assist in driving Lakwa Dáda out of the province of Méwar. Having no particular war on hand, Thomas accepted Ambaji's offer, and prepared to lead his army against the revolted chief, who had assembled a great force and taken the field in the vicinity of Udáipur.

This expedition was a more extended one than any Thomas had hitherto undertaken, and during his march southwards a mutiny broke out amongst his troops, occasioned by a delay in the payment of their arrears. To excuse their unmilitary conduct they explained, that as they were proceeding to the Deccan, their families would suffer great hardships by their long absence, and they therefore expected extra pay. Although there appeared some reason in their demand, Thomas considered that to yield compliance would form a dangerous precedent, and resolved to resist. Whereupon the mutineers grew outrageous, and plotted to seize and confine him ; but this he evaded by encamping apart from them with the soldiers who were still faithful. He then called in a body of cavalry to his assistance, upon which the mutineers advanced to attack him. Determined to repress their insolence at all hazards, he mounted his horse and rode out to meet them ; several shots were fired, but none struck him, and seizing the leaders he instantly caused one to be blown from the mouth of a cannon. Whereupon the remainder, perceiving the fate of their comrades, returned to their duty.

When nearing Udáipur, information was received that Sindhia had pardoned Lakwa Dáda, so that there no longer existed any necessity for a campaign. But Thomas, who only consulted the interest of Ambaji Inglia, in whose personal service he was now engaged, and from whom he had received positive orders to fight Lakwa wherever he came up with him, did not think himself at liberty to desist, and continued his march, and being presently joined by General Perron's Second Brigade under Colonel Sutherland, the united forces advanced against the rebel. The latter was encamped near a pass leading to Udáipur, which was so narrow that it only admitted of the passage of a single gun at a time, and here, safe in the knowledge that the Rána of Udáipur was favourably inclined towards him, he had taken up an exceedingly strong position.

A plan of attack was now concerted between the two commanders, and the following morning fixed for carrying it into execution. But during that night Colonel Sutherland, without assigning any cause, and to Thomas's utter astonishment, struck camp and marched away, leaving to the latter the sole conduct of the operations against Lakwa Dáda.

Colonel Sutherland's withdrawal inspired the rebel chief with confidence, and he became haughty and unreasonable in proportion to the improvement in the aspect of his affairs, sending letters to various chiefs in the district, summoning them to join him. But Thomas had no intention of waiting for them to do so, and three days later, leaving Ambaji with his troops to protect the baggage, advanced against Lakwa in order of battle. The action was however, prevented by the bursting of a tremendous storm of rain, thunder, and lightning, which compelled a halt. It happened that Thomas had arrived at a position favourable for cavalry to attack, and the enemy being exceedingly strong in that arm, he thought it prudent to change ground, and manœuvred so as to gain possession of an eminence where he would have no such fear. When the storm abated, Lakwa, who had been within sight all this time, advanced with his army, but, losing a number of men during his approach from Thomas's artillery fire, and per-

11

ceiving the full strength of the position to be attacked, he thought it best to retire ; and Thomas, after a severe and fatiguing service, which lasted during the whole of the day, returned to his camp in the evening.

At midnight Lakwa sent Vakils to Thomas with some letters from Sindhia, in which the Prince repeated his commands for the cessation of hostilities on both sides, and nominated Lakwa to the government of all the Maráthá possessions north of the Narbada. In consequence of this, a council of war was called, at which Thomas announced that as he was employed by Ambaji for the express purpose of reducing the province of Méwar to his authority, he could consent to no terms in which the evacuation of that country was not a leading article.

After much discussion, a proposal was made that both armies should march to the northern frontier of the district, and there await fresh orders from Sindhia. Thomas's assent was reluctantly given, as he doubted the sincerity of Lakwa, believing that the chief only desired to gain time in order that he might be reinforced by a body of troops who were marching to join him from Ajmir, which city, with the surrounding territory, belonged to him. The two armies now commenced their journey northwards, but owing to heavy rain, it took them fifteen days to cover the distance to Shahpúra, although it was only seventy-five miles. On arriving there Lakwa Dáda was joined by his Ajmir troops, whom he had been expecting, and now peremptorily refused to evacuate the territory in dispute.

Hostilities were at once resumed by Lakwa taking the offensive. Thomas had prudently pitched his camp on ground surrounded by ravines on all sides, which secured him from the danger of cavalry attacks. A council of war being called, it was decided that Ambaji's army, which was in an exposed position, should shift quarters, and encamp in Thomas's rear so as to be under his protection ; but before this could be accomplished, Lakwa, sensible of his error in not having at first occupied the ground secured by Thomas, advanced to take a redoubt that defended it, near to which one of Ambaji's battalions happened to be cooking their morning meal, the preparation of which had delayed them in falling back into a place of safety. This battalion was charged by Lakwa's cavalry and cut to pieces. Thomas no sooner heard of this than he formed his men and hastened to retrieve the disaster ; but heavy rain again coming on, the ravines were soon swollen with water, which put an end to all hostilities for that day.

The rain continued without intermission for a week, during which no opportunity occurred for a general action, though frequent skirmishes took place. In order to bring these about Thomas constantly changed the colours and uniforms of his men, and by this ruse often succeeded in getting to close quarters with the enemy, and opening a smart cannonade, which caused them considerable loss in men and horses. On one occasion he nearly killed Lakwa himself, but the chief managed to get out of range by the fleetness of his steed.

Intelligence now reached Thomas that General Perron, taking advantage of the undefended state of Jhajjar, had invaded it. This information he was most anxious to keep secret, fearing that a knowledge of it might prejudice his position; but Lakwa had been similarly informed, and, as he was strongly hostile to General Perron, he made Thomas very handsome proposals to join his standard. As Thomas was in the service of Ambaji, who was General Perron's native colleague in both the government of Hindustan and the command of Sindhia's army, this invasion of Jhajjar was a distinctly treacherous act, which might have reasonably served as an excuse for Thomas to desert his allegiance, and accept Lakwa's offer of service. But, with all his lawlessness and aggression, there never breathed a more faithful soldier of fortune than George Thomas, and he rejected the proposals, saying, that although at the termination of the present campaign he might leave Ambaji's service, he could never become an enemy to that chief, nor connect himself with those who were. This answer greatly displeased Lakwa, whose Marátha morality was unable to comprehend the European code of honour, and in open *durbar* he complained of Thomas, declaring him to be a man of the most unaccountable character: for, although he had received repeated orders from Sindhia to cease hostilities, he disobeyed them, and Lakwa could only suppose he was bent upon extirpating the Prince's authority, and establishing his own.

Lakwa now began to try other expedients to rid himself of this pertinacious antagonist, and sent emissaries into Thomas's camp to stir up a mutiny amongst his troops; but these men being discovered, were seized and put into confinement, and there detained during the rest of the campaign, whilst Thomas conciliated his soldiers by an assurance of speedily conducting them back to their own country.

Lakwa's force at the time amounted to 9,000 cavalry, 6,000 regular infantry, 2,000 Rohillas, and 6,000 mercenaries, with 90 pieces of artillery. To oppose this formidable army Thomas could only muster six battalions of infantry, much reduced by desertion and casualties in the field, 300 Rohillas, 150 cavalry, and 22 guns, the whole not numbering more than 2,400 men. The disparity in numbers was enormous; but, in addition to fighting, Thomas was called upon to provide for the safety of Ambaji, guard the camp, procure supplies of forage and provisions, and convoy them into the place.

As soon as the rain abated hostilities were actively resumed, and several actions took place, in most of which Thomas was successful, frequently driving the enemy back to their camp. On one occasion Lakwa escaped total defeat by a very narrow chance. Having formed his whole army into order of battle, he advanced suddenly against Thomas, who at the time had only two battalions with him in the front, and was obliged to fall back, the enemy following close on his rear till he reached the outskirts of his encampment. Here he was reinforced by three other battalions and a supply of ammunition, of which he had nearly run out. Whereupon he faced round, and resolutely meeting his pursuers compelled them to retire quicker than they had advanced. So great was their consternation and confusion that Thomas inflicted the greatest slaughter, and it was only the darkness of night, which had overtaken the combatants, that saved Lakwa from a crushing defeat.

But not long after this there occurred a disaster which led to the termination of the campaign. Between the rival armies flowed a nullah, or stream, the north side of which was occupied by Lakwa, and the south by Thomas and Ambaji. Shortly after the action above described, Ambaji obtained possession of one of the enemy's redoubts on the north side of this nullah, and garrisoned it with three battalions of infantry, 1,000 Ghussains, and six guns. No sooner was this accomplished than heavy rain came on, and continued without intermission for twenty-four hours. This caused two large tanks to overflow, and, breaking their banks, they discharged their contents into the nullah, which soon became so full of water as to be impassable, whereby all communications were cut off with the newly-captured redoubt. Perceiving this Lakwa attacked the post with great vigour, his men advancing to the assault through rushing water, which in places rose up to their necks. Such intrepid conduct struck terror into the garrison, who became panic-stricken, and, except the Ghussains, surrendered without firing a shot. The latter refused to yield, and after a brave, but fruitless resistance, were cut to pieces. This disaster seemed to crush all the spirit out of Ambaji's army, for directly after it his men refused to fight, and began to desert in great numbers. Lakwa, being informed of this, induced the Shahpúra chief, near to whose capital the armies were encamped, and who had hitherto remained neutral, to declare against Thomas, and withhold supplies of grain. Although the latter had provisions sufficient for twenty days' consumption of his own men, Ambaji had not more than enough for three, whilst Thomas himself was short of ammunition, his reserve having been left at Singánah, thirty miles distant. It was imperative to obtain a fresh supply, but he did not think it prudent to risk sending a small detachment for it, and therefore determined to fall back on this base. But he could not bring himself to abandon Ambaji's sick and wounded, of whom there were a large number in camp, and generously advanced money for their transport to a place of safety. During this retreat, although pursued and harrassed by cavalry sent out by Lakwa, he defended himself so successfully that after several futile attempts the enemy drew off, and he completed the remainder of his march unmolested, and brought his whole force safely to Singánah.

His conduct on this occasion appears to have touched a tender chord in Ambaji's breast. The chief had tacitly acquiesced in Perron's recent attack on Thomas's districts, both he and the general supposing at the time that Lakwa had finally evacuated Méwar, and there would be no further occasion for Thomas's services, while the distressed condition of the latter, far away from home, and weakened by a long and arduous campaign, made the opportunity for seizing his country a favourable one. But now that a reverse had been sustained, and Ambaji saved from annihilation by Thomas's faithful adherence to his interests, the chief grew ashamed of his treachery, and began to excuse the recent attacks on Jhajjar, ascribing them to the enmity of General Perron. Thomas, from prudential motives, accepted this disclaimer, and pretended to be satisfied, and shortly afterwards information reached him that the villages occupied had been restored, and so he allowed the matter to drop.

Having supplied his troops with ammunition at Singánah, Thomas returned to the attack on Lakwa, who had meanwhile invested a fort forty-five miles to the north-east of that place. Advancing by slow and easy marches through the districts of a chief named Agaji Merta, Thomas took occasion to punish this individual for his hostility on a late occasion, when he incited the country people to rise against Ambaji. A few days after this he arrived within twelve miles of Lakwa's army, and made dispositions to attack him the next morning, but the chief, deeming himself unequal to the contest, struck camp, abandoned the fort he was endeavouring to reduce, and quitted the boundary in dispute, and by a couple of forced marches reached his own district of Ajmir.

Thomas's commission was now fulfilled : he had driven Lakwa out of Méwar, and this being accomplished he turned his attention towards reimbursing Ambaji for the expenses he had been put to, and entered on the congenial task of levying contributions. Deogarh and Amét, two strong towns, were in turn attacked and forced to purchase their safety, and then Kosital and Lusain were stormed, and heavy ransoms exacted. So successful was the raid that the fines collected amounted to four lakhs of rupees, a sum considerably in excess of the expense incurred by Ambaji, and this handsome harvest would have been increased but for a new development of affairs.

Ambaji, at the commencement of this campaign, had entered into an understanding with General Perron, by which it was mutually agreed that should Sindhia at any time reinstate Lakwa Dáda, who was avowedly hostile to the General, the two should act in concert, and by their combined efforts preserve their respective possessions. A separate stipulation of this treaty was that Ambaji was to retain Méwar. But Perron now began to entertain a jealousy against Ambaji, and entered into a secret understanding with Lakwa, whom he gained over to his own interests. Such, at least, is Thomas's version of current politics; but it seems more probable that Perron, having learnt of Lakwa's restoration to favour, shaped his course accordingly, for not long afterwards the chief was appointed to his former post of commander-in-chief of the Marátha army in Upper India.

The upshot of this intrigue was that letters from Sindhia were now produced, desiring Ambaji to retire from Méwar, and Perron wrote recommending compliance, and threatening in case of refusal to assist Lakwa Dáda by force of arms. Under these circumstances Ambaji ordered Thomas to deliver over the country in dispute and withdraw his troops.

Thomas had no option but to comply, though it touched him to the quick to tamely yield up that which he had won with so much hard fighting. No sooner had he done so than he heard General Perron was marching to Jaipur, and simultaneously Ambaji desired him to proceed to Datia in Bundelkhand, a place 200 miles to the eastward. Thomas was preparing to obey, for he still considered himself bound to Ambaji, when a contrary order arrived, directing him to join the united forces of that chief and Lakwa Dáda, who had exchanged visits of amity. From such contradictory instructions Thomas suspected treachery, and knowing Lakwa was highly incensed against him, declined to place himself in his power, but determined instead to return to Hánsi.

Whereupon Lakwa threw off his mask, and would have sent a force after Thomas, but for his inability to raise funds sufficient for the purpose. Thomas retaliated by levying contributions on the province of Ajmir, through which he directed his return journey, considering himself now in a state of actual hostility with the chief.

His position had by this time become exceedingly precarious. Lakwa's army was only thirty miles to the eastward, and at Jaipur, which lay between him and his destination, General Perron was endeavouring to induce Partáb Singh to cut off his retreat. To add to his cares a grievous disease attacked his troops, who were suffering from the effects of drinking the unwholesome water of the mountainous country of Méwar, and a third of them were stricken with sickness. Fortunately Lakwa's soldiery were in a state of open mutiny, whilst Perron and the Rájah of Jaipur were overawed by the presence of Colonel Collins, the British resident. This officer, towards the end of 1799, arrived at Jaipur to demand the surrender of Wazír Ali, the spurious Nawáb of Oudh, who after occasioning much trouble by his opposition to the English in that country, sought refuge from their anger in Rájputana.

In this state of affairs Thomas, after eluding every attempt to oppose his progress, and successfully levying contributions to the extent of two lakhs of rupees, made good his retreat past Jaipur. Almost his last exploit was the capture of a strong fort named Súrajgarh, belonging to Patáb Singh, from which he exacted a fine of Rs.50,000. After this he prudently accelerated his homeward journey, and arrived at Hánsi towards the end of 1799.

Apart from the question of its morality, this flying campaign was certainly one of the most brilliant and dashing that Thomas ever executed. In less than five months he had led his little force a distance of nearly 1,000 miles, had fought a succession of battles, had obliged Lakwa Dáda to evacuate Méwar, and had finally marched his victorious troops safely home through a hostile country, from which, even as he retreated, he extorted several heavy fines. The districts he had traversed were either dry and waterless deserts, or difficult and pathless ranges of hills, and the elements had been against him during the greater part of the campaign. Yet such was the vitality and mobility of his force that he successfully overcame all these obstacles, and carried his men triumphantly back to the point from whence they started.

Thomas was now inclined to allow his troops some repose after their late exertions, but an excuse for fighting presenting itself, he could not resist the temptation of taking the field again. It occurred to him to make an incursion into the Sutlej states, and punish Sahib Singh of Patiála, who had maltreated his sister for entering into negotiations with Thomas in the previous year. Moreover, during Thomas's absence in Méwar, the chief had committed depredations in Hariána, and this was a crime that could not be overlooked. So preparations were made to chastise him, when, at the last moment, he agreed to surrender certain villages, and pay an indemnity for the damage he had done, and thus avoid hostilities.

But raid and foray had become essential to Thomas, who found it impossible to remain inactive and at peace. He and his men were prepared to fight, and were not to be baulked of their design by the pusillanimity of Sahib Singh. A pretext for another expedition was afforded by the remembrance of the dishonoured bills which Thomas had received from the Rájah of Bikanir, and he forthwith determined on an invasion of Súrut Singh's country.

This prince had recently obtained an advantage over his neighbours, the Bhattis, an extraordinary race of people inhabiting a jungle tract of country to the north-west of Hánsi. When Thomas reached the frontiers of Bikanir the Bhattis, hearing of his intended expedition, offered him Rs.40,000 to capture and deliver over to them a strong fort which Súrut Singh had erected nine miles south-west of their capital of Batinda, whereby they were much incommoded and menaced. Thomas cheerfully accepted the commission, and, altering his route, soon reached the city of Batnér, which in the geographical light of these times was regarded as the most western habitation in that part of India.

The fort which the Rájah of Bikanir had erected was garrisoned by a large force of infantry and cavalry, and, from its natural position, was almost inaccessible to an enemy, there being no water obtainable within a circuit of twelve miles. But Thomas had prepared himself for a desert campaign, and, bringing up his artillery with him, battered a breach in the walls almost before the garrison realised he was attacking them. He soon made the necessary preparations for storming the place, when the enemy capitulated on being permitted to march out with the honours of war, and Thomas put the Bhattis in possession of the fort, and received from them the stipulated reward of Rs.40,000.

He now continued his march towards Bikanir, storming and capturing several places, and fighting various skirmishes. In these his losses were heavy, which, added to sickness consequent upon the unhealthiness of the climate, reduced his fighting strength to one-third of its original number, and compelled him to suspend his advance and fortify his camp for defence. Many attempts were made by the enemy to carry his entrenchments, but his vigilance and energy foiled all, and the health of his force improving, he presently struck camp and returned towards his own country. On his way he came across a town called Futehbad, which he burnt, and would in all probability have taken possession of the adjacent country, and added it on to Hariána, which it adjoined, had not the enemy received assistance from the Rájah of Patiála, who, deeming the present moment a favourable one to work his revenge for past injuries, sent a contingent of 1000 cavalry to act against Thomas. The latter, not feeling strong enough to prosecute hostilities, returned to Jhajjar, where he allowed his people to recuperate after the distempers they had contracted during the campaign, and recruited his battalions to their full strength.

This was in March 1800, about which time Lakwa Dáda, through the intrigues of Perron at Sindhia's durbar, had been again superseded in his command. To hasten the chief's downfall, and, if possible, to take him prisoner, the General marched against him at Sounda, in the Datia district, where he stormed his camp, and forced him to fly for his life to Jodhpur. Perron, whose designs against Hariána Thomas had reason to distrust, being thus occupied, the latter did not choose to remain idle long. Large arrears of revenue were due to him from his northern districts, and he resolved to march thither and enforce payment. On his route he incidentally punished a numerous and daring banditti who had frequently annoyed him by their predatory attacks, and who, having been joined by a number of the peasantry, were assembled in considerable force at the village of Safidún, just outside Thomas's north-eastern boundary. Confiding in their superior numbers, the robbers issued boldly forth, on his approach, to give him battle on the plain in front of the town. But their temerity proved their destruction, for Thomas not only routed them, but followed so close on their heels, that his troops entered the fort with the fugitives, and put to death no less than 700 within its walls. Thomas's own loss on this occasion was considerable ; but the victory struck such a terror throughout the country that the remaining districts submitted without a struggle.

Emboldened by this success, Thomas now determined to cross the boundary and levy contributions in the district of Saharanpur, which was being administered by Sambunath, one of Lakwa Dáda's collectors, who had remained true to the chief's cause in the hour of his fall. Sambunath was in the Doáb at the head of a numerous, but disorderly rabble, and had lately sustained some smart skirmishes with the troops sent against him by Perron. Taking advantage of the anarchy in which the district was thrown, Thomas made a rapid dash through its upper portion, and extorted several heavy fines before his presence there was suspected.

Soon after this Perron advanced in person against Sambunath, and at the same time caused letters to be delivered to Thomas, which he pretended emanated from the Peshwá, and directed the recipient to assist Lakwa Dáda. These letters Thomas at once recognised as forgeries, intended to tempt him into an attitude of declared hostility against Sindhia, which would have given Perron an excuse for declaring war against him. This crafty plot made Thomas regret that he had not in the first instance taken Sambunath's part, who might then not only have saved himself from defeat, but crushed, or at least shaken the power of Perron himself. It was, however, too late to do anything now, so he contented himself with offering Sambunath an asylum at Hánsi, and advising him not to think of opposing his wretched troops to Perron's. But the former, confiding in the protestations of his followers, rashly determined to fight. He was soon convinced of his error, for on the approach of Perron, his troops deserted him, and some endeavoured by treacherous means to seize his person and deliver him up a prisoner. He effected his escape, however, and found refuge in the Sikh country.

Thomas now received intelligence that several of his own districts in the vicinity of Hánsi were in a state of actual rebellion, and had plundered the merchants resorting to them of a very considerable sum of money. Amongst others guilty of this reprehensible conduct were Balhali, Soráni, Jamálpur, and Bihál. The latter place contained 10,000 inhabitants, who enjoyed a character for remarkable bravery, having defeated several armies which, at various times, attempted their reduction, and on one occasion successfully resisted the Mughal noble Ismáil Beg, who fruitlessly endeavoured to subdue them with a force of 16,000 men and 100 guns. The population of Bihál consisted chiefly of Rathór Rajputs, who possessed the finest qualities of courage and resolution.

This rebellion broke out in June 1800, just as the rainy season was commencing, and Thomas was sensible that if it was not quickly crushed, the most serious consequences would ensue to the cultivation, on which the revenues depended. He therefore marched against the place without delay and found it garrisoned by 3,000 men, who, although well armed, were badly supplied with provisions. With a discretion he did not ordinarily display, Thomas decided not to storm it, thinking from the numbers and bravery of the defenders that the event might prove doubtful, and certainly lead to an immense loss of life. So he fell back on the slower, but surer method of a blockade, and erected a chain of forts around the town, and also completely encircled it with a ditch twelve feet deep, which prevented any provisions reaching the garrison, and soon reduced them to a condition of severe distress. This was further augmented when means were found to diminish their water supply, and force them to the necessity of drinking from the wells within the fort, which, being bitter in quality and unwholesome, soon caused sickness to break out. At last the garrison was reduced to one-third of its original number, and Thomas, desirous of putting an end to the siege, drew out his troops with intent to storm the place. Seeing this, and satisfied of his resolution, the enemy capitulated at the last moment, and paid a fine of Rs.30,000 to be forgiven and allowed to return to their allegiance.

In August Thomas returned to his quarters at Hánsi, and was soon after this visited by a man named Usuf Ali Khán, a native agent sent by Colonel Collins, the British resident at Sindhia's court, on a political mission to the Sikhs. Usuf Ali, in his report to Colonel Collins, mentions that he was received with the greatest courtesy by Thomas "on account of the Colonel's letter," and provided by him with an escort to Rohtak.

For the next four months Thomas was busy completing his ammunition and stores for his next campaign, on which he entered in December 1800. This was the last aggressive one he undertook, and also the most important, being directed against the Sikh states of the Sutlej district

CHAPTER VI.

THE INVASION OF THE SUTLEJ STATES.

1801.

IN an earlier chapter it has been shown how the range of Thomas's ambition was not confined to the establishment of an independent rule over the principality of Hariána, but nurtured far more extended schemes of conquest in the Land of the Five Rivers. The Panjab dangled a rich prize to an invader. Its fertile plains yielded harvests twice a year : it was well watered and well wooded : its annual revenues were two million sterling : it contained populous cities, the resorts of merchants and caravans from the far countries of Central Asia ; and, finally, the Sikh nation, who inhabited it, was divided and subdivided into countless clans and confederacies, whose internal dissensions and jealousies nullified the effect of their numbers, and made their country an easier prey to an invading army than if they had been a united people.

Thomas knew the Sikhs and their ways well. During fifteen years he had exchanged many hard knocks with them, and beaten them times without count. Along their frontier his name was one to conjure with, for it was feared and dreaded by the sons of Nanak. In addition to his old designation of *Jehazi Sahib*, he received about this time the more honourable one of *Jowruj Jung*, which, being interpreted, means " *George the Conqueror.*" A conqueror Thomas was, and he now proved his further claim to the title by aspiring to the conquest and consolidation under his own government of all the petty states into which the Panjab was divided, and the proclamation of his rule over the broad territory that stretched between the Jumna and the Indus.

His design is thus summarised in his memoirs by his biographer, Captain Francklin :—

" When Thomas first fixed his residence at Hánsi, he conceived, and would, if unforeseen circumstances had not occurred, have executed the bold design of extending his conquests to the mouth of the Indus. This was to have been effected by a fleet of boats, constructed from timber procured in the forests near the city of Ferozpur, on the banks of the Sutlej river. He then intended proceeding down the river with his army, and settling the countries he might subdue on his route—a daring enterprise and conceived in the true spirit of an ancient Roman. On the conclusion of this design it was his intention to turn his arms against the Punjaub, which he expected to reduce in the course of a couple of years, and which, considering the wealth he would then have acquired, and the amazing resources he would have possessed, must have established his authority on a firm and solid basis."

With the advantage of our modern geographical knowledge we are able to properly estimate the full scope of this enterprise. The territory this audacious Irishman proposed to invade, includes the two vast provinces which now constitute the entire western frontier of the British Empire in India. Their annexation cost the English three great wars. Well might Captain Francklin write that the scheme " was conceived in the true spirit of an ancient Roman." A conquest whose limits were determined by Karachi, Lahore, and Delhi, was a task worthy of a heroic age.

Although it was ambition which first led Thomas to the consideration of this delirious scheme, there were other causes that operated in commending it to his mind. He was conscious of the increasing jealousy and hostility of General Perron, whose encroaching arms and despotic power threatened to swallow up the little principality of Hariána. From such an inconsiderable base of operations as Hánsi, Thomas could not hope to successfully resist the wealth of men and material possessed by Perron. But with the Panjab at his back there was no hostile combination he would have feared, and with that magnificent recruiting ground to draw upon, he could have created an army that might reasonably hope to cope with the Brigades of Hindustan.

To the dangers and difficulties of the project Thomas was not blind : but he feared those which lurked in his rear, not those which existed in front. And it was with a view of securing himself against an attack from Sindhia that about this time he made definite overtures to the British Government. In these he announced his intention of declaring war against the Sikhs, who were, he observed, equally the enemies of the Maráthás and the English. To enable him to attack them with confidence he desired an assurance of neutrality from

General Perron, under guarantee from the Governor-General. In return for this Thomas offered "to advance and take possession of the Punjaub, and give up his army to the direction and control of the English; to take the country, and, in short, to become an active partisan in their cause. By this plan," he explained, "I have nothing in view but the welfare of my King and country; it is not to better myself that I have thought of it; but I should be sorry to see my conquests fall to the Mahrattas, for I wish to give them to my King, and to serve him the remainder of my days. This I can only do as a soldier in this part of the world? "

Political considerations made it quite impossible for the Marquis Wellesley to entertain these proposals. They were advanced at a time when he had his hands fully occupied with the expedition to Egypt, and the unsettled state of affairs in the Deccan, where signs of trouble were looming which would require all the resources of the English power to successfully oppose. In consequence of this Thomas's design of an invasion of the Panjab was never carried out in its entirety, but was confined to the short but brilliant campaign which he undertook in the year 1801.

A plausible excuse for the formality of a declaration of war against the Sikhs was afforded by the conduct of the Rájah of Patiála, who, in the preceding year, had broken his treaty of peace with Thomas, and assisted his enemies to harass him during his return from the Bikanir expedition. Sahib Singh of Patiála, whose forces consisted of 1,500 cavalry and 1,000 infantry, was at this time engaged in laying siege to a fort in which his Amazonian sister Kunúr had taken refuge from his resentment. Thomas, with his native chivalry, determined to march to this lady's relief, but on his approach Sahib Singh hurriedly raised the seige and retired within the fortifications of Sunám, a large town thirty miles to the west of Patiála. Thomas followed on his track with the intention of storming the place, but was deterred from doing so by the unexpected arrival of Tárá Singh, an ally and son-in-law of Sahib Singh, who brought with him a large force. The appearance of these reinforcements gave confidence to the surrounding peasantry, and they rose *en masse* to join the Patiála chief. Thomas accordingly determined on more prudential tactics, and striking camp marched twenty-four miles to a town called Belad. But he was followed by a large body of the enemy's cavalry, who concealed themselves in a neighbouring jungle, intending to make a sudden attack on his rear when he advanced to the storm.

Belad was a strongly fortified place, as indeed were all the towns and villages in the district, owing to its constant state of warfare.

The walls were nine feet in thickness, and it was surrounded by a ditch twenty feet deep, and defended by a numerous garrison. Nevertheless Thomas, who was apprised of the proximity of the Patiála troops, determined to storm it without any loss of time, and before the latter could form a junction with the garrison, or afford external aid.

Fortune favoured him, and he carried the place by a vigorous assault, with a loss of only eighty of his own people. A rancorous enmity had long existed between his troops, who were chiefly Muhammadans, and the Sikhs, and in the heat of racial conflict, despite all his attempts to stay the slaughter, no less than 500 of the garrison were put to the sword. Upon which the townspeople who survived, ransomed their lives by the payment of a large sum of money.

Having thus established himself in a situation of strength and safety, Thomas directed his attention to dividing the force that had followed him, and gradually increased to not less than 10,000 men, intending if possible to attack and defeat them in detail. He also experienced an inclination " to explore the neighbouring country and raise contributions." To effect these objects he presently marched to a central position between the towns of Patiála and Sunám, but soon changed his intention on a chance presenting itself of punishing Tárá Singh, whose assistance to Sahib Singh had obliged Thomas to raise the siege of Sunám. Tárá Singh's capital was at a place called Malér Kotla, which lay a short distance to the north-west of Thomas's position, and he now perceived an opportunity of attacking it by surprise in the absence of its chief, which he at once proceeded to put into execution. The road lay through a thick jungle, well adapted for ambuscade, and as his men were making their way along, a smart firing was suddenly heard in the front. Hurrying forward Thomas found his advance guard had been attacked by a superior force of the enemy, just as they were emerging into an extensive open plain, and presently discovered that this was a ruse to draw his observation away from a large and populous town named Bhát, situated close at hand, and belonging to Tárá Singh.

Having received information of the proximity of this place, Thomas marched against it. The walls of the fort were twelve feet thick and thirty feet high, with four strong bastions, well fortified with cannon, commanding the town below, as well as the plain adjoining. It was defended by 3,000 troops, and in all respects a place difficult to take ; but Thomas was determined to capture it, and resolved on an immediate assault. Dividing his force into two columns, he led one himself against the centre of the town, whilst one of his officers named Hopkins led the other against the eastern angle. The affair was desperate, for though the town was soon set on fire, the enemy made a brave and stubborn resistance. Hopkins, advancing with the utmost gallantry, stormed the quarter assigned to him, but, in the moment of victory, fell wounded, and several other officers were killed or disabled by the tremendous fire kept up from the bastions. The affair now began to present a doubtful aspect, especially when a large body of the Patiála cavalry made their appearance in the rear, just as Thomas's troops, although in actual possession of the town, were beginning to waver and show signs of retreating, either because of the excessive heat thrown out from the burning buildings, or from the uncommonly severe fire poured down upon them from above. The danger was, however, averted by Thomas's presence of mind. Bringing up a 6-pounder gun close to the gates of the citadel, he demolished them by repeated discharges. Whereupon the enemy gave up the contest, and by timely submission saved a further effusion of blood on both sides, and paid a ransom of Rs.50,000.

Although Tárá Singh was a Sikh, a great portion of the population of Malér Kotla were Muhammadans, who, when they heard of the capture of Bhát, showed a disposition to join Thomas, and eventually paid him a contribution, and united their troops with his.

Meanwhile the Rájah of Patiála had not been idle. To the eastward of his capital was the district of Shahábád, belonging to a Sikh chief of the name of Karram Singh, to whose son Sahib Singh offered his daughter in marriage if he would assist against Thomas. The proposal being accepted, 5,000 of the Shahábád troops joined the Patiála army, and on their arrival a grand council of war was held, whereat it was resolved that a general combination of the Sikh states should be formed to expel Thomas from the country.

For by this time Thomas had fully justified his claim to the title of *Jowruj Jung.* He had become a veritable scourge to the Sutlej states, and made his shadow dreaded wherever it fell. Victory followed his arms, and none seemed capable of resisting him. The confederation of such discordant elements as the Sikh clans was the best testimony to his power and prestige. Information of this alliance soon reached him through his spies, but it raised no serious apprehensions in his breast, for he considered that the diversity of interests and counsels that prevailed in the enemy's camp, and the well-known jealousies of their chiefs, would render it difficult for them to act in harmony, or carry out any preconcerted plan with loyalty to one another.

But at this juncture an event occurred which tempted Thomas

from the path of prudence, and turned the scale of circumstances against him. Adjoining the Malér Kotla country was the territory of Rai Elias, a youth who had recently succeeded his father, Rai Kallán, in his inheritance. Rai Elias's district ran contiguous with the Sutlej river, and included the important cities of Ludhiana and Firozpur. In consequence of his tender age his mother had assumed the reins of government, but from inexperience, and the disadvantages of her sex, proved wholly unable to rule a country producing a revenue of five lakhs of rupees, and surrounded by enemies eager to prey on it. Taking advantage of her weakness the Sikhs had attacked her son's districts in the previous year, and taken possession of a great portion of them, only a few strong forts remaining to the Ráni. Soon after this Zamán Shah, the King of Kábul, arrived at Lahore, which was only seventy miles distant from Rai Elias's capital, and to him the Ráni appealed for assistance to reinstate her son in his authority. Hearing of this the Sikhs evacuated the villages they had occupied, and the peasantry returned to their allegiance, and matters were beginning to assume a brighter aspect when a fresh danger arose, which reduced the Ráni to even deeper misfortunes than those from which she had just emerged.

A certain Sikh named Sahib Singh (not to be confounded with the ruler of Patiála) who was a Behdi of the race of Nanak, the founder and prophet of the Sikh nation, counterfeited religious inspiration, and having by fraud and artifice imposed on his countrymen, collected a large force and proceeded to possess himself of the country of Rai Elias. As Zamán Shah had by this time returned to Kabul, no help could be expected from that sovereign, and the Ráni was soon reduced to a truly deplorable situation, and obliged in her extremity to sue for terms from her enemies. A treaty was drawn up by which she agreed to pay a sum of two lakhs of rupees to the Sikhs as ransom, but Sahib Singh, the imposter, refused to approve it, and demanded the surrender of the whole of her country. As a last resource the Ráni sent her young son to make an appeal in person, and try to obtain an abatement of these harsh terms ; whereupon the youth was treacherously seized and retained a prisoner by Sahib Singh, but was shortly released by a Sikh chief named Karram Singh, whose credulity could no longer be imposed upon by the pretended prophet, and who detached himself from his cause and carried Rai Elias to a place of safety. Sahib Singh immediately returned to the attack of the Ráni's country, and was occupied in the siege of Ludhiana, one of the chief towns in it, when Thomas appeared upon the scene and captured Bhát.

12

In this situation of her affairs the Ráni determined to apply to *Jowruj Jung* for assistance in expelling Sahib Singh, and despatched a confidential agent to his camp, offering him a lakh of rupees to reinstate her son in power, ánd promising him an annual tribute of Rs.50,000 a year to guarantee the youth in undisturbed possession. Although this proposal seemed likely to drag Thomas into a prolonged war he was so touched by " the fallen condition of an ancient and honourable family " that he acceded to it. Lovely woman in distress never appealed in vain to this susceptible Irishman, and whether it was the Witch of Sardhána, the Amazon of Patiála, or the widow of Ludhiana, it needed but a woman's cry to bring him to the rescue.

Hearing of these negotiations Sahib Singh, the imposter, wrote to Thomas, threatening him with punishment, and warning him " if he wished for quarter " to send a Vakil at once to " the successor of Nanak and the Sovereign of the Sikh nation "—such being the dignity to which the Behdi laid claim : and he concluded his letter by recommending " implicit obedience to his commands."

The idea of Thomas " wishing for quarter " at the hand of a Sikh was distinctly precious : and there was a splendid audacity of expression in the recommendation of " implicit obedience" from *Jowruj Jung*. Equally indignant at the impertinence of the language and the menace, Thomas replied that he was accustomed to receive, not to send Vakils, and that Sahib Singh had better pay down his contribution before he was compelled, and immediately evacuate the country of Rai Elias. This answer brought matters to a point, and the imposter prepared to make good his threats.

Meanwhile Rai Elias left the Rájah of Patiála, with whom he had taken refuge after leaving Karram Singh, and came of his own accord to Thomas's camp. " The comely appearance of the youth," observes the Irishman, " his fallen condition, and above all the confidence he showed in placing his whole reliance on one against whom he was so lately leagued in enmity, altogether influenced me in his favour, and determined me to use every exertion to support his cause."

The Rájah of Patiála now joined the imposter to make common cause against their common enemy. Thomas at once advanced against them, upon which " the Sovereign of the Sikhs " incontinently fled, his followers evacuating the country faster than Thomas could occupy it. So rapid was the Behdi's retreat that in one place his bed, palanquin, tent and baggage were all found abandoned. His discomfiture was complete, and he never afterwards occasioned any disturbance.

The Ráni and her son were now put in possession of their territory, and after the most active of the rebels had been seized and punished, the authority of the young chief was re-established. But although the imposter was no more, the Rájah of Patiála still kept the field, and was joined by several other chiefs. He now advanced at the head of 15,000 men against Thomas, with the intention of driving him out of the country. Several skirmishes took place, but without any substantial results, neither party being desirous of risking a general engagement. And so hostilities continued to be carried on in a desultory manner, the Sikhs contenting themselves with cutting off supplies from Thomas's camp, and preventing him from collecting forage. But as all this occurred within Rai Elias's territory, and occasioned great loss by stopping the cultivation of the land, Thomas desired to carry the war into the enemy's country. To this, however, the Ráni would not consent, pressing him to stay by her while the Sikhs remained in the neighbourhood.

So long as prudence allowed, he listened to these solicitations, but at last a time came when his ammunition began to fall short, and he was reluctantly compelled to make preparations for his return to Hánsi to obtain a supply. And so, much against her will, he left the Ráni to sustain her authority by herself, and began his march homewards.

The Sikhs at once closed in upon his rear and began to harass him. This behaviour incited him to retaliate by devastating their country through which he passed. And there was a further satisfaction in knowing that his pursuit by the whole force of the enemy was operating favourably for Rai Elias, since it drew the Sikhs away from his districts, which, for a time at least, would be freed from their depredations.

Previous to his setting out on this campaign Thomas had effected a treaty with two powerful Sikh neighbours, Bágh Singh of Jhind, and Lál Singh of Kaithal, by which they solemnly agreed to live in amity, and particularly to abstain from invading Hariána during Thomas's absence. But now these treacherous chiefs, perceiving the strong combination that had been formed against him, broke their faith, and joined his enemies. They had not, however, rightly reckoned the character of the man whose feelings they thus outraged. Thomas, by forced marches, forged ahead of his pursuers, and led his troops against the fort of Kanhori, which belonged to Lál Singh, and taking it by storm, put the garrison to the sword. The capture of this place, which was only forty-five miles distant from Patiála, was of the greatest importance to him, for its situation near the Ghaggar river, and on the borders of his own districts, afforded Thomas an excellent advance depôt for stores and ammunition, and he accordingly repaired the fortifications and garrisoned it with a large force.

This done he collected hostages from the surrounding country as security for its peaceful behaviour, and marched to Retára, another strong fort, belonging to the Kaithal chief, and was on the point of storming this when the garrison of 500 men, dreading a similar fate to that experienced by the inhabitants of Kanhori, appealed for quarter, and were granted it on payment of a substantial contribution, and the surrender of the fort with its contents to Thomas.

From Retára Thomas returned to Hánsi, where he learnt that during his absence Bapu Sindhia, the Marátbá general, had invaded Hariána under orders from General Perron, but had fallen back on Delhi, where the main army was encamped, directly information reached him that Thomas was returning to his capital.

The main Sikh army, which had not relinquished the pursuit, now began to suffer seriously from want of water and supplies, and were eventually compelled to abandon active operations for the present, and drawing off encamped in the neighbourhood of Kaithal, there to await the bursting of the monsoon rains before recommencing hostilities. But no consideration of this sort hindered Thomas when he was on the war-path. He had still to punish the Rájah of Jhind, and marching to that chief's district, he exacted a fine, and took hostages. Thence he passed on to lay siege to Safidún, a town dependent on the same ruler. This place was built of brick and surrounded by walls of uncommon height and strength, so that it was impossible to take it by a sudden assault. Thomas therefore erected three redoubts around it, which he fortified with eighteen 12- and 6-pounder guns, and opened a bombardment, keeping up an incessant fire from early dawn till three o'clock in the afternoon, at which hour, fearing the place might be reinforced during the night, he determined on a storm. The garrison consisted of 700 men, 300 of whom remained in the fort, whilst the rest sallied bravely out and attacked Thomas's advanced posts on the first signs of his intention to assault, but most of them, including some chiefs of distinction, were put to the sword as they clambered their way out of the deep ditch surrounding the place. And now Thomas in his turn delivered his attack, and attempted to mount the breach which his guns had made. But his scaling ladders proved too short, and his men were involved in the greatest difficulty, being entirely exposed to the enemy's fire without any possibility of returning it. After a desperate conflict of two hours he was compelled to draw off with a loss of 450 of his best troops. The gallant Hopkins, who had been, as usual, conspicuous by his ardour during the assault, was again severely wounded.

But the enemy had also suffered greatly in the earlier part of the day, and now attempted to escape by cutting their way through Thomas's line. In this they were successful, and reached the shelter of a thick forest in the neighbourhood, whilst the victors marched in and occupied the abandoned fort.

It does not speak much for the national spirit of the Sikhs that during this time their main army lay within twenty-seven miles of Safidún, and yet never attempted to relieve their brethren in distress. It was also a fortunate occurrence for Thomas that Bapu Sindhia, who was encamped fourteen miles to the south, made no hostile movement. Encouraged by this immunity from attack Thomas now marched against the main Sikh army at Kaithal, to renew the war which had been suspended; but his late feats had struck a chill into the hearts of his enemies, who recognised that *Jowruj Jung* was a masterful man, to whom it was better to submit than offer resistance. So soon as his intentions became evident to the Chief of Patiála and his allies they sent four Vakils to negotiate for peace, thus admitting his advantage.

Thomas, despite his exhibition of energy and vigour, was sincerely desirous of terminating the war; for he was informed that General Perron was preparing to march from Delhi for the avowed purpose of assisting the Sikhs. Although this was not exactly the case, it was certain that Perron was bent on measuring swords with Thomas. Added to these considerations was the occurrence of disturbances which had broken out near Hánsi, and required care to avert danger. Thomas, therefore, wisely decided to profit by the enormous prestige he now enjoyed, and agreed to terms. It was settled that the Sikhs should pay him an indemnity of Rs.135,000, and renounce all pretensions to the country of Rai Elias; that the Chief of Patiála should be reconciled to his sister, Kunúr, who was to be reinstated in the property confiscated from her; that certain districts on the frontier should be ceded to Thomas; and finally that the Chief of Patiála should subsidise two battalions of infantry, who were to be stationed to keep order on the boundary, as a safeguard to either party.

It was a treaty which did honour to Thomas, not only because it asserted his complete mastery over his enemies and secured him solid advantages, but because two of its principal stipulations showed how the protection of the weak, and the rehabilitation of an injured woman had a first place in his warm Irish heart, and evoked the support of his chivalrous nature.

" Thus," he observes in his memoirs, " ended a campaign of seven months, in which I had been more successful than I could possibly have expected when I first took the field with a force consisting of 5,000 men and 36 pieces of cannon. I lost in killed, wounded and disabled, nearly one-third of my force ; but the enemy lost 5,000 persons of all descriptions. I realised near Rs.200,000, exclusive of the pay of my army, and was to receive an additional Rs.100,000 for the hostages which were delivered up. I explored the country, formed alliances, and, in short, was DICTATOR in all the countries belonging to the Sikhs south of Sutlej."

Directly this treaty was concluded Thomas made an astonishingly rapid march back to Hánsi, to the consternation and amazement of General Perron, who was actively preparing for an attack on that town, in the belief that its master was many miles away. This extraordinary display of vitality confounded Perron, who, in the changed aspect of affairs, began to consider the advisability of substituting negotiations for action.

But the star of *Jowruj Jung* had passed its meridian height and was now on the decline. Once or twice it was destined to blaze brightly out through the dark clouds that shrouded its setting ; but the campaign that carried him conquering to the Sutlej and safely back was his last victorious effort. Conceived in a spirit of the boldest enterprise ; conducted with an audacity as successful as it was splendid, and concluded with a vigour that astounded his enemies, it fitly crowns the dashing and defiant career of this gallant Irish adventurer. And more than this, it compels the belief that under a happier destiny he might have carried into effect the ambitious scheme of conquest which he marked out for achievement, but never lived to realise.

The end was drawing near: his work was nearly done. But its memory was to remain. For in many a Panjab village, for many a long year after he had passed from the scene of his exploits, the whisper of the name of *Jowruj Jung* could hush children into silence, and bring a keen alert look into the grave dusky faces of grey-bearded warriors, who remembered how, in the days of their youth, the sword blows of the sailor *Sahib* were wont to fall fast and thick amongst flying Sikh armies, scourging and scattering them like the flail of the thresher descending upon the trampled sheaves of corn.

WAR WITH PERRON. THE BATTLE OF GEORGEGARH.

1801.

THE extraordinary success of Thomas's career, the alarming growth of his power, and his singularly ambitious nature, had for some time marked him out as an object of suspicion to Daulat Ráo Sindhia and of jealousy to General Perron. More than once the Marátha prince had in the past offered service to Thomas, and these offers had recently been revived, but Thomas refused them, owing to his disinclination to serve in conjunction with Perron, whom he cordially hated. And so no arrangement was concluded, and meanwhile Thomas gradually increased his force to eight battalions of regular infantry of 750 men each, 1,500 Rohillas, 2,000 garrison troops, 1,000 cavalry, and 50 guns. This little army, from a numerical point of view, was sufficiently powerful to create distrust, but it was rendered doubly formidable from the prowess and prestige of its commander, "who had a spirit and elevation of mind not to be subdued by accident, or depressed by ill-fortune," and from the valour and confidence which animated all ranks after an almost unbroken career of victory.

The recent invasion of the Sutlej states had raised Thomas to a distinct place in the community of Indian powers, whilst the lawless and predatory instinct that swayed him made his army a source of constant terror to the neighbouring countries he so frequently devastated and laid under contribution. Even to the Marátha power itself *Jowruj Jung* had become a standing menace, for his proximity to Delhi, and the dash and daring of his system of warfare, made a *coup de main* against the capital and the person of the Emperor not outside the bounds of possibility.

This in itself was a sufficient reason for Perron's determination to measure swords with the conqueror of Hariána. But there was another consideration which influenced him, and that was Thomas's notorious hatred of Frenchmen. *Jowruj Jung* suffered from the acutest form of Francophobia prevalent at a time when the disease was very virulent. It was on this ground that he refused Sindhia's proposals, explaining that " M. Perron and himself being subjects of different nations then in a state of actual hostility against each other, it was impossible they could ever act in concert or with cordiality. He was moreover convinced that as a Frenchman and possessed of a national enmity against him, M. Perron would always be induced to represent his actions in a light most unfavourable to his interests." This inference was certainly sufficiently justified by Perron's behaviour towards the British officers in his army. He was at this time bent on the establishment of a French dominion in Hindustan, to which end he had entered into negotiations with the French Government. These schemes and ambitions undoubtedly influenced his policy towards Thomas, for it was impossible for him to view with equanimity the existence on his weakest flank of a growing power, whose sympathies were intensely British. He therefore urged upon Sindhia the necessity of crushing the army of the audacious adventurer of Hánsi, whose increasing fame threatened to eclipse that of Perron himself.

Whatever Perron suggested, Sindhia of necessity approved and sanctioned, for he was too harassed and tormented by difficulties in the Deccan to exert any real authority in Hindustan. But true to the traditions of craft and intrigue that governed the Maráthá mind, Daulat Ráo first attempted a diplomatic solution, and once more repeated his invitation to Thomas to join his standard. Thomas met the proposal with his former reply. " Principles of honour," he wrote, " forbid me from acting under the command of a Frenchman. But should you think proper to appoint me to the management of operations, either offensive or defensive, in any part of the Deccan, Hindostan, or the Punjaub, I am ready and willing to undertake the charge so soon as the necessary arrangements for the payment of my troops can be completed."

To this Sindhia, under Perron's direction, replied " That it was impossible to consent to such a proposal, as it would create an unfavourable precedent; and he recommended Thomas to curb his national enmity, and consider the matter in a light more favourable for the interests of the service."

Such was the position of affairs at the end of the Sutlej campaign, when it became evident that a conflict between Thomas and Perron could be no longer deferred. The Sikhs, smarting under the defeat they had suffered, helped to bring matters to a head by opening negotiations with Perron, to whom they offered a subsidy of five lakhs of rupees and a contingent of 10,000 cavalry, if he would undertake the destruction of their dreaded enemy.

This offer came at an opportune moment, for Perron was fully determined in his mind to bring matters to a summary conclusion, either by force of arms, or by absorbing Thomas's army in his own. So he wrote a sort of ultimatum to Thomas, requesting him to send a Vakil to confer upon the proposals recently made by Sindhia. But no sooner was this communication despatched than news reached Delhi of the disastrous defeat of Sindhia's forces at Ujjain by Holkar, which in a moment changed the aspect of affairs. Orders followed for Perron to temporise with Thomas, and proceed immediately to the Deccan with all his troops, to assist in re-establishing his master's power, which had received a serious shock.

This was an ominous blow to Perron. His personal interests were centred in Hindustan, a withdrawal from which would be fatal. The negotiations which he had recently opened with the French Government required both the consolidation of his power at Delhi, and that it should be supreme there. To detach all, or even a portion of his troops to Ujjain would be political suicide. It was far more important to him to destroy Thomas than to defeat Holkar. The temporary success of the latter might even be advantageous to his personal schemes if it weakened Sindhia : for Daulat Ráo's weakness was Perron's strength so long as the latter could keep his Brigades around him. Rumours reached him of several alliances which Thomas was negotiating with the Begum Somru, the Rájahs of Jaipur and Ulwar, with sundry Sikh chiefs, with Lakwa Dáda, and with Jaswant Ráo Holkar himself. As a fact, Holkar had repeatedly urged Thomas to commence hostilities, and promised to assist him with men and money. Thomas was also in communication with Jean Baptiste la Fontaine, who commanded six battalions of Filoze's party in the service of Sindhia. This pairing of opposite cards comes on the authority of Lewis Ferdinand Smith, who writes : " Such are the singularity and treachery of Eastern politics, that two of Scindia's Brigades, Sombre's and Filoze's, had agreed to assist Thomas against Daulat Ráo's commander-in-chief Perron ! " For the moment it almost appeared as though Thomas would be successful in forming an overwhelming combination against his enemies, whilst he was considerably augmenting his own force, having made preparations to raise six more battalions, the recruits for which were on their way to join him, and the arms ready for them. A careful review of the comparative strength of Thomas and Perron at this time seems to favour the former.

Perhaps Perron realised this; but he had gone too far to draw back. The very existence of his power depended upon the destruction of Thomas's. It was impossible for him to obey Sindhia's orders and march with his battalions to the Deccan, leaving Hindustan shorn of troops. So under various pretexts he avoided starting for Ujjain, and meanwhile cogitated on an extremely clever scheme which, if successful, would at one and the same time undermine Thomas's power, and pacify Sindhia's importunity. This was nothing more or less than sending Thomas to do the work in the Deccan, and retaining his own Brigades intact in Hindustan. With this design in his mind Perron received the Vakil Thomas sent him with marked favour, and presently requested a personal interview with his master.

Thomas consented, and the fort of Bahadurgarh was fixed for the meeting. Thither Perron sent his Third Brigade of 10 battalions of infantry under Bourguien and 2,000 regular horse, following them from his headquarters at Koïl, about the middle of August. At the same time Thomas marched out of Hánsi to attend the interview. On approaching Bahadurgarh, which was situated a few miles to the north-west of Delhi, he was met by Captain L. F. Smith, who was deputed to conduct him to the place of meeting. Thomas was not altogether without suspicion of Perron's good faith, and this distrust was increased by information which reached him that the General had recently put to death a Sikh chief, who had revolted from Sindhia, and of whose person he had obtained possession by treacherous means. Thomas, therefore, took with him as a personal escort, two of his most approved battalions and 300 cavalry, and on the 19th of August, 1801, arrived and encamped two miles' distant from Perron's lines at Bahadurgarh.

The next day an interview took place. Thomas was determined to observe the greatest circumspection, but both he and Perron were too cunning to deceive each other long. One can imagine the meeting of the vain-glorious Frenchman and the hot-headed Irishman, each in his own way typical of the European nations they represented. Both were self-made men, sprung from the same low strata of seafaring life; both had fought their way to distinction and power by similar methods, and reached an extraordinary elevation. Both, doubtless, laboured under exaggerated ideas of the etiquette and conduct required in diplomatic dealing. The mind pictures the forced Gallic politeness of the one, and the Tipperary punctilio of the other, as they attempted to disguise the racial hatred that filled their hearts. Perron with his solitary hand—he had lost one at the siege of Kánaund in 1793— waving the great, tall Irishman into the place of honour, must have

adjured the *scélérat* under his breath ; and Thomas cursed the d——d
Frenchman as he glared down on him and passed to his seat. But the
pantomime of politeness passed off well enough, and although no business was transacted, the way was paved for future negotiations.

Several conferences took place after this, and when the first sense of
distrust and awkwardness wore off, friendly relations were established,
if not between Perron and Thomas, at least between the latter and the
European officers of Bourguien's Third Brigade, with whom he dined
repeatedly. Amongst these was Colonel (then Captain) James Skinner (to whose excellent memoirs much of the following matter is
indebted), who states that "all seemed to be going on well," and
describes Thomas's troops as " looking well, but not over-disciplined ;
but his artillery was very fine and the bullocks particularly good and
strong." Captains Hearsey, Hopkins, and Birch, three of Thomas's
officers, were in his camp, as well as some Eu peans acting as sergeants in his artillery, so that he must have made a very creditable
show.

Thomas had already received information about Sindhia's defeat at
Ujjain and the unfavourable aspect of the Prince's affairs, and this
naturally strengthened his hand, and led him to hope that the negotiations would be productive of an amicable adjustment of all former difficulties, and lead to future tranquillity and a good understanding
between him and Perron. But when the latter indicated the conditions on which it was proposed to entertain Thomas's services, the
demand was equally sudden and unexpected, and quite took Thomas
aback. He was to surrender his district of Jhajjar, but to be permitted
to retain the fort of Hánsi ; he was to rank as a colonel in Sindhia's
service, with a pay of Rs.60,000 a month for his corps, but to serve
under Perron's orders. These terms were unfavourable and unacceptable in themselves, but they were made impossible by the additional
condition that Thomas, directly he agreed to them, would be required
to detach four of his battalions for service against Holkar in the
Deccan.

In Thomas's acutely suspicious Irish nature this last proviso aroused
the strongest distrust. It seemed to him that Perron wished to follow
the political maxim *Divide et Impera*, and he believed the stipulation
was a distinct attempt to undermine his power, and that as soon as
Holkar was defeated, his own turn would come to be dealt with, when
he would be compelled to accept any terms Perron might choose to
impose. He therefore peremptorily refused compliance, and abruptly
breaking off the conference, marched back to Hánsi and prepared for
war.

That he was mistaken in this step is proved by results, for service under Sindhia could never have led to such absolute ruin as overtook Thomas before four months had passed away. He has been blamed for want of judgment in neglecting "the only rational chance left him of realising with greater certainty a higher station as a soldier than he could ever hope to do by his own unaided resources against the jealous enmity of the most potent prince in Hindustan." Although by the light of subsequent events the wisdom of this criticism is made apparent, it is easy to understand the grounds which influenced Thomas in his choice. In the first place he could not foresee that all his projected alliances were to fail him, and he had in theory an exceedingly strong combination at his back. Then he was a victorious and independent leader treating for terms, not a defeated general suing for them, who had no choice but to submit to the humiliation of surrendering territory he had held and governed for nine years. He was at the head of a marvellously spirited force, fresh from a brilliant campaign, in which it had proved its superiority over enormous numerical odds. Perron might certainly bring bigger battalions into the field, but the recent defeat at Ujjain had gravely shaken the prestige of Sindhia's regular infantry. Lastly, there was Thomas's own nature, his unconquerable pugnacity, his firm faith in his own fortune, and his cherished ambitions for supreme power which prevented his giving way. Visions of glory blinded him; his eyes still turned towards the far Panjab; his mind was filled with schemes of conquest and acquisition. It was intolerable to him to serve under another in an inglorious *rôle* of subordination; but altogether repugnant when that other was a Frenchman. And it was this sentiment, more than any other, that urged him to enter into a struggle with the master of forty thousand fighting men, rather than yield up an independence which he had won with his own right hand, and lower his sword in salute to a chief whom he despised.

War was formally declared, and both sides began to make ready. But Perron set off for Koïl with such impolitic precipitation that Lewis Ferdinand Smith refers to his departure as "the flight of Perron from his army." He left Major Louis Bourguien, who was in command of the Third Brigade, to conduct the operations, and this officer, after being strengthened with 60 guns and reinforced by 6,000 Sikh cavalry, entered Thomas's territory early in September, and marching to Jhajjar, which was unfortified, occupied it without opposition. He then attempted to capture Georgegarh, a strong fort five miles to the south, garrisoned by 800 of Thomas's troops, but the officer entrusted with the attack being repulsed, Bourguien left Captain L. F. Smith with three battalions of infantry and a battering train to la; siege to it, and himself marched to Jhind, whither he heard Thomas had gone. On arriving here he was told his quarry had moved off to Patiála, and at once started in pursuit ; but this had merely been a feint on Thomas's part to draw off Bourguien's main army, and he now retraced his steps to Hánsi with incredible rapidity, completed his ammunition and other stores, left a body of Rohillas to defend the place, and then swooped down on Smith at Georgegarh, covering the last seventy-six miles in two days, whilst the blundering Bourguien, discovering too late the trap into which he had fallen, came following after.

Thomas's sudden approach was the signal for Smith to raise the siege of Georgegarh, and fall back on Jhajjar. But Thomas was not to be foiled, and without resting his men, dashed forward to cut Smith off. His troops, however, from some unaccountable reason, lost their road in the darkness of the night, and when in the early morning Thomas came up with the retreating enemy he found he had only one battalion supporting him.

Smith's rear-guard was under the command of a gallant old native officer, named Púran Singh, who immediately drew up his battalion in line in order to cover the retreat of the artillery and baggage, whilst Smith opened a slight cannonade, and then continued his flight. This gave time for some of Thomas's laggards to come up, but being in a state of extreme fatigue, and only commanded by a native officer named Martáza Khán, they incautiously advanced through a field of high standing corn, without reconnoitring their front, and suddenly found themselves attacked by Púran Singh, who charged them with great spirit and beat them back with a loss of four of their guns.

Hearing of this disaster Thomas immediately advanced to the relief, and leading his men, sword in hand, fell upon the enemy, and after a severe conflict completely defeated them, and recaptured the four guns. Púran Singh was wounded and taken prisoner, and a great number of his men killed or disabled, only a mere remnant escaping ; for although Smith was but a short distance ahead, he did not return to their assistance, but busied himself with securing the safety of his guns and baggage.

Thomas, whose loss was under 100 men, now fell back on Georgegarh, his troops being so exhausted with fatigue as to be unable to continue the pursuit ; and only a few cavalry were sent after the fugitives, and these picked up several stands of colours and small arms. Skinner, in his memoirs, blames Smith for his supine conduct on this occasion ; but Thomas observes, "Had it not been for the soldier-like precautions taken by Captain Smith in sending forward his artillery and baggage, while he made head with his infantry, the whole would have infallibly have been captured; as it was he lost the greater part of his ammunition and baggage."

This action occurred on the 27th of September, and on the following morning Thomas was preparing to renew the attack when his scouts brought information of Bourguien's approach.   His troops being fatigued and many of them dispersed in search of plunder, Thomas did not deem it advisable to hazard an immediate engagement, and the relieving force, which turned out to be Bourguien's 2,000 regular cavalry, under the command of Captain F. E. Smith, a brother of Captain L. F. Smith, made good their way to Jhajjar, and saved the two battalions and the battering train there from a very serious danger.

Bourguien himself, with his infantry, arrived on the 29th, the men harassed, fatigued, and famished after a march of sixty miles in thirty-six hours; yet, with incredible imbecility, their leader determined on an immediate attack.   On reconnoitring Thomas's position he found him drawn up in one line, with Georgegarh and a large fortified village on his right flank, a strong redoubt, in which were stationed 600 Rohillas and 4 pieces of artillery, on his left; and another large walled village in his rear.   Even under favourable circumstances the position would have been a strong one to attack, but under existing conditions an assault by Bourguien's exhausted and worn-out troops was madness.

Notwithstanding which the Frenchman ordered the advance at three o'clock in the afternoon, but, with a prudent regard for his own safety, directed operations from a point far away in the rear, where he faithfully kept his post during the rest of the fight, full of importance, but out of danger.   Obedient to orders, and with a calm intrepidity worthy of its reputation, the Brigade advanced in open columns of companies against Thomas's entrenchments.   The route lay through heavy sand, and they were exposed to a dreadful and well-directed fire from 50 guns.   Two battalions, with a couple of cannon, were detached to make a diversion on Thomas's rear, whilst the main body proceeded straight against his position.

Thomas had chosen his ground with his usual ability, and so divided his forces as to oppose a front to the enemy at each point threatened.   The position gave him a considerable advantage, for knowing that his men were unaccustomed to artillery fire, he selected a place where the soil was so loose and sandy that it deadened the shot, and prevented them from ricochetting.   The total number of troops under his command consisted of 10 battalions of infantry, 600 Rohillas, 500 cavalry, and 54 guns.

About four o'clock the two armies were within musket shot, and Bourguien's men began to push briskly on, with their guns at the drag ropes. But Thomas, with rapid discharges of round and grape shot, mowed them down by scores, whilst his own troops were in a great measure sheltered by a breastwork of sand which they had hastily thrown up. A few minutes of this hot work threw Bourguien's main body into confusion, which must have resulted in irretrievable disaster, had not his cavalry made a spirited charge on Thomas's centre, and pressed it so hard that it began to give way, and the rest of his line to waver.

This rendered an immediate movement necessary, and Captain Hopkins with the right wing, and Captain Birch with the left, were ordered to advance and charge with bayonets. Each moved out with two battalions in columns of companies, and then formed in front of the enemy " with as great calmness and precision as if they had been at review," and after delivering their fire dashed forward with fixed bayonets, and drove Bourguien's line back. But Bourguien's gunners would not abandon their pieces, and, serving them with great resolution, kept up a heavy fire, which created immense havoc, and so encouraged the cavalry, who had temporarily drawn off, that they charged again. But being bravely met and repulsed with loss, they retreated a second time, and were pursued for a considerable distance by Thomas's horse.

And now there came one of war's mischances to operate against the victory which seemed almost assured to Thomas. Captain Hopkins, his second in command and in gallantry, his *alter ego*, was struck by a cannon ball, which carried away one of his legs. On seeing their leader fall his men immediately lost heart, and retired in disorder, carrying him with them. Whereupon Bourguien's left wing rallied, and reoccupied the position they had abandoned, and after a little time attempted to advance to the storm again; but the fire along the line from Thomas's guns was so murderous, that at last the whole Brigade was ordered to lie down and avail themselves of such shelter as the undulating surface of the ground afforded. In the same way Thomas's troops crouched behind the sand hillocks that protected them, and in this position the two armies remained until sunset, neither daring to expose itself by an advance or a retreat, but continuing to keep up a constant fire. When at last night drew its curtain over the bloody plain, the worn-out soldiers, utterly exhausted, bivouaced on the open field they had so desperately contested.

At sunrise the next morning Bourguien hung out a flag of truce, and an armistice was granted for six hours, during which the wounded were conveyed to the rear and the dead buried. At noon the flag was hauled down, but neither party displayed any inclination to renew the engagement, and after a few rounds of cannon shot Bourguien drew off unmolested, leaving Thomas master of the field.

Thus ended the severest battle that was ever fought between the disciplined armies of Hindustan up to that date. The troops opposed had been nearly equally matched, for though Bourguien commanded 8,000 men, and Thomas only 5,000, the latter's deficiency in numbers was made up by the greater strength of his position, the comparative freshness of his men, and his own immeasurably superior military skill.

The loss on both sides was enormous, but from the conflicting nature of the returns it is difficult to state the exact numbers. Captain Skinner, who was present at the battle, puts down Bourguien's casualties at between 3,000 and 4,000, but Thomas assesses them at 2,000, whilst Captain L. F. Smith states "that above 1,100 men were killed and wounded, which was nearly one-third of the number engaged." But Bourguien had 7,500 infantry at the very least, so that Thomas's estimate is probably the most correct. Skinner's must certainly be accepted cautiously, for his memory for dates and figures is peculiarly incorrect as a rule. Out of seven European officers engaged in the attack, Lieutenant M'Culloch was killed, Lieutenant Emilius Felix Smith mortally wounded, and Captains Oliver and Rabells wounded.

Thomas lost 700 men by his own account, though Skinner puts it down at 2,000. The destruction of artillery on both sides was very great. Twenty-five of Bourguien's tumbrels were blown up, and fifteen of his guns dismounted, owing to the sandy soil from which they were fired preventing a proper recoil, and so causing the axle-trees to snap. In the same way Thomas lost twenty pieces of cannon, only a few of which were dismounted by the enemy's shot striking them.

But a far greater loss to him was the death of Captain Hopkins, who succumbed to his wound a few hours after the action. "He was worth more than a couple of battalions to Thomas," writes one who knew him, "and had the latter possessed another such officer the undecided day of Georgegarh would have been turned into victory." As these words are being penned, ninety years have passed to the very day since Hopkins fell in battle. The coincidence of date comes suddenly and with something of a shock, even as the ink that records his death is wet. God knows under what insignificant dot of land in that distant country lie mouldering the bones of this gallant adventurer. But laying down the pen, and musing for an idle moment, a forlorn pity steals over the mind as one thinks of how he was cut off in the bright spring-tide of his youth, squandering all that human nature holds most dear in the insignificant service he belonged to. Expatriated, remote, unknown, he died a soldier's death, acquitting himself as nobly as if he had been fighting under the flag of his own country, instead of in a cause that yielded little credit, and less renown. Thrice in these pages, within the compass of a year, the brief chronicle of Hopkins' bravery finds mention : twice wounded, the third time dead, and so forgotten—poor dropped atom in the world's dust !

Indecisive as was the battle of Georgegarh, the advantage remained with Thomas. Had he availed himself of his opportunity he would have added a crowning success to his career. Colonel Skinner admits this when he writes: "We had always heard that Thomas was a brave, active, and clever soldier, and an able general. But we were surprised that he now permitted us to remain for fifteen days without attempting to attack us, or make good his retreat to Hánsi : for there was no doubt in our minds that had he tried either plan he would have succeeded. The state of our guns and the spirits of our soldiery was such that, had Thomas shown any inclination to move towards us, we should have got out of his reach, for our commander, Major Louis Bourguien, was not only a coward, but a fool. He was one of those who got on by flattery, and had it not been for Major Bernier, a Frenchman, we should certainly have lost the day; for the Major was not seen at all during the battle, and our being saved from total destruction was entirely owing to the exertions of Major Bernier, who was a brave and able soldier."

There is a humiliating confession in this passage, and one cannot but hope that De Boigne never learnt to what a low ebb " the spirits of his soldiery " had been reduced. Perron, when he wrote to his old chief in the following February, and boasted that "he had been obliged to entirely destroy that scoundrel Thomas," omitted to touch on this incident, or to mention how Captain Drugeon, the general's deputy at Delhi, collected all the doctors in the city and bundled them off to the front to tend the wounded, whilst Perron himself raised new troops, and hurried forward reinforcements with feverish haste.

Captain Lewis Ferdinand Smith takes even a stronger view than Skinner of the possibilities opened to Thomas by the battle of

13

Georgegarh, as the following passage will show:—" Had Thomas taken advantage of Bourguien's ignorance and folly, and sallied out on the beaten troops of Perron, he would have overturned his power. But Thomas was, in this critical moment, confused and confounded, though he had shown feats of valour during the action . . . Had he acted with his usual boldness, caution and activity, the forces under Bourguien must have been destroyed ; the allies of Thomas would have thrown off the mask, and openly taken his part ; and before Perron could have collected another efficient force, Thomas would have been master of Delhi and the king's person, and probably have extinguished Perron's power and authority. Scindia would have quietly transferred that power to Thomas, for he would have been equally indifferent who governed Hindostan, Perron or Thomas, as he must, from impotency to resist, have bowed to the will and power of every aspiring mind who commanded large bodies of regular infantry."

It was in this supreme moment of his career that Thomas fell. Fell from an estate so high, that its possibilities are scarcely credible when we consider the character of the man who might have grasped them, and learn the reason why he failed to do so. That reason has not hitherto been hinted at, but it had long existed. When Thomas required his faculties to be clearest, his understanding unclouded, and his energies strung to their highest pitch, he gave way to drink ! Alas ! for the unheroing of this hero, that he should have sold himself so cheaply, so vulgarly, so wantonly. Who shall diagnose a drunkard's reasons ? Perchance Thomas was over-affected by the death of gallant Hopkins, and his impressionable Irish nature sought the solace which countrymen of his class not unfrequently fly to on such occasions : perchance it was the very devilry of drink that drove him to the bottle ; or a more charitable explanation may lie in the stimulant required by the unendurable fatigue of over-taxed physical effort, or the terrible strain of mental anxiety. It matters little which. The pitiable truth remains that in the momentous crisis of his life Thomas surrendered himself to the demon that enslaved him, and in one wild, reckless debauch, sacrificed everything.

Those who have followed him thus far in the erratic course of his adventurous career, and who, in noting each step in it, have sighed over his lawlessness and condemned his abandonment, but have yet been cajoled into admiration for the man militant, may surely, in this moment of his weakness and his folly, as they see him distraught and undone, blindly seeking his own destruction, spare one regret for the lost man. Remembering only, out of their charity, those things which lie to his credit: the loyalty that never deserted a friend, the chivalry that so oftentimes succoured the weak, the enterprise which raised him to the height from which he fell, and the invincible spirit that sustained him through twenty years of war and battle in the East.

into the breach from which he fell, and the impulsive spirit that
sustained him through thirty years of war and battle in the East

CHAPTER VIII.

GATHERING TOILS. A DASH FOR HÁNSI.

1801.

FOR a fortnight after the battle of Georgegarh Thomas resigned the
entire conduct of his affairs to Captain Hearsey, who, instead of
pressing forward to attack, or retiring on Hánsi, began to fortify the
camp—a proceeding that halted half way between an advance to
victory and a retreat to safety. The reason he gave for his action
was that he expected assistance from Lakwa Dáda, but this chief was
fully employed in defending himself against Ambaji Inglia's English
officer, James Shepherd, and was, moreover, in a state of pecuniary
embarrassment, for it had recently been publicly reported he had been
obliged to sell his jewels to raise money to pay his troops.

It is difficult to understand the considerations which induced
Hearsey to repose confidence in the faith of a Marátha, and on the
strength of it take up a position in an open camp instead of falling
back on Hánsi, which was not only Thomas's capital and arsenal and
the base of his supplies, but a fortress of great strength, and capable
of opposing an indefinite resistance to Perron. Ignoring this, Hearsey
elected to fortify what was little better than an open cantonment,
completely cut off from all resources, and without any corresponding
advantage in return.

While Thomas drank the golden moments away, and Hearsey
thought only of holding an untenable position, reinforcements kept
reaching the enemy daily. Drugeon, Perron's deputy commandant
at Delhi, hurried forward all the available troops he could spare.
Perron detached five battalions of the Second Brigade from Koil,
and five more from Hessing's corps at Agra: Bapu Sindhia, the
Marátha Súbahdar of Saharanpur, contributed a large force of cavalry,
and the chiefs of Bhartpur and Hathras supplied their quota of troops.
Last of all, a great many of the Sikh chiefs joined Thomas's enemies,

amongst them being Sahib Singh of Patiála, whose Amazonian sister, Kunúr, died on the 15th of September, at the early age of twenty-eight.

Perron, when he heard of Bourguien's defeat, was furious, and despite that officer's solemn asseveration that " God knew he had done his best," superseded him by Major Pedron, who commanded the Second Brigade. This officer immediately started for the front, and shortly after he had assumed command at Georgegarh, a cordon of 30,000 men and 110 pieces of artillery was drawn round Thomas. This army was made up of twenty-two battalions of regular infantry, including ten of the Third Brigade, five of the Second Brigade, five of Hessing's, and two of the Begum Somru's (the authority quoted is that of Colonel Skinner), with 2,000 regular Hindustani horse, and about 12,000 Sikh and Maráthá cavalry. One of Pedron's first acts was to advance his line and secure possession of a large tank or reservoir of water, a short distance outside Georgegarh, which left Thomas with only three wells to depend on. Very soon the enormous display of force brought against him overawed the surrounding peasantry, who submitted to Pedron, and discontinued their usual supplies of provisions to the beleaguered camp, by which the difficulties within it were very considerably augmented.

And now, when it was too late, Thomas pulled himself together and resumed the command of his troops. He soon realised that he was too weak to draw out his army in open field and give battle, and that all he could do was to remain within his lines and act on the defensive. Something of his old energy and resource began to return to him, and he set to work to fortify the camp in the best manner possible, building around it a hedge of the same kind of thorn trees he had utilised in his defence of Fatehpur, and found so efficacious. He then took a careful stock of his provisions, and found they were sufficient for a month's consumption. Having thus arranged everything for the security of the camp, he braced himself to hold out until assistance arrived from Lakwa Dáda, who, at the commencement of hostilities, had given him frequent assurances of support.

It was now nearly the middle of October. Soon skirmishes began to take place daily, and Thomas made frequent sorties and attacked Pedron's entrenchments, but was never able to capture any of them. Isolated duels were often fought in the open plain between the two camps by detached parties from either army, but although Thomas's troops behaved with signal gallantry, they were always overpowered by superior numbers and driven back within their own lines again. On the 18th of October a grand concerted attack was made in conjunc tion with some troops Váman Ráo had sent to Thomas's assistance, but it failed, and the latter lost 400 men without effecting anything decisive. The following day, Rahmán Khán, one of his Afghan mercenaries, made a gallant sortie with 2,000 men, but only to be driven back by a heavy cannonade from Pedron's well-posted guns. And so a fortnight passed, marked by frequent conflicts, in which nothing was gained, and by the end of it Thomas's provisions had shrunk alarmingly, for his foraging parties found it impossible to avoid the Sikh and Marátha cavalry that swarmed round the camp, and prevented them from replenishing his fast diminishing stock. Day followed day, and one week another, and there was no sign of Lakwa Dáda's coming. The investing lines were drawn closer and closer, and the weak points in them strengthened, until at last a complete blockade was established, whilst, to complete his troubles, the water in Thomas's three wells began to show signs of failing.

The Asiatic soldier, no matter how heroically led and commanded, is a fatalist at heart, and this prejudices him for defensive operations, for, curiously enough, his fatalism always anticipates the worst, and when he touches his forehead and says "*Kismet*," he is prepared to accept defeat. When food ran short, and water began to be stinted, a portion of Thomas's troops commenced crying "*Kismet.*" Previous to the declaration of war he had enlisted several bands of Afghans to swell his ranks for the coming contest, and to the untrustworthiness of these treacherous mercenaries his ruin can in a great measure be traced. Pedron was not slow to avail himself of these facts, and began to intrigue with the malcontents in the besieged camp, and bring corrupt influences to bear upon them. The families of several of Thomas's native officers resided in Perron's territory, and their dependent situation was taken advantage of to effect their master's downfall. Perron, being acquainted with their circumstances, had, at the commencement of the war, placed guards over the houses of many of these individuals, notably over those of Shitáb Khán, who was commandant of the fort of Georgegarh, and Khairát Khán, who commanded Thomas's first matchlock regiment, both of whose families resided in villages belonging to Perron. These native officers were now pressed to desert their colours under pain of their property being confiscated, and their women folk maltreated—a threat more potent in the East than fire or sword. Bribes, threats, and promises were all freely used to induce them and others similarly situated to forsake their allegiance. To this unfair and ignoble pressure many succumbed, not a few being selected men, who had been the recipients of the greatest kindness from Thomas, and whom he had raised from low stations in his army to appointments of authority and command. Yet, in the hour of his sore distress, they scrupled not to prove traitors to their salt, and joined his enemies.

But there was even fouler treachery than this at work in the camp, for incendiary fires began to break out. In the fort of Georgegarh, where Shitáb Khán commanded, several stacks of hay, which formed the chief forage supply were destroyed, whilst the small remaining store of grain was made away with by means equally nefarious. Not content with this, these perfidious men were constantly instilling into the minds of the troops the peril of their situation, and the impossibility of saving themselves except by submitting to the enemy and joining them, as they were daily invited to do. Of these traitorous designs Thomas was not informed until it was too late, when their truth was brought home to him by the sudden increase in desertions.

Meanwhile Lakwa Dáda did not arrive, and, disheartened by Thomas's misfortunes, several other chiefs, who had promised him their assistance, not only withheld it, but actually joined his enemies. Constant and authentic information of all that was passing in his camp reached Pedron, who, on the 23rd of October, hoisted a flag, and publicly announced that all deserters from Georgegarh taking refuge under it should receive quarter. That night two of Thomas's newly-raised battalions marched out, and availed themselves of this proclamation, and three days later, Sharif Khán and Hamza Khán, two Afghan mercenaries, whom he had recently entertained, followed their base example, and passed over to Pedron with all their men.

Amidst all these dangers and difficulties Thomas was the only person who never lost heart, but unceasingly endeavoured to buoy up the spirits of his people with the assurance that help was coming. To Lakwa Dáda he sent frequent and urgent messages, and as constantly heard from him, one letter, full of the usual specious promises, reaching him as late as the 3rd of November. Váman Ráo also wrote encouraging Thomas to persevere, and stating he was sending reinforcements. But they were all words, idle words, and neither Lakwa Dáda's nor Váman Ráo's standards ever appeared.

On the 6th of November Thomas determined to make a last effort, and with a body of cavalry endeavoured to surprise Pedron's camp by a night attack. But traitors had given information of the intended attempt, and the sortie was met with a discharge of musketry, artillery and rockets from an enemy fully prepared and admirably posted, and the attempt resulted in failure and defeat. By this time Thomas was reduced to the direst straits. The grain in the camp was finished, and the scanty supply that his foraging parties collected at a great expense of life, was sold at the price of blood. His cattle had nearly all been killed, his water supply was almost exhausted, and his troops were kept alive on meat rations, a form of food not only unsuitable but positively injurious to men accustomed to grain diet. Finally, his ammunition began to run short, and threatened to leave him without the means, as well as without the men, to fight. In this extremity there remained to him but one single chance. A large convoy of grain had been despatched by Váman Ráo, and his hopes were all centred on its reaching him safely. It was due on the 10th of November, but on the previous night a detachment of Pedron's horse discovered and captured it. In a spirit of Oriental brutality the noses of the camel drivers conveying it were cut off and sent with taunts into Thomas's starving camp, early on the following morning. At the same hour he learnt of the desertion on the previous night of his most trusted Afghan chief, a man named Ali Ghól, in whom he had hitherto reposed the greatest confidence, and whose loyalty had never been doubted.

In such a pass the bravest man might without dishonour have given up an unequal fight; but submission never entered Thomas's mind. "In this distress," he writes, "I had no resource but either to attack the enemy by night, to sally forth and try the event of a contest by day, or to attempt a retreat, leaving the infantry to make the best terms they could with the enemy." No idea of surrender is apparent here, though it must have been the uppermost thought in the mind of every other man in the camp. But *Jowruj Jung* never belied his reputation for a moment. The word defeat was not in his dictionary: and when circumstances obtruded it, the letters shaped themselves into defiance. Fight by day, or fight by night, or, at worst, a dash through those investing lines, sword in hand, and his horse's head pointed for Hánsi, were still "resources" left him. After a short consideration he determined to hazard the first, and attempt to fight his way past the enemy, and reach his capital.

He accordingly gave the necessary directions for carrying this resolution into effect; but his soldiers, suspecting his intention, began to pack up their baggage and openly desert the camp. Upon this, Thomas assembled his officers and inquired of them the cause of the commotion stirring in the lines. They replied that no further reliance could be placed on the troops, who, confounded by their difficulties, would no longer remain true to their colours. On hearing this, Thomas proceeded in person to the lines, and endeavoured to reanimate his men, but hunger and thirst and want and privation had laid their hands upon his followers, and with the fatalism of their race they had accepted the decree of Fate, convinced that the star of *Jowruj Jung* had set.

But Thomas relaxed not his efforts. " To encourage the drooping spirits of his people " (!) he gave orders for an attack to be made on one of the enemy's advanced posts which, from its situation, appeared easy to be taken. But a difficulty arose regarding bullock drivers, who had all deserted the camp. Some sepoys, however, encouraged by the promise of a liberal reward, undertook the office, and a select detachment quitted the camp. But whether from being infected with the depression of spirits that prevailed, or because they were really unfit for the work assigned them, the sepoys conducted themselves in so awkward a manner, and made so little exertion in getting on the guns, that it was necessary to recall them to camp.

Shortly after this his spies brought Thomas information that the enemy, having been apprised of his intention to force his way to Hánsi, had formed line ready to oppose his progress. And it now seemed to him that, in the present discontented state of his troops, if he attempted to carry out his design, the termination must be defeat and disgrace.

The end was drawing near. At sunset Thomas summoned a council of war, and submitted to his officers the circumstances of their situation. They gave it as their unanimous opinion that nothing remained but an unconditional surrender to the enemy. Long and earnestly did their leader try to persuade them that a retreat to Hánsi was still practicable; but his exertions were ineffectual, and he was forced to confess that " a dismal aspect presented itself on all sides." The spirit of resistance was crushed out of the camp, saving only the inextinguishable spark glowing by comparison more brilliantly than ever in the bosom of its chief.

Scarcely was the council of war dismissed than Thomas learnt that a body of Rohillas stationed over the wells had gone over to the enemy. Other troops were at once appointed to guard the posts thus abandoned, but to his sorrow Thomas found that the spirit of desertion had seized on the Muhammadan soldiery in general, the cavalry alone excepted. At seven o'clock in the evening the whole of the troops stationed on out-post duty followed the example of the Rohillas, and it became apparent that Pedron was making preparations for a general assault. Simultaneously an incendiary fire broke out in the last stack of hay, which, as Thomas afterwards learnt, was a preconcerted signal between the traitors in his camp and the enemy. Even as the flames leapt forth into the dark night, word was brought him that Shitáb Khán, who commanded at

Georgegarh, and although secretly in league with Pedron, had up to now preserved an appearance of loyalty, was mounting his horse preparatory to leaving the fort, attended by all his people and their effects, and that a party of the Marátha troops had approached the walls in order to escort these deserters to safety, and occupy the abandoned post.

Thomas's soldiery were now openly deserting the camp in all directions, and the only battalion that remained faithful was the one formerly commanded by Hopkins. It had entered on the campaign 700 strong, but the severe service of the last two months had reduced it to little more than 200. " These," writes Thomas in his memoirs, with pathetic brevity, " were the only men that stood true to my interests."

Even the splendid spirit of *Jowruj Jung* was dismayed now. New dangers and calamities sprung up on every side. Within and without the camp all were against him. The enemy were preparing to advance in overwhelming numbers, and it was evident that in another hour all would be over. And so, at nine o'clock on the night of the 10th of November, 1801, George Thomas mustered his Europeans and 300 of his chosen cavalry, and putting himself at their head, led the way out of the doomed camp.

Prosper him, kind Fate! Prosper a brave man's ride to-night! No worthier object of thy kind decree ever appealed for thy aid. No stouter heart ever faced thee than this gallant Irishman, who gallops now for life and liberty!

The direction Thomas took was that in which Major George Hessing's Brigade was encamped, and against its five battalions he made his last daring charge. He succeeded in breaking through them, but the alarm was at once given, and the whole of Pedron's cavalry turned out in pursuit. Overtaking the little band of fugitives before they had gone far, they attacked them with vigour, and the escort, disheartened by late events, lost their accustomed courage and scattered and melted away, leaving Thomas with four Europeans—Captains Hearsey and Birch and two sergeants—to fly for their lives. And so, alone and unattended, "into the midnight they galloped abreast."

The horse Thomas rode was a favourite animal, of a very superior Persian breed, and of the highest spirit. He proved himself " a horse without peer " that night. The enemy continuing the pursuit, Thomas was compelled to make a circuitous route to avoid falling in with their straggling parties, and traversed double the actual distance between Georgegarh and Hánsi in reaching his destination. His generous steed covered the journey of 120 miles without halt or stay, and by nightfall of the 11th of November carried his master safely into his capital.

Fifty guns and all Thomas's camp and baggage fell into Pedron's hands. The few faithful troops left behind laid down their arms, rejecting with contempt the offers of service made them by the victors. Their personal attachment to Thomas survived his downfall, and several of his old native officers, who had been in his service for a long time, "rent their clothes and turned beggars, swearing they would never serve as soldiers again."

CHAPTER IX.

ONE IRISH SWORD !

1801.

UPON reaching Hánsi, Thomas's first care was directed towards its defences, and warned by bitter experience of the treacherous disposition of his Muhammadan soldiery, he committed the charge of the fort to his faithful Rajputs, whom on all occasions, and in most trying situations he found worthy of confidence. Two pieces of artillery were all that remained in the fort fit for service, but the dilatory advance of the enemy allowed time for eight new cannon to be cast and mounted. All the wells within a radius of several miles of the city were filled up, and the tanks defiled with beef and pork, so as to render their water undrinkable to either Hindu or Musalmán. Just outside Hánsi Thomas threw up three strongly-fortified outworks—one commanding the south-eastern gate, a second the southern, and a third the western gate, and these were manned with Rohilla troops. It is difficult to estimate the exact strength of the force that remained to him : Skinner puts it down at 5,000 men, but Thomas states there were only 1,200 adhering to his interests, of whom 300 were Rajputs. The latter estimate is probably the correct one : but whatever the number of his men, he had lost confidence in all except his Rajputs, and so critical did he consider his situation that he took up his residence within the fort and was careful to keep a strict guard during the night to avert treachery.

After his success at Georgegarh, Major Pedron brought the Third Brigade up to its full strength by drafting into it a sufficient number of men from the Second to fill the vacancies created by death and casualties, and conceiving the campaign practically finished, returned to Aligarh, leaving Major Louis Bourguien with ten full battalions of infantry, 500 Hindustani horse, and 5,000 Sikh cavalry to follow Thomas and effect the *coup de grâce*.

Bourguien set forward in a leisurely way, marching by easy stages
and possessing himself of the wells in the vicinity of Hánsi, which he
stopped to clear out. It was not until towards the end of November
that he reached the town, and after reconnoitring its environs several
times, formed his plan of attack. It was first necessary to capture
the outworks which defended the gates, and an assault upon them was
ordered. Three columns, of two battalions each, advanced at daybreak, led by Captain Skinner, Major Bernier, and Lieutenant
Mackenzie. They succeeded so easily, that Thomas ascribed their
victory to treachery. It is certain that Skinner and Mackenzie met
with but a nominal resistance, the garrisons scrambling out and
running away as the stormers advanced ; but, according to Skinner's
account, Major Bernier was obstinately opposed, for, by getting
between the town and the outwork he was attacking, he cut off the
retreat of the troops defending it, who fought well and drove the
stormers back. Bernier rallied them, but was killed in the act of
doing so, upon which his men rushed forward and carried the place,
putting every soul in it to death. Considerable doubt is, however,
thrown on this account by the recent discovery of a marble tomb
stone, which was erected over Bernier's grave, and the inscription on
which states that he was killed on the 10th of December at the
storming of Hánsi. The outpost affair above described occurred in
November, and it is probable that Skinner's memory was at fault in
making it the occasion of Bernier's death. The total loss on
Bourguien's side was very small, and the three captured works
were now fixed upon as points for his trenches. Batteries being
erected, a heavy fire was opened upon the walls of the town, and,
although the defenders kept up a smart return, a breach was effected,
and three columns, numbering 1,500 men each, were told off for the
storm.

At dawn of day on the 10th of December the signal for attack was
given. Captain Skinner and Lieutenants Skinner and Mackenzie were
the officers in command of the columns. The elder Skinner found
himself opposed by Lieutenant Birch, whilst his brother and Mackenzie
stormed the points defended by Captain Hearsey and a native officer
named Elias Beg. The two lieutenants made good their way after
some resistance, but Captain Skinner was twice beaten back by
Birch, who defended his post well. Burning thatch, powder pots, and
every missile that came to hand were showered down upon the
stormers, greatly distressing and disheartening them. At a third
attempt, however, they made good their footing, and just as Skinner
clambered up the breach, he saw Birch about twenty yards off

taking aim at him with a double barrelled gun, both of which barrels he discharged. Fortunately he missed his mark and Skinner immediately " levelled his javelin," and darting it at Birch, took off his hat, whereupon the latter set off running and joined his party who had already left the walls.

Bourguien's three columns now converged towards the centre of the town, driving the enemy before them, until Thomas came up with his reserves to the relief. Attacking the younger Skinner he beat him back to the walls of the town ; but the latter, being joined by his brother, advanced again, and obliged Thomas to retire. The three columns now effected a junction in the central bazaar, which became the scene of a desperate conflict. Thomas having ordered up a 6-pounder, brought it to bear on the stormers, and by several discharges of grape expelled them from the bazaar, but they, being reinforced by a reserve battalion and two 9-pounders, were able to retake the position. The contest was now carried on at closest quarters, the fighting being hand to hand. Young Skinner approached so near to Thomas that he made a sabre cut at him and would have disabled him but for the protection afforded by his armour. Thrice the tide of battle ebbed to and fro, now one party, now the other, gaining ground. The narrow side streets were choked with the bodies of the dead, and wounded who had crawled out of the way, and the central bazaar ran red with blood. Desperate defence was opposed to obstinate attack from morning until noon, when the superiority of Bourguien's numbers began to tell, and after disputing every inch of gr nd with the most determined valour and resolution, Thomas was compelled to withdraw into the fort and abandon his capital to his enemies.

The loss of life, in comparison to the numbers engaged, was enormous. Skinner puts down the killed and wounded on Bourguien's side at 1,600, but due allowances must be made for his habitual exaggeration. Amongst the wounded was Lieutenant Mackenzie, and several native officers were killed. Thomas records that after the fight only 700 men remained to him, and this would make his loss about 500. Directly victory was assured, Bourguien, who had watched the conflict from a strategic, but safe, position in the rear, marched into the town with two battalions and 3,000 dismounted troopers, and relieved the combatants who were allowed to retire to the rear.

The following morning Bourguien's battering guns were dragged into Hánsi, and trenches dug within two hundred yards of the fort. Eight 18-pounders being run into position in the central bazaar, their fire was brought to bear upon the walls of the citadel. Thomas made every disposition to defend himself, but his troops had lost heart and were no longer the same men whom he had so often led to victory in the past. From time to time they followed him out to the attack, but they fought with the conviction of coming defeat, and although he sometimes succeeded in driving the enemy out of the trenches, he was unable to maintain any temporary advantage.

The bombardment itself produced but little effect, for the balls of the cannon merely buried themselves in the mud walls of the fort without in the least degree shaking their solidity. On this becoming apparent it was decided to commence mining, and Bourguien's sappers advanced to within ten yards of the crown-work. But meanwhile the condition of affairs within the fort fell from bad to worse. Provisions were scarce, and the danger from shot and shell so constant as not to leave a moment's rest. The spirit of mutiny appeared amongst the Muhammadan troops, and numerous desertions occurred, so that it was soon apparent that only time was wanting to complete the tale of Thomas's ruin.

Bourguien now began to intrigue with the garrison in the fort. Letters offering them six months' pay and permanent service under the Marátha flag were rolled round arrows and shot over the ramparts, and replied to by the same method. Before long these insidious proposals began to bear fruit. There were still a faithful few around Thomas, but they were in the minority, and Bourguien was assured by those he tampered with that in a short time they would be able to arrange an accommodation for the fort to be surrendered and its master delivered up.

But in this the darkest hour of that dark time *Jowruj Jung* found in his enemy's camp hearts touched by his splendid spirit, and who would not suffer this gallant soldier to become the victim of such foul treachery as that premeditated. Lewis Ferdinand Smith, the two Skinners and Mackenzie were respectable and honourable men, and unable to acquiesce in deeds of shame. Bourguien had boasted how he would ill-use "that blackguard Irishman " when he once got hold of him, vowing he should be confined in prison, a threat he was quite capable of carrying into execution. " But this," writes Skinner, " was language we did not admire, and we felt indignant at this underhand treachery, and agreed that it would be disgraceful if Thomas fell through such intrigue." And so these officers, some English, some countryborn, waited upon Bourguien and remonstrated against what was going on, and, partly by protest, partly by persuasion, prevailed upon him to allow Thomas the barren honours of a capitulation, pointing out that much more credit would result from such a course than if the end was secured by unfair means. For a long time Bourguien resisted, but "one day, after tiffin, when the wine he had drunk had put him in high spirits and good humour," they pressed their point, and at last he consented, calling out in his broken English, " Well, gentlemen, you do as you like. I give power. Only he be one dam Englishman."

Thomas was aware of the conspiracy ripening against him, but powerless to prevent it. The Rajputs still remained faithful, and it was his intention to hold out as long as it was possible ; but it was plain to see that the end was near, and that nothing could save him. When, therefore, Captain Smith was deputed to visit him, under a flag of truce, with the offer of honourable terms, Thomas received him with gratitude, and on learning he had been sent by the whole of the English officers to save him from dishonour, thanked him and begged he would return and say any terms the officers recommended would be accepted. After some trouble, Bourguien was prevailed upon to sanction the following : that Thomas should be permitted to depart with all his money and private property to British territory, and his troops allowed to march out with all their private arms, and the honours of war ; but that everything else in the fort was to be made over to the victors.

Thomas's acceptation of these terms may be best recorded in his own words :—

" Considering, therefore, that I had entirely lost my party, and with it the hopes of at present subduing my enemies, the Sikhs, and the powers in the French interest ; that I had no expectation of succour from any quarter, Luckwa having gone to Joudpore ; that if hostilities continued my resources in money would have failed ; in this situation I agreed to evacuate the fort."

And so the curtain fell on the rule of *Jowruj Jung*, and the principality he founded. Won by the sword, and held by the sword, it was surrendered at the sword's point. Crowded are its brief but brilliant annals with tales of lawless, yet dauntless daring and audacious energy, and fitly closed by the heroism of the last grand struggle, when against dangers that appalled, and overwhelming numbers that crushed, the unconquerable spirit of George Thomas resisted for long weeks of unequal strife and constant battle the might of Perron's power.

On the 20th of December, 1801, the terms of surrender were drawn out and signed, and a cessation of hostilities declared. It was agreed that possession of the fort should be given up in two days. An interview followed between Bourguien and Thomas, at the bungalow of the latter, which was situated upon the banks of the Umtee tank in the town of Hánsi. All Bourguien's officers were assembled to receive the defeated soldier. His behaviour was dignified and courteous, and he was particularly gracious to the younger Skinner, " whom he embraced," and showed him the cut he had received from him on his belt during the fight of the 10th of December. His demeanour had a marked effect on Bourguien, who treated him with great politeness and invited him and his two officers, Birch and Hearsey, to dinner on the next day.

Thomas accepted the invitation, and about seven o'clock on the following evening rode into camp, attended by 50 of his cavalry. His bearing was now greatly changed from that of yesterday, and he showed signs of deep dejection, as though bowed down by the weight of his misfortunes. At eight o'clock dinner was served in a large tent and all sat down. With the chivalrous sympathy all brave soldiers feel for a fallen foe, Bourguien's officers tried their utmost to cheer their guest, carefully framing their conversation so as to avoid all reference to recent events, and endeavouring to enlist his interest in other topics. Presently the wine began to flow, and Thomas sought comfort in its fickle cheer. By eleven o'clock at night the whole company was " pretty merry," and drinking the health of " General Perron " and " George Thomas," and Thomas himself seemed quite happy.

Suddenly, stirred by some evil and ungenerous impulse, Louis Bourguien raised his glass aloft, and from his seat at the head of the table, called loudly out : " Let us drink to the success of Perron's arms ! "

In a moment the sounds of laughter and carouse died away, and an ominous hush succeeded, as those present rebelled against the toast and in testimony turned their glasses up.

As Thomas realised the import of that action, and the generous sympathy it conveyed, his impulsive Irish nature yielded to the insult, and to the condemnation it had evoked, and he burst into tears.

But only for a moment. The next he was *Jowruj Jung* once more, fierce and furious. Springing to his feet he confronted the man who could thus taunt him in the hour of his misfortune, and laying his hand on his sword hilt, called out to Bourguien that it was to his own ill-fate his fall was due, and not to the prowess of the low braggart who insulted him. Then, drawing his sword and waving it over his head, he cried aloud :

" One Irish Sword is still sufficient for a hundred Frenchmen."

One Irish Sword ! And what a sword it was. Sikh and Rohilla

14

Rajput and Pathán had fled before it. It had shielded the Mugha provinces of Saharanpur from invasion, and reinstated the Witch of Sardhána on her throne; it had scourged the lawless Mewátti districts into submission, and established a ruler in rebellious Rewari; Jaipur and Bikanir had paid it tribute, Batinda had bought its clemency, Hariána knew its weight, and Udaipur its reach; it had carried conquest to the banks of the gleaming Sutlej, and, but three months since, had defeated the battalions that were still known as " De Boigne's." *One Irish Sword*—sufficient for a hundred Frenchman, truly, as it flashed out now in the dimly-lighted tent. More than sufficient for Louis Bourguien, who felt the magic of its latent power, and in a palsy of terror jumped from his chair, and rushing out of the tent, called for his guard to protect him.

Thomas's troopers, who were outside, crowded in at the first sound of high words. For a moment it seemed as though a fight was imminent, but the European officers present assured them that it was "only the Sahib drunk," and bade the men keep off, whilst Thomas in the midst kept wildly waving his sword and calling out in Hindustani to " See! see! how he had made the d——d Frenchman run like a jackal."

A dramatic scene. Picture the great Irishman, swaying to and fro, as he lunges and thrusts with his sword into the empty air, in the intensity of his excitement. In his face the flush of wine, in his eyes the glitter of passion, in his attitude the ferocity of insulted honour. The swarthy troopers, thronging in, press forward with clank of steel and angry cries; the turbaned servants huddle in the doorways; without the hurried cry to arms, and shouting and confusion swelling the clamour; within the tent all have risen from the littered table, and are crowding round Thomas, striving to pacify him, whilst he wrestles and towers above them, waving his sword and glaring at the empty chair from whence the master of the feast has fled.

It required the greatest persuasion to prevail upon him to sheath his weapon. The natives were hustled out, and after Thomas had been induced to resume his seat, it was explained to him that the wine Bourguien had taken was the cause of his forgetting himself, and that no insult had been intended. With the inconsistency of intoxication, Thomas agreed to make it up, whereupon the Frenchman ventured to return, and shaking hands begged Thomas's pardon.

Peace being thus restored, the wine flowed again, and it was soon evident that the banquet was degenerating into an orgies. The elder Skinner was orderly officer of the day, and seeing how matters were shaping, withdrew and rode off to the town, which was occupied by

Bourguien's troops, to caution the men not to challenge Thomas on his return to the fort. Unfortunately he omitted to warn the guard posted at the south-eastern gate, which was the one Thomas entered by, and in consequence on the arrival of the latter about midnight, he was saluted with the usual challenge "*Who-Kum-Dar*?"

"*Sahib Bahadur!*" (the great master), was the reply from Thomas's troopers, that being the name by which he was always known.

The sentry replied that he knew of no *Sahib Bahadur*, and could let no one pass without permission from his officer. Thomas heard this, and turning round to his men asked them,

"Could any one have stopped *Sahib Bahadur* at this gate but one month ago?"

"No, no!" they answered, with the effusive concurrence typical of the native character. Whereupon Thomas dismounted, and drawing his sword, made a slash at the poor sentry and cut off his right hand. The guard immediately fell in and Thomas's life was in danger, but just at this moment Skinner came up and further mischief was avoided.

He found Thomas staggering up and down, his naked sword in his hand, and Hearsey and several of his troopers trying to lay hold of him. At length one of the latter caught him from behind, and he was disarmed. He then submitted to be placed in a palanquin, and in this conveyance the Lord of Hánsi was carried into his fort for the last time.

The next morning, on recovering his senses, Thomas learnt from Hearsey what had happened. Whereupon he sent for the trooper he had maimed and gave him Rs.500, and wrote to Bourguien apologising for his conduct.

Alas, for that Irish sword! The pity that it should be sullied by the stain of this cowardly act. In all his excesses Thomas never plumbed a deeper degradation of drink than this pitiable incident displays. Would that, if happen it must, it had happened on any other night than that on which, in a flash of defiance that lifted him high above his misfortunes, he bearded Bourguien at his own table, and claimed for his Irish sword that it was still sufficient for a hundred Frenchmen!

CHAPTER X.

THE DEATH AND CHARACTER OF GEORGE THOMAS.

1802.

ON the 29th of December, 1801, George Thomas evacuated Hánsi, and three days later, under escort of a battalion of Bourguien's infantry commanded by Captain Smith, started for Anupshahr—the very place from which he had commenced his adventurous career exactly eight years before. He carried with him the wreck of his fortune, to the value of about one lakh of rupees, in money, jewelry, shawls and other property, and was accompanied by his wife and family.

From Anupshahr Thomas proceeded by river to Benares, which he reached in March. Here he met the Governor-general's fleet of boats on its way to Lucknow, and was invited by Lord Wellesley to an interview, in the course of which Thomas afforded the Governor-general a great deal of valuable information about the countries beyond Delhi, and the strength of the armies of the native princes in the western parts of India. In connection with this meeting there is a characteristic anecdote recorded, which must not be omitted. In order to illustrate Thomas's remarks a map of India was laid on the table, in which, as was and is still customary, the British possessions were coloured red. On this being explained to Thomas, he swept his great hand across the chart from end to end with the emphatic comment, " *All* this ought to be red ! "

Therein breathed the true spirit of *Jowruj Jung*. Red that map was destined to be, and the great statesman he addressed little suspected how soon. And in this connection it is curious to observe that nearly forty years later, Ranjit Singh, the old Lion of Lahore, made an almost identical observation under similar circumstances, for when a map of India happened to be placed before him and the theory of its colouring explained, he fixed on it that one penetrating eye of his, " which was equal to any other man's two eyes," and almost in Thomas's words remarked, " It will all be red soon."

CEMETERY AT BERHAMPORE IN WHICH GEORGE THOMAS IS BURIED.

[*From a photograph: The tombstones in the foreground bear inscriptions dated 1802 and 1803: the date of Thomas's death was 1802.*]

Thomas remained some time at Benares arranging his affairs, and it was here that he dictated his memoirs to Captain Francklin. "He proposed," writes his biographer, "to deliver his information in the Persian language, adding, that from constant use, it had become more familiar to him than his native tongue. This offer, for obvious reasons, was declined; but it proves Mr. Thomas's capacity under every disadvantage arising from a want of regular education, and I have no hesitation in declaring my opinion that if Mr. Thomas had found leisure to cultivate his mind, his progress in the most useful branches of literature would have been surprisingly rapid. He spoke, wrote, and read the Hindustani and Persian languages with uncommon fluency and precision."

It was Thomas's wish to return to Ireland with his family and fortune, and pass his days in retirement in his native land. With this aim in view he left Benares, and commenced his journey to Calcutta by river. But misfortunes had broken his daring mind and impaired his robust constitution, and he succumbed, a victim to his own fatal weakness, on the 22nd of August, 1802, in the forty-sixth year of his age. He died near the military cantonment of Bahrámpur, in the burying ground of which place his remains were interred.

Captain Francklin states that a monument was being erected to Thomas's memory at the time when he was finishing his memoirs. Anxious to include in these pages the epitaph which his contemporaries placed over George Thomas, particular endeavours have been made to secure the same, but without success. "I have searched every cemetery in Berhampur, English and Dutch," writes an esteemed and courteous correspondent, "but no trace of George Thomas's tomb can be found. In the cemetery now in use there are many old tombs without any name plates left on them : the plates have fallen out, and where they have been picked up whole, they have been inserted in the wall. I have no doubt that Mr. Thomas's plate has fallen out and been broken—if it ever existed." The illustration shows the probable site of his grave.

In appearance Thomas was a singularly fine and tall man, standing upwards of six feet in height, and his limbs and body were massive and well proportioned. His constitution was an iron one, and his physical strength enormous, whilst his dexterity with the sword was such that he could decapitate a bullock with a single stroke. His countenance was bold and open, and his bearing manly and erect. "From the constant and active use of his limbs, during his long and arduous warfare" writes Francklin, "he had contracted a certain elevation of the head, which gave him an air of stiffness, but, at the same time, added to his martial appearance, and seemed to indicate something of the intrepidity of spirit which wholly possessed his conduct to the last hour of his life."

The life which was brought to a premature close at Bahrámpur presents a strange admixture of strength and weakness, and the contrast enables us to see the actual clay of which the man was moulded. Although this circumstance may dispel much of the glamour that surrounds Thomas's romantic career, the knowledge of his frailty heightens our astonishment at his achievement. For it reveals the fact that this fearless Irishman, who, cutting himself adrift from all communication with his fellow-countrymen, plunged into an unknown land, raised himself from the position of a private soldier in a native army to that of an independent prince, waged indiscriminate war, invaded foreign territories, fought battles, stormed fortresses, and pillaged towns, premeditated the conquest of the Panjab, and pitted his strength against Perron when the latter was in the zenith of his power—this Irishman, we find, was a very human hero after all. From the summit of his success as independent ruler of Hánsi and self-elected scourge of the Sikh states, it is a deep drop into the abyss of that fatal fortnight at Georgegarh, and an acquaintance with these facts creates a wonder, not how he rose but how he fell. We find it, indeed, more difficult to understand his exhibition of weakness than his display of strength.

There is, of course, very much that is unrecorded in Thomas's life. Francklin's memoir is, at best, a mere summary of facts, without a comment or an explanation conceded. What Thomas did—he did. No analysis of motive elucidates his actions, even when they are most lawless. Perhaps it is better so. It is to be feared that the philosophy of *Jowruj Jung* savoured too much of "the good old plan" to permit of his history being too closely scrutinised.

But passing from his motives to his deeds there comes to us much that compels our admiration. The romanceful pages of Indian adventure contain no epic more stirring than that of George Thomas. Whether he is striding forward to conquest, or standing defiant in resistance he amazes us with his prodigious daring and his unconquerable resolution. Without a single advantage of birth or education, without means and without friends, he fought his way to success. Suffering in its acutest form from an Irishman's irresistible propensity for fighting, Thomas's Indian career was one prolonged battle. Never resting for one moment on his arms, he faced about from one victory or repulse, only to attack another foe. Nothing dismayed him, nothing stopped him. He led his flying columns thirty, forty, and fifty miles a day into the heart of an enemy's country; he sacked villages of their cooking-pots and household utensils for metal to cast him cannon; he seldom saw a fortress but he stormed it there and then; never met a foe but he forthwith offered fight. He did not know what it was to be defeated, and was most dangerous when other men would have been most despairing. And yet, with all his lust of battle and his lawless extravagance, there comes, ever and anon, some strangely touching incident to reveal the finer nature of the man, as when we find him forgiving a treacherous master, championing a deposed prince, or assisting some weak and oppressed woman in her distress, with a nobility of character, a disinterestedness of design, and a chivalry of feeling that would have become many a better man.

Let contemporary opinion speak for Thomas's character.

"Thomas was formed by nature," writes Captain Francklin, "to execute the boldest designs, and though uncultivated by education he possessed a native and inherent vigour of mind, which qualified him for the performance of great actions, and placed him on a level with distinguished officers of his day. His knowledge of the different tribes and nations that composed the interior of the vast peninsula of India was various, extensive and correct, and no man, perhaps, ever more thoroughly studied, or properly appreciated the Indian character at large. In his manners he was gentle and inoffensive, and possessed a natural politeness, and evinced a disposition to please, superior to most men. He was a loyal subject to his king, and a real and sincere well-wisher to the prosperity and permanence of the British Empire in the East. He was open, generous, charitable and humane, and his behaviour towards the families of those persons who fell in his service evinces a benevolence of heart, and a philanthropy of spirit highly honourable to his character. But with these good qualities the impartiality of history demands that we should state his errors, and endeavour to discover some shades in a character otherwise splendid. A quickness of temper, liable to frequent agitation and the ebullitions of hasty wrath, not unfrequently rendered his appearance ferocious; yet this only occurred in instances when the conviviality of his temper obscured his reason, and for this, on conviction, no man was ever readier to make every acknowledgment and reparation in his power. Perfect correctness of conduct cannot be expected from a character like the one under consideration, as a seclusion from civilised life and long absence from the exercise of those duties which constitute the chief enjoyment of social happiness, must necessarily have tinctured the manners of the man with some portion of the spirit of the barbarians with whom he was so long intimate. Upon the whole, however, we may be justified in remarking that on a review of the life and actions of this very extra-ordinary man, it is difficult which most to admire—the intrepidity of spirit by which he was incited to the performance of actions which, by their effect, raised him from the condition of a private subject to rank and distinction among princes, or the wonderful and uncommon at-tachment generally exhibited towards his person and interest by the natives of every description who fought and conquered with him in his long and arduous career, and whose assistance exalted him for a time to a height of respectability and consequence that seldom falls to the lot of an individual."

In these lines Captain Francklin has laboured much to disguise Thomas's failings ; but reading carefully between them it is easy to recognise the particular vices and shortcomings they indicate. No one could believe the debauch of Georgegarh was a new and sudden folly ; it was, alas, the climax of a long course of dissipation. And for the rest it is enough to mention that Thomas so far conformed to the customs of the country as to keep a harem. After his death an exceedingly numerous progeny found an asylum at Sardhána, through the indulgence and charity of the Begum Somru, only in process of time to become merged in the native population of the country ; although one, who bore his father's name, rose to the position of an officer in her army.

The following testimony of Lewis Ferdinand Smith is, perhaps, more valuable than that of Captain Francklin, for he was brought into earlier and more intimate relations with Thomas.

" Thomas was a bold, enterprising adventurer, who stepped over difficulties which would have disheartened many daring minds. He was coarse and illiterate, but his courage was undaunted, his perse-verance invincible, and his activity indefatigable. He had a strong judgment, cautious prudence, and great natural powers, was generous and hospitable, and often insinuating from inclination : and his ambi-tion required the operation of all these three qualities. All ambitious characters must be generous : it is one of the most powerful instru-ments to forward their views. Thomas's conduct had been sur-prisingly admirable until the moment when he required the exertion of all his uncommon powers. At this critical moment he failed, and failed astonishingly. I can only ascribe it to his being confounded at the difficulties which opposed him, to his want of European officers, and to the treachery of his native commanders.

"I was intimately acquainted with him, and had a sincere respect for his character. With some oddities, and many singularities, he was an uncommon character, and his exertions towards station, power, riches and glory, were still more uncommon. He was extraordinarily ambitious, which was the principal cause that led to his ruin. He would be all or nothing. To serve under the orders of another was an inglorious dependence in his estimation of things. Courage he possessed to an eminent degree, and he certainly had abilities, if a clear head, a solid judgment, and an acute discernment can be called by that name."

To Thomas's military talents several competent critics have borne testimony. Writes a contributor in the *Calcutta Review :*—" We find this uneducated and dissipated adventurer casting guns at Hánsi, strengthening his flanks in action against large bodies of cavalry with *abbatis*, and altogether demeaning himself as a soldier in a manner that would have done credit to the school of Wellington and Napoleon." And another in the same journal : " This remarkable man, by dint of perseverance, military skill, and great personal valour, carved out for himself a small principality, and had there been only natives to contend against would have held it. In him was preeminently displayed the energy of character which distinguishes the European from the Asiatic. We find him refusing to desert the cause of friends, bringing into subjection a district previously uncontrollable, building forts, casting cannon, and training levies. To support the widow of a Mahomedan prince, who had appealed to him for help, he marched through a hostile country, in open warfare with the chiefs of it, whom he defeated in more than one battle, and he was the first Englishman to plant his foot on the banks of the Sutlez, although that honour is usually ascribed to Lord Lake."

Colonel James Tod, the author of "The Annals of Rajas'than," thus summarises Thomas's character in the pages of the *Asiatic Journal :*

"In Thomas was seen the union of wild energy, considerable foresight, and daring intrepidity, with gigantic form and strength, which placed him among the most conspicuous of all who carved their way to fortune in that wild field. Nor is there any reasonable doubt that, but for the brilliant close of his career in the unequal but unavoidable contest with Perron, he would have made Lahore his capital. For the Sikhs quailed before the name of Thomas, who spoke of them as soldiers with contempt, and treated them to hard knocks. With 500 of his Rohilla cavalry he would at any time have disposed of thrice that number of Sikh horse."

This long list of quotations may be concluded by an extract from the *Edinburgh Review.* " If we can forgive Thomas what, at that time and under his circumstances, was rarely accounted a crime, that he shed blood, and that very largely, in the quarrels of others with which he had no concern, and that he manifested very violent outbursts of temper, we shall still, to do him justice, be obliged to admit that he displayed many and very striking traits of generosity and benevolence; that he was scrupulously true to his engagements; that he never deserted or betrayed a friend or an ally; and that he possessed in an uncommon measure those noble qualities which secured to him the devoted attachment of all, of whatsoever race, who served under him."

In estimating the character and career of George Thomas, after a lapse of nearly a hundred years, we must divest ourselves of many modern ideas, and judge him by the standard of the times in which he lived, and the scenes in which he laboured. They were barbarous times and savage scenes. In the world which he penetrated, only the strongest arm and sharpest sword, the shrewdest brain and least scrupulous conscience, met with success. Moral obligations were unknown in the Marátha Empire. The ethics of the sons of Sivaji were simple. Might was right, and the end justified the means.

The starting point from which Thomas began his career did not qualify him for the exhibition of any extraordinary virtue or forbearance. A common sailor at the end of the last century was familiarised to despotism and tyranny. His personal liberty extended no further than the hail of the press gang: his professional duties were inculcated and exacted with a Spartan severity; and he was rendered callous of life by the cheerful way in which he was called on to kill or be killed. At a time when the high seas swarmed with privateers and pirates, the lawlessness of maritime warfare was notorious, and battle and chase were the conditions, not the exceptions, of naval life. This was the school in which George Thomas was educated, and in scrutinising his conduct and his humanity, we must remember that he sprang from the lowest strata of society in a civilised country, where men were transported for pilfering trifles, and hung for stealing sheep. The brutality of the repressive laws of the eighteenth century exceeded the brutality of those who broke them, and if Thomas held life cheap in war, the country he belonged to held it cheaper in peace.

To pass from Thomas's merits as a man to his claims as a soldier is a pleasant transition. He was a born leader, a general by intuition. He enjoyed the precious gift of endearing men to his person, making them not merely soldiers but zealots in his cause. He inspired confidence, courage, and enthusiasm. He could rally panic-stricken battalions by the magic of his presence, and lead them to victory where they had but just fallen back in defeat. His troops followed him, without question or concern, on distant and hazardous enterprises into regions terrible with vague dangers and unknown risks. In the record of his military achievements it is difficult to particularise any as more brilliant than the rest, but taking them at haphazard, and as they occur to the running pen, what more dashing episode could be adduced than his isolated fight at Fatehpur ? what more masterly retreat than his withdrawal from Udaipur ? what more vigorous advance than his invasion of the Sutlej states ? and, above and beyond all, what more defiant and heroic resistance than that which his invincible resolution rendered possible at Georgegarh and Hánsi ?

To complete the estimate of his military abilities contrast the conditions under which he fought and conquered with those existing in modern warfare. In the Sikhs, Rajputs and Hindustanis, whom Thomas engaged, he found enemies as brave and daring as any existing in the present day. He met them on a common ground with common arms. His superiority lay in his genius and his gallantry, not in machine guns and breach-loaders. The troops he led were composed of the same elements as the troops he conquered ; they possessed no leaven of British bayonets. The muskets he manufactured and the cannon he cast were not a whit better than those whose muzzles were pointed towards him. The forts he stormed and captured were stronger by nature than the redoubts he erected to reduce them, or the armed camps he defended. The leagues he marched were trudged on foot, ofttimes through unexplored countries and trackless deserts, where the sun by day and the north star by night guided his daring course ; no troopships or transport trains delivered him on the confines of an enemy's country, surveyed and mapped for campaign. A commissariat system and a medical staff entered not into the philosophy of his warfare. It was not the fortuitous advantages of money, a superior equipment and an advanced civilisation that enabled him to overcome numerical superiority, but his own single intelligence and valour. No hope of public appreciation or reward spurred him on to effort : he was sustained only by his own dauntless resolve. Far beyond the farthest ken of his fellow-countrymen George Thomas at Hánsi was the splendid solitary advance picket of English Empire in the Panjab.

Surely when we reflect on what he did, we may acquit him of his lawlessness and forgive his frailty. Who can help but admire this reckless, resolute Irishman, as he emerges breathless out of the great tumult of his times, and plants his foot upon the walls of Hánsi ?

Whose heart can remain unthrilled when, with a touch that conquers it, George Thomas, begirt with enemies, fallen and defeated, draws his Irish sword and hurls defiance at his French conqueror? And who can help but love this vagabond adventurer when he sweeps his great hand athwart the map of India, and vows it should all be red?

To-day that map is all red. It is dyed deep with the blood of conquered Maráthá, Afghan, Sikh, Rajput, Mughal, Sindian, Baluchi, Rohilla, Gurkha, and Burmese. With ceaseless spread the emblematic colour has increased and covered all. What then if *Jowruj Jung* swept his neighbour's borders in foray, or seized a district and proclaimed his rule? Shall we condemn him with that map before us? Let us not seek our own justification, nor question his. Let it suffice that in our Panjab Province, where peaceful tillage has followed perpetual warfare, and battle-fields have been turned into quiet pasture lands, the spirit of British adventure was typified by George Thomas, the van of British Conquest was led by *Jowruj Jung.*

PERRON.

CHAPTER I.

HIS BIRTH AND EARLY CAREER.

1755–1796.

THE events recorded in the preceding pages will have made the name of Perron familiar to the reader, and the time has now come to deal with the career of this adventurer. But in order to do so satisfactorily, it is necessary to go back a little and bring his history up to the point when De Boigne resigned the command of the army of Hindustan, and thereafter continue the narrative which was interrupted by the interpolation of the life of George Thomas.

Pierre Cuillier, better known to history as General Perron, was born in 1755 at Chateau du Loire, Sarthe, France. His father was a cloth merchant, who failed in business whilst Perron was yet in his teens, and the boy was early thrown upon his own resources. After making a fruitless appeal for assistance to a rich relative, Perron determined to trust to his own endeavours, and early in 1774 laid out his modest capital in a speculative investment of handkerchiefs, and set out for Nantes with the object of disposing of them. Not meeting with success in this venture, he deserted commerce, and obtained a situation in the cannon foundry at Nantes, where he mastered the technicalities of casting guns. He then enlisted in a regiment of volunteers under orders for the Isle of France, where he arrived in the same year. Later on he appears to have transferred his services to the navy, for in 1780 he came out to India, according to one report as a common sailor, to another as a petty officer on board the French frigate *Sardine*, under the famous Admiral Suffrein. The period was one when French military adventurers were welcomed in the native states of Southern India, and it was doubtless a knowledge of this fact that induced Perron to desert his ship, in company with three of his messmates, and land on the Malabar coast. Making his way into the interior, he journeyed up country until he reached Upper India, where, about the year 1781, he entered the Rána of Gohad's corps, commanded by the Scotchman Sangster, under whom there were two other Europeans serving, Tom Legge, and Michael Filose.

Pierre Cuillier now discarded his patronymic and assumed the *nom de guerre* of Perron, which was the diminutive form of his Christian name. This fashion of adopting a Christian name or alias on entering the employ of the country princes was a common one at the period. Thus Walter Reinhard became Summers, which was corrupted into Sombre, and so, in native speech, to Somru. George Hessing was known as *Jorus Sahib*, Louis Bourguien, as *Looee Sahib*, George Thomas as the *Jehazi Sahib*, and James Shepherd as *James Sahib*. People who retained their surnames suffered dreadful atrocities at the lips of the natives. Robert Sutherland, for instance, was known as *Sutluj Sahib*, and Captain Symes as *Sunk Sahib*, while Captain Brownrigg was even more unfortunate, for his patronymic was twisted into *Burrandee Sahib*. The designation that Perron assumed was itself corrupted by native pronunciation into *Peeroo Sahib*—a not altogether happy one for its possessor, since *Peeroo* is the Hindustani for a turkey.

Perron began his new career in a very humble capacity, and it was not until two years had passed that he rose to non-commissioned rank. It is probable his first introduction into the native service was as an artilleryman, or at best an overseer in Sangster's Foundry. But his circumstances enabled him to marry, and he was united to a Mdlle. Deridon, whose family resided at Pondichery and whose brother "a half-caste Frenchman" was a military adventurer in Upper India.

Upon the defeat of the Rána of Gohad and the disbandment of his battalion, Perron entered a corps, commanded by an officer named Lestineau, in the service of the Ját Rájah of Bhartpur, obtaining an appointment as quartermaster-sergeant on a pay of Rs.60 a month. This was probably about the year 1784. He remained in the service some time, and was present at the battles of Chaksána and Agra, and assisted in the occupation of Delhi by the Maráthás in 1789, when his chief was in alliance with Madhoji Sindhia. It was on this occasion that Lestineau, having been detached to assist in the pursuit of Ghulám Kádir at Meerut, possessed himself of .that person's saddle-bags, which were filled with jewels looted from the palace at Delhi, and with this plunder and the regimental pay due to his battalion absconded, leaving his corps under the charge of his second in command, Mons. J. Pillet, who proved unequal to the task of keeping the exasperated soldiery in order, for they mutinied directly they became aware of Lestineau's flight, and were in consequence disbanded by Madhoji Sindhia's orders.

Perron being thus thrown out of employment applied for service to Rána Khán, a general of high standing in Sindhia's army. From this chief he received the command of a battalion, which was, however, soon broken up, and Perron found himself once again adrift on the world. A friend named Montigny now interested himself on his behalf, and recommended him to the Begum Somru for employment, but as that lady's military force was fifteen months in arrears of pay at this time, she did not feel justified in increasing her establishment, and Perron found his application unsuccessful, despite the very strong recommendations he had received. This was in 1790, by which time he had been more than nine years in India, and was apparently little further advanced in life than when he first sought his fortune in the East.

But now came the turning point of his career. General De Boigne, who had recently been commissioned by Modhoji Sindhia to raise his First Brigade, was looking out for officers. Perron was personally known to him, and he had formed a favourable opinion of his capacity as a brave soldier, and an artisan skilled in the work of a cannon foundry. So he appointed him captain-lieutenant in the new Brigade, and gave him the command of the Burhánpur battalion.

Perron soon ingratiated himself with his chief by his courage, activity and great punctuality in his duties. He was a subordinate after De Boigne's heart, being diligent, energetic and indefatigable, finding a pleasure in his work, and taking a pride in bringing his battalion to the highest pitch of efficiency and discipline.

Towards the end of 1790 there occurred the campaign against the princes of Jaipur and Jodhpur, which witnessed the battles of Pátan and Merta. Perron was present at both, and at the former particularly distinguished himself. When De Boigne returned to headquarters, Perron was left behind to settle the newly annexed district of Ajmir, and this task he carried out with considerable ability. In 1792 he marched back to the Doáb, but was soon selected for further special employment. De Boigne had determined to reduce the fort of Kanaund, which still held out against the Marátha rule, and sent Perron with four battalions to capture it.

Kanaund was an exceedingly strong fortress in the Rewari territory, and had formerly been held by Najaf Kuli Khán, one of the leading nobles at the court of the emperor Shah 'Alam. On Najaf Khán's decease the possession of the fort passed to his widow, who, when De Boigne summoned her to surrender, seemed inclined to obey, for, before his death, her husband had specially warned her not to attempt to resist the general. But whilst negotiations were going on a new ally suddenly came to her assistance. This was none other than Ismáil Beg, who after the battle of Merta, had submitted to the Marátha rule, and, it is said, accepted service under Sindhia. But his sympathies were always with the old *régime*, and Holkar, aware of this, instigated him to revolt, pointing out the excellent opportunity that offered of joining forces with Najaf Khán's Begum. This artifice, by which Takuji Holkar hoped to weaken his rival Sindhia, and so improve his own prospects in Hindustan, was a very transparent one; but the shallowest excuse was sufficient to tempt the gallant Mughal noble to strike another blow for the Faith, and he accepted the suggestion with avidity. Renouncing his allegiance to Sindhia, he wrote to the Begum to hold out against the conqueror of their common country, and hurried to her assistance with an army of 20,000 men and 30 guns.

Upon hearing of this De Boigne ordered Perron to advance with all speed, give battle to Ismáil Beg, and bring him in dead or alive. Marching to Kanaund, Perron found the allies encamped under the walls of the fort, and at once engaged them. It was the first important battle in which he held chief command, and he acquitted himself very creditably. In less than two hours he inflicted a severe defeat on the enemy, killing 2,000 of them, capturing all their guns and driving Ismáil Beg and his beaten troops into the fort for shelter.

The siege of the place was now undertaken, but Ismáil Beg, although vanquished in open fight, maintained a brave defence for four months. The thickness of the mud walls of Kanaund proved impervious to Perron's battering train, and he was unable to effect a practicable breach, whilst his strength in men was insufficient to take the stronghold by assault. It seemed as though the blockade would be a very slow business, when an accident occurred which accelerated it. One day the Begum, whilst playing a game of chess with an eunuch, was killed by a chance stone shot, whereupon the garrison became disheartened and broke into mutiny against Ismáil Beg, who had been instrumental in persuading their late mistress to resist. Hoping to gain more favourable terms for themselves they conspired to deliver him up to the besiegers, but this plot coming to his ears, Ismáil Beg anticipated their action by surrendering to Perron, who promised on his own faith and that of De Boigne's to spare his life, and honourably redeemed his word despite Madhoji Sindhia's wrath and opposition.

During the siege of Kanaund an accident happened to Perron which maimed him for life. Whilst experimenting with some hand grenades one of them burst as he was in the act of throwing it, and so shattered his hand that he was obliged to submit to amputation, and thereafter he was often known among the natives as *Ekdust*, or The One-handed. But his success at Kanaund was rewarded by his promotion to the rank of major, and on the creation of De Boigne's Second Brigade, he was appointed to the command of it, Major Frèmont, as senior officer, obtaining that of the First. Thus in less than three years from the date of his entering Sindhia's service, Perron found himself in a post almost analogous to that of a general of division, and with a force of 8,000 infantry, 800 cavalry, and 40 guns under his command, whilst his pay and emoluments were probably not less than Rs.2,000 a month. This was a rapid and wonderful rise for a man who had but recently been fruitlessly seeking service, and lamenting the loss of an employment that brought him in Rs.720 a year.

During the rest of this year and in the early part of 1793 Perron was associated with Ambaji Inglia and Rána Khán in the subjugation of Méwar, and assisted in establishing the former as Subahdar or lord lieutenant of that district. Madhoji Sindhia himself accompanied the army engaged in this work, and when the objects of the expedition were completed, marched to Poonah, whilst Perron and his Brigade returned to headquarters in Hindustan. But he was not allowed to remain here long, for early in 1794 he was transferred to the command of the First Brigade and ordered to the Deccan to strengthen Sindhia's position there. Before he arrived, however, that prince was dead and succeeded by his nephew, Daulat Ráo Sindhia, whose peaceful succession was in a great measure due to the opportune arrival in the month of March of Perron and his ten fine battalions.

In the following year there came to Perron one of those opportunities which, if rightly used, often lay the foundations of future greatness. A disagreement had long existed between the Maráthás and the Nizam of Haidarabad, relative to a claim for *chout* or tribute, demanded by the former and long resisted by the latter. The sum had now increased to nearly three millions sterling, and Nána

15

Farnavis, the Peshwá's prime minister, determined to exact it, and called upon the Nizam for an immediate settlement. An angry and insulting answer was returned, which was immediately followed by a declaration of war, and in January, 1795, both powers took the field. The Peshwá was assisted by his tributary chiefs. Daulat Ráo Sindhia supplied the strongest contingent, which included De Boigne's First Brigade under Perron, Michael Filose's independent corps of six battalions, and Colonel John Hessing's of four, and a large force of irregular cavalry. Takuji Holkar sent a brigade of four battalions of regular infantry under the Chevalier Dudrenec, who had been commissioned to raise and discipline another corps after his disastrous defeat at Lakhairi. Raghoji Bhonsla, the Rájah of Berar, and other lesser chiefs of the Deccan sent in contingents, and the allied army numbered 140,000 men, of whom 24,000 were disciplined infantry. Daulat Ráo Sindhia took command of his own troops in person, but the actual direction in the field was left to Perron.

To oppose this formidable host the Nizam Ali Khán collected an army of 110,000 men, including 17,000 disciplined infantry, of which 11,000 were under the command of Colonel Raymond, a French officer of high character and repute, and the remaining 6,000 belonged to two independent corps commanded by an American named Boyd, and an Englishman named Finglass.

Upon the 11th of March, 1795, the two armies met near a place called Purinda, whither the Nizam was marching from Kardla, by which name the battle that ensued is generally known. The Maráthás appeared in great force upon the Nizam's right, on some rising ground, from whence they were able to open a distant cannonade on the rear of the Haidarabad army. The Nizam's troops were at once drawn out in line of battle, and Raymond advancing with his infantry and 24 guns took up a position on an elevated piece of ground in front, supported by a large body of cavalry. Upon this Pareshram Bhao, the Peshwá's commander-in-chief, formed his army to receive the attack, taking the centre station himself, with the Peshwá's cavalry and the Chevalier Dudrenec's brigade, whilst he placed the Rájah of Berar's contingent on the right, and Daulat Ráo Sindhia's infantry on the left wing. The action commenced with an attack on the Maráthá centre by the Nizam's cavalry, who were much elated at a slight advantage they had gained on the previous day over an advance guard of the Peshwá's household troops. They now charged with great gallantry, wounding Pareshram Bhao, and driving the Maráthá centre back in confusion. But whilst they were thus carrying everything before them in the centre, the regular infantry on both sides had advanced to within musket shot of one another. Perron, by skilful manœuvring, obtained a decided advantage of position, and, having posted 35 guns on an eminence, opened a destructive fire. Raymond was immediately deserted by the Nizam's cavalry, but his infantry stood their ground well, and had they been permitted to fight out the duel, it is possible they might have won the day. The fate of the battle was, however, destined to be decided by one of those domestic considerations which often have a preponderating influence in Asiatic contests. The Nizam, with the imbecile infatuation of an Oriental potentate, had carried his womenfolk with him on the campaign, and early in the battle, his favourite wife, terrified by the roar of the cannon, implored him to retire. To pacify her fears he ordered Raymond's brigade to fall back for her protection. Its commander resisted to the utmost this fatal and supine act of pusillanimity, until frequent and repeated commands left him no choice but to obey, and about sunset he began to retire. Darkness soon closed over the scene of battle, but Perron, whose long experience of Indian warfare had taught him the importance of pressing home an advantage, made every effort to follow, persisting in the pursuit as long as it was possible, and keeping up a desultory fire in the dark.

Meanwhile the orders and counter-orders that reached Raymond were so confusing that in attempting to carry them out his men were perfectly bewildered, and at last, worn out with fatigue and vociferation, they sank to rest in bivouac upon the field. But about eleven o'clock an accidental encounter between the advance pickets of the two armies started the battle afresh. Perron, from his advanced position, immediately opened a heavy fire with artillery and rockets, whereupon a panic seized the Nizam's soldiery, and abandoning their guns and camp they fled towards Kardla, a small fort so surrounded by hills that it formed a veritable *cul-de-sac*.

Within the walls of this fort the Nizam took refuge, and for some time Raymond gallantly defended his master. But when Perron dragged up his heavy artillery and brought it to bear on the place, surrender became inevitable, and the Nizam sued for terms. An indemnity of three millions sterling was extorted from him, besides territory yielding a revenue of nearly three and a half lakhs of rupees annually, and for the due fulfilment of these stringent terms he was compelled to send his prime minister as a hostage to Poonah.

Kardla was a decisive battle, but never was such a substantial victory won with less bloodshed. Although there were nearly a quarter of a million men contending in the field, the losses on either side were infinitesimal, and the Nizam owed his defeat to his own cowardice and folly. But Perron's reputation as an able general was at once established, and thereafter he found signal favour in the sight of his master, Daulat Ráo Sindhia.

In 1795 Sindhia left Poonah, and proceeded as far as the Godaveri river on his return to Hindustan, where his presence was required owing to De Boigne having announced his intention of resigning his command. But on the 25th of October, Mádhu Ráo, the Peshwá, committed suicide at Poonah. In the hyperbolical language of a native historian, which is worth quoting for its quaintness, "The Peshwá was one day amusing himself flying kites on a terrace of his palace, when, as Fate ordained, the string of his life being short, his foot slipped and he fell over the parapet, and the kite of his soul flew away into the air!" Immediately on receipt of this intelligence, Sindhia, by the advice of his prime minister, Balloba Tantia, returned to Poonah with his whole army to contest the succession of Baji Ráo, whom the late Peshwá had appointed his heir, and who had been immediately installed by Nána Farnavis, the powerful and determined enemy of the House of Ujjain.

De Boigne still persisted in his determination to retire from Daulat Ráo's service and return to Europe. In after years Perron boasted that it was his intrigues which obliged the general to quit the country, but it is probable that the wish was father to the thought. Still it cannot be contested that Perron was at this time in high favour with Sindhia, and in constant attendance upon his person. In December De Boigne finally quitted Hindustan. It would have been in accordance with Indian custom had he recommended a successor, but it is established on the best authority that he did not do so; on the contrary, he advised Daulat Ráo to demolish his Brigades rather than put them under the command of one person, as such power ought not to be entirely trusted to a single will and influence. Directly after his departure a keen competition arose between Perron and Robert Sutherland for the post rendered vacant. Major Frèmont, the senior officer in the force, died about this time, leaving Sutherland at the head of affairs in Hindustan, who conceived this gave him a sort of claim to the permanent appointment. But he was too far from the seat of government to press his interests, being engaged in the reduction of Bundelkhand, which occupied him for six months. On the other hand Perron was daily at Sindhia's court, and, by the death of Frèmont, was left senior officer in the Brigades. He made the most of his opportunities, and succeeded so well that before the end of the year he was promoted to the rank of general and appointed to the chief command of De Boigne's army.

CHAPTER II.

THE army which De Boigne left behind him in Sindhia's service consisted of 24,000 infantry, 3,000 cavalry and 120 guns, besides garrison troops and irregulars. The battalions were veteran and undefeated, and their spirit and organisation unexcelled. It was an army the command of which might have filled with pride any soldier in India, whether king's or Company's officer or adventurer. Behind it was a proud record of achievement; it was well disciplined, well paid, and well equipped; and in addition animated by that *esprit de corps* which lifts men out of themselves, and by identifying them with the flag they serve, doubles their individual worth. De Boigne's battalions were proud of their prestige and jealous of their honour, and upheld by a resolution to sustain the reputation they had won on many battle-fields, and, where possible, to increase it. They were, in short, a worthy monument to the man who had created them.

Such was the army to the command of which Perron succeeded in September 1796. Making over the First Brigade to Captain Drugeon, he set out for Mattra, where he arrived in February 1797, and took over charge from Jaggu Bapu, the Maráthá general. By his commission he was invested with the full powers exercised by De Boigne, and one of his first acts was to take possession of the *Jaidad* in the Doáb. Here, in October of the following year, he fixed his headquarters, considerably enlarging the cantonment of Koil and strengthening the already formidable defences of Aligarh, which defended the place. During his first year of office he had little leisure to attend to external affairs, being fully employed in acquainting himself with the details of the Brigades, and the administration of the territory assigned for their upkeep. After he had established his power and authority within his own boundaries he turned his attention to the more extended responsibilities of his post. The first matter that occupied him was the state of affairs at Delhi. Directly after Perron's appointment to the supreme command of Hindustan, Sindhia had issued orders to the Marátha governor of Delhi to make over charge of the city. But Balloba Tantia, Sindhia's prime minister and a determined enemy to Perron, secretly transmitted contrary instructions to the capital, " an occurrence " observes a contemporary historian " by no means uncommon in the singular absurdity of Mahratta politics." The Hindu governor of Delhi, only too glad to retain his post, refused to surrender the city, and in May, 1798, Perron ordered Major Pedron, with four battalions, to lay siege to it, and obtain possession by blockade, bribery, or intrigue, but to avoid a bombardment for fear of offending the blind emperor, whose titular authority it was a matter of policy to recognise and respect. After a close blockade of five weeks Sutherland arrived and the gates were opened to the impulse of gold, and the unfortunate Shah 'Alam released from the fears and privations occasioned by the conduct of his recent guardian, Nizam-ul-Dín, the Cowrie Fakir. Perron appointed Captain Le Marchant governor of the capital and custodian of the king's person, while Pedron returned to Koil, where the Second Brigade, commanded by Sutherland, to which he belonged, was cantoned, the Third Brigade, under Colonel Pohlman, being stationed at Mattra.

The insubordinate example of the Marátha governor of Delhi encouraged the commandant of Agra to resist. This person was a brother of Balloba Tantia, and refused to yield up possession of the fort to Perron, who being at the time busily employed in strengthening the defences of Aligarh, made no move until he had completed the task. He then marched against Agra with six battalions and arrived unexpectedly before the walls on the 17th of February, 1799. The town was taken completely by surprise, and Perron entered it without opposition, proclaiming his authority by beat of drum. But the fort and citadel held out, and an investment was necessary. A siege followed and lasted fifty-eight days, at the end of which a successful mine was exploded and destroyed a salient bastion on the north-east front. Whereupon, to avoid the calamity of an assault, the garrison surrendered on condition of being allowed to march out with the honours of war. From first to last the capture of this place cost Perron 600 men, and it was an achievement not unworthy of the reputation of De Boigne's battalions, for Agra was the strongest fortress in Hindustan, and defended by a force of 4,000 men.

With the possession of the Key of India Perron's power was

completely established. "He had now the entire and merited confidence of Sindhia," writes one of his officers in a contemporary journal, "and was invested with the full and uncontrolled government of all Sindhia's possessions from the Chumbul to Pateála—a country, even in its ruinous state, yielding a revenue of one million sterling. He was authorised to raise armies and retain or discharge troops, and no European, not even De Boigne, ever possessed such confidence and power."

This at first sight may seem a strangely rapid rise, but it is intelligible when the circumstances which favoured Perron are considered. Dáulat Ráo Sindhia on his accession to power threw himself completely into Deccan politics. His predominant desire was to render his influence supreme at Poonah. But he had two obstacles to contend against: the first was the craft and power of Nana Farnavis, the Peshwá's prime minister, whose opposition prolonged the contest for ascendancy from month to month and year to year; and the second was his own natural weakness of character, and the base elements of government with which he surrounded himself. Daulat Ráo altogether lacked the genius of his uncle Madhoji, and possessed little real ability. He squandered his time in riot and dissipation, and indulged in the worst vices of a debauched Oriental sovereign. Such a nature as his, out of very inertness, surrendered the power it should have wielded to hands that were itching to grasp it. With Perron the beginning was more than half of the whole. His appointment to the command of the army of Hindustan assured everything else; since the country was held solely by that army, his battalions constituting the real power behind Sindhia's throne. Left to himself in the north, Perron assiduously employed his time and resources in increasing his strength. He made Koil an immense fortified camp, and laboured to render Aligarh impregnable. "The strength of the place cannot be described—a seventy-four might sail in the ditch," wrote Lord Lake of the fortress four years later. Its position was admirably chosen, for from his headquarters there Perron held both Delhi and Agra in check. Beneath the walls of Aligarh he built himself a palatial residence—it still existed in 1871, and was used as a settlement office—and assumed sovereign state. During the seven years of his rule the dominion of Hindustan lay not at Delhi, nor at Poonah, but in the vast fortified camp of Koil, from whence the chief of many legions issued orders to the princes of the neighbouring districts and Rájputana, and so far as Upper India was concerned was the master of both the emperor Shah 'Alam and Daulat Ráo Sindhia.

There is a very interesting article in the Asiatic Review for 1799, which confirms this estimate of Perron's power. " General Perron," (it runs) " a French officer of great experience and consummate ability, both as a statesman and a soldier, represents Dowlut Ráo Scindia in Hindostan, and is invested with the most full and absolute authority over every department, both civil and military. This power, which exceeds that of any prince, he exercises with great moderation, and at the same time with a degree of judgment and energy that evinces very superior talents. Amongst his European officers none have a character for superior capacity, although very good soldiers. Yet having risen from very low situations, and not having the advantage of education, none of them have displayed any abilities out of their professional line. But this deficiency in his officers he may easily remedy (and no doubt will) as soon as peace takes place in Europe, when innumerable military adventurers will flock to his standard, qualified for the highest situations civil and military. The Mahratta ports on the Malabar coast, from whence supply of ordnance and arms and military stores have occasionally been procured, will afford them an easy access, so that before long we may expect to see the northern parts of Hindustan swarming with needy and intriguing Frenchmen."

Whilst Perron was thus engaged in establishing and consolidating his power in the north, troubles were brewing in the south, occasioned by the rebellion of the Bhais. The Bhais were the widows of the late Madhoji Sindhia, and had never acquiesced in the accession of Daulat Ráo. There were three of these ladies, one of whom, Bhagirthi, was young and beautiful. Daulat Ráo, as in honour bound, promised to make ample provision for his aunts, and they continued to reside at his court. But time passed and no measures were taken to ensure their permanent establishment. Presently it was whispered that an intrigue was in progress between Bhagirthi Bhai and Daulat Ráo, and the two elder widows, hearing of it, were scandalised, and expressed their abhorrence at the incestuous criminality. For this they were barbarously ill-treated by Ghatkay Ráo, one of Sindhia's creatures in authority. This wretch not only imprisoned the elder widows, but caused them to be flogged. Such degrading treatment aroused the wrath of the Shenwi Brahmins, a high caste of men who had monopolised all the principal offices of government under Madhoji Sindhia ; and these now openly espoused the cause of the widows against the young chief. Much discussion and dissension ensued, until it was agreed that the Bhais should reside at Burhanpur. For this purpose they left Poonah, but had not proceeded far before they were treacherously seized and thrown into confinement in the fort of Ahmednagar, and after a short imprisonment brought back to Daulat Ráo's camp. Before long, however, they found means of escaping, and threw themselves upon the protection of Amrat Ráo, who was brother to the Pèshwá, and a very powerful personage. Just prior to this, Daulat Ráo married the daughter of his minion Ghatkay Ráo. She was a woman of singular beauty, who exercised a complete control over her husband, and her influence elevated her father to the post of prime minister in succession to Balloba Tantia. No sooner was Ghatkay Ráo in power, than he urged Sindhia to crush the conspiracy of the Bhais at once. This advice was adopted, and five battalions of infantry were detached from Drugeon's Brigade under command of Captain Du Prat to surprise Amrat Ráo's camp, and seize the refugees ; but the attempt failed, and Du Prat was beaten and obliged to retreat. Resource was now had to further negotiation, and with all the duplicity of his Maráthá nature Sindhia promised to provide his aunts with a suitable establishment if they would return to his protection. Whereupon, trusting in his good faith, Amrat Ráo come to Poonah to arrange the matter, but was attacked by two battalions and twenty-five guns under Drugeon, who, without warning, opened fire upon him and dispersed his troops. This gross act of treachery constituted a declaration of war against the Peshwá himself, in whose government Amrat Ráo now filled the post of prime minister. A coalition of chiefs was immediately formed against Sindhia, who became alarmed ; the more so as Perron was at this time occupied in the siege of Agra, which he had not yet reduced, and where the faction of the late prime minister, Balloba Santia, still held out. A general rising against Sindhia's authority in Hindustan and the Deccan threatened, and he was now anxious to lay the storm he had raised. But Ghatkay Ráo, who had been the primary cause of all the trouble, having tasted blood, thirsted for more, and disregarding Sindhia's orders to effect a settlement with the revolted chiefs, increased the danger of the situation by perpetrating innumerable fresh outrages. At last Daulat Ráo was obliged to order Ghatkay's arrest, which was accomplished by two of his European officers, Filoze and Hessing. After this a peace was patched up with the Peshwá, but in the meantime the Bhais had retreated to Kolapur, where they were joined by the leading Shenwi Brahmins, amongst whom was Lakwa Dáda, one of Madhoji's best generals, who had recently been dismissed from his appointment of commander-in-chief of the Maráthá army on account of his attachment to the ex-minister Balloba Tántia, who had naturally been one of Ghatkay's first victims, and was now languishing in a cruel confinement.

Large bodies of mounted soldiery flocked to Lakwa Dáda as soon as he erected the standard of rebellion, and openly declared for the widows of the old prince. Daulat Ráo attempted in vain to allay the increasing storm. No sooner had his regular battalions under Du Prat, Drugeon, Filoze, and Hessing repressed the attacks made on his territories by the rebels and returned to camp, than the latter faced about and followed them. The flame spread through Hindustan, and Lakwa Dáda soon found himself at the head of an army of 20,000 cavalry, 15 battalions of infantry, and 20 guns, and sustained by the immense prestige which still attached to the service of the widows of the old prince.

It was at this critical moment in his affairs that Daulat Ráo desired Perron to advance against Lakwa Dáda, and at the same time appointed another chief, named Ambaji Inglia, to the head of the Marátha army, and ordered him to co-operate with the regular Brigades.

Perron was at first disposed to underrate the strength of the rebellion, and contented himself with sending two battalions, under Captain Butterfield, to assist Ambaji. With these the latter marched to Kotah, where he met the insurgents and engaged them; but Ambaji's troops had been tampered with by Lakwa Dáda, who was a master of intrigue, and lost the battle. Of the 1600 regular infantry under Butterfield, one-third were killed or wounded, the whole brunt of the action falling upon them, whilst Ambaji's Marátha cavalry showed scarcely any fight at all.

Perron now ordered Sutherland, with the Second Brigade, to reinforce the defeated army, upon which Lakwa Dáda fell back on the fort of Chittúrgarh. Ambaji, at the same time, made great preparations to retrieve his defeat, and engaged George Thomas, with 6 battalions of regular infantry and 60 guns, on a monthly pay of Rs.60,000. Supported by Sutherland and Thomas, the chief advanced against Chittúr about the middle of the year 1799, his army consisting of 20,000 horse and 14,000 infantry. A good deal of desultory skirmishing ensued, but no really heavy fighting, nor were any substantial results achieved by either party. Meanwhile Sutherland's and Thomas's troops, being far removed from their headquarters, fell into arrears of pay, and this led to a general plundering of the country round, and very soon every village within fifty miles was pillaged and deserted.

Perron had always been jealous of Colonel Sutherland, and he now gave a ready ear to a report that he was secretly intriguing with

Lakwa Dáda instead of fighting him. The colonel was therefore suspended, and Major Pohlman sent from Mattra to take command of his Brigade. Captain Butterfield fell a victim to Perron's malice at the same time, and was driven to leave Sindhia's service; but Sutherland managed to clear himself, and after a short time was sent to the Deccan, to take over charge of the First Brigade from Du Prat, who had recently superseded Drugeon fallen into disgrace.

Major Pohlman had no opportunity of distinguishing himself against Lakwa Dáda, for scarcely had he taken over the command than news came that Zamán Shah, the King of Kabul—a grandson of Ahmed Shah Abdali, whose name was dreaded by the Maráthás—was preparing for an invasion of India, with the intention of re-establishing a Mahomedan empire. This threatened danger brought about an immediate concord amongst the Maráthás, and all internal feuds and jealousies were forgotten. Daulat Ráo Sindhia released Balloba Tantia, Lakwa Dáda's staunch friend, from confinement, and reinstated him in his former post of prime minister; whereupon Lakwa and Ambaji exchanged visits of amity, and shortly afterwards the former, through the influence of Balloba, was again elevated to the post of commander-in-chief. This typical example of the glorious uncertainty of office in a Marátha administration left Ambaji without employment; and feeling hurt at a humiliation he had not deserved, he entered into retirement for a season.

All the Marátha troops, regular and irregular, were now ordered to concentrate at Mattra, where a formidable army was collected in December, 1799, under the chief command of Perron, who marched thither from Koil. From Mattra the army advanced to Delhi, to take up a position to oppose Zamán Shah, and here for some time the immense host was encamped. It included in its ranks Perron's Second and Third Brigades, under Pohlman and Pedron, 100,000 Marátha cavalry of Lakwa's, and 200 guns. So critical was the danger considered, that Perron decided to further augment his army, and directed Major Pedron to raise a Fourth Brigade. The English also assembled a large force at the frontier station of Anupshahr under General Craig, to assist in repulsing the Afghan invasion. Fortunately for the peace and security of Hindustan, an outbreak at Kabul obliged Zamán Shah to return to his capital, and so the danger passed away.

A small insurrection in the Saharanpur district next engaged Perron's attention. Here a religious impostor, whose real name was Sultan Shah, gave himself out to be Ghulám Kádir, asserting that it was not that miscreant who had been captured and killed at Meerut in 1789, and proclaiming his authority over the territories of the

Robilla adventurer whom he represented himself to be. Perron detached Captain Smith, with three battalions and some of the Begum Somru's troops, to bring the impostor to book, and he was easily defeated, and sent flying for refuge to the Sikhs, who had assembled in force near Karnál, with the object of assisting Zamán Shah.

Perron now advanced to Karnál, and summoned all the Sikh chiefs between the Sutlej and the Jumna to appear before him and tender their submission. These included the Rájahs of Patiála, Jhind, Kaithal, and Tanésur, who had long been a source of annoyance and danger to the northern frontier of Hindustan. At first they seemed inclined to resist; whereupon Perron, with a number of local chiefs who were burning to avenge past injuries, and who brought with them 10,000 cavalry, advanced with his Third Brigade to Tanésur. This prompt exhibition of strength overawed the Sikhs, and they submitted to the terms imposed, and signed the treaty required from them.* Perron then returned to Delhi, chastising, on his route, several large villages which had been backward in paying their revenue, amongst them being some over which George Thomas claimed authority. This invasion of the latter's rights—not the first instance of its kind—tended to increase the ill-feeling already existing between the two adventurers, and sowed the seeds of troubles that were to find their harvest at Georgegarh and Hánsi two years later.

* "It was about this time that Perron sent presents to Ranjit Singh, of Lahore, with proposals for a treaty of amity and friendship. Bágh Singh of Jhind, who was Ranjit Singh's maternal uncle, was induced to use his influence in bringing about this treaty, but Ranjit declined Perron's overtures, still in such a manner as to avoid giving offence. He had, prior to this time, entered into negotiations with the Marquis of Wellesley; and he explained that it was ' a difficult matter to maintain a friendship with both parties.' In the end he patched up an understanding with Perron, explaining to Colonel Collins, who had been the medium of the English negotiations, that 'although my friendship for you and the most noble the Governor-general is great beyond the possibility of words, yet I must preserve appearances with General Perron, in consideration of what is due by me to the will of my uncle, Bhág Singh.'

"A little later Perron proposed to Ranjit Singh to join him in attacking George Thomas at Hansi, but this the Sikh chief refused to agree to."—Extract, "Bombay State Papers."

CHAPTER III.

THE BATTLE OF MALPÚRA, AND THE STORM OF SOUNDA.

1800–1801.

EARLY in the year 1800 Lakwa Dáda advanced into Rájputana, to collect the tribute due from that country. He was supported by Perron's Second Brigade under Major Pohlman, and by the Chevalier Dudrenec's corps. Partáb Singh, driven to exasperation by the exactions of Perron, had determined to throw off the Marátha yoke, if possible, and assert his independence. To this end he collected a powerful army at his camp at Sanganir, a few miles south of Jaipur, where on the 4th of April he was joined by 10,000 Ráthor cavalry from Jodhpur, who, for the first time since their defeat by De Boigne at Merta, ventured to take the field against Sindhia. Hearing of these preparations, Perron sent an ultimatum to Partáb Singh, calling upon him to pay his arrears of tribute immediately; and the demand being refused, Lakwa Dáda was deputed to enforce it.

Upon the rejection of Perron's ultimatum great activity prevailed in the Jaipur camp. The Rájah mounted his state elephant and reviewed his troops; there was a vast amount of saluting with cannons, rockets, and small arms; rich sacrifices were offered to the gods, lakhs of eleemosynary rupees distributed to the Brahmins, and alms in abundance bestowed on the poor.

By this time Lakwa's army had approached to within fighting distance, and the 15th of April being declared a propitious day by the court astrologers, Partáb Singh's forces moved out to battle. Lakwa had chosen a good position near Malpura, where he formed his army in two lines to meet the attack, the advance one consisting of the regular infantry under Pohlman and Dudrenec, and the supporting one of the Marátha cavalry, who were stationed a thousand paces in the rear; whilst 5,000 of Perron's Hindustani horse defended the flanks of his Brigade.

At four o'clock in the morning the battle began with a brisk artillery fire. Presently Pohlman, who was on the right of the line, determined on a forward movement, and led his Brigade on, but with orders to withhold their fire until quite close to the enemy. With their accustomed discipline and intrepidity the troops obeyed, but the cowardly Marátha cavalry held back, leaving the infantry, as usual, to fight the battle alone; in consequence of which Pohlman was soon hard pressed, and at one time in imminent danger of being overwhelmed by numbers. But he displayed generalship equal to the emergency. By a skilful and judicious movement he massed his six battalions into square—a formation long warfare against cavalry had made them familiar with—and presented a front to the enemy on all sides; and thus drawn up they met and resisted every charge. After a desperate defence, in which the artillery played an important part, Pohlman gradually drove the Jaipur troops back, and captured 40 of their guns and 30 stand of colours, but not without heavy loss, for 1000 of his men, or nearly 17 per cent. of the force engaged, were killed and wounded.

On the left of the line the Chevalier Dudrenec fared differently. His troops were composed of newly-raised levies, who lacked the discipline that enabled Pohlman's veterans to stand firm and avoid panic. Dudrenec himself was a gallant soldier, well schooled in adversity, and if experience of disaster could make a great general, he would have had every claim to that distinction. But he was fated to suffer yet another catastrophe on this day. It fell to the Ráthors of Jodhpur to oppose his portion of the line, and they had memories to obliterate such as could only be blotted out with blood; they had historical reproaches to silence, whose cutting echoes rang through a decade of shame, and could only be drowned in the din of battle; and ribald rhymes to put a period to, whose sting could only be stayed by the clash of steel. To-day they sought the *revanche* of Merta, and 10,000 sons of Márwar were eager to fulfil their duty.

There is a stirring and vivid description of their charge against Dudrenec's corps in Colonel James Skinner's memoirs, which depicts the episóde in language singularly glowing and graphic; and although it is not free from old " Sikander's " habitual exaggeration, no apology is necessary for quoting it *in extenso*. These are Skinner's words:

"We now saw the Chevalier Dudrenec's Brigade, which was on our left, charged by the Rhattores. He received them nobly, but was cut to pieces by them : out of 8,000 men he had not 200 left. The Rhattores, more than 10,000 in number, were seen approaching from a distance, the tramp of their immense and compact body rising like thunder above the roar of battle. They came on, first at a slow hand gallop, which increased in speed as they approached. The well-served guns of the Brigade showered grape upon this dense mass, mowing down hundreds at each discharge, but this had no effect in arresting their progress. On they came like a whirlwind, trampling over 1,500 of their own body destroyed by the cannon of the Brigade. Neither the murderous volleys from the muskets nor the serried hedge of bayonets could check or shake them. They poured like a torrent on and over the Brigade, and rode it fairly down, leaving scarce a vestige of it remaining, as if the sheer weight of their mass had ground it to pieces. Then, as if they had met with but a slight obstacle, they looked not even behind them at the fallen, but went on, unshaken, and still in their formidable mass, to attack the cavalry of the second line. These ran like sheep, while the Rhattores pursued them, cutting them down for several miles. In this charge Captain Paish and several other officers were killed, and Dudrenec only escaped by throwing himself down amongst the dead."

The impetuous frenzy of the Ráthors, drunk with victory and revenge, proved their ruin. By their blind pursuit of the Marátha cavalry, they put themselves out of the action as completely as if they themselves had been in flight, and this just at the time when their presence was most needed ; for Pohlman had now beaten back the Jaipur troops, and advancing in his turn, recaptured two of Dudrenec's lost guns. Upon this Partáb Singh, with 6,000 of his chosen body-guard, determined to emulate the feat of the Ráthors, and charge Pohlman. But the latter, seeing him moving down on his elephant, divined his purpose, and immediately ordered his guns to the front of the line ; and by the time the Rájah had approached to within two hundred yards, the word was given to fire, and a discharge of artillery instantly followed. Partáb Singh's elephant was killed, but not-withstanding this, his bodyguard twice attempted to charge, but were beaten back each time. On the second occasion the Rájah mounted his horse, and turning tail fled to his capital, followed by his cavalry, who never drew rein until they found refuge within the walls of Jaipur, forty-five miles distant.

Pohlman's battalions were now left in sole possession of the field. About midday the Ráthors were seen returning from the chase of the Marátha cavalry, beating their drums in token of victory. On nearing Pohlman's camp they observed the Jaipur colours, which had been captured, floating above it; and this circumstance led them to suppose that Partáb Singh had been as successful as themselves and was in possession, and they rode up in loose order to be cruelly undeceived by a discharge of grape poured into them from thirty guns. When they realised the fatal mistake into which they had fallen they made a gallant effort to retrieve it. Twice they charged, notwithstanding their fatigued condition, but were repulsed, although many brave individuals broke through the square formed to receive them, and met their death at the bayonet's point. But the task was an impossible one, and at last they drew off, and finding the Jaipur camp abandoned, followed the direction of flight taken by Partáb Singh, victims of their blind impetuosity and an undeserved misfortune.

Pohlman's Brigade now advanced to occupy the enemy's deserted lines. It was a magnificient encampment, crowded with sumptuous tents of the most luxurious description, belonging to the various chiefs. Two large bazaars ran down the centre, filled with movable shops, in which every imaginable article was exposed for sale. But not a trader remained behind to recommend his wares, not a trooper to strut and swagger down the streets, for the great host that had thronged this tented city but yesterday had melted away into nothingness.

In the centre of the camp was Rajab Patáb Singh's wooden pavilion, or palace. It was a beautiful structure, covered with embroidery and crimson velvet, and the interior a blazing sheen of gold and silver brocade. Two golden idols guarded it, whose flashing diamond eyes peered into vacuity—two golden idols before whom the might of Jaipur had ofttimes bowed in adoration. But, impotent as Baal of old, they were, by the irony of circumstances, the very first treasures to be looted from the camp, which soon became a scene of plunder and confusion.

The losses on both sides at the battle of Malpurah were heavy. The Marátha cavalry had been cut to pieces by the Ráthors, whose own ranks, on their return from the chase, had been decimated by Pohlman's fire. Dudrenec's Brigade, which, according to Smith's authority, numbered about 4,000 fighting men, lost between five and six hundred killed and wounded, whilst Pohlman's list of casualties totalled 136. But heavier than all of these was the slaughter that had taken place in the ranks of the Jaipur army. Partáb Singh never recovered the blow to his power and prestige which was dealt him on this eventful day. Of the eighty pieces of cannon which he had brought into the field, he lost seventy-four, together with all his camp, baggage and warlike stores.

On the 10th of May Perron arrived from the Sikh country north of Delhi, where he had been engaged in reducing his neighbours to order and obedience at Kárnál. He brought with him reinforcements of five battalions of infantry and his bodyguard of 500 cavalry, known as the *Khasi Risála.* Having taken over the chief command from Lakwa Dáda, he was preparing to advance against Jaipur, when Partáb Singh sent in his submission, and was granted peace on a payment of twenty-five lakhs of rupees.

A treaty having been drawn out and signed, the Rájah invited Perron and his European officers, sixteen in number, to visit his capital and experience his hospitality. The invitation was accepted, but not without certain qualms as to its prudence. The Rájah, with a cavalcade of twenty elephants, met his guests outside the gates of his capital, and escorted them to the "Palace of the Winds," under a salute of twenty-one guns. Colonel Skinner, who was present, describes the city as "the handsomest ever seen ; the streets were broad, the houses regular on both sides, the bazaars extremely fine, and the place full of inhabitants, who seem prosperous and happy." This description, recorded nearly a century ago, would hold good in the present day, for modern Jaipur is without exception the cleanest and most beautiful city in the native states of India, and enjoys the distinction of being the only one lighted with gas !

Perron's ceremonial visit passed off with great *éclat*, despite fear and distrust on both sides at the commencement. A grand entertainment in the Hindu style was prepared, whereat *nazzars* were presented and *khiluts* bestowed. This was followed by a banquet, at which (observes Skinner) a choice assortment of Hindustani liquors were on the table, and the whole wound up with elephant battles, tiger and buffalo fights, and the inevitable Natch Dance, when several sets of handsome girls were introduced.

The defeat of the Rájah of Jaipur had a salutary effect upon his kinsman of Jodhpur, who, without further trouble, paid up the arrears of tribute due from him, amounting to twelve lakhs of rupees, and tendered his formal submission to the Marátha rule.

Affairs in Rájputana being thus satisfactorily arranged, Perron returned to Koil towards the end of July, leaving Pohlman and six battalions to reduce the fort of Jájpur, which belonged to a chief named Kasri Singh, who had long harassed the Rájah of Kotah, an ally of the Maráthás in the late campaign. Jájpur was a stone fortress, built on the summit of a steep hill, and from its position and the solidity of its masonry, a place of unusual strength. Kasri Singh refused to surrender to Pohlman's summons, and measures were taken to forcibly dispossess him. A large battering train was brought to bear on the walls of the town, and a breach soon effected,

16

and the following night, on a given signal, the troops advanced and occupied it without much difficulty. The fort now remained to be taken, and it was found necessary to make regular approaches. A fortnight was consumed in advancing the lines to within two hundred yards, during which the Rajput garrison made many vigorous sallies. When everything was ready the bombardment was opened, and a portion of the wall being battered down, a storm ordered. The six battalions were formed into two columns; Pohlman leading one, and Captain Donelly, his second in command, the other, and just before dawn the signal for attack was given by lighting a port-fire, and the troops rushed forward. But the garrison was prepared to receive them, and saluted the assailants with a tremendous fire from cannon and small arms. The stormers pressed gallantly forward, and reached the breach, but found it impracticable. The garrison seeing this, increased their exertions, rolling down large stones and discharging powder-pots and burning thatch upon the foe below, which caused the greatest havoc and confusion in all ranks. Captain Donelly, a gallant Irishman, and Lieutenant Exshaw lost their lives in this affair, and 800 men were killed and wounded before the battalions retired. Four days later the assault was renewed, and this time, in spite of the heroic defence of the Rajputs, the fort was captured and all the garrison killed and wounded with the exception of Kasri Singh and about 400 of his followers. Pohlman, himself a gallant officer, could feel for these brave men, and offered them terms which, seeing all was lost, they accepted, and marched out with the honours of war.

During the next few weeks Pohlman was engaged in reducing several refractory local chiefs, who refused to pay their tribute until compelled by force, after which he marched his Brigade back to Delhi, after a short but successful campaign.

Whilst this expedition had been in progress in Rájputana there had been another shuffling of the cards in the Deccan. Early in the year Daulat Ráo's wife had induced him to liberate from confinement her father, Ghatkay Ráo. This wretch soon regained his former evil influence over his son-in-law, and intrigued successfully against Balloba Tantia, the minister in power. Before long Balloba fell into disgrace, and in June was seized and imprisoned in the fortress of Ahmednagar, where he shortly afterwards died by poison. This event had a disastrous effect on the fortunes of Lakwa Dáda, who owed his restoration to power to the friendship of the late minister, and now felt certain that his own downfall was at hand; notwithstanding that Sindhia, with characteristic deceit, wrote to him to be under no apprehension, but to continue zealously in the performance of his duties as commander-in-chief. But in spite of these reassurances, within a very few weeks Ambaji Inglia was summoned from his retirement and appointed to supersede Lakwa Dáda, who had already sent his family to Jodhpur for safety, where he now proceeded to join them and entered into an alliance with the prince of that country.

Directly after his restoration to favour, Ghatkay Ráo recommenced urging Daulat Ráo to crush once for all the rebellion of the Bhais, by putting to death every man of note who was suspected of sympathy with them, knowing that by such a course of policy many powerful rivals would be removed from his own path. Sindhia listened favourably to these suggestions, and sanctioned a wholesale slaughter of the leading chieftains, who had been favourite officers and ministers under his uncle Modhoji, and were all men of high rank and ability. This atrocious proceeding at once alienated the affections of Sindhia's subjects: but it did more than this, for it struck a death-blow at the Maráthá national army, and left Daulat Ráo almost solely dependent upon his regular Brigades and his European officers.

Such of the chieftains as were able to escape, fled for refuge to Sindhia's enemies, and disorders threatened on every side. Lakwa Dáda was now formally dismissed from an office which he had in practice abdicated, and this gave the signal for a general insurrection to break out. The Holkars, who, since their defeat by De Boigne at Lakhairi, had scarce lifted their heads, now began to assert themselves, and under the direction of Jaswant Ráo, a natural son of old Takúji, who died in 1797, raised the standard of their house, to which vast numbers of Sindhia's late adherents began to flock.

Scarcely had Perron returned to Koil in July than news of Lakwa Dáda's defection reached him. He at once prepared to return to Rájputana to attack the rebel and his new ally of Jodhpur, but was delayed by the breaking out of an insurrection north of Delhi, where Sambunáth, the subahdar of Saharanpur, a faithful adherent of Lakwa, declared for his patron directly he heard of his supersession, and, collecting an army, audaciously avowed his intention of invading Perron's *Jaidad.* The danger from such an exhibition of insubordination existed more in its example than in its action, and it was imperative to crush it in the bud. Captain Smith was at once detached to attack Sambunáth; but although he inflicted a slight defeat, more energetic measures were necessary. Perron therefore deferred his advance against Lakwa Dáda, and on the 22nd of July took over the command of Captain Smith's force, and gave battle to Sambunáth at Katáoli. The action was short but decisive, and resulted in a complete victory for Perron. Utterly beaten and routed, Sambunáth fled to the Sikh territory and the general returned to Delhi with such laurels as he might reasonably claim from success against an individual whom George Thomas contemptuously termed " a grain merchant."

Perron stopped a short time at the capital, watching the progress of events, and whilst there paid his respects to the blind Emperor with much pomp and ceremony. The formality of " entering into the presence " was one he never omitted to observe when occasion allowed, for the nominal authority of the Mughal was the most powerful moral factor in his hand.

Just about this time Partáb Singh was going to be married, and as Perron had promised to attend the ceremony he determined to visit Jaipur, and from thence march to the attack of Lakwa Dáda. Collecting a strong force he set out for Rájputana, but on arriving at Bálahera on the 14th of November, learnt that the rebel chief had left Jodhpur and joined the Bhais in Malwa. This necessitated a change of plans, but as it was important for political reasons that Perron should keep his Jaipur engagement, he detached Major Bourguien to capture Ajmir, which belonged to Lakwa, and himself proceeded to Jaipur to be present at the nuptials of Partáb Singh on the 26th of November, and add to the ceremonial that *éclat* so precious to Oriental minds. It was not until January, 1801, that he left this city, and in fulfilment of his original design of attacking Lakwa Dáda set out for Malwa, where that chief was last reported to be. On his way he levied a heavy fine from the Rájah of Unaria, a recalcitrant chief who had lately defeated one of Perron's detached battalions under Skinner. At this place he learnt that Lakwa had evacuated Malwa and gone to Datía in Bundelkhand, taking the Bhais with him, and tired of his fruitless hunt Perron determined to discontinue it, and retraced his steps to his head-quarters at Koil, from which he had been too long absent.

Meanwhile Ambaji Inglia, the new Marátha commander-in-chief, was ordered to take up the chase of Lakwa, who had now entrenched himself at Sounda, in the territory of the Rájah of Datía, and was at the head of an army of 6,000 cavalry, 3,000 Bundela troops, and a small party of 200 sepoys, commanded by Colonel W. H. Tone, and 16 guns. The position he had chosen was an exceedingly strong one. In his rear was the fort of Sounda: in his front a network of ravines extending for seven miles: and his flanks were defended by broken country and several strong forts. Through these natural defences there were only three clear passes or passages for the advance of an enemy, all strongly protected with infantry and artillery.

Ambaji Inglia, acting under orders from Sindhia, collected at Gwalior an army of 5,000 horse and three brigades of regular infantry. Of these latter one was sent him by Perron, consisting of eight battalions under the command of Colonel Pedron; a second was one in his own employ, officered by two Englishmen, named James Shepherd and Joseph Bellasis, and the third an inferior corps commanded by a native named Kaleb Ali. But having assembled this army Ambaji hesitated to march against Lakwa, who was not so much the enemy of Sindhia as the champion of the Maráthá chieftains against the tyranny of Ghatkay Ráo, a personage as hateful to Ambaji himself as to any one, whilst the latter's feelings towards Lakwa were, at the bottom, not unfriendly. When at length an advance could no longer be delayed, Ambaji deputed his brother Bálá Ráo to take command, and himself remained at Gwalior.

In March, 1801, the army moved towards Sounda, and a series of small skirmishes soon took place, but nothing decisive was effected. Perron now began to recognise the gravity of the situation, for Lakwa Dáda and the Bhais had by this time prevailed upon Jaswant Ráo Holkar, and Ali Bahadur, a powerful independent chief in Bundelkhand, to support the rebellion. Thus a most formidable confederation was projected which threatened Daulat Ráo's authority, and thereby shook the very foundations of Perron's own position. In fact the insurrection of the Bhais, as it was still termed, was assuming such proportions that it seemed likely to change the existing balance of power in the Maráthá Empire, and opened an actual danger of Sindhia being crushed by a hostile alliance of all the other chiefs in the Deccan.

This induced Perron to proceed to Sounda in person, and he arrived in May with an escort of a battalion of infantry and 2,000 Hindustani horse. He found anything but a satisfactory condition of affairs. Pedron, overawed by the natural strength of Lakwa Dáda's position, had done nothing except engage in a few unimportant skirmishes. This dilatory conduct angered Perron, who determined to bring matters to an immediate issue, and gave the order for a general assault on the enemy's entrenchments, and at dawn of day on the 3rd of May the troops went into action.

They were divided into three columns to attack the three passes that led to Lakwa's camp. The right consisted of four battalions under Pedron; in the centre were Shepherd, Bellasis and Kaleb Ali with their brigades; and on the left were five battalions and 2,000 Hindustani horse under Captain Symes. The pass which Pedron attacked was held by Colonel Tone, who fought with great gallantry, until he was overpowered, and with his officers taken prisoner. In the centre Shepherd and Bellasis were opposed by a chief named Barár Singh, whom they drove back. But the left wing under Captain Symes met with a serious reverse at the hands of the gallant old Rájah of Datía, and sustained great slaughter.

Perron on hearing of this disaster sent to Pedron for reinforcements of two battalions, and, placing himself at their head, advanced to Symes's assistance. After rallying and reforming the routed troops, he led them back to the assault with the greatest personal daring and courage. Inspirited by his presence and example the men answered to his appeal, and the position was now stormed with complete success. The old Rájah of Datía fought until he was killed, whilst Perron was himself wounded by a spear thrust during an attack which he pressed home until it came to hand to hand work.

This decided the battle. Barár Singh was killed fighting bravely, and Lakwa Dáda, seriously wounded by a musket shot in the foot, escaped with the greatest difficulty. The Bhais fled on horseback, and all the rebel troops dispersed, whilst their sixteen guns were taken and their camp plundered. The day was not, however, won without serious loss, for the resistance offered was obstinate. In Pedron's column nearly a thousand men were killed and wounded, amongst the latter being two European officers. In the centre column Bellasis and three other officers were killed, and 1,500 men placed *hors de combat*: whilst on the left Captain Symes and Lieutenant Paish were wounded, and nearly half their men cut up. Had it not been for Perron's prompt and gallant assistance the whole of this column would have been annihilated.

Perron behaved with great humanity and kindness to Colonel Tone, Captain Evans and the other European officers who were taken prisoners. To the former he offered service in Sindhia's army, but this was declined. Whereupon all the captives were permitted to retire to Holkar's territory, Perron furnishing them with Rs.10,000 to defray their expenses and enable them to re-establish their fortunes.

All this time Major Bourguien had been doing but little in Ajmir, which, it will be remembered, was Lakwa Dáda's own province. Having arrived before the fort in December, 1800, he endeavoured to storm it on the eighth of the month, but was driven back by the garrison. He then, in expressive Oriental phraseology, "sat down" before it, and after fruitlessly attempting its reduction by siege, bombarded it with a more powerful metal than iron, and after five long months gained possession of the place by bribery on the 8th of May, 1801; so that in one week Lakwa Dáda sustained two crushing defeats at points so far distant as Ajmir and Sounda. But before news of the fall of the former place reached Perron he was so disgusted with Bourguien's incompetence that he sent Captain Symes to supersede him.

From Sounda Perron returned to Koil, which he reached early in June, having in one short but brilliant campaign broken up the rebellion of the Bhais and asserted Sindhia's supremacy.

CHAPTER IV.

PERRON PARAMOUNT.   THE BATTLE OF UJJAIN.

1801.

PERRON was now at the zenith of his career. He had brought all Hindustan into subjection, and was supreme within the boundaries of Sindhia's northern possessions. When he succeeded to De Boigne's post two formidable enemies stood in his way, Balloba Tantia and Lakwa Dáda. The former was dead, the latter a fugitive, and for the moment no shadow of opposition stood between Perron and his will. From Kotah in the south to Saharanpur in the north, from Jodhpur in the west to Koil in the east, his power was paramount.

An enumeration of the territories Perron governed at this time, and the countries and states he dictated to, will give an idea of the enormous extent of his influence. In the vast *Jaidad* he held, and which included the richest districts of the Doáb, he enjoyed the rights and privileges, and lived in the state and dignity, of an actual sovereign. The Subahs, or governorships, of Saharanpur, Panipat, Delhi, Narnól, Agra, and Ajmir, were directly under his control : he drew their revenues and ordered their government. He directed the politics of, and received tribute from, the Rajahs of Jaipur and Jodhpur, and many lesser Rajput chiefs, and claimed authority, if he did not actually exercise it, over the Sikhs between the Jumna and the Sutlej. Within Hindustan proper he owned the monopoly of the salt and customs duties, the two most valuable sources of revenue that existed, and enjoyed the exclusive privilege of coining money, and his annual revenue was estimated at £1,632,000 sterling. His possession of the person of the Emperor, Shah 'Alam, enabled him to invoke the Imperial authority for all his actions, and he enforced his will by the terror his disciplined army inspired.

It is not wonderful that such marvellous success turned Perron's head. From hawking handkerchiefs in a French provincial town to ruling Hindustan was an advancement in life that might have dazzled the most sober brain. From serving as a sailor on board a French frigate to commanding an army of 40,000 men was a promotion that finds few parallels in history. Brave in the field, and not overbearing in the camp, Perron had hitherto been respected by his European officers and beloved by his troops, and, until now, retained the character De Boigne had conceived of him, namely, that he was a gallant soldier and a man of plain sense.

But in 1801 a change became apparent in Perron's nature which soon began to influence his behaviour. He grew intoxicated with success. The subtle oil of Oriental flattery was poured into his ears, and he learnt to love it. Great schemes suggested themselves to his mind, and he indulged in dreams of establishing an independent kingdom for himself, or winning a place in his country's history by restoring to France the dominion of the East. On his elevation to his present post he had entered into correspondence with Piron, the successor of Raymond at Haidarabad, and with the French faction of Mysore, with whose revolutionary political principles he was in entire sympathy. Had Fortune permitted such a combination Perron would have joined these countrymen of his in a concerted endeavour to establish again the French power in India. But Lord Wellesley broke up Piron's force at Haidarabad, and Tipu Sultan's French auxiliaries surrendered to the English at Seringapatam, so that the only hope remaining to the French of reviving their ancient rule in the East was centred in Perron, for he was now the sole representative of the French struggle in India. The *rôle* of a national champion appealed to his vanity and pride, and he shaped his policy accordingly, and displayed a decided preference for Republican principles. He did not realise that the presence of a French army—for so his Brigades came to be called—in the very heart of Hindustan must raise the jealousy of the English; or, if he did, he was prepared to incur the risk, for he began, without any disguise, to pursue a course of favouritism in order to advance the views he had adopted.* He ignored the claims of merit

---

* The following footnote in Kaye's " Life of Lord Metcalfe " is interesting. It is an extract from a letter of the latter, dated the 22nd of March, 1802.—" Camp, Kashulghur.—Here I found four more battalions of Perron's troops. One of the officers came to visit me, anxious to hear of his father, Colonel ——. I obtained some information from him relative to the Mahratta service. It appears that promotion depends on General Perron, who is naturally disposed to favour his own countrymen. So far, however, as the rank of captain, every officer obtains a step annually—*i.e.* in four years a man must be a captain. The rule extends no higher. The uniform of the Sepoys is the same as the Company's ; so are the accoutrements, with the exception that they carry a

and the rights of regimental seniority, and filled all the posts of command in his Brigades with his own countrymen, who were pitch-forked over the heads of Europeans of other nationalities, without justice and without desert. This policy naturally excited the enmity and dissatisfaction of all foreigners serving under him and created a spirit which weakened his army. It was a gross departure from the principles laid down by De Boigne, who, above all things, was impartial, and never gave preference to any individual, but promoted each man by seniority, or for acknowledged merit. In pursuing an opposite course Perron hardly took the trouble to dissemble. He tolerated his English officers only from necessity, fully prepared to discharge them when the occasion arose, whilst every adventurer who could boast a French extraction, was pushed forward into appointments of responsibility and emolument, irrespective of claim or talent. That eventually these favoured countrymen of his rewarded his preference by disloyalty and ingratitude was but a just retribution. His downfall, indeed, was brought about by the very men whom he now raised from insignificance to power. This can create little surprise when their characters are considered. "Low they were," writes one of the superseded English officers, "in every sense of the word. Low in birth, in education, and in principle. Perron's army became a miniature of the French Revolution. Wretches were raised from cooks and barbers to become colonels and brigadiers, and absurdly entrusted with the command of troops, and showed into paths to acquire lakhs of rupees. This was the quintessence of *egalité*, the acme of French Revolution, the principles of which were now generally affected in the Force."

As a natural consequence every English officer in the Brigades soon came to detest Perron. Their supersession by illiterate and reprobate Frenchmen was sufficient to raise their indignation. How unjustly they suffered may be gathered from the fact that in the period of twenty years between 1783 and 1803, during which De Boigne's battalions flourished, only four Frenchmen were killed in active service, whilst fifteen British-born officers met their death on the field of battle. These partisan prejudices which Perron displayed were destructive not only of the *esprit de corps* that had previously inspired his army, but of the political harmony which should have existed between the Maráthás and the English. To the promotion of a good feeling between the two powers De Boigne had particularly

sword as well as a bayonet and musket. The band, which was in full tune, as they marched by my little camp, played nothing but marches—perfectly in the European style."

addressed himself, but under Perron this friendship soon changed to mutual distrust and hostility.

But this was not the only enmity Perron raised against himself and his master. As his power and influence increased Sindhia's Marátha chiefs found their own declining, and with each augmentation of the regular Brigades their feudal troops became of less and less account, and fewer prizes fell to their share. It was evident their occupation was slipping away, and with it those hereditary privileges and emoluments so dear to the native heart. Political extinction and pecuniary ruin threatened them, and the desperate condition of their prospects soon instigated them to plot against the foreigner who had usurped their rights and to enter into intrigues to effect his ruin.

Heedless of these gathering dangers Perron pursued his course. Behind his political ambition there was an even greater incentive to personal exertion, and that was his love of money. The harvest was rich, the season prosperous, the husbandman in humour, and he reaped and reaped. His pay and allowances were enormous. As commander-in-chief of the Imperial army he drew Rs.15,000 *per mensem*, with a liberal extra for " table expenses." For the support of his bodyguard he received a monthly sum of Rs.32,000. On all the revenue collections of the *Jaidad* his commission was 5 *per centum*, and the same on the revenues of the Subahs he administered. In every political arrangement he sanctioned, or entered into with the neighbouring princes and feudatory states, he exacted a *nazzar*, or complimentary donation, of 25 *per cent.* The wealth of the man was prodigious. On the lowest calculation, exclusive of the pay of his troops, he enjoyed a monthly emolument of Rs.100,000, which, at the exchange of the day, represented an annual income of over £150,000. In addition to this there must have been many other sources of gain open to him, for his savings in seven years were variously estimated at from one to two millions sterling.

It is now necessary to turn to a contemplation of the state of affairs in the Deccan, where Daulat Ráo Sindhia had been so long delayed, to the advantage of his European deputy in Hindustan.

Early in the year 1800 Nana Farnavis, the great Marátha minister, died, and a dispute immediately broke out between Sindhia and the Peshwá over the division of the immense property left by the deceased. Daulat Ráo illustrated the practical application of the adage that possession is nine points of the law, by seizing the Nana's *Jaghir*, or territory, under pretext of a claim of a million sterling against the estate. Plot and counterplot succeeded, too long and too complicated to be detailed here, inextricably interwoven as they were with the insurrection of the Bhais, whose cause the Peshwá espoused after the barbarous reprisals and bloodthirsty executions Sindhia had ordered, and which, as explained in a previous chapter, left the latter without any friends or adherents amongst his own countrymen, except his father-in-law, Ghatkay Ráo. Disorders and turmoils broke out on every side, and their occurrence prompted Jaswant Ráo Holkar to take advantage of the difficulty in which his rival was plunged, to reassert the political influence of his family, which, since the death of Takúji Holkar, had fallen to a very low ebb.

In order to explain Jaswant Ráo's standing it is necessary to go back a little and pick up the thread of the narrative at the point where mention of the house of Holkar ceased. After Takúji's crushing defeat at Lakhairi in 1793 he retired to his capital, where, in 1797, he followed his life-long rival, Madhoji Sindhia, to the burning ghaut. Takúji left behind him four sons, two legitimate and two natural ones. Of the former, the elder and acknowledged heir was Khasi Ráo, but he was weak in intellect and deformed in person, whilst the younger brother, Malhar Ráo, was brave and aspiring. A contest for the succession took place between these two, and Khasi Ráo, with fatal weakness, applied to Sindhia for assistance. So excellent an opportunity of increasing his importance and influence was precisely what Daulat Ráo desired. He became for a time the champion of the rightful heir of the house of Holkar, and in the struggle that ensued Malhar Ráo lost his life in battle, and his infant son, Khandi Ráo, fell into Sindhia's hands. Khasi Ráo was now left nominally in full possession of the Government, but, in reality, wholly dependent on Sindhia.

During the struggle between Khasi Ráo and Malhar Ráo, the two natural sons, Jaswant Ráo and Ithal Ráo, supported the latter, and when he was killed were forced to flee. Ithal Ráo sought refuge at Kolapur, and eventually met a violent death at the hands of his enemies. Jaswant Ráo, in the first instance, found protection at Nagpur, and later on, after numerous vicissitudes, in which his life was often in danger, at Dhár. Being a chief of great personal gallantry and talent he was soon able, in the distracted state of politics, to gather around him many adherents of his father who were prevented from supporting the cause of Khasi Ráo by his connection with Sindhia. Having collected a formidable following Jaswant Ráo entered on the life of a professional freebooter, directing his enterprises chiefly against Sindhia's territories. One of his first acts was to enter into an alliance with a celebrated Pathán soldier of fortune, named Amir Khán, who was at the head of a band of free lances, and lived by rapine and foray. Amir Khán's peculiar ability, audacity, and fame in predatory expeditions marked him out as a fit auxiliary for the schemes Jaswant Ráo meditated, and the Pathán, on his part, was not blind to the advantage of connecting himself with a chief of such high dignity as Jaswant Ráo, "through whom" (to quote from his memoirs) " a road might be opened to the management of great affairs, even to the very highest, from behind the curtain."

It was not long before Khasi Ráo proved mentally incapable of ruling, and when this became notorious Jaswant Ráo had no difficulty in strengthening his position by proclaiming that he was acting on behalf of Khandi Ráo, the nephew and heir of Khasi Ráo, and in the name of this infant he assumed the headship of the house of Holkar. His singular success and the depredations he committed in Sindhia's Narbada districts soon roused the latter to action, and a detachment of regular infantry was sent against him under the command of the Chevalier Dudrenec. This officer, on the death of Takúji, had cast in his lot with Khasi Ráo, a political error which soon became apparent to him, but never more clearly than on this occasion when he was defeated by Jaswant Ráo, whose reputation was thereby vastly increased. The reverse he sustained decided Dudrenec to change his allegiance, and declaring his conviction that Khasi Ráo was incapable of governing, he passed over with all his battalions to the service of Jaswant Ráo.

Jaswant Ráo's fortunes were now in the ascendant, and he began to dream of re-establishing the old glory and infl.ence of his house. Soon his improved circumstances required that he should conform to the respectability expected in a chief of position, and he reformed his vagabond army, introduced a certain degree of discipline into its ranks, and augmented his regular battalions, so as to put himself on a more equal footing with Sindhia. Several European officers were engaged to raise corps for him, and men of character and ability tempted to enter his service by liberal terms of remuneration. As there happened to be a greater number of French adventurers in the Deccan than of any other nationality, three-fourths of the Europeans introduced into his service belonged to that country. In addition to Dudrenec's Brigade two others were raised, each consisting of four battalions. One was commanded by Captain Gardner, but he did not remain long in the service, being succeeded by Captain Dodd. The other was under Captain Plumet, " a Frenchman and a gentleman ; two qualities which were seldom united in the Mahratta army." The successes achieved by these infantry Brigades soon enabled Holkar to pay them with tolerable punctuality, and for a time he continued to devastate Sindhia's territories in the vicinity of Ujjain without opposition. Sindhia was, in fact, sacrificing everything to maintain his influence at Poonah, where the political firmament continued to be much disturbed. But a time came when he could no longer disregard the rapidly growing power of Jaswant Ráo, and he felt compelled to take action against him, or run the risk of his own Malwa districts being harried into a wilderness. And so in 1801 he left the Peshwá's court, and accompanied by an enormous army set out on his return to Ujjain.

His progress was so slow that it allowed Jaswant Ráo ample time to call in all his scattered detachments and concentrate them in the neighbourhood of Sindhia's capital, with the intention of swooping down upon it in one final raid. When Daulat Ráo reached the Tapti he heard of the threatened danger, and in his alarm sent forward Major George Hessing with three of his battalions and one from Fidele Filoze's corps to protect the city. By this time the rainy season had broken, and the country was in a state most difficult for an army to traverse, notwithstanding which Hessing made an astonishingly rapid route and reached Ujjain by the end of June. A few days after his departure from Sindhia's camp the chief's anxiety increased, and he ordered Lieutenant MacIntyre, with the fourth battalion from Hessing's Brigade, and a second from Filoze's, to follow and support the advanced column. Three days later he detached two of Sutherland's battalions from the First Brigade, under Captain Gautier, to further strengthen Hessing, and finally crowned his imbecility by closing up the rear, after another interval, with two more of Sutherland's battalions and a park of artillery under Captain Brownrigg.

There was thus an *échelle* of small isolated detachments, with twenty, thirty, and forty miles between each, marching against an enemy whose entire strength was concentrated on the objective point. Jaswant Ráo was too able a general to let such an opportunity slip, and at once prepared to attack the detachments in detail. Passing by Hessing, who had reached Ujjain, he fell upon MacIntyre at Núri and compelled him to surrender. Elated with success he pushed on to attack Brownrigg, who, on hearing of the disaster, had crossed the Narbada and effected a junction with Gautier near the town of Satwás, where he took up a very strong position. The force under his command only amounted to four battalions of infantry and a hundred Rohillas, with, however, a very strong park of artillery. Holkar's army, according to a Bombay paper published at the time, consisted of fourteen regular battalions, under Plumet, 5,000 Rohillas, 50,000

Marátha cavalry, 27 heavy guns, and 42 light field-pieces; but this appears an exaggerated estimate. Still it is certain he had an immense numerical superiority over Brownrigg. The battle commenced at seven o'clock in the morning with a discharge of round and grape shot from Jaswant Ráo's guns. An artillery duel succeeded, and lasted for four hours, when an attempt was made to advance and storm Brownrigg's position. But he defended himself with such resolution and judgment that all Holkar's attacks were unavailing, whole files of his infantry being cut to pieces by the chain shot discharged against them. Before long the men became demoralised and refused to advance, and Major Plumet being taken prisoner,* Holkar decided on a retreat, which he did not effect without enormous loss. Brownrigg's casualties were only 107, but amongst them was his gallant fellow-countryman, Lieutenant Rowbotham.

Jaswant Ráo now retired to Indore, from whence he sent urgent messages to Amir Khán to join him with all speed. But the Pathán chief was a man of obstinate metal, and preferred to retrieve Holkar's reverse rather than commit himself to a retrograde movement. So he boldly advanced against Ujjain to attack Hessing, whereupon Holkar plucked up heart, and, hurrying forward with two brigades of infantry, effected a junction with his ally. On the 2nd of July, 1801, the combined forces moved against the city. They found Hessing drawn up ready to receive them, his force in a square formation, with its rear defended by the battlements of the capital. Jaswant Ráo divided his army into two equal divisions, making over the command of one to Amir Khán and leading the other himself. The Pathán opened the action by dispersing Hessing's considerable body of Marátha horse by a charge of his own cavalry, and then directed a heavy cannonade upon the four battalions of regular infantry. These were soon thrown into confusion, upon which their commander, a half-caste son, by a native woman, of gallant old John Hessing, failed to demonstrate the doctrine of heredity, and fled at an early stage of the action, leaving his officers to meet the advance of Plumet's brigade, which was now commanded by a Frenchman named Fleury. The result was soon placed beyond doubt, for, although Hessing's officers behaved with conspicuous gallantry, freely sacrificing their lives in the defence of their colours, they were completely overpowered, and, towards the close of the action, annihilated by a spirited charge of the Pathán cavalry under Amir Khán himself. " To the end," writes a contemporary observer, " they behaved with all that cool and collected

---

* So stated in the newspaper quoted from—but the fact is doubtful.

fortitude which belongs to true heroism, and fell covered with honourable wounds." Of the twelve officers engaged, eight were killed and three wounded and made prisoners, Hessing alone escaping to Bairúngarh by a craven flight. Those who lost their lives were Captain-Lieutenant John Macpherson, a son of Captain Macpherson in the Company's service; Lieutenant John Graham, son of Ensign Graham in the same; Lieutenant Edward Montague, son of Colonel Montague of the Bengal Artillery; Lieutenant Doolan, Ensigns Haddon and Urquhart, all of Hessing's brigade, and Lieutenants Lany and Meadows of Filoze's corps. Amongst the wounded were Lieutenant Humpherstone, Captain Dupont and Major Deridon, the latter a half-bred Frenchman, whose sister Perron had married. He was eventually ransomed by Colonel John Hessing, of Agra (who was also a connection of his), by a payment of Rs.40,000, which sum Sindhia afterwards refunded with unusual generosity. The heads of the dead officers were cut off and carried to Holkar, who rewarded this atrocious act of mutilation with a payment of Rs.1,000 for each. Holkar bought the victory dear, although he captured 20 guns. In Amir Khán's memoirs it is stated that 200 Europeans were killed in the battle, which the editor, in a footnote, explains " probably included all classes of Christians, so that the number slain may have been nearly as stated in the text"; but this appears very doubtful, and the sportive fancy of the Amir's biographer, Basáwan Lál, probably added a redundant cipher to the right hand of the total. Hessing's camp was plundered and an immense booty of stores, elephants, horses, kettle-drums, and standards fell into the hands of the victors in addition to the guns. The next day the city of Ujjain was given over to pillage, and sacked with all the thoroughness peculiar to Asiatic freebooters, gifted with a genius for the discovery of *cachés* and secret hiding-places.

Holkar's prestige was enormously increased by the victory of Ujjain, and overtures for an alliance were now made to him by Lakwa Dáda, the champion of the Bhais, who, although wounded, was still able to intrigue. This chief proposed a combination between Ali Bahadur, of Bundelkhand, Jaswant Ráo Holkar, and himself against Sindhia, and a formidable alliance was thus promoted, which seriously threatened the great house of Ujjain.

Sindhia was at Burhanpur when news reached him of the disaster that had overwhelmed Hessing's brigade. " He writhed in an agony of vexation and rage at hearing of it," writes the quaint native historian already quoted. His first act was to send orders to Perron at Delhi to hurry to his support. The moment was critical. Every day helped to fan into flame the mouldering embers of long pent-up hatred and jealousy that existed against him in the Deccan, and Daulat Ráo urged on Perron the supreme necessity of using every exertion in bringing his brigades south, and simultaneously recalled to his head-quarters the troops he had left at Poonah to maintain his authority there. These included 10,000 Maráthá cavalry under Ghatkay Ráo, and the remaining five battalions of the first brigade under Colonel Robert Sutherland. As soon as they joined, Sindhia's confidence began to return, and he only awaited Perron's arrival to inflict a crushing blow on the baseborn upstart of the rival house who had lowered his pride and defeated his regular infantry.

CHAPTER V.

1801.

ABOUT the middle of 1801 a danger which had for some time past been troubling Perron began to assume formidable proportions. This was the singular rise to power of George Thomas, whose history has already been related. Between the two adventurers enmity had long existed, for they were antagonistic at every point and hated each other as cordially as Briton and Frenchman could hate at that period. Perron was both jealous and fearful of Thomas's increasing influence, which had been greatly augmented by the recent brilliant campaign against the Sikhs of the Sutlej States. More than once during the past year the Frenchman had made a sly attack on Jhajjar territory, thereby raising the wrath and indignation of its master. A common instinct told both that sooner or later their differences would have to be decided by the sword, and the Irishman, with whom there was never any time like the present for fighting, was getting ready for the fray. Perron, on his part, having disposed of Lakwa Dáda, felt himself free to approach this new difficulty. For some time past he had urged on Sindhia the necessity of crushing Thomas's power, and a treaty had been approved by the chief, framed with the object of reducing *Jowruj Jung* to a position of subordination to Perron. To impose this treaty upon Thomas, Perron came to Delhi in June, 1801, and wrote to him to send a vakil to confer on the matter. Thomas, who had concluded peace with the Sikhs, and withdrawn to his capital to prepare himself for resistance, in view of a possible rupture, so far acquiesced in Perron's wish as to depute an agent to attend the General.

Such was the condition of affairs on the 8th of July, when the battle of Ujjain occurred, and Sindhia ordered Perron to proceed at once to the Deccan with two complete brigades and all the Hindustani horse. This was tantamount to the evacuation of Hindustan, for compliance with these orders would have left Upper India defenceless, saving for a few garrison troops.

But Hindustan was as completely under Perron's sway as his own *Jaidad*, for it was held and controlled by the army he commanded. Although for the sake of form he cited the Emperor's name as authority for his actions, and from time to time, at Darbár, confessed himself Sindhia's humble and obedient servant, Perron was the paramount lord and master of the country so long as his brigades were at his back. And now these brigades were summoned to the south.

It was impossible to let them go : to proceed there himself would be an act of abdication. His own duty and Sindhia's sore distress had no weight in his mind while that terrible Irishman paraded his troops and won his victories on the western confines of Delhi. What mattered Daulat Ráo's danger, when danger threatened Perron ? Charity begins at home, and the former must be met with temporising promises, the latter with the brigades, unless perchance—it was a brilliant idea that occurred to him—he could induce Thomas to undertake the fighting in the Deccan, and leave him, with his troops intact, in Hindustan.

For some time past it had been apparent that the General was neglecting Sindhia's interests and consulting only his own. This behaviour was confirmed now, for on receiving Daulat Ráo's orders to proceed to his aid Perron at once lapsed into protestations, and with these began and ended his response to his master's appeal. His sense of loyalty and his sentiments of gratitude to a prince who had loaded him with favours and raised him to his high station were lost in apprehensions of his own danger, and with a supreme selfishness he sacrificed everything to his own interests.

There exists a very detailed record of Perron's behaviour, during this critical period of Sindhia's affairs, in some Persian *Akbars*, or newspapers, printed at the time, and the following extracts, thrown into a narrative form, exhibit the true character of the man of whom they treat.

The chronicle commences on the 28th of June, 1801, when intimation was received at Delhi that Thomas had made peace with the Sikhs, and was preparing for hostilities with Perron, from whom he had just received proposals for a political arrangement. In the success of these Thomas evidently had very little faith, for he opened communications with Lakwa Dáda, who was in Datía territory, proposing an alliance against the Frenchman.

Ten days later, on the 8th of July, Perron received information of the defeat of Hessing at Ujjain, and simultaneously urgent orders reached him from Sindhia to march to the Deccan with his brigades. To these he sent a reply saying he would start at once. On the 15th of the month he moved out one stage from Delhi, with the ostensible intention of proceeding south, but having encamped at Bárahpula, remained there fast, showing no inclination to continue his march. Here, on the 19th, he received a visit from Bapu Sindhia, his deputy-governor in the Saharanpur province. As this district adjoined Thomas's territory and that of the Sikhs with whom he had recently been at war, Bapu was certainly the person most qualified to afford information about Thomas, to obtain which was probably the reason of his being summoned to attend Perron, for a long "consultation" was reported to have taken place. The following day Perron returned to Delhi with four of his European officers, and went through the formal ceremony of being "admitted to the presence" of the Emperor, to whom the usual offerings were presented, and from whom the customary gifts were, in turn, received.

For the next fortnight Perron remained at Delhi, trying to bring to an issue the negotiations with Thomas, for on the 7th of August it was publicly given out that "the General was diverted from his purpose of marching to Scindia's aid by important business negotiations with Thomas, by which he hopes to obtain four of that person's battalions and 20,000 Sikh horsemen to send to Oojein." And yet in the very same issue it is stated that "on Perron's speedy arrival depends the fate of Scindia, whose situation has become critical."

On the 8th of August Perron "called in his detachments," and it was notified that "immediately after his interview with Thomas the General intends to march against Holker." Another day passed, and he wrote to one of his native officials that "after two or three days, having adjusted matters of great urgency, I will set out to join Scindia." On the same date, with his usual punctilio in revenue collections, he sent a warning to the Rajah of Jaipur to be up to time in the payment of his tribute.

Four days later the receipt of another urgent letter from Sindhia was announced, which conveyed the information that Holkar's army was only fifteen miles distant, and that many of Daulat Ráo's chiefs had deserted to the enemy, and once more urged Perron to join him with all speed. On the 19th of August rumours reached Delhi that matters were still more critical, "all the Deccan chiefs having joined Jeswunt Ráo Holker," but still Perron made no sign of starting, for negotiations with Thomas were coming to a head, and his whole attention was monopolised by them. The next day he moved out to Sitaram Ka Serai, near Bahadurgarh, where an interview took place between him and *Jowruj Jung.* It appears to have been hedged about with the ceremonial and dilatoriness of Oriental diplomacy, for a week later he was still at the same place.

The next entry occurs on the 5th of September. The Emperor Shah 'Alam having constantly inquired, " When is General Perron going to Oojein ? " and as constantly been informed, " In two or three days," relieved himself of the sage opinion that " he did not think the General showed any intention of going at all ! " and almost at the same date Rajah Partáb Singh, of Jaipur, who had evidently been following Perron's movements with a profound interest, announced in open court that his agent at Delhi had written him saying that " Perron holds forth an intention of joining Scindia, but that in reality he entertains no such design, and has commenced a secret correspondence with Luckwadada." Commenting on which the Rajah observed that " the General seems to have detached himself from Scindia, and has not acted well in so doing."

This side-light thrown on the negotiations between Perron and Thomas is interesting, in so far as it suggests a reason why the latter was disappointed later on in receiving the assistance he expected from Lakwa Dáda, whose notoriously treacherous character would be quite equal to encouraging Thomas to resist, and coming to a secret understanding with Perron to stand neutral.

On the 12th of September it was reported that Perron was going to the camp of Ali Bahadur, one of the allies in the confederation against Sindhia, to settle certain affairs, and about the same time the report of his negotiations with Lakwa Dáda was confirmed.

On the 16th of September Perron returned to Delhi, all attempts to come to an understanding with Thomas having proved futile. Shortly after his arrival he paid his respects to the Emperor, but " on receiving an express went off to Coel." A week later it was reported at the capital that Daulat Ráo Sindhia continued repeatedly writing to Perron, urging him by every means in his power to help him, and was at the same time so sanguine of response that he " only " awaited the arrival of the General to attack Holkar. It is instructive to read, side by side with this, that " it is publicly reported in Hindustan that General Perron has withdrawn from the contest with Jeswunt Ráo Holker ! "

On the 26th of September Drugeon, Commandant of the fort of Delhi and custodian of the Emperor's person, received a letter from Perron, the contents of which he made known. They were to the effect that Perron's "wish had been to remain at Delhi, but the necessity of sending troops to Daulat Ráo Sindhia obliged him to repair suddenly to Koil, and *he had sent a brigade*, with military stores and ammunition, to Daulat Ráo."

Here, at last, he seems to have awakened to a sense of his duty, but, as will presently be seen, the good intention withered in the bud.

On the 29th of September came the news of the defeat of Captain Smith's force at Georgegarh by Thomas, followed two days later by alarming intelligence of a sanguinary battle, in which Bourguien and his brigade had been defeated and lost 3,000 men, whilst the Irishman had regained Georgegarh, and was in possession of it. No sooner did Perron hear of this than he sent immediate orders to Drugeon at Delhi to entertain fresh levies, despatched Pedron to the front with reinforcements of five battalions, and ordered George Hessing, who had evidently arrived at Agra from Ujjain, to march to Bourguien's assistance with four battalions. At the same time he collected all the available troops at Koil, and gave out that he intended to take the command in person against Thomas.

The total force at this time under Perron's command in Hindustan consisted of three brigades of infantry, 5,000 Hindustani horse, and the garrison troops. Of these, two brigades—the third under Bourguien and the fourth under Pedron—and most of the cavalry were employed against Thomas at Georgegarh. It is probable that Pedron's brigade was the one which Perron informed Drugeon "had been sent" to Ujjain. But it is possible that when he so wrote he was referring to the second brigade, under Pohlman, whose headquarters were at Mattra. Whichever it was it is very certain that neither proceeded very far towards the destination indicated. Pedron's, as has been shown, was diverted to Georgegarh, and for Pohlman's there was a more remarkable task assigned. It appears that some time previous to this Perron, in the novel capacity of a pawnbroker, had lent Partáb Singh, of Jaipur, a large sum of money, for the security of which the Rajah had pledged his jewels. Perron now wanted his money back. It is not difficult to conjecture what doubts and fears were passing through his mind and making him anxious to realise his capital. And it is evident that the recovery of his cash was a far more important business in his eyes than the relief of Sindhia, for Pohlman, who might certainly have been spared for the Deccan, was deputed, instead, to perform bailiff's work, and obtain from Partáb Singh an immediate settlement of his account, under pain of his territory being laid waste.

It is interesting to observe how Pohlman performed this honourable commission. Having summoned Partáb Singh to pay up, he did not wait for a reply, but added a point to his demand by marching from Chaksu to Haráru, where he began plundering the country a few miles south of Jaipur. The Rajah at once sent Pohlman the balance of his debt, amounting to Rs.95,000, and asked for the restoration of his jewels. But he was met with a counterclaim from the bailiff-general in possession of his country, who presented a statement of account showing a balance of two lakhs of rupees. The debtor denied the correctness of the figures, as debtors unskilled in the casting of compound interest are apt to do in India, and his agents refused to part with the money they had brought, especially after eliciting from Pohlman the acknowledgment that he had not got the jewels with him, but had sent for them, and expected them to arrive in four or five days. This delay allowed an extension of time for pillaging, and Pohlman resumed the congenial work until the Rajah bought him off with a payment of Rs.40,000 on account. Whereupon Pohlman consented to hold his hand, and marched south to Tonk—an outlying district belonging to Holkar—where he expelled the garrison from the chief town and took possession of it.

Returning now to Delhi, news was received there on the 8th of October of the death of Emilius Felix Smith, just as Drugeon was sending off 200 newly raised cavalry to the front. On the 12th Perron, who was still at Koil, was reported to have severely censured Bourguien for his misconduct of the campaign, and superseded him by Pedron, " who will now have a chance of displaying his valour." Between this and the 25th of October there were constant reports of Thomas's brave defence (which have been incorporated in the sketch of his life), and on the latter date Perron, never unmindful of the main chance, called upon the Rajah of Jaipur to pay up his tribute, promising, if he did so punctually, that, as soon as Thomas was reduced, he would march into the Rajah's territory and put him in possession of certain revolted districts, in fulfilment of a promise previously given. On hearing which Partáb Singh, who was a prince ever in trouble with his own tributaries, sadly observed that " General Perron had entered into many similar engagements, but never performed any of them, and that he regarded nothing but his own interests." Which, on the face of it, seemed a reasonable remark to make.

Such is the tale of Perron's ingratitude, faithlessness, and treachery disclosed by the Persian newspapers of the period. Nor are all these reports mere idle gossip, emanating from irresponsible sources, for in the majority of instances the authority quoted is that of Mohan Lal

Perron's own vakil, or agent, resident with the Emperor, whose duty it was to daily report his master's actions to the King of Kings. The truth was that Perron not only had no intention of assisting Sindhia, but even desired that he should be hard pressed by Holkar.. This is confirmed by a letter from Colonel Collins, the Resident at Daulat Ráo's Court, to the Governor-general, in which the following passage occurs, which bears upon the events just recorded :—

"The Mahratta Chiefs and Sirdars, envious of Perron, do not scruple to affirm that he by no means wishes the total ruin of Holker, since in this event Scindia would be unable to repair to Hindostan to take upon himself the chief direction of affairs in that quarter. . . . General Perron has been given to understand that he must relinquish the collection of all the districts which he now possesses in Hindostan, excepting those appertaining to his *Jaidad*, the annual revenues of which are estimated at 40 lakhs, while at present the General collects nearly 80."

It must here be observed that Colonel Collins under-estimated very considerably the annual collections made by Perron, towards whom, it may be added, he entertained a very friendly feeling. Moreover, the inference that Perron's reported desire for Holkar's success were to be traced to the envy and malice of unscrupulous Maráthá chiefs seems unjust. Perron's own actions afforded very strong grounds for this suspicion, which is amply corroborated by the day-to-day record of his doings between the 28th of June and the 15th of October of the year under review. No one who has followed his sinuous course during these four months can have any doubts left as to his real character. He was no longer "the brave and faithful soldier" he once had been, but a traitor, who had thrown off all disguise, and was fighting for his own hand alone. His greed of power and gold had overshadowed everything else, and he cared not how desperate was the cause of the master who had lavished so many favours on him and raised him to so high an estate when his own paltry lakh of rupees was at stake. There was ample work for the army of Hindustan in crushing that defiant Irishman, who could not comprehend the meaning of defeat, at Georgegarh ; but if, perchance, a brigade could be spared, it might, in Perron's opinion, be more profitably employed in doing bailiff's work in Rajputana than in propping up the tottering power of Daulat Ráo Sindhia in the Deccan.

Sindhia's position was indeed critical while all this procrastination was going on. The alliance against him was overwhelming, for Raguji Bhonsla of Berar, a chief of the first magnitude in the Maráthá Confederation, had decided to join Holkar, Lakwa

Dáda, Ali Bahadur, and all the lesser chiefs who were leagued against Daulat Ráo. The only person of importance who remained true to Sindhia, was his generalissimo, Ambaji Inglia, who was in the neighbourhood of Jararu, where his battalions, under James Shepherd, were successfully holding Lakwa Dáda in check.

Sindhia, in this distressful situation, was anxious to stay the storm his ambition had been mainly instrumental in raising; but the Peshwá, who had sided with his enemies, refused to listen to any overtures for reconciliation, until Daulat Ráo had made peace with the Bhais, who continued as greatly incensed as ever against their nephew. Moreover, Baji Ráo demanded a *nazzarána,* or peace offering, of fifteen lakhs of rupees, and this was highly inconvenient to Sindhia, who was in his chronic state of impecuniosity, and engaged in a costly campaign. There seemed, indeed, to be more money in Jaswant Ráo's camp than in his rival's, for the former was constantly sending remittances and reinforcements to Lakwa Dáda, with which to oppose Ambaji's attack and Perron's anticipated march from Delhi to Ujjain, it being taken for granted that the General, as he had publicly announced, would at once proceed to his master's assistance. At Agra, Colonel John Hessing held the fort, but he was so weakened by the despatch of his son and the four battalions to Georgegarh, that he was utterly unable to help Sindhia, and, on the contrary, was continually urging Perron to send him reinforcements as Lakwa Dáda's intrigues had created great disturbances in his government. In short, as far as Hindustan was concerned, there seemed to be no possible hope of help reaching Sindhia so long as Thomas held out and monopolised the attention of 16,000 regular infantry and the Hindustani horse.

But now, when matters were at their worst and nothing but danger, difficulty, and disappointment seemed to surround Sindhia, a saviour arose in his own camp, in the person of Robert Sutherland, Colonel-Commandant of the first brigade. It will be remembered that after De Boigne's resignation Sutherland tried hard to obtain his post, but fortune had been against him and Perron won the prize. The competition left a feeling of hatred and jealousy in Perron's heart, which had on more than one occasion influenced his treatment of the Scotchman. Anxious to expel him from Hindustan, he had manufactured a charge against him of entering into treasonable correspondence with Sindhia's enemies, and found in it an excuse to transfer him to the Deccan, giving the command of his brigade to Pohlman. Sutherland had been impotent to do anything but obey. But the very measure intended to punish and undo him, now gave the Scotchman the opportunity of proving his merit, for he found himself filling the chief post of defence at his master's side, which Perron had basely declined.

For nearly three months after the battle of Ujjain Sindhia did little but wait for Perron to arrive, and endeavour, by every means in his power, to strengthen his forces. At last he gave up all hope of assistance from Hindustan, and determined to try and retrieve his fortunes with such means as he had at his disposal. On the 24th of September he crossed the Narbada, on the south bank of which he had been compulsorily encamped since the rainy season commenced, and entered Málwa with eight battalions of Sutherland's brigade and four of Filoze's. A week later he formed a junction with 14,000 Marátha horse and encamped on the banks of the Kotah Sind River. Here he remained with his heavy baggage, sending Sutherland forward to avenge the sacking of Ujjain by retaliating on Holkar's capital of Indore, an undertaking which the troops approached in the highest spirits.

Jaswant Ráo immediately advanced towards the defence of his capital, and on the 13th of October the two armies met outside its walls. The Indore force consisted of ten battalions of regular infantry, 5,000 Rohillas, 12,000 Marátha cavalry, and 15,000 Pathán horse under Amir Khán. But Holkar was without European officers, which was a serious loss to him. The reason of this is not very clear: according to one authority he had dismissed all in his employ on the suspicion that they were unfaithful to him; but Major Ambrose, an officer in his service, states that he was " deserted " by his Europeans just before this action, and that this was the cause of his defeat.

After sending off his baggage and reserves to the further side of Indore, Holkar, during the night, changed ground, and placed the city between him and the enemy, taking post behind a deep ravine to the north of it, and training his guns so as to sweep this defence, whilst Amir Khán, with 15,000 horse, threatened the enemy's rear from a place about five miles distant.

Sutherland commenced the attack on Holkar's position early on the morning of the 14th, his twelve battalions moving briskly forward, animated by a determination to avenge their officers and comrades slain at Ujjain. Owing to the change of ground made by the enemy during the night, Sutherland was obliged to manœuvre his army to the right, over some difficult and broken country, before he could form it in line of battle for attack, and it was not until three o'clock in the afternoon that the action began. Having detached his Marátha cavalry to keep Amir Khán in check, the Colonel advanced against the nullah which protected Holkar, and was met with a tremendous fire from 95 guns. But it could not stay the steady and irresistible assault of the regular battalions, who forced the ravine and captured the guns in their position. At this critical moment Amir Khán, having defeated the Marátha cavalry, came charging down to the relief of Jaswant Ráo. Whereupon Sutherland boldly faced round with a portion of his force and opened a heavy fire of grape and round shot upon the Pathán as he was struggling through the ravine from which the brigade had just emerged, and the Amir's horse being killed he fell to the ground; whereupon his men, supposing him dead, took flight. This was the turning-point of the battle. Sutherland's infantry now stormed Holkar's entrenchments, which they carried splendidly, and by six o'clock in the evening the victory was won and the enemy dispersed in full flight. Holkar lost all his guns, 160 tumbrils, and his baggage, and, attended by his cavalry, fled headlong to Maheswar; and the next morning Sindhia's standard floated over Indore, and Ujjain was avenged. An incident happened in this battle, mention of which should not be omitted. Fidele Filoze, who commanded four of the battalions engaged, belonging to his brigade, had a short while before entered into a traitorous correspondence with Holkar, and when the action commenced, with a dastardly treachery, fired into Sutherland's troops. Happily this diabolical act failed in its intention, and the perpetrator was apprehended and confined in prison, where he shortly afterwards committed suicide. Sutherland's loss at Indore was 400 men killed and wounded. It is needless to add that Holkar's capital was thoroughly pillaged, and, indeed, rased to the ground by Sindhia's predatory horse, who, however useless in fight, were masters of the art of extracting the last grain of rice from any city given over to them to loot.

The victory of Indore might have been turned into a decisive battle of Marátha history by Sindhia if he had followed up his advantage. But he over-estimated his success, and deluded himself into the idea that Jaswant Ráo's power was crushed out. But this was not the case, and Daulat Ráo's imprudent assumption led to the gravest results. Holkar and his *fidus achates*, Amir Khán, soon resumed their former course of aggression and plunder, attracting to their camp all the discontented soldiery in Central India, so that it quickly became filled with rude and reckless freebooters, who came to be known by the generic term of Pindaris, and whose deeds and misdeeds during the next eighteen years laid desolate many of the fairest provinces of the peninsula, and constituted a period to which the natives gave the expressive appellation of the *Gardi-ka-Wakht*, or, "Time of Trouble." No longer able to pay his troops, Holkar gave them free license to support themselves by plunder, though he continued to keep up his regular infantry, who, after Dudrenec's desertion to Perron, which shortly took place, found a gallant leader in the person of a young English officer named Vickers.

Sindhia's unexpected success in the Deccan gave Perron breathing space; but the relief was only temporary, and the effects that followed very serious. In a short time his personal fortunes were as seriously threatened as Daulat Ráo's had been before Sutherland's victory. Thomas still continued to hold out at Georgegarh, with that unconquerable spirit of his that upset all calculations. And now Colonel Sutherland's star was in the ascendant, and the distrust and jealousy with which Perron regarded this officer were intensified to an enormous degree, and he even began to be fearful of being supplanted by the Scotchman, who had been his rival in the past. As yet he could do nothing to avert the threatened danger, for he dared not leave Hindustan while Thomas was undefeated. And so he vacillated in an agony of indecision, uncertain whether to proceed to the west and put his fortunes to the test of an assault on the fortified camp that was resisting all Pedron's endeavours, or to hurry to the south and re-establish his influence at Sindhia's Court.

On the 10th of November Georgegarh fell, but even as Perron was congratulating himself on his long-deferred success, he heard of Thomas's escape to Hánsi. The capture of the man was far more important than the capture of his outlying camp, and the victory was robbed of its chief importance by the failure to obtain possession of Thomas's person. Then came tidings of the fresh resistance at Hánsi, and the knowledge that the task of seizing Thomas had been confided to Bourguien. The incapacity of this officer was known to Perron, and he sickened at heart as he reflected how his interests were in the keeping of a man who had always failed in every task allotted to him. Week after week Perron waited, in feverish anxiety, at Koil, eagerly drinking in the daily news from the seat of war, elevated for a moment when he heard of some temporary success, depressed again when reverses were reported : hugging himself with joy when he learnt that *Jowruj Jung* had been beaten back into his citadel, downcast when it was made evident that there was still fight left in the terrible Irishman.

To add to his troubles the constant messages that continued to arrive from Daulat Ráo were now couched in very different language to that affected before the battle of Indore. In their growing insistence there were ominous expressions of anger; they were no longer appeals, but sharp commands, with a warning ring in them that indicated danger and menace.

The tension was terrible, but at last the reprieve came. Bourguien the incompetent, for the first time in his life, was guilty of achievement. Thomas surrendered. The news reached Koil early in January, 1802, and with a great gasp of relief Perron heard that his ene   had been delivered into his hands.

CHAPTER VI.

PERRON VISITS UJJAIN. THE BATTLE OF POONAH.

1802.

THE defeat of Thomas and destruction of his power cleared a very
serious danger from Perron's path and left him free to concentrate his endeavours on re-establishing his interest at Sindhia's Court.
Whilst the Irishman was undefeated it was Perron's policy to belittle
his importance, but after the fall of Hánsi the vanquished adventurer
became a national enemy, who had threatened the disintegration of
the Marátha Empire, and in his letters to Sindhia Perron made as
much of his victory over Thomas as if he had defeated a Cæsar or an
Alexander.

The reason of this change of opinion was not far to seek. Perron
wanted an excuse to explain his long and systematic disobedience of
Sindhia's orders to march to the Deccan. The campaign against
Thomas offered a plausible exculpation, and the more he extolled its
importance the greater credit would be reflected on himself for
destroying such a formidable public enemy. Moreover, Perron was
now as anxious to proceed to Ujjain as he had before been unwilling.
Colonel Collins, the English resident, had recently joined Daulat
Ráo's camp, and Perron distrusted him, fearing he might have come to
initiate a policy hostile to the brigades, similar to that under which,
four years previously, the British Government had broken up and disbanded Raymond's corps at Haidarabad. This was one of the
reasons that made a visit to Ujjain necessary, whilst another was
Perron's jealousy of Sutherland, who, since the battle of Indore, had
risen high in Sindhia's favour—a state of affairs highly detrimental to
the General, since the Scotchman was next to him in seniority. In
fact Perron felt it was imperative to counteract the growing influence
of this successful subordinate, who already held their master's ear,
and at the same time learn the real tenor of Colonel Collins's instructions, and so he determined to proceed to the south.

THE EMPEROR SHAH 'ALAM.

[*From a plate in Francklin's "History of the Reign of Shah-Aulum."*]

Matters in Hindustan were now in a fairly settled state. Bourguien's brigade had overawed the Sikh country, and that bold brigadier was engaged in levying tribute from his recent allies, under guise of collecting a contribution towards the expenses of the war, so that the cost of expelling Thomas was defrayed by the chiefs of Patiála, Jind, and Kaithal. At Delhi Drugeon kept watch and ward over the blind Emperor—a close one, too, in every sense of the word, for in January of this year Shah 'Alam wrote to Sindhia in terms of mild remonstrance, saying that "Although General Perron certainly made a monthly remittance of the royal stipend, it would still be more agreeable if Dowlut Ráo would do so himself, under his own immediate supervision." Pedron had returned to Koil with the fourth brigade (for the command of which the Chevalier Dudrenec had lately been engaged), and George Hessing to Agra, with his four battalions, to reinforce his father in command there. All things were in order, and Perron could safely be spared. His departure was accelerated by a report which found publicity in the Persian akbars at Delhi in February to the effect that "Dowlat Ráo Scindia had several times written to General Perron requiring his personal attendance, but without effect; and that His Highness was accordingly so much exasperated at the General's neglect of orders, that he instantly broke and disbanded the regiments under his command."

This was the climax, and at the end of the month Perron left Koil, and, escorted by his bodyguard of 500 horse, started for Ujjain. A letter written by him at this period is given in the appendix of M. St. Genis' "Life of De Boigne," and the following translation of it may conveniently be inserted here:—

"Camp Bandares,
"*February* 28, 1802.

"My dear General,—Since your departure from this country there have been nothing but troubles. Four years ago the widows of the old Prince fled from their nephew, the reigning Prince, and collected a considerable force in opposition to him.

"Three years ago Luckwadáda, who also turned traitor to the Prince, took the part of the widows. I was obliged to march against these two factions who opposed us. Having brought them to action I was fortunate enough to defeat them. Luckwadáda was wounded in the battle, and since his defeat the widows have petitioned the Prince to grant them terms.

"He has just pardoned them, and they have returned to their allegiance. Luckwadáda died of his wounds; had he got the better of me he would never have spared me.

"Jeswunt Ráo, of the house of Holker, has also been at war with the Prince for the last two years. He is plundering and desolating the country everywhere, and I am on the march against him with my cavalry.

"A man named George Thomas, who took advantage of my stay in the Deccan to raise a party of 12,000 men with 60 guns, seized a considerable tract of territory on the Sikh frontier, where he built a strong fort and devastated all the countryside even up to the walls of Delhi. I was obliged to destroy his force with my third brigade, and I have allowed the scoundrel to go, but prohibited him from again entering the Prince's territory.

"You are a soldier, my dear General, and you know that we always lose brave soldiers in the time of war. M. Rostock, whom you recommended to me, was killed at the battle of Indore. M. Bernier, one of the best and bravest officers in the brigades, met the same fate; also the younger Smith, Donelly, your *protégé*, and several others whom you do not know.

"At the present moment the Prince has only Jeswunt Ráo to subdue to assure complete peace in his immense possessions. The brigades, of which you yourself, my dear General, were the creator, and in which your name is daily invoked, are as efficient as ever. It is in reality you who have conquered this immense territory.

"Following your example in the discipline which I insist on, and which is not only most necessary for an army, but the basis of its success, I have been everywhere victorious with the brigades. My command is made happy by the attachment and confidence which the troops express for me, and I have always won, remaining master of the situation even under the most critical circumstances.

"You recommended M. Drugeon to me. A year ago I reinstated him in the brigades, but in consideration of the ability which you know he possesses, I appointed him to an even more honourable situation than any I could have given him in the army itself. I have made him Governor of the fort of Delhi and guardian of the Emperor's person. In giving him this post I have overlooked his former shortcomings, and I feel perfectly compensated by the interest you take in his welfare.

"Yes; I will receive with pleasure any one whom you may recommend for an appointment in the brigades. My friendship for you demands this, and it is also due to you as the creator of the brave soldiers who compose this force. It is the least I can do for you, and both my duty and gratitude require that I should not fail in fulfilling your wishes. "CUILLIER PERRON."

After forming a junction with Pohlman's brigade on the road, Perron marched to Ujjain, which he reached on the 20th of March, 1802. Colonel Sutherland's brigade arrived at the same time from an expedition to the Barinda River, where it had been employed.

The story of Perron's reception at Sindhia's Court is so graphically related in Colonel Skinner's memoirs that the account must be borrowed *in extenso*. This is how it runs :—

" His reception was not of a nature to gratify an officer like Perron. It was not until the 25th that he was invited to call upon the Maharajah, and then, having proceeded to durbar with 200 horsemen, he was kept waiting at the gates for two hours while Scindia was amusing himself by flying kites. Not a chief came out to meet him, while he sat in company with certain discontented chiefs of note, among whom was old Gopal Ráo Bhow, who was at the head of the army. This officer, addressing Perron, said, ' Observe to what the old Pateil's reign has come ! Good soldiers are all forgotten : none but dirty time-servers and flatterers can get on. But mark my words, he will soon find out his error, but not until too late to mend it.' To this Perron replied that he was but a servant, and all he knew was to obey. This sort of conversation went on until the *choleedars* announced the approach of Scindia, when we all rose, and Perron went up and presented his *nuzzur*. Scindia just touched it, and asked him if he was well ; to which Perron made the usual reply, ' By your favour,' and then we all in turn presented our *nuzzurs*, and were desired to sit down.

" In half an hour Scindia dismissed the durbar, and desired Perron to return to camp, which he did, completely disgusted with the cold and slighting reception he had received from his master. Eight days now passed without the slightest notice or message from Scindia to Perron, and Gopal Ráo Bhow, a great friend of the latter, signified to him he had best be on his guard, as the Maharajah had resolved to lay hold of him. Several secret visits passed at this time between Perron and Gopal Ráo Bhow, whilst Colonel Sutherland and Major Brownrigg were intriguing against the former.

" Perron, aware of the intrigues of his enemies, became depressed and perturbed, when at length matters seemed likely to be brought to a crisis. A day was appointed for holding a durbar, to which Perron and all his European officers were invited. At the durbar Scindia, together with his father-in-law, Shirzee Ráo Ghatkay, had formed a plot to lay hold of him, and had employed 500 Patháns, belonging to Bahadhur Khán, a chief then at Malaghur, and several others of his

18

own favourites and companions in vice and debauchery to carry the purpose into effect.

" Perron, however, was made aware of this plot, and ordered all the native officers of both brigades, as low as the rank of jemadar, as well as all the European officers, to come fully armed to attend his visit to Scindia. Our full uniform included a brace of pistols attached to our sword-belts; and these he directed us to bring loaded. We amounted in all to 300 native and 30 European officers, and in this state of preparation marched to the durbar, which was held in a large tent pitched for the occasion.

" At the hour of nine in the morning, headed by Perron, we reached the tent. Scindia rose to receive us, and we all presented our *nuzzars.* We were then directed to sit down on the left side of the presence, the right being occupied by the Patháns, who regarded us very fiercely. When we were seated, Scindia, turning to Perron, observed that the invitation had been extended to himself and his European officers only, to which Perron replied that in arranging his *suite* he had only followed the old rule laid down by himself and his uncle ; and this answer silenced him. All this time we sat quiet, eyeing each other, whilst much whispering went on between Scindia, Gopal Ráo, and Shirzee Ráo. I believe it was Gopal Ráo who persuaded him not to attempt any violence, for that not only himself, but the whole party would be cut to pieces by the fine body of men whom Perron had brought in.

" Scindia then ordered the Patháns to retire, and they all got up, looking as if they would eat us, while our men sat laughing at them with the most perfect unconcern.

" When they were gone Scindia and Shirzee Ráo began to flatter and endeavoured to throw Perron off his guard. But he, assisted as he was by his old friend Gopal Ráo, was too old a soldier to be so cajoled ; and so *khiluts* were ordered for us all, and after receiving them we presented our *nuzzurs*, which Scindia graciously accepted. Beetul was then handed round, and we received leave to retire.

" Perron then got up, and taking off his sword, laid it down at Scindia's feet, saying that he had grown old in the service, and that it did not become him to be disgraced by dissolute knaves and bullies ; that all he wanted was his discharge. Then, addressing us, he said that henceforth we must look to Scindia, for that he, for his part, was too old now to brook affronts and must retire. Scindia on this rose and embraced Perron, telling him that he regarded him as his uncle, and that he had no idea what offended him. Compliments without measure passed between both parties, but on taking leave Perron cautioned Scindia to beware of Shirzee Ráo Ghatkay, for he would be his ruin—a caution in which all the old Mahratta chiefs joined cordially and applauded the part which Perron had taken.

" At length we reached camp, where several days were occupied in the transmission of messages to and from the Court, and in visits from chieftains who were sent to make matters up. But Perron was too indignant to be pacified. Colonel Sutherland in the meantime was sent to the second brigade and Colonel Pohlman to the first, while Major Brownrigg was put in arrest under fixed bayonets. On the 15th of April Perron marched with the second brigade for Hindostan."

The light in which Perron's conduct is here depicted is a very favourable one, but Skinner was somewhat of a partisan officer, and allowance must be made for his sympathies, and also for a certain faultiness of memory. The account of Perron's visit that comes to us from other sources somewhat modifies the impression that Skinner's version leaves. Lewis Ferdinand Smith states that " a storm was brewing at Oojein, and Perron was obliged to risk his authority, and even his personal safety, by proceeding there. But he had motives for this dangerous step, wishing to find out by closer inspection what were the views of Colonel Collins, the British Resident, Perron being jealous of the Company. Moreover, he began to dread Colonel Sutherland, who commanded the first brigade." There was good cause for this, if any trust may be placed in a report which appeared in the Persian akbars about this time, and which stated that Sindhia had actually transferred the command of the brigades to Sutherland. But Perron, although " determined to quit his station and resign his authority if he could not quell the storm that was rising against him, succeeded in doing so. Perhaps his apprehensions were greater than the real danger. Perhaps the five lakhs he gave Scindia dissipated the dangers he feared, and which threatened his ambition." Herein we have a much more likely explanation of his success than that which Skinner puts forward. It was not Perron's injured dignity that influenced Sindhia, but his hard cash. Daulat Ráo was a dissolute, vicious prince, who cared nothing for character : a good man in distress awakened no compassion in his heart. But a wicked man—and assuredly Perron had been wickedly treacherous during the past year—with five lakhs of rupees was worthy to be taken to his bosom !

While it lasted the contest between Perron and Sutherland must have been a sharp one, but the former triumphed, and secured the Scotchman's transfer to the second brigade, which was to return to

Hindustan with the General, where it is not difficult to imagine the treatment that would have been meted out to the vanquished subordinate. Sutherland, however, had no intention of subjecting himself to such a risk, for " he took some offence at an expression of Perron's and his extraordinary behaviour and left Oojein for Agra with a hundred horsemen." Whereupon the General " composed the minds of the troops when Sutherland left them without permission, and promised them another officer of equal rank to command their brigade."

Early in May Perron commenced his return march to Hindustan, and on the 14th reached Jaipur, where doubtless there was a little account to be squeezed out of Partáb Singh. But although the General returned to Koil with his former power and in perfect safety, still it was clear to every discerning eye that his influence with Daulat Ráo was diminished. This is confirmed by letters written by Colonel Collins to the Governor-general soon after Perron's departure, in which the following passages occur :—

" I hear on very good authority that it is Scindia's intention as soon as he can get to Agra to deprive Perron of the command of the fortresses he possesses in Hindostan "; and two months later, " General Perron has been peremptorily directed by Scindia to give up all the *mehals* in his possession not appertaining to his *Jaidad.* I understand that Perron is highly displeased with the conduct -of Scindia's ministers, and that he entertains serious intentions of relinquishing his present command."

The Asiatic Register, in a communication dated June 2, 1802, very clearly summarises what Perron actually accomplished by his visit to Sindhia's Court :—

" We learn by a letter from Oojein that Scindia has dismissed the whole of the British officers in his service. There is no doubt that this is to be ascribed to the influence of General Perron, who has long been jealous of the introduction of English officers into Scindia's army, and has occasionally exerted every artifice of intrigue to frustrate their views and to impress the Prince with a notion that though these men came into his dominions in the character of independent adventurers, they are generally emissaries of the British Government, in whom it was impossible and highly unsafe to confide ; and Scindia listened to these untruths and acted on them."

Perron made the best use of his renewed opportunities, and in the shuffling of commands that resulted Major Brownrigg was the only Englishman who kept his post. He was last heard of, upon Skinner's authority, under fixed bayonets, but he appears to have been restored to favour, for he was appointed to the command of the fifth brigade, which was raised shortly after this. The rest of Sindhia's army passed entirely under the hands of foreigners. Pohlman, a German, commanded the first brigade ; George Hessing, a Dutchman, and nephew to Perron, the second; Louis Bourguien, also a relative of Perron, the third; Dudrenec, a Frenchman, the fourth. This officer was also promoted to second in command, and destined to succeed the general when he retired. The independent corps, affiliated to Perron's command, were those of Jean Baptiste Filoze, an Italian, and also a relative of the general, and the Begum Somru's under Colonel Saleur, a Frenchman. John Hessing, a Dutchman, commanded the fort of Agra, Drugeon, a Savoyard, that of Delhi, and Pedron, a Frenchman, had charge of Aligarh. Deridon, Perron's brother-in-law, also filled a high post. Thus every Englishman in the force, with the exception of Brownrigg, was debarred from superior employment, although the British subjects in the brigades numbered not less than forty. Country-borns—a very large factor in the force—who could boast a British origin fared no better ; and so gross was the favouritism and injustice Perron displayed, that even the natives could not conceal their contempt for it.

These intrigues and jealousies which contaminated Sindhia's court and brigades had a lamentable effect upon his interests. His own countrymen were estranged, and their complete supersession by the regular troops shut them out from every opportunity of following a soldier's career, and they ceased to be a martial people. Daulat Ráo himself plunged deeper and deeper into the mire of vice and degradation, neglecting state affairs and ignoring the duties of government, and Perron, on his return to Hindustan, soon became as independent as he had been before his visit to Ujjain. Little of importance occurred during the rest of the year 1802, the only matters recorded being some desultory fighting against Holkar's Pindaris in the Deccan, and a visit paid by Perron to the Sutlej, where Bourguien with the third brigade was trying to reduce the Sikhs to the same state of subjection as the Rajputs, and was, as usual, " waiting for reinforcements."

All the time these matters had been taking place in Sindhia's possessions Jaswant Ráo Holkar had not been idle. He and Amir Khán engaged in an extensive and lawless campaign, during which Rajputana was plundered and Khándesh devastated. Holkar's Pindari army might appropriately be likened to the mountain torrent, which gathers volume in its course. In a predatory expedition there is nothing which succeeds like success. Malwa was full of disbanded soldiery, to whom Jaswant Ráo's remunerative rapine constituted a call to arms. From all quarters he was joined by wild Deccan horsemen thirsting to share the pillage of his route. Before a year had passed he completely recovered from the shock of Indore, and was at the head of a mighty host, full of the dash and daring acquired by a long course of successful foray, and made the more formidable by two complete brigades of regular infantry included in its numbers.

Holkar now began to turn his steps towards the Deccan, intent on once more regaining his influence in the councils of the Peshwa. As soon as his intention became apparent, the Court at Poonah took alarm, and endeavoured by every means to stay his advance. He was even desired to formulate his demands, and immediate attention was promised to them, provided he would only remain north of the Godávari. But this Holkar declined to do. Personal as well as political motives guided his course. He had a brother's murder to revenge, for Baji Ráo, the Peshwa, had in the previous year not only ordered the death of Ithal Ráo, Jaswant Ráo's younger brother, but gazed on the execution as it was being carried out with all the shocking barbarity of Oriental savagery.

On the 7th of October Holkar's infantry brigades, under the command of a trusted chief named Fateh Singh, came upon the Peshwa's army, and after a short, but decisive, action completely defeated it, and captured all its cannon. Two days later Jaswant Ráo, who had been elsewhere engaged with his cavalry, effected a junction with Fateh Singh's force, and at once marched towards Poonah.

The Deccan capital was now at Holkar's mercy, and with it the Peshwa, who was the key of the power which controlled the Marátha Confederacy. On Jaswant Ráo's approach overtures for peace were opened by Baji Ráo, but they led to nothing. Holkar's real object was to obtain possession of the Peshwa's person, but the latter would not consent to a meeting; for, in the language of a native historian, "the word treachery was in the page of his dealings with the Holkar family, and his eye fell on it, and he feared to trust himself in the power of Jeswant Ráo." But nothing short of this would satisfy Holkar, who was determined to establish himself in a position where he could enforce his ascendancy to the exclusion of Sindhia's influence

Daulat Ráo had been roused to action by Jaswant Ráo's rapid advance, and directly he realised that it was the intention of the latter to attack Poonah, he sent an army from Ujjain to assist the Peshwa. This force successfully made its way to the capital, but it was utterly inadequate for the performance of the work assigned to it.

Holkar, however, before proceeding to war, determined to make an attempt to divide his enemies, hoping to overawe the Peshwá into neutrality, whilst he himself first settled matters with Sindhia. So he wrote a diplomatic letter to Baji Ráo, saying " that the Holker and Scindia factions were the same in the balance to His Highness ; for him therefore to show partiality to the one and estrangement to the other, much less to side absolutely with either, was not the part of the High Lord of both. That it would be more becoming to his dignity to keep up a friendly understanding with the two parties, and bring about a friendly reconciliation, or if precluded from adopting this course, that at any rate he should give protection and countenance to neither, but stand aloof from the contest, and leave them to settle matters as they might."

In explanation of this it may be observed that Sindhia still held possession of the person of Jaswant Ráo's nephew, Khandi Ráo, the infant son of Malhar Ráo, and the rightful heir of the house of Holkar. For political reasons Jaswant Ráo had constituted himself the champion of the child chief, claiming to be his proper guardian. It was therefore a matter of great importance to procure the release of this youth, and Holkar informed the Peshwa that his present action was due to this necessity.

Of course Baji Ráo would not consent to disconnect himself from Sindhia, whom he had taken into favour again after his victory over Holkar at Indore. The Peshwa had no choice in the management of his political machine, except to use one chief against another, and so preserve a balance between them, which left him with the nominal control. When Sindhia grew too powerful the Peshwa sided with Holkar, Lakwa Dáda and the Bhais, and now that Jaswant Ráo's star was dominant Baji Ráo, as a matter of course, threw himself into Sindhia's arms. It is impossible in the limits of a short sketch to follow the shifting currents of Marátha intrigue and diplomacy, but the explanation afforded will make the present situation intelligible.

Negotiations being unsuccessful, both armies prepared for battle, and on Sunday the 25th of October 1802, their lines were formed for action on the plain outside Poonah. Sindhia's forces consisted of four battalions of Pohlman's brigade, under Captain Dawes, and seven battalions of Ambaji Inglia's under a Mahomedan commander, with 10,000 Marátha cavalry and 80 guns. The Peshwa only contributed four very inferior battalions of infantry, under native officers, and 6,000 cavalry. The position the allied forces took up was a strong one, their rear being protected by the city of Poonah.

Holkar brought into the field an army superior in both numbers and quality. His regular infantry consisted of four battalions under Major Harding, five under Major Vickers, and four under Major Armstrong. There were also three others under a native commander, and 5,000 irregular Rohilla infantry. His cavalry numbered 25,000, and he had 100 capital guns.

It was due to the spirited representations of Captain Dawes that battle was offered to a force so superior in every way. Dawes was a gallant soldier, and strongly advised fighting, although there were but four European officers in the allied armies. The troops were accordingly formed for action, and Jaswant Ráo eagerly responded to the challenge. Dawes himself took post in the centre, with the artillery. On the right were the Poonah troops, and on the left the Marátha cavalry. At 9.30 a.m. the action commenced with a sharp and incessant cannonade, which lasted for four hours, and showed great determination on both sides. An advance was then attempted by Dawes, and for a time the superior discipline of his battalions began to tell; for, owing to a misunderstanding, Jaswant Ráo's cavalry were ordered to make an ill-timed charge on Dawes's left flank, during which they were exposed to the grape of the artillery in such repeated discharges as to threaten the loss of the day altogether, for seeing them wavering Dawes's cavalry attacked them with fatal effect. "The confusion," writes the quaint native historian already quoted, "was like that of the Day of Judgment : no one knew where he was or what he was about. The slaughter was great, and the flight of Holker's troops had commenced."

Jaswant Ráo, who had taken up his station on an eminence, in order to direct the operations of the field, perceived this critical pass to which his arms had come. It roused him to a great and worthy effort. Springing on his horse, he drew his sword, and calling out, " Now or never to follow Jaswant Ráo!" spurred to the front, rallied the fugitives, collected a compact body around him, and turning round charged back again upon the enemy.

As he reached them he found Ambaji's battalions already beginning to waver before the steady attack of Major Harding, whose brigade had advanced to the rescue of the cavalry. Against these Holkar dashed, and scattered them like chaff, and then turned his charge upon Dawes, whose troops had up to this time behaved with a courage and discipline worthy of their reputation. As Dawes saw the Chief and his squadrons approaching, he attempted to oppose a proper resistance, but his small body of men was completely overwhelmed by the sheer weight of numbers and thrown into confusion. They fought desperately to the very last, and as became the best traditions they had inherited from the days of De Boigne. It was not until three of their officers were killed, and the fourth taken prisoner, and 600 men out of their total strength of 1,400 killed and wounded, that they surrendered. During the latter part of the action a terrible explosion took place in their very midst, caused by a cannon shot striking one of their tumbrils, and this added to their disorder, and hastened their defeat. Almost immediately after this catastrophe Dawes was killed, and a similar fate befel Captain Catts and Ensign Douglas. This left the force with only one officer—a Frenchman named Hanove—who behaved with great intrepidity, carrying with him the colours of the corps, until he was made prisoner.

Jaswant Ráo, to whose personal bravery and spirit the victory was due, was wounded in the act of spearing one of Dawes's artillerymen at his gun, to the very muzzle of which the chief had charged. Major Harding, who joined him, and rode by his side, was killed by almost the last cannonshot fired. Holkar lost 1,600 men in this action, whilst on the side of the allies the killed and wounded amounted to 5,000. Sixty-five guns were captured, of which twenty belonged to Dawes's battalions. It is worthy of note that, during eighteen years of arduous active service and continual fighting, these were the first guns lost by any of De Boigne's old brigades since their formation. The whole of Sindhia's baggage and camp were taken, and his army, bereft of their officers, was routed and dispersed, and fled in all directions.

The consequences of this defeat were far more more disastrous to the Peshwa than to Sindhia. Early in the morning Baji Ráo, not doubting success, left his palace with the intention of being present at the action. But the noise of the firing frightened him, and he withdrew to a place some distance south of Poonah. Almost before a shot was fired his troops deserted Dawes, and retired within the walls of the city, and as soon as Baji Ráo heard of the impending issue of the day, he fled, attended by 7,000 followers, to the fort of Singarh, from whence he proceeded to Mhár, on the sea coast. Here he embarked on board an English ship, provided for his reception by the Government of Bombay, and was landed at Bassein, a fugitive from his throne, and indebted for his safety to the very nation from whom it had been the policy of the Marátha nation to consistently hold aloof.

CHAPTER VII.

1802–1803.

" JESWANT RÁO HOLKER has taken possession of Poonah, and greatly harassed that city and His Highness the Peishwa. I am therefore obliged to march towards Poonah to oppose the Holkers, and immediately on receipt of this letter you will hasten your march with all your troops under your command and meet us at that place. Our endeavours must be strenuously exerted to baffle the Holkers in all their hostile designs, and to secure the country from their infamous depredations now and hereafter. It will be necessary to use every means in our power to crush and overwhelm them at once, that they may never again have sufficient ability to do us similar mischief."

Thus wrote Daulat Ráo Sindhia to General Perron on the 16th of November, 1802, after the defeat of his and the Peshwá's troops at Poonah. On receiving this letter Perron made some show of obedience by directing Bourguien, who was at Jind, to proceed to the Deccan with the third brigade. But here his efforts began and ended: the order was not carried out—probably there was never any serious intention of having it executed—and Perron confined himself to copious protestations, declaring he was about to march south "immediately "—a formula that had an elasticity about it not contemplated by the framers of language.

Other reinforcements, however, reached Sindhia. Ambaji, his Maráthá general, despatched five of the Begum Somru's battalions, and Raghuji Bhonsla of Berar sent a large body of horse. On these joining him Daulat Ráo marched with his army six or eight miles out of Ujjain on the 1st of December, with the intention of proceeding to Poonah, but his further progress was arrested by sickness which broke out amongst his troops, and by a belief that he was not strong enough to risk a conflict with Holkar, and reinstate the Peshwa, who was continually urging him to come to his assistance, and drive Jaswant Ráo out of the capital.

Perron was fully aware how critical the moment was. Holkar was not only in possession of Poonah, but had declared Baji Ráo deposed, and elevated to the *masnad*, the Peshwa's brother, Amrat Ráo, whom he desired to use as his tool, usurping the real authority himself. Driven from his country, a fugitive and afraid, it was hopeless to expect Baji Ráo to accomplish his own restoration. There were but two courses open to him : either to trust to Sindhia to reinstate him, or to throw in his lot with the English, as the Nizam of Haidarabad had done two years previously, and accept from them the services of a contingent force to replace him in power and keep him there. But this would be tantamount to the surrender of the independence of the Marátha Empire, and Baji Ráo naturally hesitated before committing himself to such an irrevocable step.

During the two months of indecision that followed, Baji Ráo repeatedly appealed to Sindhia for military assistance against Holkar, warning him that if help was deferred he would be compelled, from sheer necessity, to apply to the British Government to reinstate him. Sindhia as repeatedly despatched express messengers to Perron, commanding him to send down troops to the Deccan at once, as without reinforcements Daulat Ráo dared not risk a battle. But Perron pursued a line of conduct similar to that which he had adopted in the previous year. He was afraid of throwing too much power into his master's hands, which might ultimately be turned against himself. So long as he kept three complete brigades under his personal control in Hindustan, he had nothing to fear from his enemies at the Ujjain Court ; but the transfer of one of them from Delhi to the Deccan would destroy his preponderance of power, and prejudice the political plans he had in view. So he avoided compliance with Sindhia's commands, and affected an excuse for his disobedience in the refractory conduct of Partáb Singh.* Instead of marching to Ujjain he led his troops to Jaipur, announcing that he expected to be absent on this expedition for some time. But Partáb Singh, scared at Perron's approach, immediately paid the fine demanded, whereupon the general, instead

---

* A "news letter" in a Persian journal states that in August, 1802, the Rájah of Jaipur wrote several letters to Ghat - kay Ráo, Daulat Ráo's father-in-law, and Prime Minister, complaining of the conduct of General Perron, and stating some other matters of moment to himself. These letters were intercepted by Perron's *Harkarras*, or news runners, and brought to him. Their contents "effaced all the impressions of friendship he felt for the Rajah, and determined him to take vigorous measures to ruin the Prince."

of proceeding to the seat of war in the Deccan, returned to his head-quarters at Koil.

And this at a moment when kingdoms were toppling! The Peshwa, Holkar, Sindhia, all were threatened directly or indirectly by the existing state of affairs. One masterly stroke would have assured the complete ascendancy of Sindhia's influence; for had he driven Holkar out of Poonah, and reinstated the Peshwa, Daulat Ráo's power would have become unassailable. It needed but Perron's co-operation to make this a certainty: but that co-operation was withheld, and the failure and ruin which followed were solely due to the general's treachery. Baji Ráo, beholden for his personal safety to the English at his elbow, could hold out no longer. Sindhia was even invited by Colonel Collins, the British Resident, to assist in the restoration of his suzeraine, but his anxiety to be the sole agent in the matter would not permit him to act in concert with a foreign power, and one which he especially feared and dreaded. So he temporised with Colonel Collins, and carried on an active correspondence with Baji Ráo, promising help, which never came, until the latter grew despairing as he daily received the stereotyped reply that Sindhia " would march as soon as he was strong enough," whilst every hour consolidated the power of Holkar at Poonah, and tended to make the elevation of Amrat Ráo to the *masnad* an established and recognised state of things.

At last the Peshwa could no longer defer coming to a decision, and on the 31st of December, 1802, the die was cast, and he appended his signature to the Treaty of Bassein. It sounded the death-knell of Marátha Independence, and, by a retributive justice, of Perron's own power, for his subsequent fall was distinctly traceable to this event. By the Treaty of Bassein the Peshwa was reduced to the status of a protected prince, and accepted from the Company the services of a subsidiary force of 6,000 regular native infantry, with the usual proportion of guns, and European officers, and artillerymen. In return for this he assigned to his deliverers vast districts in Guzerat, and on the Narbada and Tapti Rivers, which yielded a revenue of twenty-six lakhs of rupees. Moreover, the treaty contained a clause directed against adventurers of Perron's class, for by the eleventh article the Peshwa agreed, in the event of a war between the English and any European nation, to " discharge any European or Europeans in his service, belonging to such nation, who shall have meditated injury towards the English, or entered into intrigues hostile to their interests."

Perron's relations with the French Government were within the knowledge of the Marquis Wellesley. Colonel Skinner mentions that in 1801 the general "was so puffed up with riches and power that he allowed himself to be persuaded by his flatterers into sending an ambassador to Bonaparte, and Monsieur Desoutée was the person despatched ; but the purport or result of the embassy was never known." But if not actually known, it may reasonably be suspected that it led to the Expedition which the First Consul ordered. His designs against India have been fully explained in the sketch of De Boigne's life, and need not be here repeated. But Perron's share in them must be noted. Perron was a Frenchman and a revolutionist, in close sympathy with the principles which the French nation affected at this period, and after his own personal advantage he honestly desired his country's welfare. He perceived how favourable was the opportunity afforded by the internal commotions in Hindustan for the establishment of a French dominion in India, and was prepared to assist that consummation. There is but little doubt that the elaborate project formed at Paris owed much to his practical suggestion, for it could scarcely have been any other person who pointed out the route by which the Expeditionary French officers were to reach his headquarters through Cuttack. It is known that Perron pressed his views on the attention of Bonaparte, and that an important communication from him reached Paris during the national rejoicing over the Peace of Amiens. It could not have arrived at a more seasonable period, for the treaty of 1802 opened every desirable avenue for the prosecution of the schemes suggested. An arrangement was actually settled for the assignment to the Government of France of all the districts that Perron held, the transfer of which was to be confirmed by the Emperor Shah Alam, in whose name, and under whose authority everything was to be done.

Perron's policy in Hindustan was subordinated to this scheme, for the success of which he worked and waited, and sacrificed Sindhia. The three brigades which Perron kept under his immediate command, refusing to spare any of them for the Deccan, were required for its accomplishment. They were regarded as "the French army of Hindustan," and contemporary writers constantly refer to them by that designation. Perron only awaited a full complement of officers from France to co-operate in any attack on the English which the First Consul might order. But, unfortunately for Perron's plot and Bonaparte's plans, Lord Wellesley anticipated them, and the Treaty of Bassein was one of the countermoves in this game of politics. It established the paramount influence of the English in the Marátha dominions, and at the same time cut the ground from under the feet of the French faction. " There is every reason to believe," writes Lord Wellesley in his " History of the Mahratta War," " that the Government of France intended to make the unfortunate Emperor of Hindustan the main instrument of their designs in India, and to avail themselves of the authority of His Majesty's name to re-establish their influence and power. A plan to this effect was actually submitted to the Chief Consul of France, in 1801, by an officer, who afterwards accompanied General Decaen to India, in 1803." This plan resulted in the despatch of the Expedition to India, which was preparing tó sail from France at the time that the battle of Poonah took place, and Perron was probably aware of it when he received Sindhia's urgent orders to join him " with all his troops "—the very troops who were to be officered by the expected French expedition. To detach them to the Deccan under such circumstances was manifestly impossible, and so, from November to February, Perron evaded obedience, expecting at any moment to hear of the arrival of the force which would so immeasurably strengthen his hand as to make him independent. But the French fleet was delayed, and did not appear off Pondicherry till June, 1803. Before that time Perron was in difficulties, for Sindhia grew " warm and positive" in his tones, and the Frenchman had not sufficient staying power to hold out. Hope deferred made his heart sick, and he submitted to pressure, which a stronger man might have resisted for a much longer time. In February, 1803, he sent Sindhia the fourth brigade, under the Chevalier Dudrenec, and half the newly-raised fifth brigade, under Captain Brownrigg, thus detaching nearly half his army to the Deccan. It was the acknowledgment of his defeat, and he confirmed it by tendering his resignation at the same time.

There is only one explanation of this sudden and complete collapse of Perron's policy. He suspected the designs of the British Government against the French military adventurers in the Maráthá service, and wished to secure his own personal safety and his large fortune before any further political complications ensued. Disappointed in the long deferred arrival of the French Expedition, it was now evident that with the English paramount at Poonah, the accomplish-ment of his plans was impossible. The auspicious moment had, in fact, passed away; and even as Sindhia's projects and ambitions had been destroyed by Perron withholding assistance from him, so were Perron's own schemes ruined by the untoward delay in the arrival of the aid from France, which he had so long expected. It is curious to note how in his downfall Perron suffered, step by step, from almost identically similar disasters as those which, through his influence, contributed to his master's undoing.

At the same time that Perron tendered his resignation to Sindhia, he applied to General Lake, the Commander-in-chief at Cawnpore, for leave to proceed to Lucknow, with an escort of 200 cavalry and 400 infantry, on his return to Europe. General Lake forwarded the application to the Marquis Wellesley, who replied that he was strongly disposed to accelerate Perron's departure from Sindhia's service, conceiving it to be an event which promised much advantage to the British interests in India. A willing guarantee was accorded for the general's safeguard from Lucknow to Calcutta, necessary orders issued for his suitable reception and treatment, with every mark of respect and consideration, and he was assured that a proper guard of Sepoys for his route would be provided, and at the Presidency the Governor-General proposed to receive him in a manner conformable to his wishes, and to use every means to facilitate his voyage to Europe.

Perron's resignation reached Sindhia towards the end of February, 1803, just as Colonel Collins, the British Resident, returned to the Maráthá prince's camp at Burhánpur, after a temporary absence, bringing with him a copy of the Treaty of Bassein, whose terms he now disclosed. In a moment the whole political atmosphere was changed. Although Sindhia affected to consider that there was nothing in the treaty he could object to, it put a period, with one dash of the pen, to the whole policy of aggrandisement to which he and his uncle before him had devoted their entire energies for the last decade; for it placed the head of the Maráthá's under the protection of the one power they most desired to keep out of the nation's councils. No instrument could have been more complete in its attack on the existing condition of things, or more unacceptable to the Maráthás at large. Every Deccan chief was startled, and, in the face of this common danger, all internal enmities and jealousies were relegated to the background. The note of alarm was sounded by Raghuji Bhonsla, of Berar, who at once proposed an alliance between Sindhia, Holkar, and himself, for the purpose of expelling the English and restoring the national independence of the Peshwa. All the minor chiefs concurred in the determination to resist, and, if possible, overthrow the new regime. In this crisis of affairs Sindhia wrote to Perron, declining to accept his resignation, and informing him of the Treaty of Bassein, and the proposed general alliance against the Company.

A false ray of hope shone out on Perron, who thought he saw the silver lining behind the black cloud of disappointment. It is not impossible that he was further encouraged by advices of the forward state of the French expedition destined to strengthen him. At any rate he decided to see out the storm that was now gathering in the Deccan, and consented to withdraw his resignation and remain in Sindhia's service for another year.

War, although within a measurable distance, was not at this time declared. But at Sindhia's request Perron drew out a plan of campaign to be followed in the event of hostilities. It was one that did credit to his ability as a general, and, although it was never carried into effect, its details are worth recording.

The forces of the Confederate chiefs were apportioned as follows : Sindhia, with 35,000 Maráthá cavalry, was to penetrate into the Haidarabad territory and compel the Nizam, who was in alliance with the English, to withdraw his forces from the seat of war in the Deccan. Raghuji Bhonsla, with 30,000 horse, was to enter Bengal, cut off General Lake in Oudh, and carry fire and sword into the rich districts of the Ganges. Holkar, with another 30,000 horse, was to invade Benares and Behar, and Shamshir Bahadur (a son of Ali Bahadur, who had recently died) and Ambaji Inglia, with 20,000 cavalry, were to desolate Oudh and the British Doáb provinces. This disposed of the mounted native armies. The infantry were detailed for defensive work. Perron, with three brigades of twenty-four battalions, was to defend the passage of the Jumna. Holkar's infantry, under Vickers, was to oppose the English in Surat. Sindhia's Deccan brigades, consisting of Perron's first under Pohlman, half the fifth under Brownrigg, four battalions of the Begum Somru's under Saleur, and four battalions of the late Fidèle Filoze's under Dupont—in all twenty battalions were to defend the Adjanta Ghát ; and, finally, fifteen irregular battalions of Raghuji Bhonsla's, under native commanders, were to bar the passage of the Kásabéri Ghát. It was a skilful and comprehensive plan of campaign, which apportioned defensive work for 94 battalions of infantry at four widely divided points, and offensive operations for 115,000 cavalry. Had it been carried out in its entirety it must have resulted in a long and bloody war. But the ignorance, distrust, and supineness of the Maráthás, and the treachery of Holkar, who withdrew from the alliance at the last moment, ruined all hope of success.

From March to August, 1803, Colonel Collins, the British Resident, remained in Sindhia's camp, vainly endeavouring to obtain from that chief and the Rájah of Berar the withdrawal of their armies from the frontiers of the Nizam's territory, where they were encamped, and which they threatened. But Sindhia, in reply, demanded the previous retirement from the territories of the Peshwa of the army of observation assembled under the command of Major-General Arthur Wellesley. To consent to this was impossible while the Marátha forces retained their commanding position and menaced Haidarabad. In the Governor-General's words, "It would have submitted the dignity, honour, and interests, if not the very existence, of the British Government in India to the most faithless, sanguinary, rapacious, and violent of Mahratta adventurers. We should have forfeited the opinion of the native powers, which forms a main pillar of the fabric of our Empire ; we should have been degraded by the native states of Hindustan and the Deccan to the rank of a secondary power in India ; of a power secondary to Daulat Ráo Scindia, whose military strength rests upon the support of French adventure, enterprise, and skill."

During these negotiations Perron strenuously advised Sindhia not to form any connection with the British Government nor to enter into their plans, vowing that he was ready to sacrifice his life and his fortune in defending the cause of his prince. No explanation is given of this newly-developed loyalty and enthusiasm, nor does any suggest itself for Perron's conduct during this period, except the arrival at Pondicherry, on the 15th of June, of General Decaen's expedition from France. Of this he probably received early intimation. Whatever professions he made to Sindhia he certainly substantiated by the uncommon energy with which he prepared for war. On the 26th of June he directed Bourguien to withdraw the third brigade from the Panjab and canton it at Panipat, whilst the second, under George Hessing, was concentrated at Sikandra, near Agra. At Aligarh, where Pedron was in command, the most elaborate preparations were made for hostilities. On the 25th of July old Colonel John Hessing died at Agra, and Perron instantly proceeded there and appointed Colonel George Hessing to the command of the fort, sending a French officer named Geslin to take over charge of his brigade, which had marched to Delhi.

Notwithstanding all this energy and the display of loyalty which these preparations seemed to indicate on the part of Perron, he was fated to feel the reaction of his former treachery to Daulat Ráo Sindhia. At the very moment when he was really working honestly in his master's interests intrigues against him were being brought to a successful issue in the Court he served. Ambaji Inglia had long coveted the *Subahdari* of Hindustan. Despite Perron's protestations of fidelity there existed a deep-set feeling of distrust against him in Sindhia's breast. His past actions rose up to condemn him, and Ambaji, by a timely gift of twenty-five lakhs of rupees, was able to gain his ends, and in the month of August, on the very eve of the declaration of war, was appointed to the chief command of Hindustan, with instructions to supersede Perron, who was to be subordinate to his orders. "By this action," writes Lewis Ferdinand Smith, "Scindia delivered Perron over to his most implacable enemy, for Ambajee would have assuredly drained Perron's purse if he had spared his life."

On the 3rd of August Colonel Collins left Sindhia's camp, and the British Government forthwith declared war, and proceeded to carry into execution the plan of military operations previously determined upon.

Perron was actually the last man in the Maráthá councils to hear of it, and even then the notification came to him from General Lake himself after the British advance had begun. In this tremendous crisis of his life the master of many intrigues was destined to find himself undone by the craft and treachery which disclosed themselves around him. He was unaware that Ambaji Inglia was hastening to Hindustan to wrench the *báton* from his hands; or that the Chevalier Dudrenec, whom he had given service to and destined for his successor, had declared his allegiance to the new commander-in-chief. But the cruellest blow of all was yet to come, for Louis Bourguien, Perron's bosom friend and most trusted lieutenant, "whom he had raised from obscurity to rank and riches, with outrage and injustice to other officers," was the first in Upper India to revolt against the hand that had lifted him from the gutter, and ere many days had past to declare the deposition and attempt the life of the man before whose frown Hindustan had trembled for seven years.

CHAPTER VIII.

LORD WELLESLEY'S DESPATCHES.

1803.

SO far the narrative has followed Perron and his fortunes from the Maráthá point of view. In order to assist a broader estimate of his political, and even international, importance, it is necessary to extract a few passages from the Marquis Wellesley's despatches and correspondence, which will illustrate the high elevation attained by this self-made soldier of fortune.

The first reference to Perron in those voluminous writings occurs in a letter, dated from the Cape of Good Hope in February, 1798, and addressed to the Right Honourable Henry Dundas, President of the Board of Control. It merely indicates Lord Wellesley's knowledge that " Scindia employs about 20,000 Sepoys, disciplined by Europeans or Americans. The commander is named Perron, a Frenchman." The next reference is in June, 1799, by which time the Governor-General has become alive to the influence French adventurers were exerting in the Maráthá States, for addressing the same correspondent, he writes :—" I shall endeavour to render the cession of territory (after the Mysore war) the instrument of annihilating every remnant of a French party in that quarter," and a few days later adds, " I am anxious to find some mode of engaging the interests of Scindia in the new settlement of Mysore, under the condition of dismissing all the French officers from his service, and (if possible) under that of his delivering them over to our Government for the purpose of being sent to Europe." On the 4th of July, in a despatch to Colonel Palmer, the Resident at Poonah, he further emphasises this desire. " The whole system of my policy is an earnest of my anxiety to expel the French from the service of Scindia."

But the action of this policy was delayed by another circumstance which demanded Lord Wellesley's attention and heavily taxed his resources. This was the invasion of Egypt by Bonaparte, which was a blow aimed directly at India, and all current intentions had to be suspended in order to assist in repelling this new danger by despatching a powerful contingent, under General Baird, to co-operate with General Abercrombie in the Delta of the Nile.

But although Lord Wellesley's local policy was necessarily deferred, it was by no means abandoned, and in 1802, on the termination of the Egyptian campaign, his attention was once more focussed on affairs in the Deccan. " The distractions in the Mahratta Empire," he writes, " occasioned a combination of circumstance of the utmost importance to the stability of the British power in India, yet pre-senting a conjunction of affairs which appeared to afford the most advantageous opportunity that has ever occurred for improving the British interests in that quarter on solid and durable foundations."

This was written just after the battle of Poonah, when Jaswant Ráo Holkar had defeated the combined armies of Sindhia and the Peshwa, and the latter, a fugitive from his capital, was indebted for his personal safety to British protection. In the diplomatic trans-actions which followed the treaty of Bassein was conceived and executed, and the road opened for the attack on the " French army of Hindustan," which the Governor-General had so long desired.

On the 27th of March, 1803, the name of Perron again appears in Lord Wellesley's despatches, on the occasion of his acknowledging a letter from General Lake, which enclosed an application from Perron to be allowed to proceed to Europe through the Company's territories. To this sanction was accorded ; but before it reached Perron he had changed his mind, and decided to throw in his lot with Sindhia in the crisis that had just arisen, and was instigating him to resist all the demands of the English. Swayed by his advice, Daulat Ráo refused all accommodation, and at last became threatening and insolent in his tone, when, as a final resource, a separate treaty was offered to him. Upon his rejection of this the Commander-in-chief was ordered to make preparations for war, and in a despatch dated the 28th of June, 1803, the Governor-General laid down the following objects to be attained by force of arms :—

1. The seizure of all Sindhia's possessions between the Ganges and the Jumna : in other words, Perron's *Jaidad*.

2. To take the person of the Mughal Shah 'Alam under British protection : he was at the time in Perron's custody.

3. The immediate reduction of the forces under the command of Perron.

4. The formation of alliances with the Rajputs and other inferior

states beyond the Jumna for the pupose of excluding Sindhia from the northern districts of Hindustan : these states were tributary to Perron.

5. The occupation of Bundelkhand.

It is very plain to see that the objective of the campaign was nothing more or less than Perron. Without the Frenchman there would have been no war at all : it was his brigades which gave Sindhia confidence to resist and the British Government the incentive to attack. As witness the Governor-General's note on the subject :—

" M. Perron's forces are said to be at present collected at Coel, and to consist of about 8,000 infantry and an equal number of cavalry.*

" Scindia, it is generally believed, has no confidence in M. Perron's attachment to his government. In the event of a war with the British Government it is probable that Scindia will endeavour to propitiate M. Perron, and the prospect of this crisis of affairs, which would render M. Perron's conduct an object of attention to both states, may have contributed to induce M. Perron to postpone his avowed intention of relinquishing Scindia's service, in the hope of more advantageous offers from Scindia or from the British Government. A considerable number of the Sepoys who were discharged from the British Army at the late reduction are said to have entered into M. Perron's service. . . . It is supposed that Scindia's European officers might be induced to resign the service by offers of present subsistence and of a future establishment in the service of some of the allies or tributaries of the

---

* These refer to the local forces at Koil only, for in the Marquis Wellesley's "History of the Mahratta War " Sindhia's army, regular, and irregular, in June, 1803, was estimated as follows :—

Names and Description of Corps.		No. of Battalions.	No. of Men.	No. of Guns.
1st Brigade.	M. Louis Bourguien	8	7,000	50
2nd ,,	M. Hessing	7	5,600	50
3rd ,,	M. Pohlman	8	6,000	80
4th ,,	M. Dudernaigue	7	5,000	70
5th ,,	,,	7	4,000	
Corps under M. Dupont		4	2,000	about 20
Major Brownrigg's Corps		5	2,250	30
Begum Somru's Corps		4	2,400	20
Late Filozé's Brigade		6	3,000	60
Ambaji Inglia's Brigade		16	6,400	84
Grand Total		72	43,650	464

N.B.—The force in this estimate is exclusive of the troops employed in garrisons, of irregular infantry Mewattis, &c., the number of which is considerable.

British Government. It must be ascertained whether it would be
safe or practicable to detach M. Perron, or any of the European
officers in Scindia's service, or any of Scindia's troops from their
employment with Scindia, and whether any and what emissary
should be sent to M. Perron or to the officers."

Ten days after the date of these instructions Lord Wellesley writes
to General Lake: "I wish you to understand that I consider the
reduction of Scindia's power in the North-west Frontier of Hindustan
to be an important object in proportion to the probability of a war
with France. M. du Boigne (sic), Scindia's late general, is now the
chief confidant of Bonaparte. He is constantly at St. Cloud. I leave
you to judge why and wherefore."

On the 18th of July a secret and confidential memorandum is
despatched to the Commander-in-chief, in which the following
passage occurs :—

"The defeat of Perron is certainly the first object of the campaign.
The Commander-in-chief will consider what advantage can be
derived from any negotiations with Perron or Hessing (for Agra).
My opinion is that it might be dangerous to attempt any negotiation
with any of Scindia's officers until we shall be masters of the field.
.. The Rajput and Jaut Rájahs are disgusted with Mahratta rule,
but their dread of Perron's power exceeds their wish to be relieved,
and the same observation applies to the Sikh chiefs. . . . Colonel
Sutherland, lately dismissed from the command of a brigade by
Perron, might be able to give much valuable information, and be
instrumental in drawing over other officers from Perron. . . . I shall
cheerfully sanction any obligations or expenses incurred for the
purpose of conciliating the officers or ministers of the Confederates."

On the 25th of July, in a secret despatch to Lord Castlereagh, the
Governor-General writes : " The state of preparation required by the
position and strength of Scindia's French corps, under the command
of M. Perron, has already compelled me to restore the native corps to
the war establishment."

Two days later, in a despatch to the Commander-in-chief, Lord
Wellesley more particularly explains his opinions : " The regular
infantry in the service of Scindia, under the command of European
officers, is supported by funds derivable almost exclusively from the
territorial possessions of that chief, situated between the Jumna and
the Ganges, and the mountains of Kamaon. A considerable portion,
if not the whole, of the territory has been assigned to M. Perron, a
French officer who has succeeded M. du Boigne (sic) in the chief
command of Scindia's regular infantry. M. Perron has formed his

territory into an independant state, of which Scindia's regular infantry may justly be termed the national army. The inhabitants of the districts comprehended in M. Perron's *Jaghir* consider that officer as their immediate sovereign, while the troops supported from the revenues of the country regard M. Perron as the immediate executive authority from which the army is to receive orders, subsistence, and pay. Possessing such means, M. Perron dictates with the authority of a sovereign state of a superior rank, and with the vigour of efficient military power, to the petty states occupying the countries to the southward of the Jumna, and by the terror of his name and arms holds in abject submission the Rajput states of Jeypore and Jodpore, together with the Jhauts and the state of Gohud, extending his influence even to Bundelkhand and to the country occupied by the Sikhs. Scindia retains no efficient control over M· Perron, or over his regular troops. Various instances must be familiar to your Excellency's knowledge in which M. Perron has either openly disobeyed, or systematically evaded the orders of Scindia, especially in the late crisis of that chief's affairs. M. Perron has for some time past manifested a systematic disposition to remove all British subjects from the command of Scindia's regular infantry, and to introduce French officers under his own immediate patronage. M. Perron is supposed to have amassed a considerable fortune, and your Excellency is intimately acquainted with his anxious desire to retire to Europe, and to dispose of his actual command, and of his territorial possessions to some person of the French nation. To these considerations it is important to add that M. Perron is in possession of the person of the unfortunate emperor, Shah Allum, and consequently is master of the nominal authority of that unhappy prince, and therefore may transfer this valuable possession, with his property of any other description, to any French adventurer or officer who may be enabled to complete such a purchase. Thus the coincidence of various extraordinary and uncontrollable accidents, and the weakness of Scindia's personal character, have contributed to found an Independant French State on the most vulnerable part of the Company's frontier. *Under the influence of a succession of French adventurers, this state must be exposed to the intrigue of the French in India, and even to the ambition and hostile spirit of the person who now rules the French nation. Nor could an instrument of destruction more skilfully adapted to wound the heart of the British nation be presented to the vindictive hand of the First Consul of France.* This French state actually holds possession of the person and nominal authority of the Mogul, maintains the most efficient army of regular native infantry and the most powerful artillery existing in India with the exception of the Company's troops, and exercises a considerable authority over the neighbouring states, from the banks of the Indus to the confluence of the Ganges and Jumna. In the present crisis, when every circumstance announces the probability of a renewal of the war with France, and urges the necessity of resorting to every practicable measure of precaution and security, the safety of the British dominions requires the reduction of M. Perron's military resources and power, independantly of any question which might exist between Scindia and the British Government."

This explicit declaration of the views and opinions of the Marquis Wellesley amply confirms the testimony previously adduced of the high political position held by Perron. His *Jaidad* was " an Independent French State," in which he " dictated with the authority of a sovereign of high rank," and his army constituted " a menace to the British dominion in India." This was the height of power and influence to which the runaway sailor from a French frigate had raised himself. It was an elevation even more astounding than De Boigne's, an usurpation of authority more audacious than that of George Thomas. Had Perron resigned his post at this moment he would have left behind him a reputation second to no adventurer's in India. But the splendour of his success was to be marred by the squalor of his dawnfall. He lacked the respectable dignity of De Boigne and the dauntless defiance of George Thomas ; and in the last few days of his power, when summoned to face the culminating crisis of his life, he showed a weakness of purpose that prejudices all his previous achievements, and his exit from the scene wherein he had played so prominent a part was that of a poltroon, clutching his money bags and crying for quarter before he had struck a single blow.

CHAPTER IX.

1803.

UPON the declaration of war by Lord Wellesley, Sindhia's Regular Brigades numbered over 39,000 men, with 5,000 Hindustani horse and 464 guns. In addition to these there were 35,000 Marátha cavalry and fifteen battalions of infantry belonging to Ambaji Inglia, and also sundry garrison troops, so that the entire strength was not far short of 90,000 men-at-arms. The Rájah of Berar contributed fifteen battalions of infantry, 30,000 horse,'and 60 guns, and Shamshir Bahadur 10,000 troops of sorts. The Confederate army was divided as follows :—

With Sindhia, in the Deccan, were Perron's First Brigade, under Colonel Pohlman, four battalions of Jean Baptiste Filoze's corps, under Dupont, and four battalions of the Begum Somru's, under Colonel Saleur. These totalled 10,400 men. The Rájah of Berar's infantry was estimated at 6,000, and the combined Marátha cavalry at 50,000. The cannon numbered 190 pieces.

En route to Hindustan were Perron's Fourth Brigade, under Dudrenec, and five battalions of the Fifth Brigade under Brownrigg —in all nearly 8,000 men. Ambaji's infantry and cavalry increased the total to about 25,000 of all arms.

At Ujjain was stationed Jean Baptiste Filoze's party of six battalions, numbering 3,000 men, with 60 guns. They were destined for the defence of the capital, and had no share in any of the historical actions of the war.

With Perron in Hindustan were the Second and Third Brigades, under Bourguien and Geslin, at Delhi. Two battalions of the Fifth Brigade and 5,000 Hindustan horse at Koil, and at Aligarh the garrison troops under Pedron, and a similar body at Agra under George Hessing. In addition there were about 10,000 Marátha cavalry.

As far back as the month of March Sindhia had ordered Perron to bring his army into a state of readiness to take the field, and these instructions were faithfully executed. By the end of June it became publicly known that war was inevitable. Perron was busy with his preparations at Aligarh, and orders were issued to all the feudatory chiefs in Northern India to rally to the standard. The Emperor's royal tent was pitched at Delhi, and it was proclaimed that Sindhia was about to take up arms against the English in order to defend the Mughal from tyrants who sought to usurp his throne. The Second and Third Brigades were massed at the capital and the Fourth was on its way to join them, after its fruitless march to the Deccan. Shah 'Alam was invited to place himself at the head of the army—a proposal the helpless old man was not in a position to decline Harsúk Rai, Perron's chief banker, was sent to the capital to advance whatsoever money might be required for the troops. In short, all that was possible was done to put the army on a sound war footing, and bring every available man into the field.

It is beyond doubt that Perron's fixed determination was to fight. However spurious his lip-loyalty had been in the past, he now girded his loins for war. One can only surmise the reason for this. It was certainly not his fidelity to his master's cause, for he had displayed his insensibility to this too often; nor was it to secure his fortune, for he had declined the offer of a safe conduct to Calcutta, which had been recently guaranteed him; nor could it have been for the pure love of fighting, for although Perron had in the past shown himself a gallant man, he was never carried away by that lust of battle which distinguished George Thomas. Lord Wellesley suggested that he stayed on, hoping in the event of war to find two powers bidding for his sword; but this was disproved by his declining overtures subsequently made to him by General Lake. There remains only one solution to account for his line of conduct—his relations with the French Government. He was too deeply committed to dare to withdraw from Hindustan, especially with the knowledge that General Decaen's expedition, which had been despatched not improbably on his application, was at Pondicherry. This in itself made his return to France without striking a blow impossible. Had he deserted his post at the eleventh hour he could never have faced the First Consul, to whom he had sent an ambassador offering him the dominion of Hindustan. It was necessity, not choice, which made him apparently loyal to Sindhia, and decided him to see the contest out; to which end he sent his family and treasure to Agra, and made every preparation to resist General Lake.

But there was one power with which Perron had not reckoned, and whose attack he had not even anticipated. This was the enmity behind him. One cannot but feel a compassion for this faithless man when one learns the reason of his downfall. For even as he was bracing himself for the momentous struggle, working with energy and ability, hurrying from post to post, and doing everything in his power to safeguard Sindhia's interests, intrigue and treachery were leagued against him in secret and plotting his downfall. As he had meted it out to his master, so it was to be meted out to him.

Just before the declaration of war, Lord Wellesley issued a very judicious proclamation inviting all the English officers in Marátha employ to quit their stations and come over to the British Government, under promise of pensions graduated to their rank. Most of the adventurers in Sindhia's army took advantage of this. Amongst them were Captain Carnegie, a Scotchman, and Captain Stewart, a country-born—both in the Second Brigade—who at an early date signified to Perron their intention of leaving the service. Hearing which the General grew furious, and summarily dismissed seven other British-born officers, ordering them to quit Marátha territory forthwith, and following this action by a general discharge of all British and British country-born subjects in the brigades. It was a swift and prompt way of cutting the Gordian knot, and was resented by not a few, who remonstrated against the sweeping decision. But Perron's wrath was roused, and the only reply he vouchsafed was a warning to them not to be found within reach of the Marátha camp after a certain date. His conduct is hardly to be wondered at: for many months past he had been unpopular with his English subordinates, whom he had mortified and disgraced in the most unjust way. Such men were not the ones to rely on in this extremity: their prejudices were fixed and antagonistic to him. Fully realising this, Perron determined to expel them from his service, and to repose his confidence on his own countrymen alone, especially on those related to him by marriage or bound to him by ties of gratitude. Herein he made his last and most fatal mistake.

On the 20th of August Perron heard of General Lake's advance. He immediately wrote to the British Commander-in-chief, expressing his surprise and demanding to be informed if war had been declared against Sindhia. In reply, General Lake explained his march in general terms, and at the same time invited Perron to send a confidential officer to confer. This was in accordance with instructions received from Lord Wellesley, who had shortly before written to the Commander-in-chief in the following terms :—

" It would be highly desirable to detach M. Perron from Scindia's service by pacific negotiation. M. Perron's inclination certainly is to dispose of his power to a French purchaser. I should not be surprised if he were found to be ready to enter into terms with your Excellency, provided he could obtain a sufficient security for his personal interests. I empower your Excellency to conclude any agreement for the security of M. Perron's personal interests and property, accompanied by any reasonable remuneration from the British Government, which shall induce him to deliver up the whole of his military resources and power, together with all his territorial possessions and the person of the Mogul and the heir-apparent, into your Excellency's hands."

Perron sent no reply to General Lake's letter until the 27th of August, when he wrote expressing an earnest desire to find some convenient means of avoiding hostilities, but declining the proposition of sending a confidential officer to the British camp, on the grounds that such a step would excite the jealousy of Sindhia. But, as a counter proposal, he suggested that General Lake should send an officer to him. With this the latter did not think fit to comply, but in conveying his refusal he mentioned that the aim of the proposed conference with a confidential officer of Perron had no reference to the public affairs of the British Government, but to the private interests of Perron, and to the means of executing with ease and safety his recent design of withdrawing from Sindhia's service.

Perron's reply was one that did him honour. He stated that it was his intention to stay by Sindhia during the present crisis, and that it was impossible for him to retire until his successor was appointed. But he added that he would send his aide-de-camp to General Lake, and, in consequence, Mr. Beckett attended the Commander-in-chief on the 29th. But the conversation that ensued was of a vague character, excepting that Beckett would not agree to any proposition for Perron's surrender, and he withdrew without any arrangement being concluded.

General Lake had during these communications steadily continued his march, and when they were concluded he was at the gates of Aligarh. Directly Mr. Beckett had left the camp the British army moved out to attack Perron, whose force consisted of about 15,000 cavalry, which included his own 5,000 regular Hindustani horse. The position they had taken up was a strong one and favourable for defence, their front being covered by an extensive swamp, which was unfordable in many parts, whilst their right flank was protected by the fortress of Aligarh, and their left derived considerable advantage from the nature of the ground. Directly Perron observed indications of the hostile movement in the British camp he struck his own tents and drew up his cavalry in line of battle.

General Lake determined to try and turn the left flank of the enemy, and, forming his cavalry up in two lines and his infantry in three or four, as the confused nature of the ground permitted, advanced to the attack. As he was executing this manœuvre a fine opportunity was afforded Perron of making a bold charge with his cavalry upon an enemy who numbered only two men to his three ; but he did not dare to strike a blow, being intimidated and confounded ; and his indecision ran through the ranks. No sooner had General Lake fired a few rounds from his galloper-guns than Perron's force turned and fled. The irregular portion disbanded and dispersed to their homes, and the 5,000 Hindustani horse followed their chief in retreat to Mandu, a large village eight miles south of Koil.

Amongst the British officers whom Perron had recently dismissed from Sindhia's service were Skinner and Stewart (country-borns), Fergusson and Carnegie (Scotchmen), and Lucan and Henessy (Irishmen)—the latter a deserter from the 14th Native Infantry, in which he had been sergeant-major. They had started from Koil on the day previous to the battle, and were proceeding southward to Agra, where their families resided. About midday on the 29th, being encamped by the roadside during the heat of noon, they saw the Marátha horse galloping towards them in a disorderly manner, as they fled from the fight. Presently Perron himself dashed up " in confusion and without his hat." Skinner, who at that time was bound by no tie to the British interest, had made up his mind to apply to Sindhia for redress, since his remonstrance against summary dismissal had been of no avail with Perron. This is how the story of what now occurred is told in his memoirs :—

" Skinner went up to Perron immediately, and told him he had come to again remonstrate against his dismissal, and had determined to remain in the service and share his fortunes. 'Ah ! no, no,' replied Perron, ' it is all over. These fellows [the horse] have behaved ill ; do not ruin yourself ; go over to the British ; it is all up with us ! ' ' By no means,' replied Skinner. ' It is not so. Let us rally yet and make a stand. You may depend upon having many yet to fight for you.' But Perron still shook his head, and after a little while said in his bad English, ' Ah, no, Monsieur Skinner. I not trust. I not trust. I 'fraid you all go.' Skinner on this got angry, and retorted, saying that in that case it was Perron who was the traitor, if he meant to proceed in that way ; if, on account of one or two ingrates, he should lose to his master the services of many faithful persons, this was the way to ruin the cause. But that if he persevered in doing all for the best, no doubt he might still hold the country and effectively serve his master. But Perron, who had made up his mind on the matter, still refused to have anything more to do either with him or any of his brother officers, on which Skinner declared he would go to Sindhia himself and complain. Perron answered impatiently, and bidding no further parley, shook his head and rode off, saying, ' Good-bye, Monsieur Skinner. No trust, no trust ! ' ' Then you may go to the devil ! ' roared Skinner after him."

Perron pursued his way to Háthras, where he made over the command of the Hindustani horse to Monsieur Fleurea, and ordered him to go to Cawnpore, destroying the country as he went. Perron himself retreated to Agra, where his family, and a great portion of his wealth in precious stones, jewels, and shawls, had been sent.

The following day, the 30th of August, General Lake sent a summons to Colonel Pedron to surrender Aligarh. Pedron was not disinclined to listen to terms, but he simultaneously received a letter from Perron, who either divined or was informed of the Commandant's weakness, and this document is worth quoting, if only to exhibit the singular effrontery of the man who, having himself shamefully avoided battle under the walls of Aligarh two days previously, could write in the strain he now adopted :—

" *To Colonel Pedron.*

" Sir,—You will have received the answer you are to make to the propositions of General Lake. I never could have believed that for an instant you could have thought of capitulation.

" Remember you are a Frenchman, and let no action of yours tarnish the high character of the nation.

" I hope in a few days to send back the English commander as fast, or faster, than he came. Make yourself perfectly easy on the subject. Either the Emperor's army or the army of General Lake shall find a grave before the fort of Alyghur. Do your duty ; and defend the fort while one stone remains upon another.

" Once more remember your nation. The eyes of millions are fixed upon you.

" I am, etc.,

" C. Perron."

Of a surety a characteristic letter, with its vainglorious vauntings and its ineffable French vanity. Nor must notice be omitted of the reference to the *Emperor's*—not Sindhia's—army, by whose valour and heroism so great store was set. And yet, even as he invoked its courage and protested its fidelity till death, that army was renouncing Perron and swearing allegiance to Brigadier-General Louis Bourguien, ex-cook of Calcutta, and *quondam* pyrotechnist of Lucknow, awhile it clamoured for the life of the man who cited its virtues.

The fortress of Aligarh had been rendered strong by all the skill and pains which science could bestow, and Perron reposed the most implicit confidence in Pedron. But the latter—" a stout, elderly man, dressed in a green jacket with gold lace and epaulets "—was not made of that stern metal requisite for defending a place " while one stone remained upon another." On the contrary, he would have hailed capitulation with relief, had not the garrison refused to agree with him. The troops in the fort consisted of 800 regulars, 1,000 Rajputs, and 1,200 irregulars, and a squadron of horse. These men resolved to defend the place to the end, and deposing Pedron, elected for their commander a Bahadari Rajput named Baji Ráo, who signalised his accession to office by confining " the stout, elderly man in green," and occupying the place of honour in charge of the gate and outer fort.

General Lake, finding his summons disregarded and his terms refused, assaulted the stronghold on the 4th of September, with 500 Europeans and three battalions of Sepoys. This force left the camp at 2 a.m., and reached the walls a little before dawn. Lieutenant Lucan, the Irishman who had recently left Sindhia's service, and had since been received by General Lake, volunteered to lead the storming party. A picquet of 50 men with a 6-pounder gun had been stationed by Baji Ráo about fifty yards from the fort, and this was quickly driven back by the forlorn hope, who captured the gun after a desperate tussle. They then made for the moat, which was so broad and deep that a three-decker might have floated in it, and crossed it by a narrow causeway leading to the gaté, which was raked by two or three guns, and flanked by a bastion, from whence a most destructive fire was kept up. Scaling-ladders were now applied to the walls and an attempt made to mount them, but the stormers were repulsed. A 12-pounder was then run up to the gate, and after five shots it was blown open. The conflict now became a hand-to-hand one, the garrison fighting with stubborn bravery, but by degrees the attacking force made good its footing, and eventually succeeded in capturing what had hitherto been regarded as an impregnable fortress. The Rajputs " fought like lions," and Baji Ráo was killed, with 2,000 of the defenders. Gallant and loyal men they were, as the following extract from General Lake's letter of the 4th of September shows : "I had tried every method to prevail upon these people to give up the fort, and offered a very large sum of money, but they were determined to hold out, which they did most obstinately, and, I may say, most gallantly. From the extraordinary strength of the place, and being obliged to win it inch by inch, it being so determinedly defended, in my opinion British valour never shone more conspicuous."

The English loss at the storming of Aligarh was very heavy, no less than 223 officers and men being killed and wounded. One hundred and nine guns were captured, exclusive of wall-pieces, and a vast quantity of warlike stores and material, including thousands of regimental uniforms, chiefly blue jackets with red facings, made after the French fashion. Pedron, in spite of himself, had the honour of being made a prisoner of war.

The intrepid *coup de main* on the fort of Aligarh was a mortal blow, not only to Perron, but to Sindhia. It created a panic in the minds of the natives, and astonished every prince in Hindustan, giving them exaggerated ideas of European valour and prowess.

It will be remembered that M. Fleurea had been detached with Perron's 5,000 Hindustani horse to harry the country towards Cawnpore. He carried out his orders, and to him belongs the single success achieved by any portion of Sindhia's regular army during the war. Making his way to Shikohábád, a small out-post in the Company's frontier district of Etáwah, held by Lieutenant-Colonel Coningham, with five companies of the 11th Native Infantry and one gun, Fleurea attacked it on the 2nd of September. From four in the morning till two o'clock in the afternoon the garrison resisted all his attempts with great spirit and resolution, and ultimately obliged him to fall back. The attack was, however, resumed on the 4th, and Colonel Coningham, through the failure of his ammunition, was compelled to capitulate after two hours' fighting, and to give his parole that none of the garrison should serve against Sindhia during the continuance of the war. He retired to Cawnpore with his arms, ammunition, and all his private property, the cantonment being burnt and pillaged, but Mrs. Wilson, an officer's wife, was carried off by the Mahrattas. Colonel Coningham lost four of his officers and 63 Sepoys killed and wounded, whilst Fleurea purchased his victory dearly, at the expense of seven officers and 500 men. No sooner had these terms been arranged than news arrived of the fall of Aligarh. Fleurea's troopers refused to believe the fort had been taken by assault, but maintained that it had been treacherously surrendered by Perron, and immediately made their way to Agra in great indignation, expecting to find the general there. He had, however, removed with his family and effects to

Mattra, taking with him his bodyguard of 800 horsemen, mounted from his own stable, and here Fleurea's horse joined him—a reinforcement which, as events happened, proved highly inconvenient.

For within the period of one short week that had elapsed since his flight from Aligarh Perron was destined to see the whole fabric of his power fall in fragments to the ground, and the army he had so long commanded arrayed in revolt against him. More bitter to bear than this was the revelation that his bosom friend Bourguien was at the head of the mutiny which declared their chief's deposition.

Bourguien had received early intelligence of Ambaji's appointment to supersede Perron, and on the first rumour reaching him began to plot and intrigue against his chief, and publicly announced that he had gone over to the English. A semblance of confirmation was given to this by Perron's supine conduct at the battle of Koil; and no sooner did news of the abortive resistance reach Delhi, than Bourguien threw off all disguise, and called on the Third Brigade to elevate him to the supreme control, which they forthwith did. He then attempted to win over the Second, under Monsieur Geslin, but this officer stood true to Perron, and denounced Bourguien. But the spirit of mutiny was abroad, and his men placed Geslin and all their officers of the Second Brigade in arrest under fixed bayonets, and declared for Bourguien. The latter now demanded an audience with the Emperor, and procured from him a *Khilut* of investure as Commander-in-chief of the Imperial army. The blind and helpless monarch, in no position to withhold favours, acquiesced with the simple faith that distinguished all his actions whenever he was complimented by the request for an exhibition of his regal authority. Never, surely, did such a stalking horse exist for knaves to veil their designs, as poor old Shah 'Alam, who deputed more authority from a prison than many a sovereign has done from a throne.

But Bourguien had not reckoned with Captain Drugeon, the keeper of the King. Drugeon had been in trouble once, but had experienced Perron's clemency and forgiveness. He remembered this now, and in the moment of his chief's downfall struck a loyal blow on his behalf. Resisting Bourguien's demand to deliver up to him all the public treasure, Drugeon turned out his garrison of 5,000 men and expelled the usurper from the fort, at the same time informing the Emperor that he would obey no one except he had Perron's orders.

Bourguien immediately laid siege to the citadel of Delhi, and planted a battery of eight guns in front of the Rajghát bastion, which he battered for two days and laid level with the ground. Whereupon the Emperor begged him to suspend operations, saying he would

20

contrive to make Drugeon obey orders. Bourguien having in the meantime secured the person of Perron's chief banker, Harsúk Rai, found sufficient occupation in squeezing several lakhs of rupees out of him—at which interesting point the story stops.

The usurpation of Perron's office was not sufficient for Bourguien, who, with truly Oriental thoroughness, determined to avoid half measures, and complete the work he had begun. He now wrote to the native officers of the Hindustani horse at Mattra, denouncing Perron as a traitor, and ordering them to seize him, and, if necessary, put him to death. It seems scarcely credible that a man who owed everything he possessed to Perron should have been guilty of such black and dastardly treachery. But its confirmation comes circumstantially, and on the authority of Skinner, Smith, and Perron himself, who adds that his assassination was only prevented by the presence of mind of his aide-de-camp.

This was the last drop in the bitter cup, already filled to overflowing. A concatenation of disasters, misfortunes, and dangers was crushing Perron as suddenly as swiftly. First came the fall of Aligarh; then his supersession by Ambaji Inglia, his implacable enemy. Simultaneously the revolt of the Second and Third Brigades, and the news that the commander of the Fourth Brigade had already pronounced for Ambaji, despite the fact that Dudrenec had been selected by Perron as his own successor. Lastly came this attempt on his life, instigated by Bourguien, at the hands of the cavalry who had come hurrying in from Shikohábád, already incited against Perron by the news of the fall of Aligarh, which seemed to them *primâ facie* evidence of his treachery. All these slings and arrows of outrageous fortune crowded in together, and struck home, one after another, within the period of a few hours.

No wonder that Perron was "confounded with the dangers which surrounded him," and determined to throw himself on the liberality of the British Government for protection and safety. But in order to accomplish this he was obliged to employ stratagem. Mustering his Hindustani horse he harangued them, condemning Bourguien's conduct, and assuring them of his own loyalty. He declared he would at once march to punish the mutineers and then, if they would follow him faithfully, drive the British out of the Doáb. These were brave words, but he had braver material behind them. As an earnest of his good intentions, he handed over three lakhs of rupees to the native officers to be distributed amongst the men. It was an astute piece of liberality, and resulted, as Perron had counted, in the soldiery quarrelling over the division. Meanwhile he prepared their minds for his departure, by announcing that he would cross the Jumna that evening, with his bodyguard, *en route* for Delhi.

Everything turned out according to his desires. By sunset he had placed the river between him and his Hindustani horse, and, by bribing the ferrymen, secured the retainment of every boat on his side of the stream for the rest of the night. He then left, saying he was going to encamp a short distance ahead; instead of which he made a forced march of thirty miles to Sasni, sending on an express to General Lake to inform him that he had resigned Sindhia's service, and desired to renew his application to retire within the Company's territories to Lucknow.

In this letter, which reached General Lake on the 7th of September, Perron mentioned that he had just heard of the appointment of his successor, which relieved him of all obligations to remain at his post, and further observed that the treachery and ingratitude of his European officers convinced him that further resistance to the British was useless.

The Commander-in-chief immediately complied with Perron's request, and detached a British officer to meet him and conduct him in safety to Lucknow. He also permitted Perron to retain his body-guard as an escort, and provided for his reception in the Company's territories with every mark of respect and honour. This course of action was later on approved by the Governor-General, who wrote : " I consider the retirement of General Perron in the present crisis of affairs to be an event highly favourable to the success of the British arms, and to the interests of the British Government in India. It must also diminish the confidence which the Native powers of India have been accustomed to repose in the fidelity of their French officers."

Thus in ten days from General Lake's arrival before Aligarh Perron's power was dissolved, and himself a fugitive in the British camp. Never surely did a master of so many legions fall so swiftly, and so ignominiously Not a single blow had he struck to uphold that sovereign power which he had wielded for seven years. All his brave schemes, his elaborate plans of campaign, his protestations of fidelity, his vauntings, and his vanity had melted into nothingness at the first sight of the British flag flying in the heart of his domain. With a lie on his lips, and his trembling hands squandering gold to bribe the soldiery he dared not trust, Perron fled from his kingdom, followed by the execrations of his troops and the exultant denunciation of his fellow-countrymen.

The causes which led to this dramatic downfall were many. In the first place Perron had calculated that the British army would wait for the termination of the rainy season before starting from

Cawnpore, whereas General Lake marched out in mid monsoon. He considered that Aligarh would sustain a siege of at least two months, during which time he would be able to bring up his brigades and fight an advantageous battle beneath its walls. But his impregnable fortress fell in a single day, and this, in itself, appalled him. His sudden supersession by Ambaji, under whom he was ordered to serve, confronted him with actual danger to his person and property. The defection of his brigades, one after another, paralysed him and left him helpless. But, above all, the treachery of his bosom friend Bourguien crowned his tribulations, and forced from him the *et tu Brute* that bows its head in despair, and resigns itself to fate.

CHAPTER X.

1803.

PERRON'S flight left the road completely clear for Louis Bourguien, who was a man as weak as he was wicked, as conceited as he was incompetent, and as timid as he was treacherous. It was in keeping with his character that he should seek to make a stepping-stone of his benefactor. From time to time Bourguien's shadow has fallen across these pages, yet never once gloriously. Whether at Ajmir, endeavouring to bribe an enemy he could not beat, or at Georgegarh keeping out of range of fire, or at Hánsi, entering into foul intrigue to ruin a brave man, he is always an inflated, low-born fellow, fitted only to handle his native skewers, or discharge the rockets of braggadocio. But he never fell so despicably low as when he proved a traitor to Perron, who had paid him the compliment of believing in him. At the first whisper of omen, this renegade braggart, whom every consideration should have impelled to remain true to his chief, was the first to declare against him, and on the lofty grounds—forsooth—of loyalty to Sindhia's service! Louis Bourguien apostrophising the code of honour is an idea too precious to be lost!

It has been shown how Bourguien tampered with the brigades at Delhi, and induced them to elect him to their head, and how Geslin and Drugeon opposed him without success. He gained the day, and was for a time in nominal command of the Imperial army. "But," says Lewis Ferdinand Smith, "he baffled his own ends. If once the reins of subordination are thrown aside, and the soldiery encouraged to revolt, it is difficult to check or repress the commotion which often, like a dangerous instrument in feeble hands, recoils on him who holds it. Such was the result of the mutinous spirit Bourguien had infused into the troops of the two brigades. Licentious with impunity, they despised the orders of him who had taught then to despise their own Commander-in-chief."

After the fall of Aligarh Delhi became the rallying point for the troops Perron had deserted. Thither rode Fleurea's 5,000 Hindustani horse, convinced now that Bourguien was a true man, since he had warned them of the general's defection. When they arrived at the capital they found the brigades—which included eighteen battalions and 110 pieces of cannon—in a state of mutinous confusion and anarchy. Simultaneously news arrived that General Lake, with rapid marches, was approaching. A change at once came o'er the spirit of Bourguien's dream, and he endeavoured to persuade the troops to retire to Hariána.

This opened their eyes and convinced them that their new general was as craven and untrustworthy as their discarded one. Never in the history of the brigades had battle been shirked, as it was now proposed to shirk it. The spirit of the men rebelled against the cowardice of their officers, and they forthwith deposed Bourguien and placed him in confinement, electing a Native name Sarwar Khán to the chief command.

Such is Skinner's version of the progress of events at Delhi during the few days preceding General Lake's arrival. But Bourguien must have been released almost immediately, for he personally superintended the preparations for defence, and was in command at the battle that shortly took place. On the 9th of September he moved his two brigades down to Patbarghát and began to cross the Jumna, and by the 11th twelve battalions of infantry, 5,000 Hindustani horse, and 70 pieces of cannon had effected the passage, when the arrival of the British army compelled him to form his troops for battle, which he did in tolerably good order, but taking care to keep himself, with some cavalry, out of reach of fire.

General Lake was unaware of the proximity of the enemy, for they were entirely concealed from view by the high grass jungle which intervened. Having completed a fatiguing march of eighteen miles, and reached the banks of the Hindun river, six miles distant from Delhi, the British army began to pitch their tents ; and some of the Sepoys were actually engaged in cooking their food, when a large body of Bourguien's horse suddenly appeared so close at hand that the grand guard and advanced pickets were at once turned out. The enemy's numbers increasing, General Lake went to the front to reconnoitre, accompanied by three regiments of cavalry. He found Bourguien's army drawn up in complete order of battle, on rising ground, and with their guns strongly posted.

It was not a favourable hour to accept battle, for the time was mid-day, and the British troops wearied with a long march, having been in motion since three o'clock in the morning. The heat was intense, and under the fierce rays of a September sun many of the Euro-peans had been prostrated by sunstroke. General Lake's entire force consisted of 4,500 men, and included one King's regiment (the 76th), seven battalions of Sepoys, the 27th Dragoons, and two regiments of Native cavalry. With these he had to oppose nearly 10,000 regular infantry, 5,000 Hindustani horse, and 70 guns, posted in an advan-tageous position.

Bourguien opened the action with a heavy cannonade, which caused General Lake to send orders for the infantry and artillery to move up instantly to the front. They were quickly formed, and marched for-ward in columns of grand divisions from each battalion, but it was at least an hour before they joined the general ; and all this time his cavalry was exposed to a constant and well-directed artillery fire, which occasioned heavy loss. At last the Commander-in-chief (whose horse had been shot under him), perceiving the enemy were so strongly posted as to make an attack not only difficult but hazardous, determined to draw them on to more level ground by a feint, and ordered the cavalry to retire with the double object in view of enticing the enemy from their position, and effecting a more rapid junction with the infantry, than if he had waited for them to come up. The manœuvre was entirely successful, for Bourguien's battalions immediately left their ground, and pursued the retreating cavalry with exultant shouts of victory. But they halted dead when suddenly the British infantry came in sight. General Lake's cavalry at once opened from the centre to permit the infantry to pass through to the front, then the line was swiftly formed, whilst the cavalry massed and took up a position about forty yards in the rear of the right wing.

The order was now given for a general advance. Led by the Com-mander-in-chief in person, and amidst a tremendous fire of round, grape, and chain-shot, the regiments pressed forward in one steady desperate assault of bayonet against cannon. The men fell by scores, but they never took their muskets from their shoulders till within a hundred paces. Then the charge was sounded, and immediately the whole line gave a single volley and doubled forward upon Bourguien's guns and battalions with such impetuosity, that the latter refused to meet them, and, turning rightabout face, fled from the field. As soon as the infantry charge was spent, General Lake gave the order to break up into columns of companies, leaving gaps through which the cavalry charged with the galloper guns, and falling upon the flying foe, rendered the victory a complete one. The battle was fought within sight of the minarets of Delhi, and before sunset the British army was encamped on the east bank of the Jumna, opposite the city.

It was the first time in their famous career that De Boigne's battalions had given way without showing stubborn fight. Had he who created them commanded them, there would have been a different tale to tell, but, deserted by their officers, and left without proper control or direction, they obeyed the instincts which have always asserted themselves in Asiatic troops when bereft of leaders. Bourguien and his French officers were the first to fly from the field, and, accompanied by a few horsemen, who afforded them an example of fidelity, they sought refuge in Delhi. " Here the miscreant" (to quote General Lake's despatch), "after plundering the city, took himself and his vagabonds off on the morning of the 12th, and the country people were so enraged at being plundered by Bourguien, that they retaliated by plundering the baggage of his fugitive troops."

In the battle of Delhi General Lake lost 477 men killed and wounded, of whom 131 belonged to the ranks of the gallant 76th. In Bourguien's army 3,000 men were killed and wounded, and 68 guns, 37 tumbrils of ammunition, and two tumbrils of treasure captured. The report of the ordnance taken is an interesting document, and reflects credit on the handiwork of Sangster. Colonel Horsford thus describes the captured pieces : " The iron guns (eight in number) are of Europe manufacture. The brass guns, mortars, and howitzers have been cast in India, one Portuguese three-pounder excepted. Some bear an inscription of having been made at Muttra, others at Agra ; but the whole are evidently from the designs and execution of an European artist. The dimensions are in general those of the French, and the workmanship is of as high a finish as any in the Company's arsenal. The whole of the guns are furnished with well-made elevating screws of the latest French improvement."

Three days after the battle of Delhi General Lake began the crossing of the river, and on the 16th of September paid his first visit to the Emperor, Shah 'Alam. His progress to the palace was slow, for the streets were thronged with the populace, eager to behold the English general who had emancipated them from the bondage of the French adventurers. General Lake found the great Mughal seated under a small tattered canopy in a mockery of regal state. The aged monarch showed signs of all the oppressions of old age, degraded authority, and extreme poverty, and his miserable appearance was eloquent of his recent sufferings. " It reflected," writes Major Thorn, " indelible disgrace upon the merciless oppressors who had usurped his dominion," and Lord Wellesley records that, "in the metaphorical language of Asia, the Native news-writers, who described this extraordinary scene, have declared that His Majesty's deliverance restored the sight to his eyes from excess of joy." In addition to many other marks of royal favour and condescension, the Emperor was graciously pleased to confer upon General Lake the pleasing if voluminous title of " The Sword of State; the Hero of the Land ; the Lord of the Age; and the Victorious in War." His Majesty, it may be observed, was a poet, and given to composing verses. A not inelegant translation of one of his elegies is given in the Appendix to Francklin's " Life of Shah Allum."

The views expressed above concerning the actual condition in which Shah 'Alam was confined must be accepted with a certain amount of reserve. It was almost an axiom in 1803 that a Frenchman could do no good. Mills, the historian, is inclined to consider that the Emperor was very fairly treated, even though Lord Wellesley talks of his " deliverance from degradation and bondage." That the poor old man was most cruelly used in the past has been shown in the sketch of De Boigne's life, but there is evidence that his condition was much ameliorated when Drugeon was appointed his keeper. Up to that time Shah 'Alam was nearly starved by Sháhji the Fákir. After this there is an indication that the Emperor was far from satisfied, for he wrote to Sindhia, requesting that his allowance might be paid by that Prince himself, and not allowed to filter through channels which evidently showed a leakage. The income allotted to Shah 'Alam was nine lakhs of rupees annually, but Major Thorn asserts that "not more than Rs.50,000 were actually appropriated for that purpose, so that the descendant o Timur (who was at the time eighty-three years of age) and his immense household were often in want of the common necessaries of life." The suggestion immediately forces itself forward—who had the eight and a half lakhs unaccounted for ? Not Drugeon, for his savings amounted to only Rs. 30,000. He was, moreover, merely the deputy of Perron, to whom Sindhia granted the Soubahdari of Delhi in place of Shahji.

Lord Wellesley thus summarises the situation after the occupation of the capital. " By the success of our arms interesting purposes of humanity were accomplished, and so far as the object is regarded in a political point of view, His Majesty Shah 'Allum being placed under the protection of the British Government, no other power can now avail itself of the weight and influence which the Emperor's name must ever possess amongst the Mahomedan inhabitants of Hindostan. The attention of the Governor-General is now directed to the formation of a permanent arrangement for the future dignity and comfort of His Imperial Majesty. . . . He has also given directions to provide for the nobility and the great officers of state at Delhi, whose fortunes have been destroyed by the successful usurpation of Scindia's French adventurers."

Thus, after a life of singular trial and vicissitude, Shah 'Alam found a suitable repose in his extreme old age. But the fact must not be lost sight of that the British Government never attempted to restore that authority and power which "Scindia and the French adventurers had usurped," but merely appropriated it itself. The moral justification for this does not appear to be discussed in any official work on the subject.

Three days after the battle of Delhi Louis Bourguien surrendered, with four of his officers, whose names are given as Gessin (? Geslin), Guerinnier, Del. Perron, and Jean Pierre. It is also probable that Drugeon asked and obtained quarter at the same time, for there is a reference in one of General Lake's despatches to a sum of five and a half lakhs of rupees " captured in the hands of M. Drugeon," which was divided as prize-money. Bourguien and the officers with him were confined under a strong guard, and a little later sent to Fatehgarh, from whence they were deported to the Presidency. Their surrender was accelerated by the dangers that threatened them from the enraged populace of the capital, to escape whose resentment they were very glad to solicit British protection.

Thus, within the space of a fortnight (including the interregnum during which he was imprisoned by his own troops), began, flourished, and ended the reign of Brigadier-General Bourguien. Begotten in treachery, conducted with cowardice, and concluded in defeat and dishonour, Louis Bourguien's Indian career found a fitting termination. It will not, perhaps, surprise the reader to learn that on the achievement of his last fortnight he founded a claim to having valiantly endeavoured to save the Maráthá Empire from destruction.

CHAPTER XI.

LASWÁRI AND ASSAYE.

1803.

AFTER establishing matters on a sound footing at Delhi, General Lake marched, on the 24th of September, for Agra, leaving the capital and the Emperor's person in charge of Colonel Ochterlony, who was supported by a battalion and a half of the Company's Native infantry, and two newly-raised regiments of *Najibs*, recruited from men recently in Perron's service, and commanded by Lieutenants Birch and Woodwill, ex-officers in Sindhia's employ. It should also be mentioned that immediately after the battle of Delhi eight Risálas or squadrons of the Hindustani horse came over to General Lake, and were taken into British employ, Captain Skinner being appointed to command them. These subsequently became a famous regiment, known as Skinner's Irregular Horse.

There were six battalions of Perron's Second and Third Brigades which had failed to cross the Jumna in time to participate in the battle of the 11th. So soon as the day was lost they fled to Fatehpur Sikri, where they divided. Three, under Sarwar Khán, effected a junction with the Fourth Brigade, which was on its way from the Deccan, under Dudrenec, to join the army at Delhi. The Chevalier, and two of his officers, Major Lewis Ferdinand Smith and Lieutenant Lapenet, now left their troops, and surrendered to Colonel Vandeleur at Mattra on the 30th of September, the command of the Fourth Brigade being taken over by Sarwar Khán. The other three Delhi battalions pushed on to Agra, where they joined four battalions and twenty-six pieces of cannon belonging to Perron's Fifth Brigade, which had also been dispatched from the Deccan, under Major Brownrigg, to strengthen the forces in Upper India. These seven battalions, being denied entrance to the fort by the garrison, took up a position on the glacis outside. The troops in Agra consisted of 4,000 fighting men, under Colonel George Hessing. They had broken

315

into mutiny after Perron's defection, and made Hessing a prisoner, as well as the European officers under him. In the fort was treasure amounting to twenty-five lakhs of rupees (£300,000 sterling), which had been sent there by Perron for safety when hostilities first threatened, and of which particular mention will be made later on. The revolted garrison desired to divide this treasure, but their mutual jealousies prevented them from agreeing to any plan of apportionment, and the singular circumstance was presented of these mutineers guarding their precious charge from each other with the utmost vigilance. When they heard of the arrival of Brownrigg's battalions, and those from Delhi, they dreaded their strength and unanimity, and refused to admit them into the fort. But still they did not dare to broach the treasure themselves, being intimidated by their European prisoners, Colonels George Hessing and Robert Sutherland, Majors Brownrigg and Deridon, and Captains Harriot, Marshall, and Atkins, who warned them that if the money were tampered with their lives would answer for it when the British arrived.

On the 2nd of October General Lake reached Mattra, and, forming a junction with Colonel Stevenson's detachment, moved on to Agra, where, at 2 p.m. on the 4th, a summons was sent to the garrison to surrender. But within the fort all was anarchy and confusion, and not even a reply was returned.

The seven battalions, however, who were encamped on the glacis had preserved their discipline, and now prepared to show fight, which, considering that they were locked out of the fort by their fellows, exhibited uncommon spirit and resolution. So long as they held their position it was impossible for General Lake to make any approaches against Agra, and accordingly he determined to dislodge them. This he effected on the 10th, with nine battalions of Native infantry, but it cost a long and severe fight, and his loss was nine officers and 218 men killed and wounded. The seven battalions resisted stubbornly, and it was not until they had lost 600 men, and all their twenty-six guns that they yielded. "The enemy," wrote General Lake in his despatch describing the action, "fought most desperately. I understand they are supposed to be the best Perron had, and they were so advantageously posted that it was almost impossible to get at them." Two days after the battle the survivors of these seven battalions, amounting in all to about 2,500 men, tendered their submission, under promise of being taken into the Company's service on the same pay as they had received in Sindhia's, and marching over to the British lines on the 13th of October, encamped along side of their conquerors.

The siege of Agra was now commenced. Although Sarwar Khán with the Fourth Brigade, the three Delhi battalions (in all about 9,000 infantry), and 1,500 Hindustani horse, was encamped within thirty miles, he made no attempt to relieve the fort; this could not have been from want of spirit, for his troops had plenty of fight in them, as they showed before the month was out, and their supine attitude can only be attributed to the want of intelligent direction, due to their desertion by their European officers.

A breaching battery having been erected within 350 yards of the south-east side of Agra fort, preparations were made for a bombardment. But before it was opened the garrison released Colonel Sutherland from confinement, and sent him to ask for terms. He brought a letter signed by Hessing, as commandant of the fort, who wrote that "his soldiery had become a little more reasonable from his having repeatedly told them that any further resistance on their part would avail them nothing, but on the contrary exasperate the English." They were now prepared to deliver up the fort, guns, stores, &c., on condition of protection to themselves and their private property. "But," added Hessing, "should any unforseen deviation from this proposal take place, as we are still their prisoners, we hope your Excellency will not impute to us the blame."

In reply, General Lake sanctioned the terms asked for, but particularly specified that no treasure was to be taken out of the fort. He granted one hour's grace in which to confirm the agreement. This answer was taken by Captain Salkeld, but after receiving it fresh difficulties and divergences of opinion arose amongst the garrison, and in the midst of them the firing recommenced from the fort, whereupon Captain Salkeld immediately retired.

In consequence of this treacherous act all negotiations were decreed ended, and the breaching battery opened on the morning of the 17th, doing considerable damage to the high stone bastions and rampart. A few hours sufficed to bring the garrison to their knees, and the next morning the place capitulated, and the English marched in. The defeated troops, amounting to 4,000 men, were permitted to depart, and some of them joined the British service, whilst others dispersed to their homes. Twenty tumbrils laden with treasure, amounting to twenty-four lakhs, were taken, and the amount distributed as prize-money. The ordnance captured consisted of 76 brass and 86 iron guns, including a famous piece known as "The Great Gun of Agra," which was composed of many metals, including all the precious ones, and discharged a ball measuring twenty-two inches in diameter, and weighing 1,500 lbs. General Lake attempted to send this "Agra

Infant " as a trophy to Calcutta, but it was swamped in the Jumna, and under the golden sands of that river found a final resting-place.

In less than two months Aligarh Delhi and Agra had been captured, and three battles won, by which the Second, Third, and Fifth Brigades had been practically destroyed—only the Fourth, and three of the escaped Delhi battalions, remained undefeated, but this force had been gradually swollen by the daily arrival of refugees and small, dispersed parties from Delhi and Agra, so that it now numbered twelve or fourteen battalions, furnished with seventy-four pieces of artillery. Against this formidable force General Lake turned his arms. "If I can get hold of the brigades of the Deccan," he writes, "not a Frenchman will be left in the country." He had information of their position. and at first made overtures to their commander, Sarwar Khán, to desert Sindhia's cause, offering him very tempting pecuniary inducements. But this native was as faithful as he was gallant, and rejected them. It speaks well for the loyalty and discipline of De Boigne's battalions that in those dark days, when they were deserted by all, or nearly all, their European officers, and were aware that every action hitherto fought had gone against them, they still maintained themselves as an army and stood to their guns. How nobly they held out to the very end let the story of Laswári show.

When Sarwar Khán heard of the fall of Agra he marched from Fatehpur Sikri, where he was encamped, to Bhartpur, to gain the protection of the fort. The Rájah, however, refused him admittance, whereupon he prevailed on a local Marátha chieftain to join him with about 5,000 irregular cavalry, and commenced his march towards the Mèwatti country, levying contributions as he went.

General Lake started from Agra in pursuit of these troops on the 27th of October, and on the 1st of November overtook them at the village of Laswári, after a forced march of twenty-six miles, performed at night, during which the cavalry had outstripped the infantry. When he came upon the enemy at sunrise he had only three regiments of dragoons and five of Native cavalry with him, but with these he determined to make an immediate attack without waiting for the arrival of the infantry. So he placed himself at their head, and led them forward. There never was a more gallant general than Gerard Lake, who was " a man of action " in the boldest sense of the word. Throughout this Marátha war we find him ever heading charges in person, just as if he had been the colonel of a cavalry corps, and constantly having his horses shot under him on the field of battle.

He now attacked and forced the enemy's first line in the face of a tremendous discharge of grape and musketry, which created great slaughter amongst his squadrons, whose progress was seriously impeded by chains fastened to the enemy's cannon and running from one battery to another. " Sarwar Khán's battalions reserved their fire," writes Major Thorn, " till our cavalry came within a distance of twenty yards of the muzzles of their guns, which, being concealed by the high-grass jungle, became perceptible only when a fierce discharge of grape and double-headed shot mowed down whole divisions, as the sweeping storm of hail levels the growing crop of grain to the earth. But, notwithstanding the shock of this iron tempest, nothing could repress the ardour of the cavalry, whose velocity overcame every resistance. Having penetrated the enemy's line, they immediately formed again, and charged backwards and forwards three times amidst the continued roar of the cannon and an incessant shower of grape, and chain-shot, with surprising order and effect. The scene of horror was heightened and the work of destruction increased by the disadvantage under which our cavalry had to act ; for no sooner had they charged through than the artillerymen of the enemy (who, to save themselves, had taken shelter under their guns), directly our men had passed, reloaded them and fired upon our rear." So determined was this resistance and so galling the fire, that at last General Lake found it necessary to withdraw out of reach of the enemy's guns, and await the assistance of the infantry to continue the battle.

It was not until noon that the rest of the troops came up, after having covered a distance of twenty-five miles since three o'clock in the morning. A short rest being absolutely necessary, two hours were allowed the fatigued troops in which to recover themselves. Taking advantage of this delay, Sarwar Khán fell back and concentrated his battalions around the village of Mehálpur, placing the Fourth Brigade on the left, and the refugees of the Second and Third Brigades, who had redeemed their character, lost at Delhi, by repelling the cavalry charge, on the right, whilst the cavalry was stationed in the rear. In front of his position was a tank or large pond of water, the embankment of which he cut, and so flooded the space between the two armies. His front was covered by his guns, which were posted with great judgment.

Soon after noon General Lake formed his infantry into two columns, and directed one to support the other in turning the right flank of the enemy, while the cavalry were detached to make a hostile demonstration against their front. The renewed action opened with a tremendous cannonade, and as soon as Sarwar Khán perceived the plan of the attack, he threw back his right wing so as to bring it at almost

right angles with his front and left wing, both rears being protected by
the village of Mehálpur. The gallant 76th led the way against this
position, supported with equal alacrity by the 12th Native Infantry.
When they arrived within a hundred and fifty paces of the enemy's
line their ranks were being so mown down by Sarwar Khán's admir-
ably-served guns, that, sooner than risk a temporary halt whilst waiting for th eserves to come up, General Lake ordered a bayonet
charge. The men responded magnificently, and rushing forward with
a ringing British cheer, were soon in the thick of a *mêlée*, wherein not
even a spirited charge of the enemy's cavalry could dismay them;
and when, in turn, the British cavalry spurred forward to attack, the
day was won.

But splendid as was the advance, equally splendid was the resistance. On the field of Laswári De Boigne's battalions surrendered not
only their glorious career, but their existence as an army and their
lives as men. There was no confusion, no fear, no rout: to the end
they were staunch, disciplined veterans, on whose colours were em-
blazoned Pátan, Merta, and Lakhairi, and worthily they sustained their
proud heritage. Their breasts met the opposing British bayonets
as inch by inch they contested every point, refusing to give way until
they had lost the whole of their guns, and even then, although their
situation had become desperate, they continued to maintain the same
courage and disposition. When at last, out-fought by British
persistance, they fell back, it was in steady retreat and good order.
But it was too late to escape. They were broken in column, and cut
to pieces by the British cavalry, who detoured and took them in rear,
sabreing all except 2,000 men. These, being hemmed in on all sides,
and without a loophole for escape, surrendered as prisoners of war.
They were the sole survivors of fourteen battalions numbering 9,000
men who had been ranged in the field that morning! The annals of
Indian warfare contains no more dreadful sacrifice at the shrine of
duty.

The battle was over by four o'clock in the afternoon. The enemy's
camp was captured as it stood, with all their baggage, 74 guns, and 44
stands of colours. The loss on the British side amounted to 834 men
killed and wounded of all grades, including 42 officers. Major-
General Ware and Colonel Vandeleur were amongst the killed. The
Commander-in-chief had two horses shot under him, and his son,
Major George Lake, was wounded in the act of tendering his charger
to his father.

No sketch of the battle of Laswári could do complete justice to the
vanquished, if it omitted to quote General Lake's secret despatch to

Lord Wellesley, dated from the field of battle on the 2nd of November, 1803. The following is an extract from it :—

" The enemy's battalions are most uncommonly well appointed, have a most numerous artillery, as well served as they possibly can be, the gunners standing to their guns until killed by the bayonet. All the Sepoys of the enemy behaved exceedingly well, *and if they had been commanded by French officers, the affair would, I fear, have been extremely doubtful.* I never was in so severe a business in my life, and pray God I never may be in such a situation again. Their army is better appointed than ours ; no expense is spared whatever, and they have three times the number of men to a gun we have. Their bullocks, of which they have many more than we have, are of a very superior sort. All their men's knapsacks and baggage are carried upon camels, by which means they can march double the distance. . . . *These fellows fought like devils, or rather heroes, and had we not made a disposition for attack in a style that we should have done against the most formidable army we could have been opposed to, I verily believe, from the position they had taken, we might have failed.*"

Skinner, in his memoirs, strikes a more human note, as indeed he often does in his record of these stirring times.

" As General Lake was returning from the battle some of the Europeans cheered him. He took off his hat and thanked them, but told them to despise death, as those brave fellows had done, pointing to the Mahrattas who were lying thick about their guns. All these guns were captured, with several thousand prisoners, besides killed and wounded, the number of which on the Mahratta side was very great. But it was never properly ascertained, as I believe the field was never cleared, and the poor fellows were left to the wild beasts ! "

At Laswári the destruction of the last of Perron's battalions in Hindustan was completed. Twelve had been routed at Delhi, seven at Agra, and ten more here, exclusive of the dispersed fugitives from the previous battles. In the fortresses of Aligarh, Agra, and Delhi, about 13,000 garrison troops had been broken up, and the 5,000 Hindustani horse never paraded again. The total amounted to nearly 40,000 men, of whom twelve weeks after the declaration of war not a vestige remained in opposition. At least one third of them had been actually killed or wounded in fight—a return which illustrates their bravery and devotion to a lost cause far better than any words can hope to do. Without detracting from the merits of the victors, the observation may be permitted, that had it been possible to deprive the British army, suddenly and without warning, of all their commissioned officers at the commencement of the campaign, it is doubtful whether the record at the end of it would have illustrated such devotion true to death as ennobled the passing of De Boigne's Battalions.

Whilst General Lake was winning victories, and Perron's army crumbling away in Hindustan, the same process had been going on in the Deccan, where Sindhia and Bhonsla were opposed by General Arthur Wellesley. The force in the south consisted of the First Brigade under Major Pohlman ; four battalions of the late Fidèle Filoze, now commanded by Major Dupont, and generally referred to as Dupont's Corps ; five battalions of the Begum Somru's under Colonel Saleur ; and Sindhia's grand park of artillery of 52 guns, which, added to those of the Brigades, brought up the total to 115 pieces in the field. In addition to these troops there were 35,000 irregular Marátha cavalry.

General Wellesley's first exploit was the capture of Ahmednaggar, a strong fortress near Poonah, garrisoned by 3,000 men, " including 1,000 Sepoys, in white jackets, commanded by three French officers, a little dark coloured, who wore blue clothes." The General then marched against the combined armies of Sindhia and the Rájah of Berar. These, on the 24th of August, had entered the territories of the Company's ally, the Nizam of Haidarabad, by the Adjanta Ghát, and reached Jálnapur, a place forty miles east of Aurangabád. After some marching and countermarching, which only gave opportunity for a little skirmishing, General Wellesley managed to come within striking distance of an enemy, whose disposition had been to avoid action. Although at the moment a considerable portion of his troops was detached at a distance under Colonel Stevenson, whereby he was much weakened, the General determined not to lose the chance afforded for a battle. Leaving his baggage under guard of a battalion and a half of Sepoys at Naulnér, he marched, on the 23rd of September, with the 74th and 78th King's Regiments, the 19th Light Dragoons, four battalions of Native infantry, and four regiments of Native cavalry to the place where the enemy were known to be encamped near the fortified village of Assaye, where he arrived at one o'clock in the afternoon, after a fatiguing march of twenty-two miles, and found the enemy strongly posted in a triangular piece of ground, between the junction of two small rivers, the Káitná and Juah. He determined to attack at once, and having crossed the former by a ford, near its junction with the Juah, formed his infantry in two lines, with the cavalry as a reserve in a third, and from the apex of the triangle wheeled down upon the foe, who quickly ran their guns into line to oppose him. Notwithstanding the terrible artillery fire poured into them, the British troops advanced with undaunted firmness, but the execution in their ranks was so great, and especially amongst the men and bullocks of the artillery, that their cannon had to be left behind, and the infantry and cavalry, led in person by General Wellesley, advanced without any support whatever from their artillery to attack a line of 115 guns.

The Maráthás, numerous and daring as they were, stood astounded and appalled at the audacious spirit of the comparatively insignificant array that thus presumed to attack their formidable host. The total number of men under General Wellesley's command did not exceed 4,500, of which only one third were Europeans, whilst the enemy numbered 50,000, of whom 10,500 were disciplined infantry.

Moving rapidly forward the British troops fired but a single volley, and stormed the first line of guns at the point of the bayonet. Then advancing again, in equally good order to the second line, they captured that as well. But meanwhile many of the artillerymen of the first line, who had thrown themselves down and simulated death as the British regiments passed over them, rose, and manning their guns again, turned them round and poured grape and chain shot into the rear of the victors, who were obliged to return and drive them away from their pieces. Encouraged by this seeming retreat, some of Sindhia's battalions, who had been retiring in good order, halted, faced about, and advanced to the attack, whilst their cavalry were emboldened to charge.* This was the critical point of the battle,

* The following interesting Native account of the battle of Assaye from the pages of "Pandurang Hàri" is perhaps not generally known, and is here inserted as confirming with singular accuracy the account above given, which has been culled from English sources: "At Assaye we opposed a great English general. He attacked our left wing, and we changed the position of our guns and infantry. The English advanced to the attack; our fire was dreadfully destructive to them, and we so thinned the right of their line, that a body of our cavalry was induced to charge it, of which number I was one. We thought ourselves to be doing business pretty satisfactorily, until we found that the enemy's cavalry was in reserve to intercept us. They repulsed us with great slaughter. These English are large, powerful men—perfect war-tigers—and the weight of their sabres almost annihilated my poor troopers. They unhorsed numbers of us merely by riding against us—I was so served for one, and, with many others, feigned myself dead. Our army being routed, fled, and the English pursuing them, left the guns they had captured in the rear. These I proposed to turn upon them; we got up and did so with great effect. It was clear we made our shot tell pretty well, for a body of the Topee Wallahs, with their general at their head, rode up to put a stop to the firing. The General had

and, realising the danger, General Wellesley put himself at the head of the 78th Regiment and charged the Maráthás who had manned the guns, whilst at the same moment the 19th Dragoons, who drew only 350 sabres, and the Native cavalry delivered their attack. After a bloody and perilous contest General Wellesley, who had a horse shot under him, and was exposed to the most imminent danger, achieved his object by recovering the cannon, whilst Colonel Maxwell, with the cavalry, so vigorously attacked the enemy's main line of infantry, which had reformed, that he completed their overthrow, but with the loss of his own life.

Although defeated and thrown into confusion, Sindhia's regular infantry fought to the end with the desperate fury of men stung by a sense of shame at having to yield to an inferior force. For three hours the sanguinary conflict raged, at the end of which British resolution triumphed over Asiatic valour, and the glorious name of Assaye was added to the battle-roll of England's victories. Daulat Ráo Sindhia and the Rájah of Berar fled from the field soon after the commencement of the action, as did the Maráthá cavalry, who behaved in a dastardly way. Pohlman left 1,000 men on the field, whilst the country round about was covered with his wounded. The whole of the enemy's camp equipage and military stores, with 98 guns and 100 tumbrils, fell into General Wellesley's hands. On the British side the loss in killed and wounded amounted to 1,566 (of whom 600 were Europeans), or more than a third of the total number engaged. Such a percentage of loss had never previously been recorded in any general action since the establishment of the English power in India. The 74th King's Regiment was half annihilated, 17 officers and 384 men being struck down : they were 700 strong when they went into action. Sindhia's Prime Minister, Jádu Rao, received a wound, from the effects of which he afterwards succumbed, and an European of distinction was found dead on the field. It is difficult to surmise whom this could have been ; he was probably one of the following, whose names appear in General Wellesley's despatches as serving with the enemy.

Brigade-Major D'Orton.	Ensign Perrin.
Captain Gautier.	Ensign Mars.
Captain-Lieutenant Mercier.	Ensign Cameron.
Captain-Lieutenant Honoré.	'Ensign Brown.
Ensign Wroughton.	Cadet Songster (? Sangster).

his horse killed under him. At this time our troops still hovered about one part of the English line. At length we fled, leaving ninety-eight pieces of cannon and seven standards in the hands of the English."

Reviewing the battle of Assaye, it was acknowledged by all the officers present, who had witnessed the power of the French artillery in the wars of Europe, that the enemy's guns on this occasion were equally well served, and that they fought with a prowess worthy of a European nation. "The battle," wrote General Wellesley in a private letter to Colonel Collins, "was the most severe I have ever fought in India. Sindhia's infantry behaved well. They were driven from their guns only by the bayonet, and sòme of their corps retreated in great order and formed again." Lord Wellesley, the Governor-General, termed it a matchless victory. It swept out of existence all that remained of De Boigne's battalions, and cleared the way for the treaty made with Daulat Ráo Sindhia on the 30th of December, 1803, by which Hindustan was closed to French influence and intrigue for ever.

The two great battles won by Lake and Wellesley rank amongst the most notable gained by the English in India, because our arms overcame a brave and powerful enemy, whose defeat meant something more than the mere addition of another inscription on the crowded page of British achievement. The foemen were worthy of our steel; the fight was hard and desperate; the victory one to be proud of; the results commensurate. For they added to our Eastern possessions the rich Doáb districts between the Ganges and the Jumna, including the cities and forts of Delhi, Agra, and Aligarh; the greater portion of the province of Bundelkhand; the whole of Cuttack and Orissa; and a large extent of territory in Guzerát. It left us in possession of the entire seaboard of India, and was the most important extension of frontier our Indian conquests have ever known, since it secured to us not merely the supremacy, but practically the annexation of the whole of the peninsula; for round the independent states that still remained the cordon of the red line was closely drawn, supported in its rear by the oceans of which our navy was the master. Finally, there was left to our enemies but a single road to India—the long and dreary one through Central Asian deserts, over which they are still toiling.

Commenting on these two battles, thus writes an eloquent historian in 1807 : "At Assaye and Laswaree the infantry of the enemy stood till the English bayonets came to their breasts; the artillerymen served their guns without receding an inch, till they fell under the wheels of their own cannon; the cavalry charged to the very muzzles of the English firelocks. There is not in the records of human courage a more desperate engagement than that which was fought between the British army commanded by Sir Arthur Wellesley and the Mahrattas, aided by the French regular battalions, on the plains of Assaye,

Had the liberties of Europe been contested with equal bravery, the Continent would not at this day be laid prostrate at the heel of France."

Thus passed away De Boigne's battalions, which had in twenty years increased from two to forty, and preserved an almost unbroken record of victory until they met the English. Great in their rise, they were not less great in their fall, but worthy to the last of the traditions and achievements which made their career illustrious.

CHAPTER XII

A FTER his surrender to General Lake, Perron, with his secretary and aide-de-camp, Beckett, an Englishman, and his cavalry commandant, Fleurea (who had effected his escape with great diffi- culty from the Hindustani horse), proceeded to Lucknow, which they reached on the 1st of October. Under special orders from the Governor-General, Perron was treated with the respect and distinc- tion due to his rank in Sindhia's army, and received the customary salutes and marks of attention. The Resident at Lucknow was, how- ever, ordered to accelerate his departure for Calcutta, but notwith- standing this his start was delayed by several circumstances.

Soon after his arrival at the Oudh capital Perron wrote to Lord Wellesley, stating that at the time of quitting Sindhia's service he had deposited twenty-two lakhs of rupees in the keeping of a Native banker, besides other valuable personal property, and that, on re- quiring their restoration, he was informed the money and valu- ables were at Agra, and could not therefore be delivered up. In consequence he was obliged to leave the money behind him, and now requested that it might be restored.

This was the treasure which had induced the garrison at Agra to depose and confine their European officers; but they had been fright- ened to divide it owing to the warnings of Colonel George Hessing, and the money was found intact when General Lake captured the fortress. He questioned all Sindhia's European officers about it, who declared it was public treasure, and not Perron's private property. It was clearly in the possession of the garrison at the time of taking Agra, and although the terms of capitulation permitted the troops to carry their private property away with them, they left this money behind. General Lake, on these grounds, declared it to be lawful prize money, and in this view he was supported by the Governor-General, who, in answer to Perron's application, informed him that when he was allowed to retire into the Company's territory, the safeguard granted only extended to his person and the property he carried with him, and that the British Government could not guarantee the safety of anything he had left behind in the hands of an enemy with whom the English were at war.

Of this incident Perron, who was naturally much exasperated at losing more than a quarter of a million sterling at one fell swoop, made considerable capital on his return to Europe, by which time the sum in question appears to have more than quadrupled itself, whilst its confiscation came to be described as an actual robbery on the part of the British Government. Major Thorn distinctly traverses this statement, for he says, " Perron, with a singular effrontery, but with an address peculiar to adventurers, being no doubt well acquainted with the deposit of the treasure at Agra, laid claim to twenty-two lakhs taken there." In this there is a suggestion of *mala fides*, which is not confirmed by Louis Ferdinand Smith, who states that " before the declaration of war Perron sent all his ready money to the fort of Agra." It is not improbable that the treasure was derived from his *Jaidad* revenue collections, and that technically it was Perron's ; but it had passed out of his keeping and control into that of his mutinous troops, and he lost it, not unfairly, but by the chances of war. Its loss by no means crippled him, for in addition to the property he was able to convey away, he had a large sum of money (estimated by one authority at £280,000) invested in the East India Company's funds ! In pecuniary investments this shrewd Frenchman ran with the hare and hunted with the hounds.

On the 8th of October Perron left Lucknow for Calcutta, from whence he retired to Chandernagore, where he resided for some time in the neighbourhood of the French settlement. It was not until the following year that he embarked for Europe, nor until September, 1805, that he landed at Hamburg, where de Bourienne was the French Consul, from whose memoirs the following passage is extracted :—

"Every one has heard speak of the famous General Perron, who has played such a great *rôle* amongst the Mahrattas. In 1805 he arrived at Hamburg and applied to me for a passport, and I had a most interesting conversation with him about his truly extraordinary adventures. He said that he had possessed more than fifty million francs, but that in order to obtain permission to leave India he had been obliged to pay the English three-quarters of the money. Most of his goods were magnificent cashmeres. He was good enough to offer me one. General Perron had only one arm. He was accompanied by two copper-coloured children—a boy and a girl—the offspring of an Indian mother. Their costume attracted considerable attention wherever they went. They did not speak a word of French. Their father exhibited great affection for them, and caressed them continually.

" Some days after General Perron's arrival Bourguien also arrived and applied for a passport for France. He was at daggers drawn with Perron, who spoke of him with similar bitterness. They professed a profound contempt for each other, and accused each other of being the cause of the ruin of the Mahrattas. Both had immense fortunes. I do not know what has become of Bourguien, but General Perron retired to a magnificent estate which he bought in the neighbourhood of Vendôme."

Perron, after landing, proceeded to Paris, where he was coldly received by Bonaparte. He did not remain long in the capital, but withdrew to a domain which he purchased at Fresnes, near Montoire, in the department of Loire et Cher. His mother and sisters were alive when he returned to France, and received him with open arms. Soon after he had settled down he married a Madamoiselle Du Trochet, by whom he had a large family. Two of his daughters by this union were subsequently married to two members of the Rochefoucauld family, one of whom, the Countess Frederic de Rochefoucauld, died so recently as March, 1892, whilst the " copper-coloured damsel " gave her hand to M. Alfred de Montesquiou. In his luxurious retirement at Fresnes Perron passed nearly thirty years, but towards the end of his life he was suspected of republicanism and subjected to police surveillance by the French Government, and, in the words of a French author, "found in his own country misery and persecution."

Of the three careers of military adventure which have been sketched in this work, Perron's was, without doubt, the most remarkable. Starting from a beginning as humble as that of George Thomas, he obtained a political power exceeding that of De Boigne, notwithstanding which he leaves us with the conviction that of the three he was the inferior man. He lacked the daring and the personal attraction that distinguished Thomas, and he wanted the dignity and straightforwardness of De Boigne. Not that Perron was deficient in personal courage or self-esteem : no one could impugn his spirit during the earlier part of his career, nor deny his appreciation of position towards its close. But there came a time when he pre-

ferred to gain his ends by cunning and intrigue rather than by good
honest fighting, when he stooped to grossest favouritism, and was
guilty of injustice and treachery, and when his proper pride degenerated into vulgar vanity, and his actions gave the lie to his protestations of courage and fidelity.

It is, perhaps, difficult for an Englishman to approach the consideration of Perron's character without prejudice. Had he carried his
pronounced hostility towards the British nation to its legitimate end,
and fought us in the field of battle, he might have claimed more
from our generosity than he can from our impartiality. But he
declined to cross swords, preferring rather to accept quarter, which he
repaid by copious abuse when his personal safety was no longer at
risk, and this rouses our indignation and ranges us against him.

And when we come to judge his career as a whole we cannot but
condemn much that was evil in it. His later loyalty to Sindhia, and
his creditable rejection of General Lake's overtures, do not condone
his long course of faithlessness and treachery during the war with
Holkar, when he sacrificed his master's interests with callous unconcern. His courage at Sounda is obliterated by his craven retreat at
Koil. We cannot help reading with contempt his appeal to Pedron to
hold the fort at Aligarh, when we remember his own spiritless surrender a week later. And if his fall was due to his desertion by his
chosen favourites, Bourguien and Dudrenec, their defection suggests
how little there must have been that was lovable in their chief.
The recriminations Perron entered into with Bourguien at Hamburg
display his smallness of mind, as does also his vainglorious boast that
by his intrigues he compelled De Boigne to resign his post. This
latter assertion comes to us on the authority of General Belliard, who
was in a confidential post under Bonaparte in Egypt, where he had
charge of all the First Consul's intrigues and correspondence with
the Native states of India. This officer records that, on his return to
Europe, Perron boasted that he had compelled De Boigne to quit
Sindhia's service. De Boigne never stooped to notice, far less
to reply to these allegations, which only leave in our minds
a wonder that Perron should so self-convict himself of baseness.
That Perron was cunning, grasping, and avaricious, his financial feats
clearly show. Who shall say from how many helpless wretches,
and by what dire exactions, his fortune was accumulated? If—as he
stated—it amounted to two millions sterling, its very magnitude is
its own condemnation, for such a vast sum could never have been
honestly accumulated in the time and circumstances which were open
to him.

This is the dark side of the picture. On the other hand it cannot be denied that Perron made the most of his opportunities, and if he succeeded to a great position by favour of fortune and intrigue, he held and improved his station by his own energy and determination. He was as industrious as he was able. Colonel Collins bears testimony to the former quality in a letter addressed to the Governor-General in March, 1802, just after Perron's visit to Ujjain. " I noticed " (he writes) " the unwearied attention of General Perron to improve and strengthen the works of the different fortresses garrisoned by his troops, and mentioned [to the Mahratta ministers] the high estimate in which he was held by all the Rajpoot and Sikh *sirdars*, who were chiefly guided by his counsel and direction." As to Perron's ability, the singular success with which he wielded the power left to him by De Boigne admits no doubt of it. His methods may have been questionable, and his administration unjust and venal, but he held the reins with a firm and skilful hand. His reputation as a soldier was established by the capture of Kanaund and the victory of Kardla. His subjugation of Rajputána and his defeat of Lakwa Dáda were masterly, vigorous, and brave demonstrations of military capacity. The plan of campaign which he proposed for the war against the British does credit to his powers of organisation and his talent as a general, and had it been carried out in its entirety would have resulted in a long and bloody struggle for supremacy. Of his contest with George Thomas perhaps the best that can be said of it is that Perron won ; if he exhibited signs of personal weakness in its conduct ; if, as has been suggested, his courage was doubtful, he at least continued to keep his grip on Hindustan throughout the crisis, and when it was over immediately advanced his power to the Sutlej. Even when his influence with Sindhia was gone, and he was peremptorily ordered to give up possession of all the districts he held, except his own *Jaidad*, he evaded obedience, and to the end retained his government intact. Throughout his career he was opposed by many enemies, but he triumphed over all. The three most powerful ones were Balloba Tantia, Lakwa Dáda, and George Thomas : they all died in flight or defeat. Ambaji Inglia alone prevailed over him, and the victory he purchased with gold was a dear and empty one.

In addition to these internal foes, there was a far more powerful external hostility opposed to him. The consideration in which the Marquis Wellesley held Perron's influence towards the end of his career has been shown. But it was not only in 1803 that the Governor-General considered him dangerous ; so far back as 1798, when Zeman Shah's invasion threatened India, Lord Wellesley wrote to

Colonel Collins in the following terms : " Your particular attention must be given to the conduct of M. Perron. *We must counteract any attempt from him to establish a state in Hindustan.* He would undoubtedly assist Zeman Shah, and perhaps enter into his service in the event of Scindia's fall. . . . I cannot believe that M. Perron would give a cordial support to any cause that we might favour. *We must never forget that he is a Frenchman.*"

In the face of this determination Perron did establish " a state in Hindustan," as Lord Wellesley admitted four years later. " Géneral Perron," he recorded, " has obtained the exercise of sovereign authority over a territory whose annual revenues amount to near two millions sterling, and has negotiated treaties and alliances with several petty states in his own name."

When we consider what Perron was—a runaway sailor from a French frigate—and what he became—a person exercising sovereign authority over Hindustan—and this in spite of the active opposition of many enemies in the court he served, and Lord Wellesley's expressed intention of opposing him, we must allow him the full credit of an achievement as extraordinary as it was great.

It has been asserted that the Marquis Wellesley over-estimated Perron's power, and that the adventurer was not such a dangerous individual as the Governor-General found it convenient to make out. It was not the man but the principle that Lord Wellesley feared. He regarded Perron as the active representative of the French interest in India. It is known that Perron was in friendly communication with Raymond, and after that officer's death with his successor, Piron, at Haidarabad ; and also with the French faction in Mysore. The alliance of these three parties, which was solely prevented by Lord Wellesley's sagacity and statesmanship, would have threatened the English with a graver peril from French ambition than any actually experienced. When Piron's corps was broken up, and Tipu's French auxiliaries surrendered at Seringapatam half the danger of the situation was demolished. But there still remained sufficient to require the most eager vigilance and precaution ; and when Perron sought the countenance and help of Bonaparte, the final contest could no longer be safely delayed, nor the means taken to secure success too carefully guarded. The simultaneous and marvellously rapid victories of Generals Lake and Wellesley gave rise to an impression that the enemy they vanquished could not have been so formidable as the Governor-General asserted, and on these grounds he was publicly attacked by many persons, notably by Sir Philip Frances—one of those virtuous instruments of chastisement not altogether unknown in modern parliaments—and by the discredited historian James Mills. But their argument that because Perron's Brigades were so soon defeated and dispersed, therefore they could not have been as powerful as Lord Wellesley represented, was unjust to many. It was unjust to De Boigne's stubborn battalions, who displayed such heroic courage at Laswári and Assaye, and although deserted by their European officers fought with a valour that has never been equalled by any Native-led armies in India. It was unjust to Perron, for no one can deny that he kept his army up to its ancient standard of excellence— and indeed the rank and file who fought to the death were far more worthy of praise than the officers who left them before a shot was fired. It was unjust to General Lake and General Wellesley, since it belittled their achievements by suggesting that their victories were too cheaply won, when the very opposite was the case. And, lastly, it was unjust to the Governor-General, whose statesmanlike policy had weakened the effect of Perron's power by previously destroying those who would have been his allies in an international struggle between France and England for the possession of India.

As regards Perron himself, it is true that his influence was waning when the war broke out. He had passed his zenith, and his personal power was on the decline. At a defined period in his career this change became manifest, and it was due in a principal degree to his own faults and failings. Skinner describes the commencement of this moral decadence in 1801. " Perron now began to feel his power, and to change his manner. Instead of being, as formerly, a good, plain, honest soldier, beloved by his soldiery and esteemed by all about him, he began to turn his ears to flattery, and to neglect merit, while his favourites got all the good appointments, and he himself only thought of amassing money." No personal government could safely pursue such a course without risk : it was bound to end in danger and disaster. When once the controlling hand entrusted the reins to incompetent subordinates, and began to grope for gold, the whole fabric of administration was weakened. Lewis Ferdinand Smith confirms this. "Unfortunately for Perron," he writes, "every low Frenchman he advanced with outrage to others repaid his unjust preference with ingratitude. His army was a miniature of the French Revolution. Wretches were raised from cooks, bakers, and barbers to majors and colonels, and absurdly entrusted with the command of brigades. . . . I speak the calm language of impartiality. I have no personal dislike to Perron, nor have I received more injury from him than any other British subject who had the mortifying misfortune to resort to him for service. Every low Frenchman was put over us in rank.

This would not have been so unjust if they had superior, or even equal merit."

As regards Perron's final surrender, Smith judges it leniently. " I do not approve of Perron's principles, nor do I admire his character, but impartiality obliges me to declare that I do not think he wanted either sense, prudence, or principle in quitting Scindia's service when he did, and seeking protection to his person and property from the British Government. I condemn him for not advising Scindia to avoid hostilities."

De Boigne's opinion of Perron has been quoted in an earlier part of this sketch : he described him as " a man of plain sense, of no talent, but a brave soldier."

Such are the views of three of Perron's contemporaries. De Boigne's we may accept as reflecting truthfully Perron's character and disposition in the earlier part of his career, and before success had turned his head. With regard to Skinner's and Smith's opinions, even admitting the unavoidable prejudice that existed in their minds, there is no reason why we should hesitate to give weight to their judgment. Had Perron's resignation occurred just after he won the battle of Sounda, his name might have been handed down to posterity with De Boigne's. But, like many another great man, his meridian splendour was dimmed by the dark clouds that shrouded his decline.

"We must never forget that he is a Frenchman," wrote Lord Wellesley of Perron, in 1798. Assuredly we never can forget it, for he was a typical son of France, and displayed all the strength and all the weakness of the national character. How earnest he was in his patriotism it is difficult to estimate ; how much may be forgiven him on the plea of it is still more difficult to decide. " Remember you are a Frenchman, and let no action of yours tarnish the character of your nation" were Perron's own words to Pedron, when he exhorted him to hold the fort of Aligarh against the English. " Once more remember your nation," he reiterates ; and then with a true touch of Gallic vanity, " The eyes of millions are fixed upon you." If those were Perron's actual thoughts, how much more focussed, must he have considered, the eyes of France upon himself ? But the knowledge, however much it influenced his actions, did not make him strong, and within a week he was tendering in surrender the sword which he had never drawn from its sheath.

The severest condemnation of Perron comes from one of his own countrymen. " Perron," writes a French critic in 1822, " under the protection of the British Government, escaped the just vengeance of the Maráthás, Sikhs, Rajputs, and all the people of India. He has returned to France to exhibit before our eyes, as a trophy of his infamy, the diamonds and the millions he stole from the miserable Sindhia whom he betrayed. His infamous treachery was so odious to the Indians that his·name was long execrated by them. The conduct of this traitor assured to the English the supremacy of Hindustan, and has done more harm to the name of France than fifty years of misconduct and misfortune could have accomplished."

He died at his Château of Fresnes in 1834, in the seventy-ninth year of his age, and there he lies buried. And though it may seem strange, yet it is true, that Death, "Eloquent, Just, and Mighty," has denied to this famous Frenchman "those two narrow words, *Hic jacet.*" For Pierre Cuillier, the last representative of the French power in India, and who, for seven years, ruled in kingly state and with sovereign authority the fairest provinces of Hindustan, sleeps in an unmarked grave, above which posterity may not even read the name of *Perron.*

LIEUT.-COLONEL JAMES SKINNER

[From a plate in the " Military Memoir of Lieut.-Col. James Skinner, C.B."]

APPENDIX.

A MBROSE, R. L., MAJOR.—Major R. L. Ambrose was an English officer in Jaswant Ráo Holkar's service, of whom little or nothing is known, excepting that he was the author of an Indian tract entitled " A letter on the present crisis of affairs in India, addressed to Edward Parry, Chairman of the Honourable Court of Directors of the Honourable East India Company." The following extracts from the pamphlet are of interest, as touching on the subject of military adventure in India :—

" Holker detested—justly detested—the name of a Frenchman, when he reflected that by the Chevalier Dudernaigue and Monsieur Plumet, to whom in the first instance he entrusted the command of his brigades, he was deserted on the near approach of Scindia's army, and left with his infantry, deprived of officers, to the defeat which he experienced at Indore. So highly irritated was he that he never mentioned the country without signs of abhorrence, and it was his express orders to the commanders of brigades subsequently appointed, that on no account whatever should they afford employment to individuals of a nation by him entitled the *Duggerbáz*, or Faithless. . . .

" It is well known, to those conversant with the affairs of the East, that there are in that country many hundreds of thousands, soldiers by profession, who wander continually from service to service, from prince to prince, as the pressure of the moment requires their assistance and promises them employ. Gain is their god, and it is so perfectly immaterial to them whom they serve, while they are paid, and the *minutiæ* of their caste attended to, that an utter stranger, with efficient funds, might at any time raise an army in Hindustan, who would follow him and fight his battles as long as his resources were sufficient for the current expenses of the day. Born soldiers, without any other profession than that of arms, these men eagerly flock to the standard of any adventurer, however desperate his prospects, if he only possesses the *summum bonum* of their happiness. In the minds of these people no such sentiment as *amor patriæ* is to be found, above affection for a few clods of earth or stumps of trees, merely from their having been imprinted on their recollection from the sportive period of infancy. The Indian is, in this point, a citizen of the world. It not unfrequently happens that fathers, sons, and brothers embrace different services, and meet in battle array on the ensanguined plain against each other, perhaps unwittingly to fall by each other's hands."

ARMSTRONG, MAJOR.—Major Armstrong succeeded Major Plumet in the command of Holkar's Second Brigade of regular infantry in 1802, and distinguished himself at the battle of Poonah in the same year. On the breaking out of the war with the English in 1803, Armstrong determined to quit the chief. But he did not effect this without the greatest difficulty, and was obliged to sacrifice all his arrears and most of his property, barely saving his life by a secret flight. Had his intention been suspected he would assuredly have shared the cruel fate of Vickers, Dodd, and Ryan, whom Holkar barbarously put to death for refusing to fight against their own countrymen. Major Armstrong lived to enjoy a pension of Rs.1,200 a month from the British Government, as a compensation for his loss of employ.

BAOURS, MAJOR [orthography doubtful ; also written Bahors].— Major Baours was a Frenchman, and began his career in the Begum Somru's force, to the command of which he succeeded in 1783, after the murder of Pauly at Delhi. When De Boigne raised his first brigade Baours gladly left the Begum's employ to take the command of a battalion in Sindhia's service. His career was, however, soon cut short, for he was killed at the battle of Pátan in 1790.

BELLASIS, JOSEPH HARVEY, CAPTAIN.—This fine young adventurer was probably a cadet of a well-known Bombay family of the same name, one member of which rose to the command of the artillery in the Peshwa's service. Captain Bellasis was originally an ensign in the Honourable Company's Corps of Engineers, but was impelled by his pecuniary embarrassments to seek to retrieve his fortunes in the service of the Native princes, and in a rash moment resigned his commission, and penetrated into the Maráthá dominions. He had seen and heard of many adventurers who had reached the summit of ambition, power, and riches as soldiers of fortune in the interior of India, and who did not possess greater talents or stouter resolution than himself ; for he was a young man allowed by all to be an honour to his profession. His courage was undaunted, his integrity irreproachable, and his generosity unbounded. He had an excellent knowledge of military science, was elegant in person, and endowed with great activity of body and energy of mind, and was, moreover, an excellent scholar, conversant with Greek and Latin, and understanding music and painting. To these accomplishments he added a fascinating address and an open disposition. Such was the young English gentleman who in 1796 cut himself adrift from his fellow countrymen, and entered the service of the Marátha chief, Ambaji Inglia, for whom he raised four battalions of regular infantry. He soon found out the mistake he had made. Ambaji was " tainted with the worst principles of the worst Asiatic," and Bellasis lacked the powers of intrigue, the assiduity and the duplicity necessary to rise in such a service. Yet he tried hard to do his duty, and it is recorded that Ambaji's battalions would have been " as fine as any in Hindustan, if the parsimony of the chief had not rendered futile their commander's labour and genius." In 1797 Bellasis was engaged in the storm of Lohár, and in an assault of uncommon boldness his battalions suffered heavily. Notwithstanding this, he was ordered, immediately after the capture, to march his shattered and fatigued corps to storm another fort, named Gopálpur, fifteen miles distant, leaving his dead unburied, and his wounded unattended to. Such inhuman orders could only be justified by the most cruel necessity, and Bellasis, with the fine feelings of a soldier and the propriety of a commander, refused to obey them. This refusal, which was eagerly expected, was made the pretext for discharging him and his battalions, and plundering their effects. Two years later his distress and his necessities drove him once more into Ambaji's service, and he obtained the command of two battalions in James Shepherd's party. With these he took part in the siege of Sounda, and whilst gallantly leading his men on to victory was shot through the head in the assault on Lakwa Dáda's entrenchment.

BERNIER, AUGUSTINE, MAJOR [spelt Bunnear and Burnear by contemporary writers].—Major Bernier was a French adventurer, and began his Indian career in the service of the Begum Somru, and was one of the witnesses to that lady's marriage with Le Vassoult in 1793. Later on he commanded a battalion in Perron's Third Brigade, under Louis Bourguien. Bernier was a brave and able soldier, and Skinner states that at the battle of Georgegarh in 1801 he saved Bourguien from a disastrous defeat by his ability and courage. He was killed a few weeks later at the grand assault on the town of Hánsi—a fact which, it is curious to note, was brought to light so recently as November, 1891, for Skinner erroneously states that Bernier was killed in the attack on Thomas's outposts whilst rallying his men, who had been beaten back. A correspondent of a Lahór paper thus writes on the date above mentioned :—

" A marble tomb, in a broken condition, has been found by Mr. Stanley Skinner in his village of Rarsi, close by Hánsi, bearing an inscription to this effect : ' *To the memory of Augustine Bernier, late Major in the service of H.H. Dowlut Ráo Scindia. Killed in the storm of Hánsi, on 10th December*, 1801, *while gallantly leading on his troops. Aged 32 years.*' "

Bernier was a great favourite with his soldiery, by whom, as well as by his fellow officers, his death was deeply regretted.

BIRCH, LIEUTENANT.—Lieutenant Birch was originally an officer in George Thomas's army, in which he fairly distinguished himself. He proved faithful to his chief during the long and trying siege of George-garh, and accompanied him in his flight to Hánsi, which he helped to defend until Thomas was forced to capitulate. Birch then appears to have joined Perron's service, for he remained in Hindustan, and was one of the officers in Marátha employ who took advantage of Lord Wellesley's proclamation offering pensions to all British subjects who, on the declaration of the war, left the Maráthás and passed over to the English. Birch appears to have been awarded a pension of Rs.300 a month, and after the battle of Delhi, when General Lake left Colonel Ochterlony in command of the Capital, received the command of two Najib battalions raised to assist in holding the city. Soon afterwards they were detached against Bapú Sindhia, Daulat Ráo's governor in the Saharanpur district, but were shockingly beaten, and lost four of their guns—a catastrophe which so incensed Colonel Ochterlony that he refused to entrust any more of the Company's artillery to Sindhia's late officers, many of whom were now in the British service and in command of newly raised levies, recruited from the dispersed remnants of Perron's Brigades. Birch, after his defeat by Bapú, re-assembled his battalions, and was stationed on the Punjab frontier, where, in 1804, he assisted Skinner to defeat a large body of Sikhs.

BOYD, J. P., COLONEL.—Boyd was an American. When Raymond increased his corps at Haidarabad to such an extent as to make it too formidable, the British Government, as a counterpoise, suggested to the Nizam that he should raise two fresh corps, to be commanded by officers whose sympathies were with the English. Boyd, who owned a party described as " a ready formed and experienced corps of 1,800 men," was engaged, and in 1795 took part in the battle of Kardla. In the following year, when Raymond was at the height of his power, and it was rumoured that he premeditated an attack on the British Resident's camp, Boyd and Finglass (another English adventurer in command of a corps) at once paraded their troops, and signified their intention of supporting the Company's cause. The trouble, however, passed over, and they were not called upon to act. A few months later misunderstandings arose between Boyd and the Court of Haidarabad, fermented probably by Raymond, and the American quitted the service, taking his party with him. He was next engaged by the Peshwa of Poonah, who paid him a salary of Rs. 3,000 a month. In October, 1796, Boyd assisted in the operations which resulted in Baji Ráo being seated on the *masnad* as Peshwa, after the tragical death by suicide of Madhu Ráo. The next year he was raised to the command of the Peshwa's regular Brigade, and the last mention of him is in connection with some local disturbances which broke out at Poonah in 1797.

BOURGUIEN, LOUIS, COLONEL [spelt also Bourguienne, Bourquoin, Bourquin, and Bourkin].—This individual, who was known amongst the Natives as *Looee Sahib*, was a Frenchman, whose real name was Louis Bernard. He came to India in Admiral Suffrein's fleet, landing at Pondicherry, where he remained some time. He then made his way to Calcutta, and enlisted in a mercenary regiment of foreigners in the Company's service, known as Captain Doxat's Chasseurs. Upon the reduction of that force Bourguien turned his attention to civil pursuits, and for some time exercised the calling of a cook at Calcutta, his craft in culinary matters being superior to his skill in military ones. Later on he started business as a manufacturer of fireworks, and in this capacity accompanied a gentleman named Gairard, the proprietor of the Vauxhall Gardens at Calcutta, to Lucknow. He then returned to the military profession, and obtained an appointment in the Begum Somru's force, from which he entered that of De Boigne about the year 1794, when he is found rated as a lieutenant on a pay of Rs. 200 a month. No mention of his name appears again until August, 1800, when he joined the Rájah of Jaipur, with one of Perron's battalions, to assist against Lakwa Dáda. Soon after this he was detached to capture Ajmir, but the fort proved too strong to be taken, and he was defeated in December and obliged to fall back. He then invested the place, and on the 7th of May, 1801, secured its surrender by bribery. But meanwhile General Perron had become greatly dissatisfied with his conduct of the siege, and sent Captain Symes to supersede him.

Bourguien was so enraged at this that he offered his services to the Rájah of Jaipur, but Partáb Singh declined to accept them for fear of disobliging General Perron, by whom he had recently been reduced to a state of abject submission. So Bourguien swallowed his mortification, and retained his appointment in Sindhia's army. He seems to have been undeservedly fortunate, for in a few weeks he was promoted to the command of the Third Brigade, and in August entrusted with the conduct of the war against George Thomas. A full account of this campaign has been given in the sketch of Thomas's life. Although at the head of ten fine battalions of infantry and a large body of Hindustani horse, Bourguien was outwitted and outmanœuvred by Thomas, and finally defeated at the battle of Georgegarh. This led to his supersession for incapacity for the second time within the year, but after Pedron had retrieved affairs Bourguien was once again entrusted with the command of operations, and eventually forced Thomas to surrender at Hánsi. He was then detached with his brigade to collect tribute in the Sutlej states, and in November, 1802, we find him at Jind negotiating matters of considerable importance with Rájah Bágh Singh. He remained in the Sikh country till the middle of 1803, his last exploits being the capture of Rohtak, and the levying of a tribute of Rs.15,000 from the Karnal district. In June of this year, when war with the English was imminent, Perron ordered Bourguien to encamp at Pánipat, and shortly afterwards to march down and occupy Delhi. In August hostilities broke out, and simultaneously Ambaji Inglia was appointed to supersede Perron. Bourguien, although a "bosom friend" of the General —Skinner states they were relatives—was the first to revolt against him, and the chief instrument in effecting his downfall. The events leading up to the battle of Delhi, and Bourguien's brief tenure of power, have been fully recorded. He surrendered to General Lake shortly after the British victory, and was deported to Calcutta, from whence, in course of time, he found his way to Hamburg, and so to France. He retired with "an immense fortune," and there his history ends. "He was not only a coward, but a fool," was Skinner's brief commentary on him, and Smith describes him as being "as wicked as he was weak." He gained a certain reputation from the mere fact of his being in nominal command of the enemy at the battle of Delhi, but it was a totally spurious one, for he was the first to fly the field. With the exception of Sombre, and perhaps Michael and Fidèle Filoze, there is no more contemptible character amongst the military adventurers of Hindustan than Louis Bourguien, cook, pyrotechnist, and poltroon.

BROWNRIGG, MAJOR.—Major Brownrigg was known as *Burandee Sahib* amongst the natives, but there is no proof that this derogatory designation was anything but an unhappy corruption of his proper name. He was an Irishman by birth, and a very brave and able officer, much liked by his soldiery, and highly esteemed by Daulat Ráo Sindhia, for whom he raised an independent corps. He is first heard of in 1799, when he stormed and captured the fort of Kolapur, near Poonah. During the next year he was chiefly employed in opposing Pareshram Bháo, the Peshwa's commander-in-chief, during the political revolutions and disorders that prevailed in the Deccan. He then accompanied Sindhia to Malwa, and in July, 1801, made his famous defence against Jaswant Ráo Holkar, who, after defeating MacIntyre, attacked Brownrigg's entrenched camp near the Narbada. Brownrigg's force was vastly inferior in numbers, not exceeding four battalions, but his position was an exceedingly strong one, with the river in his rear, and his front and flanks intersected by ravines, which prevented Holkar's cavalry from acting. He was, moreover, well supplied with artillery, being accompanied by Sindhia's grand park. He defended his position with great judgment and intrepidity, and finally obliged Holkar to retreat, leaving two guns behind him. Three months after this Brownrigg assisted Sutherland in winning the notable battle of Indore, in which Holkar's entrenchments were stormed at the point of the bayonet, and all his guns taken. By this time Brownrigg had risen very high in Sindhia's favour, which made him an object of jealousy to Perron, who, when he came to Ujjain, in March, 1802, found means to encompass his disgrace, and Skinner mentions him as having been " put in arrest under fixed bayonets " for intriguing against the General. What became of Brownrigg's corps after this is not quite clear, but it is possible it was incorporated in Perron's army, for a few months later Brownrigg was at Koil, from whence, a little while before the breaking out of the war with the English, he was sent back to the Deccan in command of five battalions of the newly raised Fifth Brigade. Sindhia, however, soon ordered him back to reinforce Perron's army in Hindustan, and he reached Agra just after the battle of Delhi had been fought. Although Brownrigg's battalions were refused entry into the fort, he was permitted to join Hessing, Sutherland, and the other European officers residing there, and shared with them the confinement they were presently placed in by the revolted garrison. After the fall of Agra, Brownrigg entered the British service, obtained the command of some irregular levies, and was employed in the war against Jaswant Ráo Holkar. He fell in an unequal conflict before Sirsa, in the Hariána district, on the 19th of February, 1804, his troops being overpowered by superior numbers and defeated for want of good arms. It was the first repulse he had experienced in the course of twelve years of active and arduous service. He was an amiable man and a fine soldier, whose defeat of Holkar in 1801 was one of the most brilliant episodes of Marátha civil strife.

BUTTERFIELD, CAPTAIN.—Captain Butterfield was the son of an officer in the Honourable Company's service. He appears to have sought a career in the Native courts early in life, and before 1790 was employed by the Rájah of Karaoli, whom he quitted in order to enter the service of Thakúr Dúrjan Lál, a Rajput chief, from which he was tempted away by the superior inducements of Sindhia's army. It is probable that he joined De Boigne when the Second Brigade was raised, for in 1794 he had risen to the rank of a captain, though on a pay of only Rs. 200 a month. Some years later he was still a captain in the Second Brigade under Colonel Sutherland. When Lakwa Dáda joined the rebellion of the Bhais, Ambaji Inglia was ordered to attack him, and Butterfield, with two battalions and ten pieces of cannon, acted under the chief. Marching to Kotah they engaged the Bhais army at a place called Chand-khori, when Ambaji's irregular troops deserted, and the whole brunt of the attack fell upon Butterfield's two battalions. After fighting for two hours it became apparent that not only cowardice but treachery was rife in Ambaji's army, for some of his troops went over to Lakwa, in consequence of which Butterfield was forced to retire, and lost a great number of men before he could get to a place of safety. Eventually he made good his retreat to Shérgarh. For his conduct on this occasion he received a very flattering letter from Perron. No further mention of his services can be found.

DAWES, CAPTAIN.—Captain Dawes was an officer in Perron's First Brigade under Sutherland. Little is known of his career. In February, 1802, he was detached by Daulat Ráo Sindhia to pursue Holkar after his defeat at Indore. Dawes had only four battalions of regular infantry and six ragamuffin battalions belonging to Ambaji, and was unable to effect anything of importance, or stay Holkar's rapid predatory course, though he carried on a desultory campaign in Khandésh for some months, and won a few small skirmishes. When Holkar advanced against Poonah, Dawes was sent to oppose him. His army was utterly inadequate for the work, and inferior in every respect to Jaswant Ráo's, notwithstanding which he strongly urged

Sudáseo Bhao, the Marátha general, to force a battle. The defeat which followed is historical, and was the indirect cause of the war between the English and Sindhia in the following year. Dawes's battalions behaved with signal courage, fully sustaining their reputation, but they were completely overpowered. Of their four officers, three — Dawes, Catts, and Douglas — were killed, and one taken prisoner. The guns lost on this occasion were the first ever captured in action from any of De Boigne's battalions.

DERRIDON, LOUIS, MAJOR [spelt also Deridan, Derridoven, and Dareebdoon].—Major Derridon was a half-bred Frenchman and brother-in-law to General Perron, who married his sister. He was also related to Colonel John Hessing, probably in the same degree, for the Colonel's son, George Hessing, is described by Skinner as Perron's nephew. Major Derridon commanded a battalion in Hessing's corps, and was present at the battle of Ujjain, when Holkar defeated four of Sindhia's battalions, and killed nearly all their officers. In this action Derridon was wounded and taken prisoner, and Colonel John Hessing paid Rs. 40,000 to ransom him from Holkar, though Sindhia, according to ·a local paper published at the time, subsequently refunded the amount. Derridon then repaired to Hindustan, and when Perron discharged most of his English officers in 1802, received a high appointment in his army. He was at Agra when the fort was captured by General Lake in 1803. Lady Fanny Parkes, in her "Wanderings of a Pilgrim in Search of the Picturesque," incidentally mentions that this officer was living at Koil in 1838, "in a house formerly the property of General Perron." His grandsons were owners of the same property as late as 1871.

DODD, MAJOR.—Major Dodd was an Englishman, and succeeded Captain Gardner in the command of a brigade in Jaswant Ráo Holkar's service, which was composed of four battalions of infantry, 200 cavalry, and 20 guns. It is probable he took part in the battle of Poonah. He was one of the British officers beheaded by Holkar in 1804 for refusing to fight against their own countrymen.

DONELLY, CAPTAIN.—Captain Donelly was an Irishman, and commanded a battalion in Perron's Second Brigade, under Colonel Pohlman. All that is known of him is that he was killed at the storming of Shahpúra in 1799, when Pohlman was beaten back with a loss of a thousand men killed and wounded. Perron in a letter to De Boigne mentions the death of this officer, whom he refers to as "your *protegé*, Donelly."

DRUGEON, CAPTAIN.—Captain Drugeon was a Savoyard by birth, and a countryman of De Boigne. He was born at Hyenne, near Chambéry where his father resided in the château of Bergen. The circumstance of his brother having risen to the rank of a general in the Sardinian army seems to indicate that Captain Drugeon was a man of good family. In 1787 he was at Paris, and probably came out to India in the French service. He was one of De Boigne's oldest officers, and in May, 1794, was Brigade-Major of the Second Brigade, and drawing Rs. 400 a month pay. When Perron was transferred to the command of the First Brigade and sent to the Deccan, Drugeon accompanied him, and succeeded to his command in 1797, when he was promoted to De Boigne's vacated post. Drugeon saw some fighting at Poonah, but not of a very creditable kind. In June, 1798, after the Bhais had fled for protection to Amrat Ráo, that chief was induced by Sindhia to repair to Poonah for negotiation. But no sooner had he encamped on the out-skirts of the city than Ghatkay Ráo, Sindhia's father-in-law, made a treacherous attack upon him with two Brigades of infantry under Drugeon's command. Opening fire from twenty-five guns upon Amrat Ráo's unsuspecting troops, he speedily threw them into confusion, and then charging with the infantry put them to flight and plundered their camp. Soon after this Drugeon appears to have fallen into some grave trouble, for a local paper records that he was deposed by his own officers, and, under orders from Perron, superseded by Colonel Duprat. He attributed his disgrace to the machinations of his enemies. In 1800, partly at the request of De Boigne, who appears to have retained a regard for him, he was restored to Perron's favour, and appointed to the commandantship of the fort at Delhi, and ten months later to the charge of the Emperor's person, on a salary of Rs. 800 a month. About this time he wrote an interesting letter to De Boigne, from which many of the following particulars are gleaned. He mentioned he had saved Rs. 30,000, which he had invested in the Company's Funds, and hoped to be able to pay for his passage to Europe without trespassing on this capital, which would constitute a sufficient provision for his old age. He deplored De Boigne's departure, declaring that his presence was necessary to re-establish Sindhia's fortunes on a sound basis, and that his return would be hailed like that of a Messiah, "in such veneration and adoration are you held, especially by the troops, who invoke your name only in their songs." As for Perron, Drugeon describes him as "like the King of Prussia for power, and like a Crœsus as regards riches, which fall on him night and day like the most abundant rain, in the form of rupees. He is courted by all the rájahs and chiefs of the country and also by Sindhia, who is afraid of him. You have made the soup, which he has only the trouble of supping." His own misfortunes, Drugeon goes on to state, had been very heavy. "If my jealous enemies," he protests, "had not done me an ill turn with Perron, I would have been a rich man to-day. I try to forget them—for what can I do? God Almighty cannot undo what has already been done." Such is his philosophical reflection, but doubtless he found a balm to his wounded spirit in the fact that the Emperor's person, his correspondence, and all his household were entrusted to his care. After detailing some local news, which has been incorporated in the sketch of Perron's life, Drugeon goes on to say: "I very much desire to return to Europe, but I am hindered from doing so by an entanglement with a lady of the country, whom I love very much, and whom I have taken up with to assist me to forget my past cares. As to taking her with me, can I do so? I do not at all wish to desert her. Kindly give me your advice. She is a niece to the Nawáb Súliman Khán, and a widow, seventeen years old, and is incessantly telling me she would rather die than leave me. I am speaking to you as a confessor, and I await your answer before deciding anything."

Drugeon remained at Delhi till the breaking out of the war with the English, and is constantly referred to in the Persian newspapers of the period. Much of the information concerning Perron's movements recorded in the life of that adventurer has been gleaned from the published reports which Drugeon made to the Emperor. In August, 1803, when Bourguien revolted against Perron, and stirred up a mutiny in the Second and Third Brigades, Drugeon resisted him, and after refusing to surrender the treasure he had charge of, turned him out of the fort, which he prepared to defend with the 5,000 men forming its regular garrison. After the capture of Delhi by the British, Drugeon, who seems to have stuck to the treasure, attempted to "deposit it" with the Emperor, but the transaction was regarded by General Lake as a "fraudulent transfer," and it was distributed as prize money to the troops. Drugeon was deported to Calcutta, and eventually found his way to Europe, and died at Nice in 1824.

DUDRENEC, THE CHEVALIER [written also Du Drenec, Du Dernaig, Duderneg, Du Dernec, Dodernaigue, Dudernaigue, and Dudernek. Known to the natives as *Hazur Beg*].—Had the history of the Chevalier Dudrenec been properly recorded, it would without doubt have afforded as interesting a career of romance and adventure as any in these pages. The following fragmentary particulars have been pieced together from a great variety of sources, and even in their skeleton form suggest a remarkably eventful life. Dudrenec was a native of Brest, in France, and a gentleman of refinement, education, and agreeable manners. He came of a good family, his father being a commodore in the French navy. The Chevalier arrived in India about the year 1773, as a midshipman on board a French man-of-war. Leaving his ship, he made his way to Delhi, where he obtained employment in Madoc's corps in 1780, two of his fellow officers being the Count de Moidavre and the Chevalier Cressy. With Madoc's party he served in turns the Rájahs of Bhartpur and Gohad, and Najaf Kuli Khán, the Wazír of the Emperor Shah 'Alam. About the year 1782 Madoc retired, and Drudenec entered the service of the Begum Somru, whose force was at this time commanded by Pauly. With this lady he remained till 1791, a little previous to which he obtained the command of her troops. But he resigned the appointment to enter the service of Tukaji Holkar, who offered him Rs. 3,000 a month to raise and discipline a brigade of four battalions of regular infantry. In the following year this force suffered an annihilating defeat from De Boigne, at the battle of Lakhairi, when all its guns were captured, and its ranks broken and dispersed. Dudrenec only saved his life by throwing himself down amongst the dead, and simulating death. But his battalions had shown such stubborn fighting powers before they were destroyed, that Tukaji Holkar listened to their commander's representations and consented to raise another brigade, advancing Dudrenec a large sum for this purpose. The new force was enlisted in 1793, and two years later took part in the battle of Kardla, being associated with Perron's battalions and sharing with them the honour of a somewhat easy and bloodless victory. From the seat of war they returned to Indore, where they reposed in peace for three or four years, and by 1797 their strength had increased to six battalions. On the death of Tukaji Holkar, Dudrenec was much puzzled whether to cast in his lot with the imbecile but rightful heir, Kasi Ráo, or with the dashing but illegitimate Jaswant Ráo. He declared for the former, and for a time carried on a campaign against Jaswant Ráo, whom he at first defeated, but at whose hands he sustained a serious reverse in 1798. After this Amir Khán, Holkar's brilliant ally and *fidus achates*, found means to tamper with Dudrenec's troops, and by offering them increased pay gained over a great number, and created a mutiny amongst the rest, when they were encamped at Mahéshwar. The Pathán chief, galled at a defeat received at the hands of the Chevalier, had vowed not to wear a turban till he had reduced Dudrenec. This came to the knowledge of the latter when he was at Mahéshwar, in great straits for want of provisions, and he sent a vakil to Amir Khán offering to come to terms with Jaswant Ráo. The Amir reported the overture to Holkar, who, with characteristic perfidy, proposed to allure the Frenchman to an interview and then assassinate him. But the Pathán, though not a man of many scruples, could not bring himself to consent to this, and, after some persuasion, extracted a promise of honourable terms for the Frenchman. Armed with this authority, he proceeded to Jámghát, near Mahéshwar, to receive the Chevalier's surrender. Dudrenec met him some distance out from his camp, gave him a salute with all honours, and invited him to his tent, where he first desired him to be seated, and then pointing to the silk handkerchief Amir Khán wore in lieu of a turban, took off his own head covering, and, with joined hands, said: "As your vow prevents you from wearing a turban till you have conquered me, see, the object is accomplished! Bareheaded I lay my head's covering before you, and acknowledge my defeat. Nay, if you wish to make me your prisoner, here is my sword. I surrender it, and you may take me to your camp." This, being conformable with the European custom, pleased Amir Khán very much, and he expressed himself fully satisfied with the speech. The Chevalier then gave the Amir his own turban, and put on the silk handkerchief the Pathán was wearing, after which he escorted him to Mahéshwar. Having transferred to him all his jewels, stores, and treasures, he accompanied him to the Marátha camp, to be presented to Jaswant Ráo. In consequence of the protection extended by Amir Khán, Holkar dared not harm Dudrenec, but he still designed evil against him in his heart. "Whereupon," to take up the thread of the narrative from the pages of a Native historian, "it happened that on that very night the Maharajah was sitting on the bank of the Narbada river, amusing himself with firing at a mark, when the matchlock burst and inflicted a severe wound in the eye, by which he entirely lost the sight of it. Of a truth He that knows all things, secret and divulged, is not to be deceived! In the twinkling of an eye, upon the eye of the Maharajah fell this just retribution for the treacherous designs he meditated against *Hazur Beg*." In the end Holkar accepted Dudrenec's submission, and restoring him to the command of his brigade, sent him, in 1798, to occupy and administer the districts of Tonk and Rampúra, where he remained two years.

In 1800, when Lakwa Dáda was restored to favour by Sindhia, he appears to have obtained Dudrenec's assistance for the subjugation of Jaipur, in which Holkar was probably interested. On the 12th of March of that year the Chevalier effected a junction with Perron's second brigade, commanded by Pohlman, and shortly afterwards was engaged with his corps at the battle of Malpura. A spirited account of the charge of the Ráthor cavalry, which destroyed 500 of his force, exists in the pages of Skinner's memoirs, and has been already quoted in the sketch of Perron's life.

In August of the following year Dudrenec, having made up his mind to leave Holkar, showed an inclination to follow the fortunes of Lackwa Dáda, who had been again disgraced and deposed from office by Sindhia, but he eventually decided on joining Perron's service, being invited to do so by the General himself, who offered him the post of second in command, *vice* Sutherland dismissed, and a brigade. Dudrenec was at this time at Rampúra, where he always kept his family and property under the protection of Zalim Singh. He had the greatest difficulty in escaping, for his troops, who refused to follow his fortunes, pelted him out of camp, and then, at the instigation of a Native named Shamrao Nadik, surrounded his house, with the intention of putting him to death. He was saved by the intervention of Zalim Singh, the regent of the ruler of the territory. Jaswant Ráo, on hearing of this, demanded his surrender from the old Rajput, but the latter refused to perpetrate such an act of treachery, and in the end a small sum of money was paid by Dudrenec to Holkar, by way of compensation, and he was permitted to depart to Hindustan with all his money and belongings.

On arriving at Koil Dudrenec entered Perron's army, and early in 1803 was given the command of the Fourth Brigade. In February of the same year he marched to the Deccan to reinforce Sindhia, but just before the breaking out of the war with the English he was sent back to Hindustan, and left Daulat Ráo's camp at Jalgáon on the 18th of July. About this time Ambaji Inglia was appointed to supersede Perron in the command of the Brigades, and Dudrenec exhibited more attachment to the Native than to the European Commander-in-chief —a desertion which stung Perron acutely. On his way to Delhi Dudrenec received information of Bourguien's defeat, and seeing little prospect of ultimate success, abandoned his command, and on the 30th of November surrendered to Colonel Vandaleur at Mattra. Thus ended a career full of adventure, incident, and peril. The Chevalier seems to have been a singularly unfortunate commander, for he suffered several disastrous defeats. His faithlessness had such an effect on Jaswant Ráo Holkar, that he withdrew all countenance from any whose nationality was French, and after the Chevalier's defection gave orders that no adventurer of his nation should be allowed to enter his service. As will be seen by this slight sketch (in which, it is to be feared, there are many inaccuracies due to an attempt to reconcile divergent statements and dates), Dudrenec served no less than seven different masters during the period of his Indian career. It is difficult to see how he deserves the many encomiums that have been passed on him by various writers, for there is no record of his having won any substantial victory. His surrender to Amir Khán was singularly spiritless, and his notions of loyalty were decidedly questionable.

DUPONT, JOHN JAMES, MAJOR. — Major Dupont was a native of Holland, and an officer in Filoze's corps. After the suicide of Fidèle Filoze he succeeded to the command of four of the battalions and was with Sindhia when war with the English broke out. His force took part in the battle of Assaye, where they shared in the defeat and dispersion of Daulat Ráo's army. According to one account Dupont was engaged in the battle of Ujjain in 1801, where he was wounded and made prisoner with Derridon and Humphertson.

DUPRAT, COLONEL.—Colonel Duprat was a Frenchman and an officer in Perron's army. He succeeded Drugeon in the command of the First Brigade at Poonah in 1798, but only held the post for a year, being relieved by Colonel Sutherland. He was in command of five battalions of infantry which attempted to surprise the camp of Amrat Ráo, the Peshwa's brother, after the Bhais had fled to him for protection. This occurred on the night of the 7th of June, 1798. He failed in the attempt, and being briskly attacked in return, was compelled to draw off, and it was not without considerable loss that he made good his retreat. In the negotiations which followed the affair Amrat Ráo was prevailed on to come to Poonah, when Drugeon treacherously attacked and defeated him. Duprat's name does not appear in any subsequent records.

EVANS, CAPTAIN [also spelt Evens].—Very little information is available concerning this officer. He appears to have commanded the Begum Somru's party after Baours left it in 1789. He then entered De Boigne's service and rose to the rank of captain on a pay of Rs. 400 *per mensem*. Skinner mentions an officer of this name as having been taken prisoner with Colonel W. H. Tone at the storm of Sounda, and from another passage it is made apparent that he passed into Holkar's service. When war broke out with the English in 1803 a Captain Evens availed himself of Lord Wellesley's proclamation and "came in," receiving a pension equal to the pay he drew in the service of the state he was serving. But it is difficult to believe that an officer who commanded Somru's party so far back as 1789 was only a captain in 1803, and there may have been two adventurers of the same, or similar, names.

FILOZE, FIDÈLE, COLONEL [also spelt Filose, Felose, and Feloze].
—Fidèle Filoze was the son of Michael Filoze by a Native woman. When his father found it prudent to hastily resign Sindhia's service and leave Poonah, the command of his eleven battalions was divided between his two sons Fidèle and Jean Baptiste Filoze. Fidèle, however, retained eight of these with him in the Deccan and sent three only to his brother who was at Delhi. The first mention of Fidèle is in 1798, when he and George Hessing were directed by Sindhia to arrest Ghatkay Ráo, whose gross misconduct and contempt for the prince's authority had become intolerable, and this task they effected with great dexterity. Soon after this Fidèle succeeded to the command of his father's battalions. In 1801 he accompanied Daulat Ráo to Malwa, and on reaching the Narbada one of his battalions was detached under Colonel George Hessing to protect Ujjain, and a second shortly followed under Captain MacIntyre. Both were defeated and dispersed, the former at Ujjain, the latter at Núrí. The remaining six battalions took part in the battle of Indore in October of the same year, and directly afterwards Fidèle was accused of a foul act of treachery, in having fired into Sutherland's troops as they advanced. It was asserted he had entered into a secret understanding with Holkar, and on these grounds he was seized and confined. According to one account he cut his throat in prison, in order to avoid the disgrace of condign punishment, but another states that the act was done in a fit of delirium following fever. Smith, though admitting his treason, somewhat unaccountably describes him as " on the whole a good, ignorant man," but he has been depicted in a much less favourable light by others, and Drugeon condemns him as a traitor who worked to ruin a master who had loaded him with favours. This is probably the more correct estimate of his character.

FILOZE, JEAN BAPTISTE DE LA FONTAINE, COLONEL [known to the Natives as Ján Batteejis].—Baptiste Filoze, as this individual is always called, was the younger son of Michael Filoze. When his father fled the country Baptiste was at Delhi, where his brother Fidèle sent him three of the eleven battalions they had inherited, and to these Baptiste added three more which he raised in Hindustan. This force assisted in the war against George Thomas in 1801, but was in a sorry state of discipline, and extremely insubordinate, the three original battalions being on one occasion expelled from Delhi by the

Emperor Shah 'Alam's orders on account of their atrocious conduct. This appears to be the single recorded instance of that king of kings having voluntarily promulgated a decree which was carried into effect, and both the order and its prompt execution seem to indicate that Baptiste's battalions were a public nuisance. After the fall of Georgegarh Baptiste—who, according to Thomas's memoirs, carried on a traitorous correspondence with him—returned to Delhi, and Smith says that Perron procured the transfer of these six battalions to his command by intrigue, and that they formed the foundation of the Fourth Brigade. This was probably the case, for in 1802 Baptiste proceeded to Ujjain to take over the command of the Deccan battalions left vacant by the suicide of his brother Fidèle. When war broke out with the English his force consisted of eight battalions of infantry, 500 cavalry, and 45 guns. Four of these were beaten and dispersed at Assaye under Dupont, and Baptiste, with the remaining four, escaped a similar fate by the circumstance of his having been left to guard Ujjain. When he heard of Sindhia's crushing defeat, he saved himself by hurrying off to Rajputana, but rejoined the prince on the conclusion of the war, and remained in his service for many years afterwards, being the single military adventurer of Hindustan who survived the disasters of 1803. People of his name, and probably his descendants, are to this day employed in the court of Sindhia, and Sir Michael Filoze is a highly respectable architect at Gwalior. In Broughton's " Mahratta Camp " there are several references to Baptiste Filoze, whose circumstances in 1809 were far from happy, for serious disturbances were constantly occurring in his corps, which was seldom out of a state of regular mutiny, owing to the men being in arrears of pay, and the tyrannical treatment they experienced from Baptiste. On one occasion he was removed from the command, after he and his European officers had been seized and confined, some being flogged, while others, with a refinement of cruelty, had their ears nipped in gunlocks, after which they were all expelled from the lines. They numbered forty, chiefly half-castes, but two or three were Englishmen. A little later on Baptiste was reinstated, through the interest of friends at court, who described him as " one of the greatest generals of the day " ; which elicited the shrewd comment from Sindhia " that he had generally found these very great generals were also very great rogues." However, Baptiste obtained his reappointment, and evidently prospered, as the following extract from Colonel Sleeman's " Rambles of an Indian Official " testifies :—

"After the Dusera festival in November every year, the Pindaris go ' Kingdom taking ' as regularly as English gentlemen go partridge shooting on the 1st of September. I may give as a specimen the excursion of Jean Baptiste Filoze, who sallied forth on such an expedition at the head of a division of Scindia's army just before the Pindari War. From Gwalior he proceeded to Kerowlee, and took from the chief of that territory the district of Sùbughur, yielding four lakhs annually. He then took the territory of the Rájah of Chundeylee, one of the oldest of the Bundlecund chiefs, which yielded about seven lakhs of rupees. The Rájah got an allowance of Rs. 40,000 a year. He then took the territories of the Rájahs of Ragooghur and Bahadhurghur, yielding three lakhs a year, and the three princes got Rs. 50,000 a year for subsistence amongst them. He then took Lopar, yielding two lakhs and a half, and assigned the Rajah Rs. 25,000. He then took Gurha Kotlah whose chief gets subsistence from the British Government. Baptiste had just completed his Kingdom taking when our armies took the field against the Pindaris, and on the termination of the war in 1817 all these acquisitions were confirmed and guaranteed to Scindia." Writing in 1833 Colonel Sleeman adds : "The present Gwalior force consists of three regiments of infantry under Colonel Alexander, six under Apajee, eleven under Colonel Jacob (Broughton mentions them as excellently disciplined in 1807, their commander enjoying a *Jaidad* and paying them regularly), and five under Colonel Jean Baptiste Filoze."

Baptiste remained at Gwalior till the breaking out of hostilities between the ruling Sindhia and the English in 1843. He was then commander-in-chief of the State army, which consisted of 30,000 regular troops and the famous park of artillery which had remained with it since the days of De Boigne. Just before the battles of Maharajapúr and Panniár, Baptiste arranged that he should be locked up by his own men so as to avoid fighting the English. The reason of this was that he had £40,000 invested in Company's paper. With the exception of two, all the other officers of his army withdrew from the contest, knowing the hopelessness of success. The war was begun and concluded with these two battles, both fought on the same day, and after it Baptiste and his officers were removed from their commands and employment of every kind.

Thus Baptiste's career is traced for forty-seven years in the service of Sindhia—a record no other military adventurer can boast of.

FILOZE, MICHAEL, COLONEL. — Michael Filoze was a low-bred Neapolitan of worthless character, yet not without a certain address and cunning that enabled him to advance his interests. In his native country he had followed the calling of a muleteer, before he enlisted in the French army and came out to Madras, from whence, after several vicissitudes, he made his way to Delhi, and enlisted in the Rana of Gohad's service, in the corps commanded by Madoc. De la Fontaine, a Frenchman, was a fellow officer, and it was evidently after him that Michael named his son Baptiste, who was born at Gohad in 1773. In 1782, when the Rana was defeated by Sindhia and his battalion broken up, Michael Filoze lost his employment, and it has been stated that during the next eight years he served one of the Native states of Southern India. But if so, he evidently returned to Hindustan, for about the year 1790 he found means to recommend himself to De Boigne, who appointed him to the command of a battalion in his First Brigade. It was some time before he rose to any substantial rank, for in May, 1794, he was only rated at a pay of Rs. 300 per month. In the previous year he had been selected to accompany Madhoji Sindhia to the Deccan, and later on he successfully intrigued to get his battalion made into a separate command, independent of De Boigne's. It formed the nucleus of the corps he raised, which eventually numbered eleven battalions. In 1797 Michael Filoze found it prudent to fly from Poonah, under the following circumstances. Nana Farnavis, the Peshwa's prime minister, and the most able statesman in Marátha history, was induced to return a formal visit of ceremony paid him a few days previously by Daulat Ráo Sindhia, of whom he was suspicious and distrustful. But Michael Filoze pledged his word of honour for the safety of the old minister, and so overcame his scruples; notwithstanding which the Neapolitan seized Nana and made him over a prisoner to Sindhia. This perfidious act excited the just indignation of all the European officers in the service of the Native states, whose general character was impugned by it, and who, in Grant Duff's words, " though mere soldiers of fortune, were as distinguished for good faith as daring enterprise." The Maráthás themselves excused Michael's treachery, saying that he was ignorant of what was intended, and ascribing it to sudden coercion by Ghatkay Ráo. It should further be mentioned that in a letter to a current newspaper Michael Filoze strenuously denied his guilt. The Nana was too powerful a personage to be kept a prisoner long; for a time he was confined in the fort of Ahmednagar, but in the following year he obtained his liberty by a payment of ten lakhs of rupees. Directly Filoze heard he was treating for his liberty, and likely to obtain it, he decamped to Bombay, leaving the command of his eleven battalions to his sons. Drugeon, who brands Michael Filoze as a traitor, mentions that he set out for Europe, " but died "—whether on the voyage or after his arrival there is not specified. Grant Duff confirms Drugeon's estimate of this adventurer's character, as does Smith, who describes Filoze's party as one that " never performed any action of military or political consequence."

FINGLASS, CAPTAIN.—This officer was an Englishman, and formerly a quarter-master in the 19th Dragoons, where he bore a good character. He and Colonel Boyd, at the head of two independent parties, were introduced into the service of the Nizam of Haidarabad as a counterpoise to Raymond's overgrown power. In the year 1795 Finglass's corps numbered about 800 men, and took part in the battle of Kardla, where it shared in the defeat the Nizam brought upon himself by his pusillanimity. After this it was increased, and in 1798 numbered 6,000 men. Early in this year Raymond died, and was succeeded by Piron in the command of the " French army " of 14,000, which was disbanded in the following October by Lieutenant-Colonel Roberts, under orders from the Governor-General. With the dispersion of these troops, and the cessation of the danger they threatened, it became a question whether or not Finglass should be allowed to retain his corps. In the end Lord Wellesley sanctioned its continuance, and, furthermore, permitted Finglass from time to time to purchase ordnance, ordnance stores, and muskets at Fort St. George. It is possible that the Haidarabad reformed troops, now in the service of the Nizam, can carry their traditions back to the days of Captain Finglass.

FLEUREA, CAPTAIN [also written Fleury].—Captain Fleurea was a Frenchman and a cavalry officer in Perron's army. After the battle of Koil in 1803, when Perron precipitately fled to Agra, he detached Fleurea, with 5,000 Hindustani horse, to carry fire and sword into the Company's district of Cawnpore. Fleurea came across a small British outpost at Shikóabad, commanded by Colonel Coningham, and after four days' fighting forced it to surrender. It was not a very brilliant performance, but still the single advantage gained by any of Perron's troops during the war. On hearing of the fall of Aligarh, Fleurea's troopers carried him back to Agra, from whence he made his escape with great difficulty after Perron's flight, joining the General at Lucknow, and accompanying him to Calcutta.

FRÉMONT, COLONEL [spelt also Frimont and Fremond].—Colonel Frèmont was a Royalist and commander of the French forces at

Chandernagore. But he quitted the service, as did most of the other officers in 1790, on the breaking out of the French Revolution. Proceeding up country, he applied to De Boigne for employment, and was appointed to the command of one of the two original battalions, and, when the Second Brigade was formed, promoted to the head of the First with a salary of Rs. 1,400 a month. In 1792 he distinguished himself at the storm of Balahiri, a hill fort forty-five miles east of Jaipur, on which occasion Captain Bulkeley was killed. An interesting account of this campaign appears in *The World* (a newspaper printed at Calcutta), in the following letter, dated from a place called " Ringhass," on August 6 and 10, 1792 :—

"We arrived at this place on the 5th, our force consisting of the Second Brigade and 15,000 regular Mahratta horse, but excluding irregulars. This is a stone fort, upon a scientific plan of construction, surrounded by a ditch thirty feet deep, twenty-four feet wide, and capable of defence with such men and discipline as ours. It belonged to the Rájah Deby Sing, a tributary to the Jeypore Rájah, to whom he has refused the established tribute, amounting to two lakhs and a half, offering only a small portion. We arrived early, and after summoning the place to that effect, at nine o'clock we opened our trenches, and kept up a severe fire on the place till ten o'clock, by which time we had effected a capital breach between one of the bastions and a head of the curtain. The garrison had but few guns, with which, and musketry, they contrived to annoy us heartily. We opened two mortars after dark, which created, as was intended, dreadful confusion among them.

" Captain Chambaud's battalion and a select body of Rohillas were ordered for the storm in two divisions, with orders *not to spare the sword*. The time, three in the morning. However, the order had reached the garrison, and by a capitulation at half-past two they saved the lives of the remaining people. Deby Sing had quitted the fort previously, leaving injunctions to his officers not to surrender on any terms. The garrison are all prisoners now with us, and the stock of provisions and stores is valuable to us. The valuable property was carried off to the Rájah ; however, what was left more than pays the amount offered.

" Deby Sing has another strong fort, called Sikker, about eight *cos* distant, where he has resolved to hold out, and we are determined to bring him to implicit obedience or bondage. He has a chosen force, a strong fort, good guns, and three months' provisions, and the country around is without water."

Frèmont brought this expedition to a successful conclusion. The next mention of him is two years later, at Datía, whither he was sent to punish the Rájah. The following account of this campaign is extracted from the " Asiatic Researches." " Gopal Ráo Bhow marched against Dutieya (in 1794) to compel payment of tribute and exact a fine. He was opposed. An engagement ensued, in which the Dutíeya troops charged, sword in hand, the veteran battalions of De Boigne, which were commanded by Major Frèmont, an officer of ability and experience. The Bundélhas showed no fear of the musket and bayonet, and there were several instances of grenadiers cut down, while their bayonets were buried in the breast of their assailants' horse. The Brigade lost 300 men in the attack, and Major Frimont himself assured me that nothing but a continual discharge of grape from the guns prevented it from utter destruction." In another account the victory is attributed to the judicious disposition of Frè-mont's artillery, and the gallantry of his men in some severe close fighting, in which they routed the enemy with considerable slaughter.

In 1795 or 1796 Frèmont died, and this left Perron the senior officer in the force, and paved the way for his promotion to the chief command.

GARDNER, WILLIAM LINAEUS, COLONEL. — In its social aspect Colonel Gardner's life is the most romantic of any recorded in these pages. Born in 1770, he was a great grandson of William Gardner, of Colleraine, and a nephew of Alan, first Baron Gardner, a distin-guished admiral in the British navy, who received the thanks of Parliament for his services. Colonel Gardner was educated in France, and came out to India in the King's service, and after rising to the rank of captain quitted it to enlist under the banners of the Native princes. There was a Scotch officer of the same name who entered Sindhia's service in 1792, was Brigade-Major of the First Brigade in 1793, commanded the Second Brigade in 1794, and was at the storm and capture of Sohawalgarh in 1795, where he was assisted by George Thomas. But as his Christian name is given as James in one place it is doubtful whether he was the same individual as the officer under notice. Colonel William Gardner entered Jaswant Ráo Holkar's service in 1798, and raised a brigade of regular infantry for that chief. But a disagreement arose between them, and Gardner left him. The story of his escape is thus told by himself:—

"One evening, when in Holkar's service, I was employed as an envoy to the Company's forces, with instructions to return within a certain time. My family remained in camp. Suspicion of treachery was caused by my lengthened absence, and accusations were brought forth against me at the durbar held by Holkar on the third day follow ing that on which my presence was expected. I rejoined the camp while the durbar was in progress. On my entrance the Maharajah, in an angry tone, demanded the reason of my delay, which I gave, pointing out the impossibility of a speedier return. Whereupon Holkar exclaimed, in great anger, ' Had you not returned this day I would have levelled the *khanáts* of your tent.' I drew my sword instantly and endeavoured to cut His Highness down, but was prevented by those around him; and before they had recovered from the amazement and confusion caused by the attempt, I rushed from the camp, sprang upon my horse, and was soon beyond the reach of recall.''

To account for Colonel Gardner's indignation it must be explained that he was married to a Native lady, and that the *khanáts*, or canvas walls of his tent, represented the privacy of the *zenána*, and to have cut them down implied the exposure of the inmates, an insult for which there could be no atonement. Through the influence of friends Colonel Gardner's wife and family were allowed to join him shortly afterwards—a piece of generosity hardly to be expected from such a character as Jaswant Ráo Holkar.

The story of Colonel Gardner's marriage, as related by himself to Lady Fanny Parkes, is one of romantic interest. He was married by Muhammadan rites to a princess of the house of Cambay, a state on the western seaboard of India, and probably when he was an officer in the British service. This is his description of the incidents leading to the union :—

" When a young man I was entrusted to negotiate a treaty with one of the Native princes of Cambay. Durbars and consultations were continually held. During one of the former, at which I was present, a curtain near me was gently pulled aside, and I saw, as I thought, the most beautiful black eyes in the world. It was impossible to think of the treaty: those bright and piercing glances, those beautiful dark eyes completely bewildered me.

" I felt flattered that a creature so lovely as she of those deep black, loving eyes should venture to gaze upon me. To what danger might not the veiled beauty be exposed should the movement of the *purdah* be seen by any of those present at the durbar? On quitting the assembly I discovered that the bright-eyed beauty was the daughter of the prince. At the next durbar my agitation and anxiety were extreme to again behold the bright eyes that haunted my dreams and my thoughts by day. The curtain was again gently waved, and my fate was decided.

" I demanded the princess in marriage. Her relations were at first indignant, and positively refused my proposal. However, on mature deliberation, the ambassador was considered too influential a person to have a request denied, and the hand of the young princess was promised. The preparations for the marriage were carried forward. ' Remember,' said I, ' it will be useless to attempt to deceive me. I shall know those eyes again, nor will I marry any other ! '

" On the day of the marriage I raised the veil from the countenance of the bride, and in the mirror that was placed between us, in accordance with the Mahomedan wedding ceremony, I beheld the bright eyes that had bewildered me. I smiled. The young Begum smiled too."

This young princess was only thirteen years old when she was married : " An event," says Colonel Gardner, " which probably saved both our lives." She was eventually adopted as a. daughter by Akbar Shah, who succeeded Shah 'Alam as Emperor of Delhi. For over forty years husband and wife lived a life of perfect happiness, and she died of a broken heart in August, 1835, six months after Colonel Gardner.

Subsequently to his departure from Holkar's service Colonel Gardner had another very narrow escape for his life. In 1803 he was confined a prisoner by Amrát Ráo, who, when war broke out with the English, caused Gardner to be fastened to a gun, and threatened with immediate execution if he refused to take the field against his fellow countrymen. The Colonel remained staunch, and in the hope of wearying him out, his execution was suspended, and he was placed in charge of a guard, who had orders never to quit sight of him for a single instant. Walking one day along the edge of a steep cliff, which led by a precipitous descent to the river Tapti, Gardner was suddenly inspired to make a daring dash for liberty, and perceiving a place fitted for his purpose, he called out " Bismillah ! " (" In the name of God "), and flung himself down a declivity some forty or fifty feet deep. None were inclined to follow him, but an alarm was sounded. Recovering his feet, he made for the river, and plunged into it ; but after swimming for some distance he found pursuers were gaining on him, and sought shelter in a friendly covert, where, with merely his mouth above water, he waited until they had passed. He then landed on the opposite side, and proceeded by unfrequented paths to a town in the neighbourhood, which was under the command of a Native whom he knew, and who afforded him protection. After remaining in hiding for some time, he ventured out in the disguise of a grass cutter, and reached the British outposts in safety.

At one time it would appear, from a passage in Major Thorn's "War in India," that Colonel Gardner was in the service of the Rájah of Jaipur ; but in 1804 he returned to his allegiance to the British Government and raised a famous cavalry corps known as " Gardner's Horse," which achieved a great reputation. His best services, both in the field and in diplomacy, were performed under the King's flag. He had a profound knowledge of the native character, and had adopted many of the ideas and opinions of the people with whom he passed a great portion of his life. But this did not prevent him from being an acceptable companion to his own countrymen, with whom he was always a great favourite. Lewis Ferdinand Smith describes him as " a gentleman and a soldier of pleasing address and uncommon abilities." His figure was tall and commanding, and his handsome countenance and military air rendered his appearance very striking. Lady Fanny Parkes, from whose interesting " Wanderings of a Pilgrim " many of the foregoing facts have been gleaned, formed an intimate friendship with Colonel Gardner, and speaks of him, in his old age, in terms of the warmest admiration and regard. For many years prior to his death he resided on his *jaghir*, or estate, at Khasganj, sixty miles from Agra. His Begum bore him two sons and a daughter. His eldest son James married a niece of the Emperor Akbar Shah. The younger, Alan, was united to Bibi Sahiba Hinga, and left two daughters, Suzan and Hármuzi. The latter was married in 1836 to her relative, William Gardner, a nephew of the second Baron Gardner. Their son, Alan Hyde Gardner, succeeded to the title, and is the present holder of it. He married in 1879 Jane, a converted princess of the House of Delhi, and has an heir, born in 1881. There is a most interesting pedigree of this family on p. 420 (vol. i.) of the " Wanderings of a Pilgrim," which illustrates in a very curious way the thread of connection by intermarriage between the heirs and descendants of an English Barony, the Imperial House of Taimúr, the Kings of Oudh and the Princes of Cambay. The degree of relationship is too intricate to be explained in detail, but the present Lord Gardner is grandson of a Prince of Cambay, and nephew to a late Emperor of Delhi, and a late King of Oudh. This sketch cannot be more suitably concluded than by an extract from Dod's Peerage.

" GARDNER (Ireland) created 1800. Baron Gardner, 1806 (United Kingdom), by which title he holds his seat in the House of Lords. Baronet, 1794 (Great Britain). Alan Hyde Gardner, son of the late Stewart William Gardner, grandson of the first baron. B. 1836 : M. 1879, Jane, daughter of Angam Shekoe. Succeeded his kinsman in 1883. Residence, Village Munowta, near Nadri, Etah district. Heir, Son Alan Legge, born October 25, 1881."

GESLIN, MAJOR.—Major Geslin was a Frenchman, and commanded a battalion in Perron's Second Brigade. When the war of 1803 broke out he was appointed to succeed George Hessing in command of the brigade, the latter being sent to take up the commandantship of the fort of Agra, rendered vacant by the death of his father, Colonel John Hessing. Geslin, meanwhile, joined Bourguien at Delhi, and opposed him when he revolted against Perron's authority, and usurped his command. Bourguien, having failed in every attempt to seduce Geslin from his allegiance, incited the brigade to mutiny and place the Major under arrest, which they did. After the battle of Delhi, Geslin was one of the officers who surrendered to Lord Lake, and were deported to Calcutta.

HARDING, MAJOR.— Major Harding was a very gallant young English adventurer, whose career though short was brilliant. He raised a brigade of four battalions for Jaswant Ráo Holkar, which he brought to a high state of efficiency and discipline. He met his death at the battle of Poonah, whilst charging Dawes's guns side by side with Holkar. In the very moment of victory he received a cannon shot in the shoulder, almost the last one fired in the action. Jaswant Ráo, although wounded in three places, immediately hurried to the spot where Harding was lying, to afford him assistance and consolation. But the wounded officer was sinking fast, and he only had time to express a wish to be laid to rest by the side of his fellow countrymen in the burial place of the British Residency at Poonah—a dying request that was scrupulously fulfilled.

HARRIOTT, CAPTAIN.—Captain Harriott was an Englishman, and an officer in Perron's Fifth Brigade. He was one of the Europeans confined by the mutinous troops at Agra, previous to the capture of that fortress by General Lake. Taking advantage of the terms of Lord Wellesley's proclamation, he passed over to the British Government, and obtained the command of one of Sindhia's battalions which were taken into the Company's service after the war, and saw some fighting with it in the Hariána district in 1804.

HEARSEY, CAPTAIN.—Captain Hearsey was one of Thomas's officers, and assumed temporary charge of the camp at Georgegarh after the memorable battle of the 4th of September, 1801. It was owing to his error of judgment in not retiring to Hánsi, that Thomas's fall was indirectly due. He appears to have possessed very little military ability, but was faithful to his chief, and not only accompanied him in his flight to Hánsi, but fought bravely to the end. After Thomas's fall Hearsey entered the service of some Native state, whether Sindhia's or Holkar's it is impossible to say; but he was one of the officers who availed themselves of Lord Wellesley's proclamation in 1803, and received a pension of Rs. 800 a month from the British Government.

HESSING, GEORGE, COLONEL.—George Hessing was a half-caste Dutchman, being a son of Colonel John Hessing by a "Native woman." But though Grant Duff describes the mother in these terms, there is little doubt but that she was a sister of Major Derridon and Madame Perron, for Skinner mentions that George Hessing was the General's nephew. Hessing was known amongst the Natives as *Jorus Sahib*, a corruption of his Christian name, which cannot bear comparison with the sonorous *Jowruj* applied to Thomas. The first mention of George Hessing is in 1798, when, in conjunction with Fidéle Filoze, he expertly effected the capture of Ghatkay Ráo. In 1800, on the retirement of his father, he succeeded to the command of a brigade of four battalions, which he quickly increased to eight. The next year he accompanied Sindhia to Malwa, and on reaching the Narbada was sent forward to protect Ujjain against a threatened attack by Holkar. Although it was in the rainy season, and the country flooded with water, Hessing made an astonishingly rapid march, and arrived at the capital in June. Amir Khán soon attacked him, and kept him in play till Holkar defeated MacIntyre and attempted to repeat the success against Brownrigg; but being repulsed by the latter officers, he joined Amir Khán, and made a concerted assault on Hessing's entrenchments outside the walls of Ujjain. Hessing behaved in a most cowardly manner, flying at an early period of the action, and leaving his troops to be annihilated, and his eleven European officers killed or wounded and taken prisoners. Just previous to the battle of Ujjain he had despatched four of his battalions to his father at Agra, whither he now made his way. He was soon called upon to march with these to assist in the war against George Thomas, and it was through his lines that *Jowruj Jung* cut his way when he escaped to Hánsi. After this Hessing returned to Agra. Smith states that his four battalions were taken over by Perron in 1803, and made the foundation of the Fifth Brigade, Hessing being promoted to the command of the Second, in succession to Robert Sutherland; but he did not hold the appointment long, for his father died in July, and he was transferred to the commandantship of Agra. He was here when General Lake captured the fort, but not in command, for he had been previously deposed and confined by his mutinous troops. At the last moment he was put forward to negotiate terms for the garrison. Skinner asserts that he was " too rich a man to defend the fort well, and soon found means to dissatisfy the garrison," but this opinion seems ill founded. Hessing's fortune was estimated at five lakhs of rupees, besides money in the Company's funds. After his surrender he retired to Chinsúra for some time, and eventually removed to Calcutta, where he died on the 6th of January, 1826, aged forty-four years.

HESSING, JOHN, COLONEL.—Colonel Hessing was a native of Holland, and was born in 1740. He came to India in 1764, and entered the service of the Native princes. After many adventures, no records of which appear to exist, he joined De Boigne, and obtained the command of one of the first two battalions the General raised. He was present at the battles of Lalsót, Chaksana, Agra, and Pátan. After the latter he quarrelled with his commander and left him. Soon after this he was specially employed by Madhoji Sindhia to raise a body-guard for that chief, and accompanied him to Poonah in 1792. By degrees Hessing increased his party to a small brigade of four battalions. In 1800 ill-health obliged him to resign his command in favour of his son George, and, " covered with wounds received in war," the fine old Dutchman retired to fill the post of Commandant of the Fort of Agra. Here " in his judicial capacity he so tempered justice with mercy, that he was universally loved and esteemed, and in this honourable retreat passed the remaining years of his life, spending with liberality a well-earned fortune." He had many opportunities of extending hospitality to British officers, who visited Agra for amusement or curiosity. Lord Metcalfe, then a young civilian and Assistant Resident at Daulat Ráo Sindhia's camp, met John Hessing at Agra in March, 1801, and thus describes the incident:—" I breakfasted by invitation with the Dutch Commandant, Colonel J. Hessing. I found him with his son, who commanded in the engagement at Oojein, where his battalions were defeated ; a Mr. Marshall, an Englishman, and two others, whose names I have not learnt. The breakfast consisted of *kedgeree* (rice and eggs), fish, game, fowls, curry and rice, stews, oranges, pears, pomegranates, eggs, bread-and-butter, cakes of all kinds, pancakes, and a number of other dishes which have escaped my recollection—amongst others I have forgotten to enumerate cheese. The Dutchman was as polite as a Dutchman could be, and very well meaning, I am certain. On the following day I breakfasted and dined with him again."

John Hessing died on the 21st of July, 1803, aged sixty-three years, of which thirty-seven had been spent as an adventurer in military service in India. From some passages in Skinner's "Memoirs" it appears the Colonel was father-in-law to Robert Sutherland, and it seems certain that his wife was a sister of Madame Perron. Smith describes John Hessing as "a good, benevolent man and a brave soldier." A beautiful mausoleum was erected to his memory in the Catholic burial ground at Agra. It was designed in imitation of the Táj, and cost a lakh of rupees!

HOPKINS, CAPTAIN.—Captain Hopkins was the son of a field officer in the Honourable Company's service, and one of George Thomas's officers. He was an extremely gallant man, greatly beloved by his chief, whom he accompanied in the invasion of the Sutlej States, where he was twice wounded whilst gallantly storming Native forts. He met his death at the battle of Georgegarh. Thomas was deeply affected by his loss, and thus refers to him in his memoirs :—"The firmness of his behaviour during the whole period of his service, as well as the manly resignation which he exhibited at the close of life, stamps his character as that of an amiable man and a brave and gallant soldier." And Skinner gives it as his opinion that, "had Thomas possessed another officer like Captain Hopkins, he would have gained the day at Georgegarh." Hopkins's battalion was the only one that remained faithful to Thomas to the last. When Thomas retired into British territory, after his surrender at Hánsi, he sent a present of Rs. 2,000 to Hopkins's sister, who had just been left an orphan by the death of her father, with a promise that if this sum was not thought enough, he would extend further benevolence to her out of his ruined fortunes.

LEGGE, THOMAS.—The name of "Tom Legge" has been rescued from oblivion by the graphic pen of Coloned Tod, the author of "The Annals of Raj'asthan," and from a contribution of his to the *Asiatic Journal* the following particulars are excerpted :—Legge was a native of Danagadee, in the north of Ireland, his father being a shipowner in a small way, and engaged in the emigrant-carrying trade to America. Tom Legge was very wild in his youth, and, rejecting all his father's offers to establish him in a respectable calling, ran away from home and shipped on board the *Swallow*, sloop of war, bound for Madras. Arrived in India, his vagrant principle asserted itself, and, deserting his ship, he tramped his way to Haidarabad, in Sind, supporting himself by begging. This must have been about the year 1775. He stayed in the lower Indus districts for five or six years, and then proceeded to Multan, and from thence through the desert to Jaipur. After a short residence in Rajputana he entered the service of the Ját Rana of Gohad, being appointed to a post in Sangster's corps. From this officer Legge learnt the art of casting cannon and whatever belonged to their management, and with the possession of this knowledge, and the revival of the errant principle within him, he resumed his travels. Bidding farewell to Sangster, he steered his course to Kabul, where his talents gained him a situation on a pay of three rupees a day. Here he remained some years, receiving very kind treatment, and rendering himself so useful that, when he desired to leave, he was obliged to escape by stealth. Journeying north, he crossed the Hindu Kúsh and entered Badakshan, and was so well received that he stayed there for a considerable time and contracted a left-handed marriage. On quitting this country he went to Bokhára, where he exercised his art for some time, and there, as elsewhere, his only difficulty was to get away. He afterwards visited Herát and Kandahár, and in this mode of life spent twenty years, serving almost every power between the Indus and the Caspian. At length, tired of this nomad existence, he set out for Jaipur, where he determined to settle down for the rest of his days. Here he married a daughter of Dr. de Silva, a grandson of the celebrated Favier de Silva, whom the King of Portugal sent out to assist the astronomical studies of Jai Singh, the prince who founded Jaipur. This alliance obtained for Legge the command of a Najib battalion in the Jaipur army, but his first service with it proved his last, for in storming the stronghold of a refractory chief he received two wounds. It was shortly after this that he came to Colonel Tod's camp to obtain medical assistance. " I was poked down with a pike, and shot through my thigh, and I've come to your honour's camp to get cured, for they can make no hand at it at Jaipur," was his explanation of his appearance, and the speech was intermingled with forcible and patriotic expressions of joy at seeing the British flag waving in front of the Colonel's tent. His stay here extended for some months, during which Colonel Tod heard all the incidents of his adventurous life, and records the pleasure he felt " in listening to the variegated history of this singular being, who had retained, amidst these strange vicissitudes, an artlessness of manner and goodness of heart which were displayed in many notable instances during his abode of some months in our camp." Legge was in many ways an eccentric and cosmopolitan character. He practised the healing art, alchemy, and divination. He was very benevolent, and his accurate memory had mastered and retained an extraordinary stock of wild Central Asian legends, which he used willingly to retail to any one who would listen to him. He suffered from a delusion that during his wanderings he had discovered the Garden of Eden. The road which led to it was through a spacious and dark cavern, and an angel with flaming wings guarded its entrance. Deep down in the heart of a mountain was situated a beautiful garden, filled with delicious fruit, with piles of gold bricks at one end, and of silver at the other, and various other marvels. The location of this imaginary spot was in the Hindu Kho. Another striking and praiseworthy characteristic of Tom Legge's was his reverence for the Bible, a copy of which he carried about with him in all his travels and wanderings. The doctor who attended Tom Legge was a Scotchman, and although his patient's brogue could not be mistaken, there was blended with it a strong Scotch accent, and the doctor fancied he recognised a countryman. "At this Tom's meek spirit took fire ; the *quaere* involved a double insult, to his country and to his veracity, and he exclaimed with warmth, ' You may take me for a Spaniard or a Portugese, or what you *plase*, sir, but I tell you nothing but the truth, your honour, when I say I'm an Irishman.' Colonel Tod instantly poured the oil of gladness on his wounded spirit by saying he did not doubt his word, but that the doctor was a Scotchman, and wished to know whether, from his accent, he might not claim Tom as a fellow-countryman. Tom's countenance brightened as he rejoined, with a tone and expression which could only come from a genuine son of Erin, ' Sure, an' was not me mother a Mackintosh ? ' "

Tom's wound did not heal, and he felt himself slowly wasting away. " I do not fear death, your honour," he said to Colonel Tod, "and could I get my life written and my boy sent to Calcutta I should die contented." At length he expressed a desire to return to Jaipur, and everything necessary was provided him ; but he had not long quitted the camp before despair overtook him, and, throwing away his clothes, he took up his post in a deserted tomb and proclaimed himself a *Fakir*. In this condition he was discovered by the wife of Sindhia's General, Jean Baptiste Filoze. She acted the good Samaritan towards him, but it was too late, and poor Tom Legge died shortly afterwards in the year 1808. Alas! the pity of it that his book was never written. Literature might have been the richer by another work like " Tom Coryat's Crudities."

LE MARCHANT, CAPTAIN [also written Le Marchand].—Captain Le Marchant was a Frenchman, and entered De Boigne's service about the year 1792. In 1794 he had risen to the rank of captain, and was drawing Rs. 300 a month pay. Four years later Perron appointed him

"Prefect" of Delhi, and there, in command of two battalions, he faithfully discharged the trust reposed in him, and proved himself an active and diligent officer. He died in November, 1799, and his widow assumed the command of his battalions, and refused to surrender them to a successor. In March, 1800, a Native was appointed to the post, but the spirited widow declined to recognise his authority, and Perron was obliged to send Emilius Felix Smith to dislodge the defiant lady. She had taken up a strong position, and fortified it with four guns, but despite her gallant resistance she was eventually compelled to surrender, after having held her late husband's appointment for four months. The custom of a widow succeeding to the command and emoluments enjoyed by her husband was not an uncommon one in India. The example of the Begum Somru naturally suggests itself, but others can be adduced as illustrating this somewhat singular system of succession. There was in 1790 in the Peshwa's service a corps commanded by a European named Yvon, on whose death an Englishman named Robinson was appointed to succeed him. But Mrs. Yvon immediately hurried to Dharwar, where the corps was stationed, deposed Robinson, caused him to be imprisoned, and assumed the command herself. Another instance occurred in the service of Haidar Ali of Mysore. A Portugese officer named Mequinez, who had on one occasion rendered signal service to the prince, was slain in a battle with the Maráthás. Haidar Ali immediately conferred the command of his battalion upon the widow, Madame Mequinez, and invested her with the rank of colonel, which she was to enjoy until her son became old enough for thé post. This lady accompanied the regiment everywhere ; its colours were carried to her house, and she had a private sentinel at her door. She received the pay of the force, and caused it to be distributed, and the deductions made from it, in her own presence. When the regiment was drilled and paraded she inspected it herself, but in time of war her second in command led it into action. Her fate was rather a humiliating one. She married a "mongrel Portugese sergeant " ; whereupon Haidar Ali reduced her to a sergeant's rank and pay, because, by her own voluntary action, she had degraded herself!

LESTINEAU, MONSIEUR [also written Lesteneau].—Lestineau was a Frenchman, and commanded a regular corps in the service of Ranjit Singh, the Rájah of the Játs, about the year 1788. After the defeat of Lalsót, Madhoji Sindhia entered into an alliance with Ranjit Singh, and thus it happened that Monsieur Lestineau's corps acted with the Maráthás in the battles of Chaksána and Agra. In the former his troops were stationed on the right wing, and shared with De Boigne's two battalions the barren honours of the day, and after making a staunch and gallant resistance, were forced to retire owing to the desertion of the Maráthá cavalry. Lestineau and his corps accompanied the Maráthás to Delhi after the victory of Agra, and he was detached to assist in the pursuit of Ghulám Kadir, who had fled to Meerut. When Ghulám was captured, his saddle-bags, stuffed with the jewels which the miscreant had looted from the Emperor's palace, fell into Lestineau's hands, who with these, and the pay of his battalion, absconded shortly after his return to the capital. He reached British territory in safety, and eventually found his way to Europe, with his ill-gotten wealth.

LE VASSOULT, COLONEL [spelt also Le Vassou, Le Vaisseau, Le Vaisseaux, Le Vaissaux, Le Vassoo].—Le Vassoult—assuming this to be the proper orthography of his name—was a Frenchman, and a person of talent, good birth, and pride of character. He entered the Begum Somru's corps, and after rendering his mistress essential service in the management of her artillery, was promoted to the command of it in 1793. Two years later, in order to obtain complete control of her party, he married the Begum. He always felt a profound contempt for the officers in the force, and refused to sit at meals with them, treating them in a haughty manner, and attempting to reform the character of the troops with stern severity. This speedily led to a mutiny, and Le Vassoult lost his life under circumstances which will be found fully related under the heading of " Sombre."

LUCAN, CAPTAIN [also spelt Luccan].—Captain Lucan was an Irishman, and an officer in Perron's army. When the war of 1803 occurred, he availed himself of the Governor-General's proclamation, and left Sindhia's service. At the storm of Aligarh he volunteered to show Lord Lake's troops the way to the gate, and the Commander-in-chief mentions him in the following terms in his despatch of the 4th of September, 1803, announcing the capture of the fortress :—"I feel I shall be wanting in justice to the merits of Mr. Lucan, a native of Great Britain, who recently quitted the service of Sindhia to avoid serving against his country, were I not to recommend him to your Lordship's particular attention. He gallantly undertook to lead Colonel Monson's storming party to the gate, and point out the road through the fort, which he effected in a most gallant manner, and Colonel Monson has reported having received infinite benefit from his service." Lucan was rewarded with a commission in the 74th Regiment, and a donation of Rs. 24,000—" for the job," as Skinner somewhat disparagingly puts it. General Lake mentions Lucan again in his despatch of the 10th of October following :—" To Mr. Lucan's information and exertions on this occasion [the battle before Agra] as well as on every other, I feel myself very much indebted." Subsequently Captain, or as he ought perhaps to be called, Lieutenant Lucan was appointed to the command of a large body of irregular cavalry, and attached to the force under Colonel Monson, which was employed in keeping Holkar in check. Monson met with a disastrous defeat after a short campaign in Holkar's territory, and Lucan was detached to protect his rear. When the troops were leaving Rampúra he might have saved himself if he had retreated directly Jaswant Ráo's advance guard came in sight. But he desired to win a name for himself, and thought he might do so by making a brilliant charge before falling back. He was deserted by most of his men, and soon surrounded by Holkar's best cavalry, and after sustaining a gallant fight, in which his few faithful troops were cut to pieces, he was wounded and taken prisoner. He was confined at Kotah, and shortly afterwards died, according to various accounts, by poison, by torture, or from the effects of his wounds. In the "Life of Amir Khán," by Bhosawan Lal, it is made to appear that Lucan fell in hand-to-hand conflict with Holkar himself, and the apocryphal exploit is commemorated by some Persian verses, of which Prinsep gives the following metrical translation :—

" The Maharaj at Lucan flew,
    As swoops the falcon on its prey,
His water-tempered blade he drew
    And streams of gushing blood found way !

The broken host took flight and fled,
    Death was among them freely dealt,
Sepoys and soldiers, black and white,
    The sword's keen edge in plenty felt.

A Raging Lion, Jeswunt Ráo,
    Came upon Lucan, brave and bold,
And striking at his neck one blow,
    His head upon the green sward rolled.

The army saw their leader's fate
    And forthwith in confusion turned ;
Such the reward of those, whose hate,
    Like Lucan's against Holkar burned."

It is, perhaps, as well to mention that, despite these circumstantial and gory details, the above incident is purely imaginary.

MacINTYRE, CAPTAIN.—Nothing is known of this adventurer, except that he was an officer in Hessing's or Filoze's brigades, and was detached by Sindhia in June, 1801, to support the former at Ujjain with two battalions. He was cut off by Jaswant Ráo Holkar at Núri, twenty-seven miles distant from the capital, and compelled to surrender.

MacKENZIE, LIEUTENANT.—Lieutenant MacKenzie was an officer commanding a battalion in Perron's Third Brigade under Bourguien. He was present during the campaign against Thomas, and behaved with gallantry at the final assault on Hánsi, where he was wounded.

MADOC, COLONEL [spelt also Médoc].—Next to Sombre's, Madoc's was the oldest "party" in Hindustan. Madoc was an illiterate and ignorant Frenchman, who had formerly been a private in the French army in Southern India, from which he deserted in 1774, and found his way to Delhi, where he entered the service of Najaf Khán, for whom he raised a corps of five battalions of infantry, 500 cavalry, and 20 guns. He gathered around him several very respectable and competent officers, amongst whom were the Count de Moidavre and the Chevaliers Dudrenec and Cressy. Colonel Malleson states that Madoc commenced his career as early as 1757, and that he was one of Sombre's officers, and served at the battle of Buxar. He was a gallant man, but deficient in military knowledge, and with more enterprise and bravery than prudence and science, and his battalions generally failed in their attacks from the rash impetuosity of their commander. After leaving Najaf Khán's service, Madoc entered that of the Rána of Gohad in 1776, and a little later experienced a disastrous defeat in the defiles of Biána in the Méwatti district, where his force was attacked by a large band of Rohillas, during a heavy storm of rain, and annihilated, twelve of his European officers being killed, and all his guns and baggage captured. Madoc escaped by flight, and found refuge at Fatehpur, from whence he repaired to Agra, and set to work to cast new guns and raise and discipline another corps. When it was ready for service, by a species of transaction not uncommon in those days, he sold it to the Rána of Gohad in 1782, and its command devolved on Major Sangster. Madoc, having realised a small fortune, retired to Europe, where he was not long afterwards killed in a duel.

MARSHALL, JAMES, CAPTAIN.—Captain Marshall was a Scotchman, and a gentleman of good family and education. He began life as a midshipman in the Company's navy, but in a spirit of adventure left the sea, and took service with the Native princes, obtaining the command of a battalion in Hessing's corps. He is spoken of by a contemporary as a brave soldier, an intelligent officer, and a man of liberal sentiments and amiable manners. Little is known of his active career in Sindhia's service, except that he was one of the officers who was confined by the revolted troops at Agra in 1803, and it is probable he was engaged in the war against George Thomas. Having surrendered to General Lake in terms of the Governor-General's proclamation, he was awarded a pension of Rs. 500 a month by the British Government, and shortly afterwards appointed to the command of some newly-raised levies, and sent to keep order in the Hariána district. He was shot through the heart about the year 1804, whilst gallantly storming a town, in the discharge of his duty to his King and country. "Such characters are rarely seen," writes Lewis Ferdinand Smith. "I knew him long, and he was esteemed and respected by all who were acquainted with his many excellent and amiable qualities. He was cut off in the flower of his life. As he received the fatal bullet, he grasped the hand of his friend, Captain Harriott, smiled at him, and dropped back dead."

MARTINE, CLAUDE, GENERAL [also written Claud Martin].—Claude Martine was a Frenchman. He was born in the year 1732 at Lyons, where his father carried on the business of a silk manufacturer. It was intended that he should follow the same calling, but his adventurous spirit would not submit to so tame a career, and running away from home at an early age, he enlisted in the French army. He soon distinguished himself by his activity and energy, and was advanced from an infantry to a cavalry regiment. In 1757 the Count de Lally was appointed to the government of Pondicherry, and requiring volunteers for his bodyguard, Martine made application to be enrolled, and was accepted. Accompanying Lally to India, he arrived there in 1758, but had not been long in the country before he began to experience trouble. Lally's ideas of discipline were inordinately severe, and his behaviour and manners toward his subordinates harsh and tyrannical. His treatment might have been necessary, for a large portion of his bodyguard had been recruited from military criminals and deserters under sentence, who were drafted into it as a punishment. But Lally's sternness had the effect of increasing rather than diminishing the insubordination, and when, a little later, Coote advanced and laid siege to Pondicherry, the whole of the Governor's bodyguard deserted *en masse* to the English, by whom they were well received. On the return of the British troops to Madras, Martine volunteered to raise a corps of French chasseurs from amongst the prisoners of war, for service under the Company's flag. His proposal was entertained, and he received a commission as ensign. Shortly afterwards he was ordered to Bengal with his corps, but, during the voyage, the ship in which he sailed sprang a leak, and it was only with the greatest difficulty that he saved his men in the boats, and eventually landed them safely in Calcutta. In due course he was promoted to the rank of captain, but in 1764 his men mutinied, notwithstanding his exertions to keep them faithful, and the corps was broken up. Martine's conduct on this occasion was greatly commended by the authorities, and, being an able draughtsman, he was rewarded by an appointment in the north-eastern districts of Bengal, where he was sent to survey the country. His work was so satisfactory that, on its completion, a similar appointment was found for him in the province of Oudh.

This was the turning-point in his career, which had hitherto been more eventful than profitable. Having fixed his headquarters at Lucknow, he employed his leisure in exercising his ingenuity in several branches of mechanics, and, amongst other things, manufactured " the first balloons that ever floated in the air of Asia." This brought him under the notice of the Nawáb, who conceived so high an opinion of his abilities, and especially his skill in gunnery, that he solicited permission from the Bengal Government for Martine's services to be transferred to him, and this being granted, the adventurer was appointed superintendent of the Nawáb's park of artillery and arsenal.

Martine did not neglect the opportunities thus opened out to him, and speedily ingratiated himself with his new master, whose confidential adviser he became. In the many political changes that took place in Oudh during the next twenty years the Frenchman always contrived to remain on the right side, making himself indispensable in negotiations between the Nawáb and the Company. At the same time he was careful not to push himself forward into public notice, preferring to remain the power behind the throne; and although he seldom appeared at Darbar, he had more real influence than the Nawáb's ministers in shaping the course of events.

Martine's salary was largely increased, and he enjoyed, in addition, extensive sources of emolument, such as were always open to men in positions of confidence in the Native courts. He became the recognised channel for petitions from all who desired any favour from the

Government, and in this capacity enormous bribes and presents of great value found their way into his hands. He educated the Nawáb into an appreciation of the products of Europe, and then acted as his agent in procuring them. He established extensive credits with the Native bankers, and so obtained a large share in the profitable public loans made to his master. Finally his position at Court was esteemed so secure that, in a country distracted by war and internal troubles, he soon became a sort of " safe deposit " for the valuables of the Nawáb's subjects, charging a commission of 12 per cent. for the custody of articles committed to his care. By these and similar methods he acquired an immense fortune during his long residence at Lucknow.

Martine's pleasure in life seems to have been limited to the mere accumulation of riches, for he derived none from spending them. In his peculiar way he was sufficiently hospitable, but his table was not calculated to attract guests, either by the elegance of the entertainment or the geniality of the host. Of his private bounty during his life very few instances are recorded, though it is known that from time to time he assisted his family at Lyons. The principal object of his ambition or vanity seems to have been the attainment of military rank, a fact the truth of which is emphasised by the epitaph he wrote for his own tomb. During the time he resided at Lucknow his promotion in the Company's service continued ; for although he relinquished his pay and allowances, he retained his commission. In 1790, at the commencement of the first war with Tipu Sultan, he presented the Company with a number of fine horses to mount a troop of cavalry, and in return was gazetted to the rank of colonel, thus achieving the object for which the gift was made. Six years later, when the Company's officers received brevet rank from the King, Martine's name was included in the *Gazette*, and to his infinite satisfaction he became a major-general. Lord Teignmouth described him in 1797 as a man of much penetration and observation, whose language would be elegant if it corresponded with his ideas; but he talked very broken English, interlarding every sentence with " What do you call it ? "—" Do you see ? "

Amongst the most remarkable points connected with Martine was his house at Lucknow, which was a castellated edifice built on the banks of the River Gúmti, and designed for defence if necessary. It was constructed strictly on hygienic principles, for it contained a series of rooms—or flats, as we should call them in these modern days— adapted to the varying temperature of the different seasons of the year. Thus in the hot season he resided in a subterranean suite of chambers, which were always cool and sheltered from the fierce glare and heat outside. When the rainy season came on, he ascended to an upper story high above the ground level and its malaria. In the cold weather he changed quarters again, and descended to the ground-floor. The house was fitted with many curious mechanical contrivances for comfort; the ceilings of the different apartments were formed of elliptic arches, ornamented most elaborately, whilst the exterior decorations were equally fanciful and florid. The furniture was on a par with the building, and the walls of the rooms were covered with glasses, prints, and pictures, estimated at many thousand pounds in value. Not the least curious feature in this building—which was called *Constantia*, from the motto *Labore et Constantia* carved on its front—was a room containing a vault designed for Martine's place of sepulture. He built this because the Nawáb refused to pay him the price he asked for the edifice; whereupon, in a fit of pique, he declared that his tomb should be handsomer than any palace in the kingdom. His subsequent interment therein had the effect of desecrating the place in the eyes of the Muhammadans, for no followers of the Prophet can inhabit a tomb.

For the last fifteen years of his life Martine suffered greatly from stone. He cured himself once by a successful though crude and painful course of treatment; but a recurrence of the disease terminated his life in the year 1800, at the age of sixty-two.

On the 1st of January of the same year he executed an extraordinary will, which he drew up himself. It contained over forty clauses, and began by acknowledging with penitence that self-interest had been his guiding principle through life. His fortune, amounting to nearly half a million sterling, he bequeathed in innumerable legacies. Amongst them were three to the poor of Calcutta, Chandernagore, and Lucknow, the interest of which was to be doled daily at certain fixed places, distinguished by tablets bearing an inscription in English, French, or Persian, according to the location, and notifying that the alms distributed were the gift of General Martine, and to be so disbursed in perpetuity. He left a large sum in trust to the Government of Bengal for the establishment and endowment of a school to be called *La Martinière*, which still exists, and where on the anniversary of his death a sermon was to be preached, followed by a public dinner, at which the toast of "The Memory of the Founder" was to be drunk in solemn silence. To his relatives and the town of Lyons he bequeathed large legacies, and two separate sums to that city and Calcutta, their interest to be devoted to releasing poor debtors from gaol on the anniversary of his death. He left directions that his house Constantia should never be sold, but serve as a mausoleum for his remains, and he committed it to the care of the ruling power in the country for the time being. Such were the elaborate precautions taken by this eccentric man to keep his memory alive and hand it down to posterity.

The thirtieth clause in his will was perhaps the most remarkable of all. It ran as follows : " When I am dead, I request that my body may be salted, put in spirits, or embalmed, and afterwards deposited in a leaden coffin made of some sheet lead in my godown, which is to be put in another of sissoo wood, and then deposited in the cave in the small round room north-east in Constantia, with two feet of masonry raised above it, which is to bear the following inscription :—

" Major-General Claude Martine,

Born at Lyons, January, 1738.

Arrived in India as a common soldier, and died at [Lucknow, the 13th of September, 1800] a major-general ;

and he is buried in this tomb.

Pray for his soul."

His wishes were faithfully fulfilled, and when Lady Fanny Parkes visited the tomb in 1831 she mentions that a bust of the General adorned the vault, lights were constantly burning before the tomb, and the figures of four Sipahis, as large as life, with their arms reversed, stood in niches at the side of the monument. In the centre of the vault was a large plain slab bearing the inscription above recorded.

Perchance it sufficiently summarises Martine's life, for his career was disfigured by much that was ignoble and inglorious. Yet, conning it after the lapse of nearly a hundred years, one cannot help reflecting on the achievements of the man epitomised in the few terse words. Dynasties have died out, thrones have tottered and fallen, kingdoms have crumbled into dust and been forgotten since this private soldier sought to perpetuate his name ; and it is not an unpleasing thought that the atonement of his testamentary charity still keeps alive the pious memory of the founder of *La Martinière.*

Montague, Edward, Lieutenant.—Lieutenant Montague was the son of Colonel Montague, of the Bengal Artillery, and an officer in Hessing's brigade. He was killed at the battle of Ujjain in 1801. He is described in an obituary notice published at the time as a most accomplished young man, who had been educated at the Royal

Military Academy at Kensington, and received a more ample education than was generally esteemed necessary for the army. *Tempora mutantur;* as witness the groups of great-brained, young aspirants, who periodically cluster round the doors of Burlington House to prove their sufficient intellectual powers.

MORRIS, JOHN.—John Morris was an Englishman, and commanded one of George Thomas's battalions. He is only mentioned once in Thomas's memoirs—namely, in the description of the battle of Fatehpur, where he distinguished himself and was wounded. " He was a brave man," wrote his master, " but better adapted to conduct a forlorn hope than direct the motions of troops on the field of battle."

PAISH, CAPTAIN.—There appear to have been two officers of this name. One, a captain in the Chevalier Dudrenec's corps, was killed at the battle of Malpura in 1799, in the charge of Ráthor cavalry that overwhelmed the force; the other, a lieutenant in Perron's Fourth Brigade, was wounded in the storm of Sounda, in 1801. As both incidents are gleaned from Skinner's memoirs, it is possible that they refer to one and the same individual, and that he was only wounded, not killed, in the first action.

PAULY, COLONEL (PAOLI).—Colonel Pauly was a German, and selected by the Begum Somru to command her husband's party after Sombre's death in 1778. He engaged too much in Oriental politics, and espoused the cause of Prince Jiwan Bakht, who, in 1782, desired to rid Shah 'Alam of some of his unruly nobles, and undertook to secure the arrest of a powerful minister named Mirza Sháfi Khán; whereupon the latter fled, and the Emperor appointed Jiwan Bakht Amir-úl-Umra, or Chief of the Nobles. But Mirza Sháfi entered into an alliance with several other rebel nobles, and, collecting a large army, marched against Delhi, sending forward a *vakil* to Shah 'Alam, demanding his restoration to power. The Emperor was intimidated, and summoned a council, at which Jiwan Bakht proposed to sally forth and fight the rebels, a line of action which Pauly strongly supported, undertaking to defeat Mirza Sháfi's following with his battalions of regulars. But the Emperor was too frightened to act boldly, and ordered Pauly to enter into an amicable arrangement. The German obeyed, and a general reconciliation of all parties was outwardly agreed to, but scarcely had Pauly entered the rebels' camp to arrange for carrying the agreement into effect, than a party of horse, who had been placed in ambuscade, fell upon him, and, dispersing his escort, "by a bloody process cut off the head of Mr. Pauly."

PEDRON, COLONEL.—Colonel Pedron was a Frenchman, and a native of Hennebon, near L'Orient. He served in Monsieur Law's corps at Lucknow in 1760. Law, it may be mentioned, was a son of the financial genius known as "Mississippi" Law, whose speculative enterprises in France produced a parallel to our South Sea Bubble in England. Law was at Chandernagore in 1756 when Clive captured it, but managed to make his escape into the Upper Provinces with about 250 of his countrymen, whom he kept together till the year 1761, when he was defeated and forced to surrender to Major Carnac. But prior to this a great number of his Europeans deserted, and amongst them was Pedron, who returned to Oudh, and took service with the Nawáb Wazir at Lucknow. When the French were expelled from that ruler's dominions at the instigation of the English, Pedron obtained employment under the Rájah of Berar. After this a great blank occurs in his history, for he is not heard of again till 1790, when he entered De Boigne's First Brigade as a lieutenant, and was posted to Mattra, and shortly afterwards purchased his majority. In 1795 he was promoted to the command of the Third Brigade, and must have been a man of considerably over fifty years of age. In 1799 he was engaged in the siege of Delhi, which the Native commandant, despite Sindhia's orders, refused to deliver over to Perron. After a blockade of five weeks the gates were opened "to the impulse of gold," but whether to Pedron or to Sutherland is doubtful, as the honour has been assigned to both. In 1800 Pedron raised the Fourth Brigade when the threatened invasion of Hindustan by Zemán Shah caused Perron to increase his army. His next service was against Lakwa Dáda at Sounda in 1801, but he affected so little with his eight battalions that Perron proceeded in person to the seat of war, and stormed the rebel chief's entrenchments. Soon after this hostilities were declared against George Thomas, and when Bourguien demonstrated his utter incapacity, Pedron was sent to supersede him. That he was successful was again due, in a great measure, to the "impulse of gold"—a metal in which he seems to have had more faith than in steel, for he displayed little military talent, and no courage, whilst the methods he adopted of tampering with Thomas's troops were not such as commend themselves to European notions of honourable warfare. But he gained his ends, and after Thomas's flight to Hánsi, made over the command to Bourguien again, and returned to Aligarh to recruit his brigade, which had been weakened by casualties and transfers to the Third.

Here he remained for eighteen months in charge of Perron's head-quarters, and when the rupture with the British Government occurred in 1803 he was entrusted with the defence of the fort, and was the recipient of the famous letter from Perron which exhorted him to hold the place while one stone remained upon another. But this desperate resolution was not in Pedron, and he was anxious to surrender without a blow, and only prevented from doing so by the spirit of the troops under him, who, on the first indication of his weakness, deposed and confined him, and elected a Rajput named Baji Ráo to the command. Aligarh was taken by storm on the 4th of September, and Pedron was made a prisoner of war, or to be more exact, was transferred from Marátbá to English bondage. Thorn describes him as " an elderly man, clad in a green jacket, with gold lace and epaulettes "—which is the last record discovered of this adventurer.

PILLET, J., CAPTAIN.—Captain Pillet was a Frenchman, in Lestineau's corps, in the service of the Rána of Gohad, to the command of which he succeeded by seniority when Lestineau absconded after securing Gúlam Kádir's saddle-bags. He was, however, unable to control the men, who broke into mutiny and were disbanded. Pillet subsequently entered the service of the Rájah of Jaipur, and about the year 1794 made a long report to the British Government on the resources of that country, with a view to an alliance. As the leading feature of the proposal was that the Rájah should keep up an army of 50,000 men, and the Company pay for it, it did not receive that attention which doubtless both Partáb Sing and Pillet fondly hoped.

PIRON, COLONEL [often mis-spelt Perron].—Colonel Piron, who is constantly confounded in historical books with General Perron, was a native of Alsace. He was in the service of the Nizam of Haidarabad, and second in command to the famous adventurer Raymond, who raised a brigade of seventeen battalions for that ruler. Piron was an outrageous Jacobin, and in close touch with the French Republican faction in Mysore. On Raymond's death, in March, 1798, he succeeded to the command of the 14,000 men comprising the force, which was supported by a *Jaidad* yielding eighteen lakhs of rupees annually, and included a strong train of artillery and a complete military equipment. One of his first acts was to send to Perron, Sindhia's general, a silver tree and Cap of Liberty as a souvenir. His corps always hoisted the French national flag, and the lapels and epaulettes of the Sepoys' uniforms were embroidered with the words *Liberté et Constitution.* Piron and all his officers entertained ambitious designs, and considered themselves as forwarding the interests of France. Their undisguised hostility to the English and pronounced principles soon compelled Lord Wellesley to take action against them, and he determined to effect the disbandment of the force. Lieutenant-Colonel Roberts, assisted by John Malcolm, was told off for the task, and effected it with complete success on the 22nd of October, 1798, the operation being facilitated by the fact of the troops being in a state of open mutiny, and Piron and his officers in danger. The following account of the dispersal of this " French Army " (as Lord Wellesley calls it) is extracted from Kaye's " Life of Malcolm."

" Having reported to Colonel Roberts the favourable aspect of affairs, Malcolm drew up his detachment on the heights facing the French lines. There he was speedily joined by the European officers of the French corps, elate with joy at their escape from the hands of their infuriate soldiery, and actually, in the conjuncture that had arisen, regarding the English as friends and deliverers. The rest was soon accomplished. The Sepoys left their guns, laid down their arms, and in the presence of the two lines of British troops, moved off in a deep column to a flag planted on the right of the ground. Not a shot was fired, not a drop of blood was shed. Eleven or twelve thousand men were dispersed in a few hours ; and before sunset the whole cantonment, with all their storehouses, arsenals, gun foundries, and powder mills, were completely in our possession. The celebrated French corps of Hydrabad had passed into tradition."

Piron and his compatriots confessed themselves very grateful, not only for their rescue from a grave peril, but for the humanity with which they were subsequently treated. It is difficult to estimate the exact qualities of this adventurer. Major Kirkpatrick, the Resident at Haidarabad, writing in 1797, describes him as younger than Raymond, and far more enterprising and active, and particularly fond of the military profession. But Sir John Malcolm, then Kirkpatrick's assistant, who had equally good opportunities of forming an opinion, records that " Piron is a rough, violent democrat, a man with more hostile dispositions to us than his predecessor Raymond, but less dangerous ; being a stranger to that temper and those conciliatory manners by which the latter won his way to greatness. Piron has no ability, and his authority is far from being generally acknowledged." Events proved Piron was totally unfitted to step into the post made vacant by Raymond's death. He died at Chandernagore in 1805.

PLUMET, MAJOR.—Major Plumet was " a Frenchman and a gentleman—two qualities which were seldom united in the Mahratta Empire." Such is Smith's *dictum.* Plumet raised a party for Jaswant Ráo Holkar in 1798, and had a principal share in securing the victory of Ujjain, although a short time previously he had sustained a reverse when he attacked Major Brownrigg's position on the Narbada. According to one historian, he was wounded and taken prisoner in the latter affair, and not present at Ujjain; but another, with equal insistence, accords to him the honour of that day. He soon found Holkar "too cruel, cunning, capricious, and ungrateful," and left his service. Major Ambrose states that Plumet deserted his chief on the eve of the battle of Indore, and so conduced to the defeat which Jaswant Ráo sustained, and that this behaviour caused Holkar to brand all Frenchmen as "Duggerbáz," or Faithless. Major Plumet, after his brief career in the Deccan, retired to the Isle of France.

POHLMAN, COLONEL [also written Pholman and Balaman].—Colonel Pohlman was a native of Hanover, and a sergeant in a regiment composed of men of that nationality, formerly quartered at Madras, and one of several similar mercenary corps of foreigners in the Company's service, such as Doxat's Chasseurs, the Swiss *Regiment de Meuron,* and Claude Martine's company. Pohlman entered De Boigne's brigades about the year 1792 or 1793, and was a captain on the modest pay of Rs. 200 a month in 1794. In April of the following year he was in command of a Najib battalion in the Second Brigade at Mattra, to which James Skinner was posted when he first joined the service. Between this and 1799 he probably saw a good deal of service, for it is a period of which Skinner has much to relate. Early in 1799 Perron distrusted Sutherland, who was in command of the Second Brigade, and removed him from his post, which he bestowed on Pohlman, who shortly afterwards sustained a severe reverse in an unsuccessful attack upon the fort of Shápúra, when six of his battalions were beaten back with a loss of two officers and 1,000 men killed and wounded. Eventually he captured the place, when, it is pleasant to record, he treated the gallant Rajpút garrison with great humanity and consideration, permitting them and their women-folk to march out with all the honours of war, and the respect due to their heroic defence. In the following May, Pohlman commanded at the important battle of Malpúra, when his force consisted of his own brigade of eight battalions, five of the Chevalier Dudrenec's, and 5,000 cavalry. He inflicted a severe defeat on Rájah Partáb Singh, and captured 74 of his guns. This was the action in which Dudrenec's corps was ridden down by the Ráthors, and the victory was solely due to Pohlman's good generalship. For the next two years he appears to have been quartered in Rajputana, to enforce payment of the tribute due, and keep the country under control whilst Perron's other brigades were engaged in the wars against Holkar, Lakwa Dáda, and George Thomas, in none of which Pohlman seems to have had any part. In 1802 he escorted Perron to Ujjain, and here, for the second time, superseded Sutherland, whó was obliged to leave the service owing to Perron's hostility. Pohlman and the First Brigade remained with Sindhia in the Deccan till war broke out with the English. It is uncertain whether he was in command of Sindhia's infantry at the battle of Assaye, in which his brigade fought well, the artillery being splendidly served, and the men sustaining a stubborn fight against the genius of Wellesley and the valour of British troops for three hours. Pohlman eventually entered the Company's service, though without rank, and re-enlisted some of his old soldiers to form an irregular infantry corps. He is described as an exceedingly cheerful and entertaining character, who lived in the style of an Indian prince, kept a seraglio, and always travelled on an elephant, attended by a guard of Mughals, all dressed alike in purple robes, and marching in file in the same way as a British cavalry regiment; notwithstanding which melodramatic weakness, Pohlman was certainly one of Perron's most competent officers.

RAYMOND, FRANÇOIS DE, GENERAL.—François de Raymond (whose name Colonel Malleson gives as Michel Joachim Marie Raymond) was born at Serignac, in Gascony, in 1755. He came out to India early in life, and in 1775 obtained employment as sub-lieutenant in a battalion commanded by the Chevalier de Lassé, in the service of Haider Ali of Mysore. His conduct brought him to the notice of the military authorities, and he received a commission as captain in the French army in 1783, and was appointed aide-de-camp to the famous Bussy. Three years later, on Bussy's death, Raymond entered the service of the Nizam Ali Khán of Haidarabad, for whom he raised a small corps of 300 men, hiring the weapons with which they were armed from a French merchant on the coast, at the rate of eight annas *per mensem* for each musket. When the confederate war against Tipu Sultan broke out, and the English, Maráthás, and the Nizam were leagued against the ruler of Mysore, Raymond's command was raised to 700 men, and he distinguished himself so much in the campaign that he grew into great favour with Ali Khán, and his force was augmented to 5,000 men, his own pay being increased to Rs. 5,000 a month. At the battle of Kardla in 1795 Raymond's battalions numbered 10,840 men, with 28 guns and 46 tumbrils. The regularity with which this force was paid enabled him to fill its ranks with deserters from the Company's services, to whom he held out tempting inducements. He is also said to have encouraged French prisoners of war on *parole* to escape and take service under his flag. The battle of Kardla was the only occasion except the Mysore war in which, during a service of seventeen years, Raymond met a foreign foe. He was forced to retire from the field, but was not defeated, for the retreat was solely due to the Nizam's pusillinamity, and ordered at a moment when Raymond's battalions were stoutly and, peradventure, successfully holding their own. He was next employed in reducing to submission the Nizam's rebellious son and heir, Ali Jáh. In this he met with stout resistance, and was obliged to send for reinforcements to one of his subordinates named Baptiste, on being joined by whom he quickly brought the expedition to a conclusion, and secured the person of Ali Jáh, who committed suicide, leaving Sikander Jáh heir to the throne. This Prince was accustomed to swear "by the head of Raymond," whom he regarded as the first of men, with the single detraction that he belonged to a nation that had murdered its king and queen. After the battle of Kardla Raymond tried hard to obtain the Karpa district, which would have enabled him to co-operate with any French force making a descent on the Coromandal coast, with or without the concurrence of the Nizam. He already possessed an immense military territorial assignment which yielded fifty-two lakhs of rupees a year, in addition to an estate or *Jaghir* of his own, the income of which was Rs. 50,000. His salary was princely, and in the style of his domestic life he collected round him every luxury and elegance within the reach of a European in India. Previous to his death he further increased his force, which he considered "A French body of troops, employed and subsidised by the Nizam," to over 14,000 men, with a complete train of artillery, chiefly brass ordnance, worked by a well-trained corps of Europeans, and drawn by 5,000 bullocks. His cavalry numbered 600. He possessed, in his own right, all the guns and military equipage belonging to the force. The physique of his soldiers was not to be compared with that of the stalwart and warlike warriors whom De Boigne and Perron enlisted from the fine recruiting grounds of Upper India, but the men were well disciplined, and their parade appearance was good, whilst the service itself was extremely popular with the Natives.

Raymond was an ambitious and intriguing man, and one who understood the art of gaining his ends by engaging manners and conciliatory demeanour. After the battle of Kardla he began to

assume an almost kingly state, for his power made him the arbitrator
of Haidarabad. All his regimental returns were headed *Corps de
François de Raymond*, and he was received in his own cantonments
with a royal salute. He stood in a position which would have enabled
him, in the event of the Nizam's death, to elevate whom he pleased to
the throne, and the overpowering influence which he acquired in the
country was a serious menace to English interests. He was in close
touch with the Government of France, and with Tipu Sultan of Mysore,
and engaged in intrigues which had for their object an alliance against
the British power in the East. He was also in correspondence with
some of the European officers in Sindhia's service, and an interesting
letter exists which he addressed to Michael Filoze in January, 1798,
on the subject of the treacherous seizure of Nana Farnavis, the
Peshwa's Prime Minister. This is worth quoting as showing Raymond's honourable feelings, and because of a rather quaint adaptation
it contains of the "Rights of Man" theory to eighteenth century Marátha
politics—probably the first and last time the argument was used in
such a connection. "A report prevails," writes Raymond, "that
Nana Farnavis has been arrested contrary to the Rights of Man and
to the clauses of the treaty for which you [Filoze] were security. I have
no other interest in speaking of this but that which I take for every
European whose reputation is dear to me." Then he goes on to request
Filoze to obtain the Nana's restoration to liberty, and offers him a
position and emoluments, "one-fourth more than you have with
Scindia, and a *jaghir* of one lakh of rupees annually." The reason
of this liberality is not obvious in the letter, but it suggests many
inferences. The epistle concludes : "I will be shortly on your
frontiers, when we shall be able to keep up a correspondence. Burn
this letter if it should not suit you ; but write to me. Raymond."

Two months later Raymond died—according to some accounts by
poison—at the early age of forty-three, and in the enjoyment of a
degree of power and consequence never reached by any other military
adventurer in Southern India.

Raymond's character has been variously estimated by different
writers. Major Thorn describes him as "a man of extensive knowledge and equal activity." Kaye, in his "Life of Malcolm," views
his character in the following light: "Raymond was a man of great
ability and address. . . . Had he lived the taking of his men (in 1798)
would not have been an easy task. . . . His troops were admirably
disciplined and equipped. Their store-rooms well filled with arms
and accoutrements, and clothing from Europe of excellent quality,
and they could with ease have armed 12,000 more men in a few

months. They cast excellent cannon, and made serviceable muskets in their different foundries, all of which, as well as their powder-mills, were under the direction of able and scientific Europeans." Malcolm's opinion has already been quoted in another page, namely, that Raymond was a man of " temper and conciliatory manners, by which he won his way to greatness." But it has been reserved for a contemporary historian, on grounds which it is a little difficult to understand, to elevate Raymond to the position of a national hero. " This remarkable man," writes Colonel Malleson, " is referred to by many English writers simply as ' an adventurer named Raymond.' That he was an adventurer is true, but he was one in the best sense of the term—chivalrous, daring, trustworthy, and a splendid organiser; one of those adventurers who, like Garibaldi in our own days, leave their mark on the history of the country in which their deeds have been achieved. . . . It may be said that no Indian Prince, not even Madhajee Scindia, or his successor, Dowlut Ráo, ever had a finer or more efficient body of troops in his service [than those which Raymond raised]. In the campaign against the Mahrattas in 1796 (?), it was Raymond and his troops who repulsed the charge of the Mahratta cavalry and would have beaten them back altogether had not the Nizam and his troops abandoned the field. His reputation, great at the time, still survives, and it may be said with truth that the name of no European connected with India has survived seventy-six years after the demise of his body, to live with such eternal greenness in the hearts of the people of the country as does the name of Raymond in the memories and traditions of the great families of Hydrabad."

Those who have read these pages will hardly feel inclined to agree with this estimate of Raymond's superior talents as a military adventurer. A soldier of fortune is judged by his deeds, and Raymond's achievements in the tented field cannot for a moment bear comparison with those of De Boigne, Perron, or Thomas.

Passing to the other side of the picture, we have the opinion of Major Kirkpatrick, who was British Resident at Haidarabad in 1797, and wrote of Raymond as "by no means a man of vigorous mind or decided character, and very hard, and wanting liberality in pecuniary matters, which makes him much disliked by all his officers, except one or two he favours. He never showed himself to be much of a soldier, but was artful, and had an arranging head and conciliating manners when they suited his purpose." Captain Fraser, in " Our Faithful Ally the Nizam," describes Raymond as wanting in character, promptitude, and decision. Colonel Beatson, in his History of

25

the war with Tipu Sultan, has recorded the following opinion of the adventurer and his party :—" The corps commanded by Colonel Raymond, which, during the last war in Mysore, amounted to no more than 1,500 men, was at that period so defective in point of discipline as to be rather an object of contempt than jealousy to the Government of India. It has gradually augmented its numbers and improved its discipline under the command of the late Monsieur Raymond, until it nearly reached the number of 14,000, and had obtained a degree of discipline superior in every respect to that of any Native infantry in India, excepting the Sepoys in the Company's service. The corps formed the largest and most efficient branch of the military establishment of His Highness the Nizam, and the French officers had acquired a considerable ascendancy in his dominions and councils, and had manifested on several occasions the symptoms of a disposition so arrogant, overbearing, and adventurous, as to excite alarm in the minds of His Highness and his ministers."

The last quotation must be from the despatches of the Marquis Wellesley. " Raymond's force was avowedly designed to cope with one De Boigne had created for the Mahrattas, and was organised on very similar lines. Each regiment was officered by two Europeans, and there was a field train of fifty guns, and a small body of disciplined cavalry attached. The former was served by European gunners, many of them deserters from the Company's service. The parade appearance of the force was good, but the discipline was far from strict, and the slackness in this respect, combined with the regularity of pay, made the service a very popular one with the Natives, so that there was no difficulty in keeping the brigade up to its full strength. All the officers were Frenchmen, devoted to the doctrines of Jacobinism, and any amongst them who evinced Royalist tendencies were speedily dismissed. They fought under the French flag, and the Cap of Liberty was engraved on their buttons. Raymond was not a man of any great capacity or vigour, but in craft and intrigue he was an adept, and sustained his position by surrounding himself with a few favourites, who supported him through thick and thin. With his other officers he was far from popular, being a hard man, and in pecuniary matters extremely illiberal ; for, although he derived vast revenues from enormous territorial assignments, he could never divest himself of his inherent avarice and meanness."

ROBERTS, LIEUTENANT.—Lieutenant Roberts was an Englishman, and commanded a battalion of infantry in De Boigne's First Brigade in 1790. He was present at the battles of Páthan and Merta, and was severely wounded at the latter by a missile from a weapon known as an "organ," and which consisted of several gun barrels so joined together as to fire at once. Whereby it would seem that the Mitrailleuse was of Rajpútanic origin!

RYAN, MAJOR.—This unfortunate officer was an Irishman, and commanded a battalion in the service of Jaswant Ráo Holkar. His only claim to be remembered is as a victim to that chief's treachery, for he was one of the three British subjects who were cruelly beheaded in 1804 for refusing to take the field against their fellow countrymen.

SALEUR, COLONEL [also spelt Suleur and Saleure].—Colonel Saleur was a Swiss or French officer, who succeeded to the command of the Begum Somru's corps, after the suicide of Le Vassoult in 1795. He had taken no part in the mutiny which led to his predecessor's death, but had, on the contrary, done everything in his power to prevent it. He was described as the "only respectable officer" who signed the Covenant entered into between the Begum and her rebellious soldiery. Saleur, who had been in the force almost since its commencement, increased its strength to six battalions, with 40 guns and 200 cavalry, and in 1802 marched with five battalions to join Sindhia in the Deccan after the defeat of Ujjain. The men were in a state of mutiny the whole way, as many of the colonel's letters, written in French, to his mistress testified. When war broke out with the English, Saleur's troops were with Sindhia, but only one battalion took part in the battle of Assaye, the other four having been left behind to guard the Marátha camp and baggage, and owing to this circumstance they escaped destruction; and Colonel Saleur marched them safely to Burhanpur, and from thence back to Sardhána. Saleur was one of the witnesses of the Begum's marriage to Le Vassoult in 1793.

SANGSTER, MAJOR.—Major Sangster was a Scotchman, and a person of skill and ingenuity. In 1782 he obtained the command of the disciplined battalion of infantry which Madoc raised at Agra and sold to the Rána of Gohad. It consisted of 1,000 well-trained Sepoys and a respectable train of artillery. Sangster was skilled in the art of casting cannon, and those he turned out could compare with the best the Company manufactured, whilst his muskets, produced at a cost of ten rupees each, were excellent in every respect. When De Boigne raised his first two battalions, he engaged Sangster (whose master had been forced to surrender to Sindhia), and appointed him to the charge of the arsenal at Agra. He appears to have led a very busy life, for in process of time other arsenals and magazines were established at Mattra, Delhi, Gwalior, Kalpi, and Gohad, of all of which he had the superintendence. The cannon balls were cast at Gwalior, where there were very fine iron mines, and gunpowder was manufactured at Agra, the saltpetre and sulphur being imported from Bikanir. No mention of Sangster can be found after De Boigne's resignation, though in 1801 a report appears in one of the Persian journals that "Lakwa Dáda has employed Mr. Sangster's son to raise and discipline a battalion for him," which seems to indicate that the father was still in the country. Young Sangster was probably the cadet "Songster" who surrendered to General Wellesley after the battle of Assaye.

SHEPHERD, JAMES, COLONEL [known to the Natives as *Jamus Sahib*]. —James Shepherd was an Englishman of unusual enterprise and courage. When hardly emerged from childhood, he deserted his ship in Calcutta, and accompanied an officer to De Boigne's camp in the quality of a menial servant. He afterwards lived in the same capacity with a gentleman at Fatehpur. Shepherd was described as well calculated for the Native service, being a good-looking man and endowed with pliability of temper. About 1799 he took service under Ambaji Inglia, for whom he raised a brigade of regular infantry, which numbered five battalions, with 500 cavalry and 25 guns. Ambaji was a penurious chief, and stinted his officer in money, or he would have created a much more efficient force than one which is sometimes alluded to as the "ragamuffin battalions." Shepherd was engaged in the attack on Lakwa Dáda's position at Sounda in 1801, when he materially assisted in defeating that chief, but lost four of his European officers killed or wounded—poor Bellasis amongst the former—and a great number of his men. He was detached to pursue Lakwa Dáda after his flight, and kept him in play during Perron's campaign against George Thomas. It is a pity there is no detailed record of Shepherd's services, for he is stated to have seen much and been frequently wounded. "Without birth, education, or protection," writes Smith, "he rose from obscurity to consequence by his bravery, his perseverance, and his fidelity; his diligent toil and bold enterprise deserved all the success he won." On the breaking out of the war with the English, Shepherd and his party passed over to the Company's service, and he distinguished himself in Bundelkhand in 1804, where he gave the celebrated Freebooter Amir Khan a sound beating at Maltáon Ghaut, and on the 24th of June completed his discomfiture by entirely defeating and dispersing his force near Kúnch. Shepherds corps at this time consisted of 3,180 men, and was highly praised for its efficiency when General Lake reviewed it in 1805.

SKINNER, JAMES, LIEUTENANT-COLONEL, C.B.—This compilation is so much indebted to "The Military Memoirs of Lieutenant-Colonel James Skinner, C.B.," that although that delightful and graphic biography of the stout old adventurer exists, a sketch of his career must be included in these pages, and the following has been condensed from the above work :

James Skinner was born in 1778. His father was a native of Scotland, and an officer in the Company's service, and his mother a Rajpútni, the daughter of a Rajpút landholder in the Mirzápur country. She was taken prisoner in the war with Chait Singh, the Rájah of Benares, during an action near Bijaigarh, and came under the protection of Ensign Skinner, to whom she bore six children, three sons and three daughters. The latter were all married to gentlemen in the Company's service. David, the eldest son, went to sea; James, the second, and the subject of this sketch, became a military adventurer; and Robert, the youngest, followed in his footsteps.

Skinner's mother died by her own hand in 1790, because it was decided that her daughters should be sent to school, and she conceived this would be a violation of the sanctity of the purdah, and that their Rajpút honour would be destroyed in consequence. After her death James and Robert were sent to a charity school, their father being still only a lieutenant, and unable to pay for their education. However, when he obtained his captaincy in 1793, he removed his sons to a boarding-school, where the charge was Rs. 30 a month for each. Two years later James was bound apprentice to a printer, on a seven years' indenture, and sent to the office to learn his business.

Three days sufficed to disgust him with his proposed calling, and he determined to run away to sea. On the third night he effected his escape, with sixpence in his pocket, on which he contrived to live for six days. When his money was exhausted he wandered about the Calcutta bazaar, working for any one who would hire him, and for some time picked up a precarious living by carrying loads or pulling the drill for Native carpenters at a pay of threepence a day. But before long he was recognised by a servant of his elder sister, Mrs. Templeton, who forthwith bore him away to his master's house

After getting a good rating from his uncle, he was set to work to copy law papers, and remained so employed for three months, until his godfather, Colonel Burn, arrived at the Presidency. This gentleman, finding that young Skinner burned to be a soldier, gave him Rs. 300 and sent him to Cawnpore, where Captain Skinner's regiment was stationed, and whither the Colonel was soon returning.

Here Skinner arrived in April, 1795, and a fortnight later his godfather followed, and furnished him with a letter of introduction to General de Boigne at Koil. Proceeding there the youngster was very kindly received by the great man, who gave him an ensign's appointment in his brigades, on a pay of Rs. 150 a month, and posted him to a Najib battalion, commanded by Captain Pohlman, at Mattra.

Shortly after this De Boigne retired, and the temporary command of the army devolved upon Colonel Robert Sutherland, who was at the head of the Second Brigade, to which Skinner's battalion belonged. Skinner's first experience of active service was during a campaign in Bundelkhand, where Sutherland and Lakwa Dáda were engaged in reducing several refractory chiefs and rájahs to obedience. Here he assisted in two field-battles, and the storm and capture of five or six forts, which intensified his military aspirations. He now made it his study to master all the modes of Native warfare, and became proficient in the use of the Marátha spear, the bow and arrow, and the sword exercise.

In 1796 Perron was appointed to the supreme command of the army of Hindustan, and arrived at Mattra in February of the following year. Soon after this the rebellion of the Bhais broke out, and a large force was ordered to assemble at Gwalior, under Captain Butterfield, to which Skinner's battalion was attached. The first action in the campaign was the battle of Chandkhori, where, owing to his desertion by the Marátha cavalry, Butterfield was defeated and obliged to fall back with a loss of 500 men. Skinner defended his rear during the retreat to a fort called Shérgarh, behaving very gallantly in the face of great difficulties and dangers, and bringing off his guns with safety. For this he received great commendation from Captain Butterfield, and General Perron hearing of it promoted him to the rank of lieutenant with the pay of Rs. 200 a month.

The Bhais had now been joined by Lakwa Dáda, and retired to Chiturgarh in Udaipur, and thither Ambaji Inglia, the new Marátha commander-in-chief, followed them. Captain Butterfield was again in command of the infantry, and Skinner, now promoted to the charge of two battalions, accompanied him. A great deal of skirmishing took place, but nothing decisive was effected. Nor were matters mended when Ambaji was joined by Colonel Sutherland and George Thomas, who had been temporarily engaged by the chief. The campaign, which was not without adventure for Skinner himself, was cut short by political considerations, and Colonel Sutherland being suspected of treachery by Perron, was superseded, and his command conferred on Major Pohlman, an officer under whom Skinner subsequently saw much service. It may be observed that Skinner did not care much for Sutherland, and there was a quarrel between the two before the Colonel left the brigade.

Soon after assuming command Pohlman was directed to take a fort called Jájpur, which was in the possession of a refractory Rajpút chief named Kasri Singh. In the first assault he suffered a severe repulse, but four days later succeeded in carrying the place by storm. This was one of the hottest affairs Skinner was ever engaged in. In Pohlman's life the name of this fort is given as Shapúra on very good authority, but from internal evidence it seems more likely that Skinner's location of the scene is the right one, there being a strong fort at Jajpur and none at Shapúra. From here the brigade marched to Delhi, at the siege and capture of which, as well as at that of Agra, Skinner was present, both cities having refused to acknowledge Perron's authority.

The next action in which Skinner was engaged was the battle of Malpúra, in which he showed distinguished gallantry. Lord William Bentinck, when he was Governor-General of India, mentions an incident in this battle in one of his political despatches to the Court of Directors on the subject of Skinner's public services. "I cannot refrain," he writes, "from relating an anecdote told me by an old Sirdar in the Jeypore service. He had a command in the battle of Buxar in 1764, and he must have been a hundred years of age; but he had still retained the erectness of youth, a fine martial appearance, and his faculties unimpaired. He described to me, with a manner and expression glowing with gratitude, how in the battle of Jeypore (*i.e.*, Malpúra), Colonel James Skinner, then a youth, led a charge of cavalry, captured a field battery which the Sirdar commanded, and then, by his humane and decided interference, saved his life." It is worthy of Skinner's habitual modesty that he does not relate this incident in his own description of the battle, but merely mentions how he nearly lost his own life in the final repulse of the Ráthors, being attacked by one of them, who charged into the centre of the square and killed his horse, Skinner only escaping with his life by an undignified retreat under a tumbril. After the battle Skinner was the first to reconnoitre the Jaipur camp, into which he rode boldly, only to find it deserted. Here he looted two golden idols with diamond eyes, belonging to Rájah Partáb Singh, and trinkets to the value of Rs. 2,000, amongst them being "a brass fish, with two *chowrees* hanging down like moustachios." This curious object proved to be the *Mahi maratib*, or *Fish of Dignities*, a decorative symbol conferred by the Mughal emperors on rájahs of the highest rank, and equivalent to the Three horse tails of the Turkish Empire, or the Button of the Chinese mandarin. In this instance the decoration had been conferred on Rájah Partáb Singh. Skinner presented this valuable acquisition to the Marátha General, and received in return a handsome *khilat* and considerable commendation.

A few days after this Perron joined the army, and Skinner visited Jaipur in his *suite*. From here he was detached, in independent command, to attack a fort near the Chambal river, belonging to a Rajpút chief named Ram Pal Singh. On arriving before this place, he found the low mud walls so nearly level with the crest of the glacis, that there was no touching the bastions with the battering train. He therefore opened trenches, and advanced by regular approaches to the glacis, and then ordered a mine to be carried under it. When this was sprung his three battalions rushed forward to the assault, and after one rather severe check the place was taken. Skinner was next ordered to assist the Karaoli Rájah, who had fallen out with his neighbour of Uniára, and hired several battalions, (amongst them Skinner's from Perron), to fight his battles for him. The force consisted of six battalions of infantry, 2,000 cavalry, and twenty guns; of these the only efficient troops were Skinner's.

The scene of the campaign was between the territory of Tonk and the Banás river, and here the two armies came in sight of one another. But the Karaoli chief was a coward, and an impecunious one to boot, and could not find money to pay his mercenaries, who became so dissatisfied and insubordinate, that Skinner sent for reinforcements to Colonel Pohlman. But before they arrived the Uniára Rájah took advantage of the troubles in his enemy's camp, and intrigued with the discontented levies, and a little later moved out to give battle; whereupon the whole of the Karaoli infantry, with the exception of Skinner's battalion, deserted to the enemy.

On seeing this, Skinner commenced a retreat towards a deserted village in his rear, which he gained with difficulty, driving off two of the enemy's battalions who charged him. Then the whole of their cavalry and infantry, amounting to 6,000 men, came on to the attack, and upon this Skinner recognised it was hopeless to attempt to hold

the village.   So he decided to retreat, if possible, to Tonk, which was
six miles distant, and evacuated his position, but was immediately
attacked by the two battalions who had previously charged him,
and were now aided by their cavalry.   These Skinner repulsed, but
not without the loss of one of his five guns, and his horse was killed
under him.   The remainder of the enemy now came up fast, and
Skinner found further progress impossible, so he drew up his men on
a level plain, and then made them a short but spirited speech, telling
them they could but die once, and exhorting them to fight, and, if
needs be, fall like good and brave soldiers.

Allowing the enemy to approach to within fifty yards, Skinner gave
them a volley and then charged.   Those in front gave way, and he
captured their guns; but their flanks wheeled into action, and galled
him terribly; whereupon Skinner threw his men into a square, and,
as a last resource, attempted to gain some ravines about three quarters
of a mile away.   But it was to no purpose; the enemy, inspirited by
his retreat, charged again and again, captured three more of his
guns, and destroyed so many of his men that he had but 300 and a
single field piece left.   Driven to desperation, he called on his men
to make a final sally, but as he was in the act of leading them forward
he was shot through the groin by a matchlock man, and fell to the
ground, and the remnants of his brave but unfortunate battalion were
destroyed.

This happened about three o'clock in the afternoon, and he did not
regain consciousness till the next morning, when he found himself
despoiled of everything except his pantaloons.   Around him were
heaps of his dead and wounded Native officers and soldiers, among
them a Subahdar with his leg shot off below the knee, and a Jemadar
with a pike thrust through the body.   All were tortured with thirst,
and unable to move; and thus they remained in helpless agony
through the long hot day, praying for death.   Night came at last, but
neither release from suffering nor assistance.   The moon was full and
clear, and about midnight it was very cold.   So dreadful did the
night appear that Skinner vowed to himself that if he survived it he
would never go soldiering again, and if he lived to recover, that he
would build a church to the God of his white father.   The wounded
on all sides were moaning and crying out for water, and the jackals
kept flitting about like four-legged ghouls, tearing the dead, and
coming closer and closer to the living, and were only kept off by
stones feebly thrown at them.

Next morning an old man and woman came to the battlefield
carrying a basket and a pot of water.   To every wounded man the

latter gave a piece of *joari* bread and a drink of water. This revived Skinner, but as the woman was a *Chumarin* (an outcaste) the Subahdar, who was a high-class Rajpút, would take nothing from her hands, saying that a little more or less suffering was nothing, and that he preferred to die unpolluted.

Skinner was eventually rescued by a party of the Uniára Rájah's men, who came to the field to bury the dead, and send the wounded into camp. The poor Subahdar now got some water, and he and Skinner and the rest were lifted in sheets and taken to the Rájah's encampment. After a month the chief gave Skinner his liberty. It is pleasant to learn that the brave Subahdar also recovered, and that Skinner sent the poor *Chumarin* woman a present of a thousand rupees, and a message that he considered her in the light of a mother.

His wound now obliged Skinner to take leave, and in February he went down to Calcutta, where he stayed several months with his sister, Mrs. Templeton, returning to his duties in the month of January, 1801. In the May following he was engaged in the storm of Sounda, having in the interval been transferred from the Second to the Third Brigade, which, under Pedron, had been entrusted with this attack. The column to which Skinner was attached lost three officers and 1,000 men killed and wounded, but captured Lakwa Dáda's guns. The casualties are Skinner's, and the prudent reader will do well to divide all his figures by three or four, and sometimes more; but in this sketch they are all given as he estimates them. After the victory Skinner returned with his corps to Aligarh.

Two months later he was again sent on active service, this time against George Thomas. The Third Brigade was now commanded by Louis Bourguien, an officer for whom Skinner had no respect whatever. The events of the war have already been very fully detailed (chiefly from Skinner's memoirs), and need not be repeated; although it may be noted that Skinner considers the battle of Georgegarh the severest one in which he was present during his military career. Later on he had a creditable share in securing for Thomas the terms which enabled him to surrender with honour to himself, and Skinner's conduct on this occasion, unassumingly related by himself, is worthy of the highest praise.

In March, 1802, Skinner, who had been posted back to his old brigade, the Second, accompanied Perron to Ujjain, and was present at the memorable Darbar when Daulat Ráo Sindhia's intended treachery was averted by the cunning and precaution of Perron. Skinner returned to Hindustan with the General, and a period of comparative inaction followed, till war broke out with the English in

August, 1803. On the 28th of that month all the British subjects in Perron's brigades were summarily dismissed the service, and a few days later Skinner joined General Lake's camp, under circumstances which his dark complexion rendered somewhat mortifying to the *amour propre* of a gallant man. But this was compensated by the treatment he received from the Commander-in-chief, who took a great fancy to him, and shortly afterwards, when 2,000 of Perron's Hindustani horse came over to the English after the battle of Delhi, appointed him to the command. On this occasion occurred an incident which shows how Skinner was beloved by his soldiery. When the troopers were asked whom they would have for their commander, with one voice they shouted—"*Sikander Sahib*," that being the appellation, half name, half sobriquet, given Skinner by the Natives. His own cognomen they pronounced *Is-kinner*, which they changed into *Sikander*, associated in their minds with Alexander the Great, as a compliment to Skinner's dauntless valour, which was a bye-word amongst them.

With Skinner's subsequent career it is not in the province of this compilation to deal. Perron's 2,000 Hindustani horse became a famous British irregular cavalry corps, known as *Skinner's Horse*, or more familiarly and affectionately as *The Yellow Boys*. They and their leader covered themselves with glory during the next thirty years, and their exploits and achievements won for Skinner the substantive rank of Lieutenant-Colonel in the British Army, and the coveted distinction of the C.B. A valuable jaghir in the Aligarh district was also conferred upon him. For many years his headquarters were at George Thomas's old capital of Hánsi (near to which some of his descendants are still living), and he performed able service, although his after life was not unchequered with some disappointments which he did not deserve. He made a host of friends, and found many admirers, amongst them such distinguished men as Lord Lake, Sir John Malcohn, Lord Metcalfe, Lord Minto, the Marquis of Hastings, Lord Combermere, and Lord William Bentinck. It is goodly roll of patrons and acquaintances for the offspring of a Company's ensign and a Rajpútni girl, and one whose only introduction to high society was his own sterling worth !

Many anecdotes are related of Skinner, but only two or three can be here recorded. Perhaps his most remarkable characteristic was his modesty and utter contempt of all assumption. To the end of his life an old spoon was placed on his breakfast table every morning to remind him of his own humble origin and early days. In fulfilment of the vow he made on the battlefield of Uniára, to build a church to the God of his father if his life were spared, he erected the edifice of St. James at Delhi, at a cost of £20,000, and in the same spirit of modest humility before noted, often expressed a desire that when he died he should be buried, not within it, but under the door sill, so that all persons entering might trample upon " the chief of sinners."

Skinner's domestic habits were in some respects more Muhammadan than Christian, and he left behind him a numerous family by sundry wives, of whom he had at least fourteen. His e.dest son, Hercules Skinner, was educated in England, and through the influence of Lord William Bentinck received a commission in the Hydrabad Contingent, much to his father's delight. In 1836 Colonel Skinner was confirmed, and during his latter years was sincerely pious, constantly studying the Bible, and preparing himself for his end. He died at Hánsi on the 4th of December, 1841, aged sixty-three years, and was buried there with military honours. But a little later his remains were disinterred, and carried to Delhi to be deposited by the side of his dearly loved friend and comrade, William Fraser (brother to his biographer), under the altar of St. James's Church. It had been his wish to be buried near Fraser, and it was felt proper that this wish should be fulfilled.

On the 17th of February 1842, accompanied by the whole of his corps, and a great concourse of people, the coffin was carried from Hánsi to Sitaram-ka-Sarai, on the outskirts of Delhi. Here all that was mortal of the gallant old adventurer was met by the civilians and military officers of the station, and a vast multitude from the city, and so escorted to its final resting-place. " None of the Emperors of Hindustan," said the Natives, " were ever brought into Delhi in such state as *Sikander Sahib* ! "

Skinner, Robert, Major.—Robert Skinner was the younger brother of Colonel James Skinner. He entered Perron's army in November, 1800, with an ensign's commission, and was posted to do duty with his brother's battalion. The introduction of the young subaltern to his men was a characteristic one. The elder Skinner called his most trusty Native officers together, fine old soldiers, with scarred faces and grizzled beards, and steady, intrepid fellows every one of them. Then he drew himself up in military fashion, and pointing to Robert, said, " This is my brother; see ye be his protectors ! " The veterans, stroking their beards, and carrying their hands on their foreheads, replied with grave emphasis—" On our heads be it ! " James Skinner was not quite confident of his brother's discretion, and selected this method of safeguarding his inexperience.

Robert Skinner was present at the attack on Ram Pal Singh's fort near the Chambal, where he was wounded by a bullet in the neck, and obliged to return to Aligarh to recover. He rejoined his brother after the defeat of Uniára, and was soon afterwards promoted to the rank of lieutenant, and given the command of a battalion in the Second Brigade under Pohlman. The next occasion on which the two brothers served side by side was in the war against George Thomas. At the battle of Georgegarh the following incident occurred, touchingly related by Fraser in Skinner's memoirs : " James and Robert Skinner were engaged at different parts of the field, so that neither knew how the other fared. The cannonade was so fierce and continuous, and the slaughter so great, that all was smoke and carnage, and there was little communication between the different battalions engaged. When the battle ceased, a report came to James that his brother had been killed, whilst a similar one reached Robert as to James. Both, moved by one impulse, ran to the bloody field, without thinking of rest or refreshment, and sought all over for the body of the brother, but in the darkness, amidst the thousands of corpses, torn and mutilated by the cannon shot, neither found what he sought, and after a weary and fruitless search, they returned to the tent of their commanding officer to make their report. By a singular chance they entered from opposite sides at the same moment, and the first thing that met their eyes was the object on which their thoughts were dwelling. They saw nothing else, but ran and embraced, calling out each other's names before the officers that filled the tent."

Robert Skinner was engaged at the siege and storm of Hánsi, and at the latter led one of the three assaulting columns. In the hand to hand street fighting he approached so close to Thomas on one occasion, that " he got a cut at him, but his armour saved Thomas." It was characteristic of Thomas's generous nature that after his surrender he was "particularly gracious to the younger Skinner, whom he embraced, and showed him the cut he had received from him on his belt."

On the occurrence of the war with the English in 1803, Robert Skinner, after being dismissed from Perron's army, repaired to Sardhána, and took service with the Begum Somru, and when General Lake arrived at Sikandra was deputed by that lady to make terms for her, which he did successfully. Subsequently Skinner entered the Company's service, and was given the local rank of lieutenant, and appointed to the cavalry corps his brother commanded. In this he continued to serve for many years, performing excellent services, and winning many encomiums. In 1815 James Skinner, with the

generosity of disposition and brotherly affection which so distinguished
his nature, desired to sever from his corps a portion to be made into
a separate command for his brother, whose interests he thus hoped
to forward. But Lord Hastings, the Governor-General, preferred the
force being left intact, and Robert Skinner remained in command of
the second regiment in it, but was promoted to the rank of local
Major. In 1819 the Government granted him in perpetuity a small
jaghir in the district of Aligarh ; but he did not live to enjoy it long,
for his death occurred in 1821, before he had reached his fortieth
year.

SMITH, LEWIS FERDINAND, MAJOR.—Major Lewis Ferdinand Smith,
as the historian of the military adventures of Hindustan, and as an
adventurer himself, and a writer of considerable ability, deserves a far
more complete biography than can, unhappily, be compiled ; for he
was a modest soldiery man, who preferred to write of the achievements of others, not of his own deeds. Of his early career little is
recorded. He was the son of Major Lewis Smith, an officer in the
Honourable Company's service, and entered Sindhia's army during the
time that De Boigne was in command, though at what precise date it
is impossible to say. He evidently knew De Boigne well and intimately, for in 1796 and 1797 he contributed two excellent letters, de-
scriptive of the General's life and career, to the Calcutta *Telegraph*—
a curious name for a newspaper in the last century, although, so far
back as 1767, Edgeworth had invented his *Telelograph*, contracted
into *Tellograph*, " a machine which describes words at a distance."
This digression is, however, parenthetical. In the two letters alluded
to, Smith indicates that he had a long daily intercourse with De Boigne.
His first independent command on active service seems to have been
in 1798, when he defeated the forces of the Bhopal State in an engagement, when he was at the head of a battalion of infantry and 100
cavalry. In December of the following year he was entrusted with
the conduct of a more considerable campaign. An impostor named
Sultan Shah gave himself out to be Ghulam Káder, the miscreant
who blinded the Emperor Shah 'Alam in 1788, and whom he declared
had never been killed, but escaped and reached Mecca. Sultan
Shah, claiming this personality, pretended he had been ordered
by the Prophet to recover Hindustan from the Maráthás, and
re-establish the Muhammadan Empire. He appeared in arms in the
province of Saharanpur, where he was opposed by a Marátha official
named Ramchander Palkia, whom he easily defeated. The *éclat* of
this victory brought him a number of followers, and Perron found it

necessary to send Major Smith with three battalions against him. Smith was strengthened by some of the Begum Somru's troops, and the combined force marched against Sultan Shah, and on the 22nd of November, 1799, came upon him at the village of Délun, near the Káli Nádí. Smith at once crossed the river, but the Begum's battalions remained where they were, " for more security," as a contemporary chronicler quaintly puts it. An action took place, and the Impostor's army, which consisted of 10,000 Rohillas, 400 cavalry, and some small field pieces showed poor fight. Smith advanced quickly to within grape-shot range, and then poured several discharges into the enemy, who forthwith took to flight, and were chased for a considerable distance.

The next record of Smith's services is during the war with George Thomas, in which his achievements at first were less satisfactory. He was in command of a battalion of Bourguien's Brigade, and detached with this and two others to beseige Georgegarh, whilst the Colonel followed Thomas on a wild-goose chase into the Sikh country. The latter doubled back, shook off his pursuers, and swooped down on Smith, with a greatly superior numerical force. Smith at once raised the siege, and retreated upon Jhajjar. " Why Thomas did not follow me," he writes in his book, " I cannot say. If he had continued the pursuit I must have lost all my guns, and my party would have been completely destroyed. But Thomas spared me and remained at Georgegarh." Smith was rescued from his perilously weak position by his brother's arrival next day; but he did not forget Thomas's moderation, and amply repaid it. He was present throughout the whole of the campaign, and accompanied Bourguien to Hánsi; and when the latter had "subdued the garrison with gold, which in India is more irresistible than in Europe," Smith came forward to assist Thomas to obtain honourable terms of surrender.

In 1803 Smith accompanied Dudrenec's Brigade to the Deccan, and later in the year returned with it to Hindustan, and surrendered to Colonel Vandeleur at Mattra, a few days after the battle of Delhi, availing himself of the Governor-General's proclamation offering pensions to all British subjects in the Maráthá employ who resigned their posts, and being awarded one of Rs. 1,200 a month. "I have lost," he writes, " the hopes of an independent fortune, which I would have acquired from my rank, the result of my long service, in spite of Perron's injustice ; and I should have starved had it not been for the political and munificent generosity of the Most Noble the Governor-General in allowing liberal provisions to the British officers, who were obliged to quit Scindia's service on the declaration of war. We should have been wanting in principle, and in duty to our country, had we continued to serve its enemies." Besides being the author of "A Sketch of the Regular Corps in the Service of the Native Princes of India," Smith contributed several papers to the Asiatic Annual Register and other publications, for his style of composition can easily be recognised in many of the "Newsletters" which appeared in Indian newspapers during the time that Perron flourished.

SMITH, EMILIUS FELIX, CAPTAIN.—Captain E. F. Smith was a younger brother of Lewis Ferdinand Smith, and was born in Rohilkhand in 1777. He entered Sindhia's service at a very early age, but left on obtaining a commission in the 36th Regiment. This, however, he subsequently resigned in order to remain with his brother, and to this end re-entered Sindhia's service in 1800. Soon after this he was engaged in the reduction of two rebel battalions, commanded by the widow of Captain Le Marchant, who had refused submission to Perron's orders. He then obtained an appointment in the Hindustani Horse, and accompanied Bourguien on the campaign against George Thomas. When his brother was defeated at Georgegarh, and obliged to fall back on Jhajjar, Emilius hurried to the relief at the head of his cavalry, and "performed an astonishing rapid movement of eighty miles in ten hours, fraternal affection giving impulse to his course." Two days later he commanded the left wing of Bourguien's army at the battle of Georgegarh ; and whilst gallantly leading it to the charge, his leg was severely shattered by a four-pounder cannon-ball. He was removed to Jhajjar, where he bore the tortures of an unskilful operation with manly fortitude, but sank under the fever which the wound and shock to the system induced. He died on the 8th of October, 1801, aged twenty-four years. Just before he expired he said with a sigh—" Ah, why did I not fall on the plains of Egypt with my regiment. I should then have died without a regret." He fell a sacrifice to his ardour for his profession. He was a young man of fine character, affectionate disposition, and good education. Something of a poet, too, for many fugitive pieces from his pen found a corner in the Calcutta periodicals of the day.

SOMBRE, OR SOMRU.—His infamy rather than his achievements have rescued the name of this notorious adventurer from oblivion, and awarded it an unenviable niche in Indian history. Sombre's real name was Walter Reinhard, and he was reputed to be the son of a butcher at Saltsburg, where he was born in 1720. At the age of thirty he came out to Pondicherry on board a French frigate, from which he deserted in order to enlist in the French army of Southern India. To hide his identity he assumed the name of Somers as a *nom de guerre*, but his saturnine features and lowering mien soon caused its corruption into the *sobriquet* of Sombre, which in turn was twisted by Native pronunciation into Somru.

Sombre appears to have spent some years in the Carnatic and Southern India before he made his way to Bengal. Arrived here, he first of all enlisted as a private soldier in a Swiss battalion in the employ of the Company, but eighteen days' experience of it sufficed, and he crossed the boundary into Chandernagore, and was appointed a sergeant in Mons. Law's force. But he was soon discontented with this, and once more abandoning his allegiance, proceeded to the Upper Provinces, where he assumed the Native style of dress, and entered the service of Suráj-ud-Daula, the Nawáb of Bengal, as a common trooper. This situation proved even less to his liking than his previous ones, and for the next two or three years he appears to have led a restless and vagabond existence, till 1760, when he joined the rebel *Faujdár* of Parnea, by whom he was appointed to the command of a small force, with instructions to drill it in the European method and bring it into discipline. In a few months the *Faujdár* suffered a reverse, which naturally determined Sombre to desert him. The adventurer now accepted a similar post under an Armenian name, Gregory, a member of a Calcutta family of repute, and the virtual minister of Kassim Ali Khán, who had succeeded Suráj-ud-Daula as Nawáb of Bengal. Fortune favouring Sombre, he was promoted to the command of two battalions. In 1763 a rupture occurred between Kassim Ali and the Company, and the former, enraged at the ill success of his arms, treacherously attacked and captured a large body of English residents at Patna, and in a spirit of wanton and blood-thirsty revenge, ordered them to be executed.

But the deed was too dark and foul a one for any of Kassim Ali's Native officers to undertake, and it was reserved for Sombre to ingratiate himself with his master by carrying out the crime. The details of this "execrable villainy" are thus given in the "Annual Register." "Somers invited above forty officers and other gentlemen, who were amongst these unfortunate prisoners, to sup with him on the day he had fixed for the execution, and when his guests were in full security, protected as they imagined by the laws of hospitality, as well as by the right of prisoners, he ordered the Indians under his command to fall upon them and cut their throats. Even these barbarous soldiers revolted at the orders of this savage European. They refused at first

26

to obey, and desired that arms should be given to the English, and that they would then engage them. Somers, fixed in his villainy, compelled them with blows and threats to the accomplishment of that odious service. The unfortunate victims, though thus suddenly attacked and wholly unarmed, made a long and brave defence, and with their plates and bottles even killed some of their assailants, but in the end they were all slaughtered. Proceeding then, with a file of Sepoys, to the prison where a number of the prisoners then remained, he directed the massacre, and with his own hands assisted in the inhuman slaughter of one hundred and forty-eight defenceless Europeans confined within its walls—an appalling act of atrocity that has stamped his name with infamy for ever." Justice requires it to be added that in one account of this tragedy, it is asserted that Sombre's own life would have been forfeited had he refused to carry out Kassim Ali's commands.

British troops were soon marching up from Calcutta to avenge this foul deed, and Kassim Ali Khán's army was defeated. But before this happened Sombre had been invited by the Nawáb Wazir of Oudh to enter his service, and seizing the opportunity of Kassim Ali's distress, renounced his allegiance, extorted by violence the arrears of pay due to him, and then marched his two battalions to Lucknow, where he entered on his new appointment.

By the end of 1763 Sombre's force had increased to four battalions of infantry, one of cavalry, and a strong complement of artillery, and their commander enjoyed a high influence at Court, until war broke out with the English, and the Nawáb Wazir was defeated at the battle of Buxar, and compelled to sue for peace, when one of the principal conditions insisted on by the English was the surrender of Sombre. The Nawáb accepted the stipulation in theory, but pointed out that, in practice, Sombre was in command of an armed force, which made his apprehension impossible. He proposed, as an alternative, to poison or assassinate the adventurer, but this suggestion was declined. Meanwhile Sombre, suspecting the tenor of the protracted negotiations, took advantage of the delay to surround and plunder the Nawáb's Begums, who had been entrusted to him for protection, and also to rob his late master, Kassim Ali, who was at the time a refugee at the Oudh Court. Having thus acquired a large sum of money by methods perfectly in keeping with his past career, he secured the fidelity of his force by paying it up in full, and then marched to Rohilkhand. Here he entered the service of the Afghan chief, Hafiz Raimat Ali—the benevolent Rohilla ruler of Macaulay's essay on Warren Hastings. But fear of the English soon drove him to leave

THE BEGUM SOMBRE.

[*From a medallion in Sleeman's " Rambles and Recollections of an Indian Official."*]

the neighbourhood, and marching to Díg, he enlisted under the banners of the Ját Rájah of Bhartpur. His connection with this potentate was of a very short duration, for in a few months he was serving the Rájah of Jaipur in a similar capacity, but the Rajpút prince soon dismissed a mercenary whom he found too villainous for his service, and Sombre finally tendered his sword to Najaf Khán, the Wazir of Shah 'Alam, the Emperor of Delhi, and a nobleman who seldom refused the proposals of any military adventurers, and who agreed to pay Sombre Rs. 65,000 a month for the services of his party.

Up to this period of his career Sombre had served twelve or fourteen different masters, but he remained in the service of the Court of Delhi until his death. This fixity of employment was probably due to his having been assigned a rich *jaghir* or estate at Sardhána, a district some forty miles north of the capital, where he built and fortified his headquarters, and settled down.

From the time that he had quitted civilisation and Chandernagore, Sombre had adopted the native dress, and with it the custom of keeping a harem. At Sardhána he fell in love with a very beautiful, and eke remarkable woman, concerning whose parentage there are various accounts. One historian asserts that she was the daughter of a decayed Mughal nobleman, another that she was a Kashmiri dancing-girl, and a third that she was by birth a *Syudani*, or lineal descendant of the Prophet. Sombre was already married to a woman of the Massalman faith, who was still alive ; but this did not prevent him from repeating the ceremony with this girl who had taken his fancy. His connection with her laid the foundation of the fortunes of his family, for the Begum Somru, as she came to be called, was not less notable for her beauty than for her extraordinary cleverness and force of character. She soon gained a great ascendancy over Sombre, and it was in a great measure owing to her influence that he abandoned his roving life and settled down permanently at Sardhána.

Sombre was an illiterate man who could neither read nor write, though he spoke Persian and Hindustani fluently. It is to his credit that he was never ashamed of his humble origin, and although his services were eagerly courted and bid for, and he enjoyed a position of considerable political power in the country, he despised show, and preferred a plain unostentatious mode of life. But with this single statement the category of his virtues is begun and ended. He possessed a certain degree of low and crafty intelligence, but was utterly destitute of military skill, martial spirit, or personal courage, whilst, considering the possibilities open to him, he was singularly devoid of enterprise and ambition. Shortly after entering Najaf Khan's service, he was offered a large and important *Jaidad,* or military assignment of territory, which would have raised him to a princely position, but he preferred a monetary monthly payment, and refused the proposal. It is probable he feared the risk involved in occupying an extended territory necessitating the distribution of his troops, and preferred to keep them together and concentrated about his person. For it is known that after the massacre of Patna he suffered agonies of remorse and fear, and lived in the miserable and constant terror of being betrayed into the hands of the English to expiate his crime. To prevent such a fate he always carried poison about his person, with which to terminate his existence if necessary, and if his courage served him.

Sombre's disposition was merciless, cruel, and bloodthirsty, and he was totally wanting in honour and fidelity. Avaricious and unscrupulous to an astounding degree, he bartered his sword to the highest bidder, with the eagerness of a huckster disposing of perishable goods, and changed his fealty with the same unconcern that he changed his coat. His force was officered by Europeans, but few, if any, of them were men of respectability, and those he engaged were generally the very dregs and dross of society. The consequence was that his troops were generally in a state of pronounced mutiny and insubordination, committing every imaginable outrage upon the persons of their officers, whom they despised. They seldom obtained their pay until they had put their commander into confinement, and made him dig up his hidden treasure, if he had any, or borrow from bankers if he had none. If the troops were impatient it was their custom to divest Sombre of his trousers and straddle him across a hot gun. When one battalion had extracted its dues, he was often handed over to another to be further squeezed. In later years the Begum herself was subjected to the starving process, but Colonel Sleeman is the authority for stating that she was never actually grilled on a gun. The same writer states that it was Sombre's invariable rule when engaged in active service to draw up at a safe distance and await the course of events. If victory declared for the enemy he sold his unbroken force to the foe for a cash payment; if his own friends won, he promptly assisted them in plundering, and so secured all the tangible fruits of victory.

Lewis Ferdinand Smith has left on record[1] a scathing criticism of Sombre's character as a soldier, and of the merits and qualities of his corps. "Sombre's party," he writes, "have never been conspicuous for their military achievements, nor famed for their military trophies. They never lost a gun and never gained one, until they were defeated by the British army near Adjanta Ghát (Assaye). But they were remarkable for their excellent retreats. Sombre made it a rule in every action to draw his men out in line, fire a few shots, and then form square and retreat. This rule his party has ever since adhered to with inflexible exactitude ; by which singular mode of prudent warfare they have acquired no laurels, yet preserved their reputation. They have been the most mutinous troops in India, and woe to the unfortunate European who was compelled by his necessities to enter into this party. Disgrace, if not death, attended them, from the frequent revolts of the soldiers, when they regularly wreaked their ire with clubs upon the shoulders of their European officers."

The latter years of Sombre's life were rendered a perfect purgatory to him by his distrust and suspicion of all around him. He died at Agra on the 4th of May, 1778, aged fifty-eight years, and was buried in the garden of his residence there. But three years later his widow, the Begum Somru, on being baptized and received into the Roman Catholic faith, caused his remains to be disinterred and deposited in the churchyard of that city. The following is the Portugese inscription over his resting-place, in Padretola, Agra :—

AQUIIAZ	EO AOS4
OWALT	DE MAYO
ERREINHA	NOANNO
RD. MORR	DE 1778

After Sombre's death the command of his party, its pay, and the *jaghir* of Sardhána, were continued to the Begum Somru, who was always known by that name, although on her entry into the church she had been christened Joanna Nobilis. By means of her uncommon ability, gallantry, and masculine force of character, she proved herself equal to the responsibility. She gave the command to a German named Pauly, perhaps because he was a countryman of her husband, but, it has been suggested, from more tender reasons, and gradually entertained a considerable body of Europeans, both as officers and to work her artillery, which numbered forty pieces of cannon. These Europeans were of all nationalities, English, French, Germans, Swiss, Portugese, Armenians, and half-castes, many of them being deserters from the Company's service. At one time the Begum employed over two hundred in her force.

But she was unfortunate in her officers, for the respectable ones all left her, and the others were a worthless, dissolute set of men, whose outrageous conduct often incited the troops to mutiny. Pauly was murdered " by a bloody process " in 1783 ; Baours, who succeeded him, retired, so next did Evans and Dudrenec, all three disgusted with the "beastly habits" of their European subordinates. It was about this time that George Thomas rose to a position of importance, if not the actual control of her force ; he, too, was forced to leave. It will be remembered that he was the officer concerned in the spirited succour which the Begum afforded to the Emperor Shah 'Alam, when he was trying to reduce Najaf Kuli Khán in 1788. Thomas departed about 1793, when the command of the party devolved upon Le Vassoult, a gallant and good-looking soldier, with whom the Begum carried on an intrigue. She was presently married to him by Father Gregorio, a Carmelite monk, Major Bernier and Colonel Saleur being the witnesses of the marriage, which was kept secret. Colonel Sleeman states that Le Vassoult proposed for her hand as the best method of securing his ascendancy over Thomas, to whom he was always hostile. Le Vassoult was a gentleman by birth and education, and a soldier of honourable feelings ; but he was stern and haughty by nature, and so thoroughly despised his subordinates that, after his marriage, he refused to associate with them on equal grounds, or admit them to a seat at his table. The Begum in vain endeavoured to persuade her husband to alter his demeanour, urging that their personal safety required that the officers should be conciliated. But her warnings were disregarded. They proved too true ; Le Vassoult's subordinates took umbrage, and declared that no man should command them who would not meet them on terms of perfect social equality. The troops sided with the officers, and determined to depose the Begum, and elevate Balthazar Sombre, a son of Sombre by his first wife, to the government. This woman was still living, nor, indeed, did she die till 1838, when she must have been over a hundred years old. She was buried at Sardhána, the cemetery of which place, it is curious to note, contained the bones of many centenarians.

Matters with the mutineers were brought to a crisis by Le Vassoult's harsh treatment of a German officer named Legois (a friend of George Thomas), who was degraded for endeavouring to dissuade the Begum from making an attack on Hariána. This arbitrary abuse of power disgusted the troops, who had fought under Legois for many years, and were incensed at seeing him superseded by a junior officer. After remonstrating in vain with Le Vassoult, they suddenly broke out into open mutiny. The Begum and her husband now became frightened, and determined to seek an asylum in the Company's territory. Neither of them understood English, but Le Vassoult, with the aid of a grammar and dictionary, managed to communicate his wishes to Colonel McGowan, who commanded the advance post of the British army at Anúpshahr. After some difficulty sanction was accorded, but a stipulation was made that Le Vassoult should be treated as a prisoner of war on *parole*, and reside with his wife at the French settlement of Chandernagore. This was in May, 1795.

The Begum's troops had, however, obtained information of what was going on, and immediately summoned Balthazar Sombre—or, as he was more commonly called, from a title bestowed on him by the Emperor Shah 'Alam, Zafar Yáb Khan—from Delhi to assume the government of the Sardhána State. Meanwhile Le Vassoult and the Begum managed to slip away, but their departure being discovered, a detachment was sent in pursuit to capture them. An agreement existed between the Begum and Le Vassoult, that in the event of their falling into the hands of the mutineers, neither should survive the other. In the commotion that ensued, consequent upon their being overtaken and surrounded, the Begum drew a dagger, and in a half-hearted way slashed herself slightly in the breast. Her attendants seeing the blood flow shouted out that their mistress had killed herself. Le Vassoult, who was riding a short distance ahead, hearing the tumult, inquired what it arose from. He was told that his wife was dead. A second time he repeated the question, and received the same answer. He then drew a pistol from his holster, and although he might easily have galloped off and saved himself, placed the muzzle to his mouth and pulled the trigger. The ball passed through his brain, and he sprang from his saddle a full foot into the air, before he fell dead to the ground. His corpse was subjected to every indignity and insult that the gross and bestial imagination of his officers and men could conceive, and left to rot, unburied, on the ground.

The Begum, who was only slightly injured, was carried back a captive to Sardhána, and kept chained to a gun for seven days, and deprived of all food except such as was conveyed to her by stealth by her female servants. Balthazar Sombre was seated on the *masnad*. He was a detestable compound of ignorance, weakness, cruelty, and debauchery, and it was not long before it became evident his rule had not a single element of stability.

The actual instrument of his deposition, and the Begum's re-establishment in power, was George Thomas, with whom she found means to communicate. He generously laid aside old animosities, and responded to her appeal for help. Balthazar Sombre was sent a prisoner to Delhi, where he died, some say by poison, in 1803, leaving a daughter, subsequently married to Colonel Dyce, whose son became famous as the principal personage in the great Dyce-Sombre law-suit.

The command of the Begum's force was now bestowed on Colonel Saleur, who, with thirty other European officers, signed a document swearing fidelity and allegiance to their mistress. As illustrating the class of men who filled the posts of command in this party, it may be mentioned that Saleur was the only one who could write his name, most of the others affixing their seals, whilst a few, to show the superiority of their accomplishments, subscribed two or three letters of the alphabet, not necessarily those representing their proper initials, but such as they happened to be able to form. The covenant was drawn out by a Muhammadan scribe in Persian, and as his conscientious scruples prevented him from acknowledging Christ as the son of God, the precious document was superscribed—" In the name of God, and of His Majesty Christ ! "

The Begum never publicly declared her marriage to Le Vassoult, and immediately after his death resumed her former name. So anxious was she to bury in oblivion an episode which certainly evinced weakness in a woman usually strong minded, and already well advanced in years, that she stipulated in her will that her heir, whose family patronymic was Dyce, should in addition assume the name of Sombre. To complete the story of poor Le Vassoult's fate it should be added that doubts have been cast upon the *bonâ fides* of the agreement which the Begum originated, that in the event of capture at the hands of the mutineers neither should survive the other. This and her subsequent mock wound have been denounced as a piece of treachery on her part, designed to rid herself of her husband. There is, however, no actual proof of this, and Colonel Sleeman, writing in 1836, mentions that he heard "from grave old Native gentlemen, who were long in her service, that there really was too much truth in the story of her intimacy with the gallant young Frenchman, though God forgive them for saying so of a lady whose salt they had eaten for so many years." Under these circumstances the inhuman atrocity of the above suggestion is hardly conceivable.

Colonel Saleur raised the Begum Somru's party to six battalions of infantry, increased the artillery, and added a cavalry force. The corps is often mentioned in the political history of the next eight years, but it never distinguished itself, nor did the Begum lapse a second time rom the path of prudence. Amidst the kaleidoscopic changes of Hindustan, she managed to preserve her power and independence intact, until her army, famous in peace, if not in war, met the English on the plain of Assaye. But even here fortune favoured them, for four of her five battalions, being left to guard the Maráthá camp, made good their escape, and only one was destroyed.

Just before the declaration of war in 1803, Robert Skinner joined the Begum's service, and after the fall of Aligarh was deputed to arrange for her submission to General Lake. James Skinner tells the story so well in his memoirs that its quotation cannot be resisted. "When the Begum came in person to pay her respects to General Lake, an incident occurred of a curious and characteristic description. She arrived at head-quarters just after dinner, and being carried in her palanquin at once to the reception tent, the General came out to meet and receive her. As the adhesion of every petty chieftain was, in those days, of consequence, Lord Lake was not a little pleased at the early demonstration of the Begum's loyalty, and being a little elevated by the wine which had just been drunk, he forgot the novel circumstance of its being a Native female, instead of some well-bearded chief, so he gallantly advanced, and, to the utter dismay of her attendants, took her in his arms and kissed her! The mistake might have been awkward, but the lady's presence of mind put all right. Receiving courteously the proffered attention, she turned calmly round to her astonished attendants and observed, 'It is the salute of a *padre* (priest) to his daughter.' The Begum professes Christianity, and thus the explanation was perfectly in character, though more experienced spectators might have smiled at the appearance of the jolly red-coated clergyman exhibited in the person of the General."

The Begum lived for many years after this in friendly intercourse with the British. Bishop Heber saw her in 1825, and described her as "a very queer looking old woman, with brilliant but wicked eyes, and the remains of beauty in her features." "Queer and wicked" she had been in some of her actions, as the following anecdote shows. One day two of her slave girls set fire to her houses at Agra in order to make off with their paramours, two soldiers of the guard left in charge of them. These houses had thatched roofs, and contained all the Begum's valuables. The fire was put out with much difficulty and great loss of property, and the two slave girls were soon after discovered in the bazaar at Agra, and brought into the Begum's camp. She ordered the affair to be investigated by a drum-head court-martial, and in the usual summary fashion. Their guilt being established they were first of all flogged until they were senseless, and then buried alive in a pit dug in front of her tent. Another version of this atrocious story, related in Heber's narrative, states that the girls were buried in a hole dug in the floor of the Begum's own chamber, and that she had her bed drawn over it, and smoked her *hookah* unconcernedly over this living grave. But Colonel Sleeman, who was at the pains of sifting the story, vouches for the correctness of the former version—although it is but one degree less horrible—which he heard from an old Persian merchant named Aga, to whom the slave girls originally belonged. "The Begum's object," explained the old Aga, "was to make a strong impression upon the turbulent spirit of her troops by a severe example, and she was entirely successful."

When the Begum submitted to the English, her force consisted of six battalions of infantry, 400 horse, and a party of artillery served chiefly by Europeans. She possessed a good arsenal, well stored, and a foundry for cannon, both built within the walls of the fortress of Sardhána. The cost of the upkeep of her military establishment was about four lakhs of rupees a year, and her other expenses were not less than two, but the revenues from her *jaghir* of Sardhána were sufficient to cover both. When she accepted British protection her income increased very greatly, and there were no longer any calls for the payment of her troops, which were disbanded. She thus became immensely rich, and devoted large sums to charitable and religious institutions. Amongst other gifts, she sent to the Pope at Rome Rs. 150,000, to the Archbishop of Canterbury Rs. 50,000, and to the Bishop of Calcutta Rs. 100,000. To Catholic Missions in India she subscribed Rs. 130,000 ; and for distribution to the deserving debtors of Calcutta Rs. 50,000. She also built a handsome Roman Catholic Church and a Protestant Chapel at Meerut, to which place she removed her residence during her latter years. The Roman Catholic bishop here was an Italian from Milan, named Julius Cæsar. He was the medium of her donation to the Pope, for which he received his bishopric. His Holiness made the Begum's recognised heir and step-grandson—Dyce-Sombre—a Chevalier of the Order of Christ, besides presenting him with a splint from the real cross as a relic.

The Begum was very diminutive in person, but possessed a wonderful dignity of carriage, and an uncommon resolution of manner. At Meerut she entertained from time to time several Governors-General and Commanders-in-chief. During the closing years of her life an immense army of pensioners enjoyed her bounty, and she acquired the character of a kind-hearted and benevolent woman. She died in 1836, leaving behind her a fortune of £700,000, a large portion of which was bequeathed to charities, and the rest to Mr. Dyce-Sombre, who married an English lady of title, and his two sisters, one of whom married an English officer, Captain Troup, and the other an Italian gentleman, Signor Sabroli.

SUTHERLAND, ROBERT, COLONEL [known to the Natives as *Sutlej Sahib*].—Sutherland was a Scotchman, and originally an officer in the

73rd Regiment, from which he was cashiered. He entered De Boigne's First Brigade in 1790, and in May, 1794, was still only a lieutenant on a pay of Rs. 200 a month. Soon after this promotion came to him, and he obtained the command of the Third Brigade, and on the death of Colonel Frèmont in 1795 was transferred to that of the Second. When, at the end of this year, De Boigne retired Sutherland was senior officer in Hindustan, and acted as chief commander of the troops. Perron was, however, considerably senior to him, and being in the Deccan with Daulat Ráo Sindhia, had little difficulty in obtaining the succession to De Boigne's appointment, in spite of all Sutherland's endeavours to secure it for himself. This was the beginning of a long and jealous feud between the two adventurers, which only terminated with the Scotchman's resignation in 1802. It is probable, though not actually recorded, that Sutherland was present at the battles of Pátan and Merta. In 1796 he was employed in the reduction of some revolted districts in Bundelkhand, bringing into obedience several petty rájahs, during which (in Skinner's words) he fought two general actions and captured half-a-dozen forts. His next service was against Lakwa Dáda at Chitúrgarh. This was the occasion when Thomas complained of Sutherland's conduct in having arranged a concerted attack on the rebel chief over night, and then unaccountably drawn off his forces without any assigned reason. Skinner records an incident which happened during this campaign, and does not rebound very much to Sutherland's credit. It appears that during the desultory progress of the war, Skinner was one morning exercising his horse " in full armour," and chanced to meet Harji Sindhia, a Marátha chieftain, and a relative of Daulat Ráo. Harji invited Skinner to join him in his ride to a river close by, whither he was bound, at the request of the Marátha General, Ambaji Inglia, to look for a ford. This expedition was subsequently proved to be a snare laid by Ambaji, in collusion with Lakwa Dáda—the enemy he was supposed to be fighting against—to bring about the destruction of Harji, to whom both the chiefs were hostile. As they rode along Skinner's suspicions were aroused, and he warned Harji, who was attended by 500 of his men, to be on his guard. His fears were not ill-founded, for almost immediately afterwards they fell into an ambuscade, and were attacked by a thousand of Lakwa Dáda's cavalry. Skinner and Harji immediately offered fight, and eventually succeeded in beating the enemy off, though not before the former's horse was wounded by a sabre cut, and he himself had received two or three sword blows on the body, from which he was only saved by his armour. Harji was wounded, but Skinner fortunately cut down the man who was attacking him. Returning to camp, Harji invited Skinner to his tent, where all sat down in Darbar. Then the chief arose and said, "All those who fought with me this day were my servants, and did but perform their duty; but you are my friend, and fought for me as a friend." He then took a pair of gold bangles set with diamonds, and put them round Skinner's wrists, and also gave him a sword, a shield, and a fine horse.

When Colonel Sutherland heard of this he blamed Skinner for what had passed, and told him he should report the circumstance of his accompanying the chief, without leave, to Perron. But a little later he caused intimation to be conveyed to Skinner that if he would give him the horse he had received from Harji, nothing should be said of what had happened. Skinner sent back word he would give the bangles, but not the horse, the sword, or the shield. At this Sutherland was much incensed, and his anger was increased when he learnt that Harji had himself written to Perron praising Skinner's conduct.

" Soon after this," adds Skinner, with quiet satisfaction, " the Colonel himself was discovered intriguing with the Maráthá chiefs, and Perron discharged him, bestowing his command on Major Pohlman." This incident is related because it shows the existence of an old-standing quarrel between Sutherland and Skinner, and, in a measure, explains some of the strictures the latter, in his memoirs, takes occasion to pass upon the Scotchman.

Not long after this, Sutherland, having been forgiven through the interest of his father-in-law, Colonel John Hessing, was sent to the Deccan to take over the command of the First Brigade. The side-light here is interesting, for it establishes a connection by marriage between Perron and Sutherland, since the General and Hessing had married sisters. In another part of his memoirs Skinner mentions that Filoze and Bourguien were both related to Perron, but without mentioning the degree of connection. It would thus appear that there was a regular family party in command of Sindhia's brigades, for Perron, the two Hessings, Sutherland, Derridon, the Filoze's, and Bourguien must all have been more or less connected by marriage ties. Sutherland, indeed, was nephew by marriage to Perron, having married the General's niece ; but, despite this, they cordially hated one another, and the Frenchman lost no opportunity of mortifying and vexing the Scotchman, with the object of getting rid of him, for it did not suit his policy that his second in command should be a British subject.

Sutherland assumed command of the First Brigade in 1799. Previous to this his principal services had been the storming and capture of Narwár with four battalions in 1795, and the siege and capture of Tori

Fatehpur in 1796, at the head of eight battalions. In the Deccan he was chiefly engaged in helping Daulat Ráo Sindhia to consolidate his power at Poonah, and it was not until 1801 that an opportunity occurred for him to really distinguish himself. In this year Sindhia returned to Malwa, leaving Sutherland and a portion of the First Brigade behind to support his interests at the Deccan capital during his absence. Then came the disastrous defeat of Ujjain, and Sutherland was at once summoned to his master's aid. As soon as the rainy season slackened, and the Narbada became fordable, Sutherland was detached to retrieve the defeat sustained in June. With fourteen battalions of regular infantry and 20,000 Marátha horse he gave battle to Jaswant Ráo Holkar and Amir Khán on the plain outside the city of Indore, where the latter had taken up a strong position. After an obstinate contest he gained a complete victory, drove Holkar and his troops from their entrenchments, took 98 guns, 160 tumbrils, and all the baggage, and wound up the exploit by plundering Indore. He lost 400 men in the action, which was a very severe one. Although a detailed account of this battle has been given in the sketch of Perron's life, it will not be out of place to quote the following description of it from the pages of " Pandurang Hàri," which gives a graphic idea of the fight from a Hindu point of view. Pandurang Hàri, it may be mentioned, was at the time a cavalry officer in Holkar's Marátha Horse.

" I had just entered upon my new service when despatches arrived with orders for us to march to Indore, Holker's capital. . . . A Mahratta army consists in general of horse and foot of every neighbouring nation, religion, and costume. It makes a very motley appearance, as it is under no discipline, and destitute of regular uniform. Few of the men in the same line, either cavalry or infantry, have weapons of a like form. Some are armed with sword and shield, others with matchlocks or muskets. Some carry bows and arrows, others spears, lances, or war rockets. Many are expert with the battleaxe, but the sabre is indispensable to all. The men in armour, of whom there are many to make up the variety, cut a very curious appearance. A helmet covers not only the head and ears, but protects the shoulders. The body is cased in iron network, or in a thick quilted vest. They give preference to the two-edged sword before the curved one used by the Persians and Arabs. . . . Every rájah, prince, or leader is responsible among the Mahrattas to the Peishwa, or head of the empire, for his general conduct. He pays tribute for his district, and attends when summoned with his quota of men, which is regulated by his wealth and population. He is supreme in command over his corps, which is attached alone to him and to his fortunes, and adheres to whatever party he supports. . . . After a fatiguing march we reached Indore, the capital of Jeswant Ráo Holker. Our preparations were now complete, and we were confident of success. Our cavalry was a strange rabble, mounted on tall and short horses of every colour and kind. Saddles were always slipping off for want of girths ; strings fastened to any old pieces of iron by way of bits, supplied bridles ; old turbans served for martingales, and tent ropes for cruppers. The infantry was just as wretchedly accoutred as the cavalry. Everything was wanting and nothing regular. Here voices might be heard roaring out for ball, and there for muskets or arms. Those who were not fortunate enough to procure any weapon at all, supplied the deficiency by a bamboo pole, which they dignified with the designation of a spear. . . . The eventful day at length dawned. I awoke early, and opening my tent, looked abroad. All was dark and misty. Soon it was all alive in the camp, and as the day advanced clamour, turmoil, and preparation increased. The drums roared on every hand the call to arms. The war-elephants, caparisoned and ready, yelled with impatience, and towered loftily over all other living objects. The neighing of horses, the clash of arms, the buzz of impatient voices, the sounds of command, the march of the irregular and confused masses to their stations, was an impressive scene. Soon the firing of guns, at first slow and irregular, then more rapidly, convinced me the work of death had begun in some quarter, and it seemed speedily extending itself towards the station of my troop, which I had joined, well mounted, and with which I remained, with a fluttering heart, in awful suspense. The current of battle now rolled close by me, and action soon took away all reflection, for we had enough upon our hands. Our men were all lean kine, and too scantily fed to be much heavier than skeletons. Our horses were in little better condition, and when Scindia's cavalry came down on us we were knocked off on the ground before we could strike a blow. In vain I tried to rally and remount my men. I succeeded in prevailing upon only a few to rally ; the best part of them turned tail and fled without once looking behind. Thus the division to which I was attached was speedily disposed of. Our infantry getting mixed with the cavalry that had been driven back by Scindia, was taken by it for the infantry of that chief, instead of our own, and the sabre began to cut among them as if they were a field of standing corn. I laboured in vain to rectify the mistake, and stay the carnage of our own men. My voice was lost in the scene of death and discord, the rush of rockets, and the groans of the dying. How long this scene might have continued before it could have been put an end to I cannot tell, if the attention of the cavalry had not been drawn to something, which even in the heat of battle was truly appalling to the sight, and made them, even there, think of self-preservation. A wounded elephant rushed in among them, mad with the pain of a ball he had just received, and rolled his unwieldy bulk through and over the slashed infantry, and among the terrified horse. Beast and rider were overturned and crushed beneath his tread, and all that lay in his path became victims to his fury. This effectually put a stop to the havoc the cavalry had begun, as the horses took fright and bore their riders off the field of action, leaving their own broken infantry to be trampled to death by the enraged beast. At this moment the cavalry of Scindia charged our artillery and captured it all together with our baggage. This was decisive. Jeswant Ráo Holker saw his world-conquering heroes disperse in every direction, and the battle terminated in leaving Scindia no enemies in view, the pursued soon leaving their conquerors far in the rear. The virtue of leanness, which served us so ill in the battle, was now of singular service in making our escape."

Pandurang Hàri makes a mistake in describing Sindhia as present in person at the battle, for he was some miles in the rear with his baggage, and Sutherland was in command of the victorious army. It is curious that no mention is made of the regular infantry in this spirited description of the fight. The victory established Sutherland's reputation and confirmed him in his master's favour; so much so that at one time it was announced he had been appointed to supersede Perron, whose jealousy operated as much as any other cause in bringing him to Ujjain in March, 1802.

Perron soon obtained Sindhia's ear, and although Sutherland intrigued assiduously, he was disgraced and transferred to the command of the Second Brigade, which had escorted Perron down from Hindustan. This humiliation and " a remark of Perron's " caused the Scotchman to throw up his commission in disgust, and he returned to Agra " without leave," accompanied by a hundred cavalry. Sindhia, it was stated, was very much distressed at his departure, and Perron went personally to pacify his brigade, and promised them a new commander of equal rank.

Sutherland remained at Agra till the breaking out of the war with the English, and was one of the officers confined by the mutinous Agra garrison. He was associated with George Hessing in arranging the terms of capitulation, and the bearer of the letter to General Lake which "demanded a cessation of hostilities " on the 13th of October, 1803. Two or three days after this he and all the European officers in the place found protection under the British flag.

On the whole, Sutherland seems to have been a good officer, though doubtless his social qualities were not so commendable as his military abilities. His victory at Indore justifies his claim to be considered a more competent commander than most of his contemporaries. On his withdrawal from Sindhia's service he obtained a pension of Rs. 800 a month, under favour of the Governor-General's proclamation, which he enjoyed for some years. He died at Mattra, but the date of his death is not known.

SYMES, CAPTAIN [known to the natives as *Sunk Sahib*].—Captain Symes was the commandant of a Najib, or matchlock, battalion in Perron's First Brigade, and was wounded at the storm of Sounda. After this he was sent to supersede Bourguien, who had been fruitlessly endeavouring to capture Ajmir. From thence he proceeded to Tonk, which place he garrisoned for some time, until Jaswant Ráo Holkar attacked him, and forced him to retreat to Rampúra. He died at Sikandra a short time before the war broke out with the English.

TONE, WILLIAM HENRY, COLONEL.—Colonel W. H. Tone was an Irishman, and brother to the famous Irish rebel, Theobald Wolfe Tone. William was born in August, 1764, his grandfather being a respectable farmer near Naas, in county Kildare, and his father a coachmaker, who was ruined by litigation over the family property. Tone was intended for a commercial life, and bound apprentice at the age of fourteen to an eminent bookseller. This enabled him to indulge his passion for reading, and he perused every book of voyages and travels which he could find, and also some of military history and adventure. This literature heated an imagination naturally warm and enthusiastic to such a degree that, at the age of sixteen, he ran away to London, and entered as a volunteer in the East India Company's service. His first experience was unfortunate, for instead of finding his way to India, as he desired, he was sent to the Island of St. Helena, on which barren rock he remained in garrison for six years, and then returned to Europe. It was highly to his honour that, though he entered into such execrable society as the troops in the Company's service were composed of, and at such an early age, he passed through the ordeal without being affected by the contagion of their manners or their principles. He even found means in that degraded situation and remote spot to cultivate his mind to a certain degree, so that his brother, Wolfe Tone, was much surprised when he met him in London, after a separation of eight years, to find him with the manners of a gentleman and a considerable acquaintance with the best parts of English literature. Tone had a natural talent for poetry, which he much improved, and composed several very elegant sets of verses. He was a handsome, well-made man with a good address, and extremely well received among women, whom he loved to excess. He was as brave as Cæsar and devoted to soldiering.

Having remained three or four years in Europe, by which time his father was utterly ruined by the law-suit alluded to, Tone resolved to try his fortune in India, from which step his brother did not attempt to dissuade him. Re-entering the Company's service in 1792, he arrived at Madras at the end of that year. With an advantageous figure, a good address, and considerable talents, he recommended himself so far to the colonel of the regiment in which he served, that he obtained his discharge and letters of introduction to persons at Calcutta, where he was advised to push his fortunes. A small military command enabled him to defray the expenses of the voyage, and procured him a gratification of £50 on his arrival at his destination as a reward for his exertions in quelling a dangerous mutiny which broke out amongst the black troops under his command on board, who had formed a scheme to run away with the ship. At Calcutta the persons to whom he had come recommended introduced him to a French officer named Marigny, who was second in command of the Nizam of Haidarabad's army, and happened to be at the Presidency purchasing military stores for his master. Marigny gave Tone an appointment in the Nizam's service, and promised him the command of a battery of artillery as soon as they should arrive at Haidarabad. The stores being purchased, Tone marched with the First Division, of which he had the command, and arrived safely at the Nizam's capital. After some time, Marigny followed; but by an unforeseen accident all Tone's hopes were blasted. A quarrel took place between Marigny and Raymond, the Frenchman in command, in which Tone, with an honourable indiscretion, sided with his friend. The consequence was that Marigny was put in irons, and Tone only escaped a similar fate by appealing, as a British subject, to the Resident at the Nizam's Court for protection. This circumstance, together with the breaking out of the war between the French and English, put an end to all prospects of his advancement, as all the Europeans in the Nizam's army were Frenchmen.

So Tone set out to return to Calcutta. On his journey, having travelled four hundred miles, and with two hundred yet to travel, which must have brought him into the district of Orissa, he dismounted from his horse to shoot in a jungle by the roadside. On his return he found his servants and horses in the hands of five ruffians, who were engaged in plundering his baggage. He immediately ran up and fired at them, and shot one in the stomach, whereupon another returned the fire with one of Tone's own pistols, which they had seized, and wounded him in the foot. They then made off with their booty, and in this distressed condition the unfortunate Irishman had to travel two hundred miles in a burning climate and without resources. But his courage and good constitution supported him, and he at length arrived at Calcutta, where he speedily recovered his health. His friends there had not forgotten him, and when an opportunity offered of Major Palmer proceeding to Poonah to take up the appointment of Resident at the Court of the Peshwa of the Maráthás, they procured Tone a strong recommendation to that Court, and he set off with Major Palmer in high spirits and health, and with expectations of the command of a battery of artillery at least.

So far Tone's history has been extracted from the memoirs of his brother Wolfe Tone. Carrying the narrative forward, it would appear he reached Poonah about the year 1796, and found employment in Boyd's corps. Two years later he was selected by Amrat Ráo, the Peshwa's brother, to command a proposed brigade of regular infantry, all the officers of which were to be British subjects, but the idea was abandoned. In 1801 he was in command of two hundred Sepoys assisting Lakwa Dáda and the Bhais at the defence of Sounda, where he was defeated by Perron's troops and obliged to surrender. The General behaved very kindly to him and his officers, supplying them with a handsome camp equipage, such as tents, camels, horses, &c. To the Colonel he offered service in his own army, but it was declined, and Tone was permitted to retire to Mahéswur, the capital of Holkar, and furnished with Rs. 10,000 for his expenses, and to enable him and his comrades in misfortune to recover their shattered fortunes.

Tone was killed in the following year, being struck by a bullet in the right temple in an action near Choli Mahéswur while serving with Holkar. His brother's biographer (his own nephew), writing in 1827, does not seem to have been aware of this, or, at least, does not specifically mention it.

Tone was the author of a pamphlet entitled "Some Institutions of the Mahratta People," which has been frequently quoted by various historians, so that he evidently cultivated his taste for literature to the end. Grant Duff, in his "History of the Mahrattas," refers in very appreciative terms to three letters which Tone had published, giving an accurate account of affairs at Poonah in 1796. "I have examined minutely," he writes, "all which that intelligent gentleman wrote respecting the Mahrattas. What he saw may be relied upon ; as to what he heard, I am less surprised that he should have fallen into error than that he should have obtained information so nearly correct." Smith describes Tone as a man of "undaunted valour and persevering enterprise ; an unfortunate gentleman whose abilities and integrity were as great as his misfortunes had been undeservedly severe," and criticises his "Institutions" as "both elegant and accurate." Every one who was brought into contact with William Henry Tone writes well of him, and leaves us with the impression that he was a brave and amiable man.

VICKERS, MAJOR.—Major Vickers was a half-caste, and an exceedingly gallant young soldier. He entered Perron's army as a lieutenant in the Second Brigade, under Major Pohlman, and commanded one of the trenches in the siege of Jhajgarh, displaying great bravery in leading the storm of that formidable place. When the Chevalier Dudrenec deserted Holkar's service, Vickers was appointed to the command of his corps, and behaved with great courage at the battle of Poonah, in October, 1802, his intrepidity and steadiness conducing much towards the victory, and being at the time a theme of admiration amongst all military men. In 1804, when war broke out between Holkar and the British, the chief sent for Vickers, and asked him if he would fight against his countrymen. The young man positively refused to do so, as did also two other adventurers—Dodd and Ryan. Whereupon Jaswant Ráo, assigning as a justification a treasonable correspondence which he accused them of carrying on, ordered all three to be beheaded, and the sentence was carried into effect at Nahar Maghána (Tiger's Hill) in the month of May, 1804. Their heads were fixed on lances in front of Jaswant Ráo's camp, and a public crier proclaimed that such would be the fate of any European who might fall into Holkar's clutches.

FINIS.